G00129965

DEATH, WAR, AND SACRIFICE

DEATH, WAR,

THE UNIVERSITY OF CHICAGO PRESS/CHICAGO & LONDON

BRUCE LINCOLN

AND SACRIFICE

STUDIES IN IDEOLOGY AND PRACTICE

Foreword by Wendy Doniger

Bruce Lincoln is professor of humanities and religious studies at the University of Minnesota.

The University of Chicago Press, Chicago 60637
The University of Chicago Press, Ltd., London
© 1991 by The University of Chicago
All rights reserved. Published 1991
Printed in the United States of America

00 99 98 97 96 95 94 93 92 91   5 4 3 2 1

Library of Congress Cataloging-in-Publication Data

Lincoln, Bruce.
    Death, war, and sacrifice: studies in ideology and practice /
  Bruce Lincoln; foreword by Wendy Doniger.
      p.   cm.
    Includes bibliographical references and index.
    ISBN 0-226-48199-9 (cloth). — ISBN 0-226-48200-6 (paper)
    1. Mythology, Indo-European.   2. War—Religious aspects.
  3. Death—Religious aspects.   4. Sacrifice. I. Title.
  BL660.L44   1991
  291.1′3—dc20   90-26902

In Memory of
Mircea Eliade

CONTENTS

FOREWORD

For years I have been engaging in a kind of one-woman Samizdat: handing around, to my students and colleagues, an increasingly dog-eared copy of a collection of Xeroxes of Bruce Lincoln's articles on Indo-European mythology. I kept doing this because I felt, and still feel, that these articles represent the most reliable and at the same time the most original essays yet written on this important subject, remarkable both for their extraordinary breadth of erudition and for the numerous insights that they bring both to the methodological problems of Indo-European studies and to the actual consideration of the nature of Indo-European religious thought.

But as my bootleg Lincoln volume kept getting lost and I got tired of recopying it all out, I awaited with great eagerness the publication of his book on the subject, which I naïvely assumed would incorporate, perhaps in a revised form, these intrinsically connected essays. When the book finally appeared—*Myth, Cosmos, and Society: Indo-European Themes of Creation and Destruction* (Cambridge, Mass.: Harvard University Press, 1986)—I realized how foolish I had been. I should have known that Bruce, whose thoughts progress at roughly the speed of light, would not have reworked the old articles but had, instead, written an entirely new book with an entirely different methodology. Indeed, as his essay on "The Two Paths" in this volume indicates, even since writing *that* book he has had other, major transformations in his thinking. This is but one of the many signs of his enormous vitality and integrity.

But, praiseworthy as it may be as a quality in itself, this constant retransformation in Bruce Lincoln's work left me in my original quandary. *Myth, Cosmos, and Society* is certainly a very fine book about Indo-European religion, but it does not cover the ground covered by the articles. There is, I think, an irony in the fact that Bruce is, like his old sparring partner the late Georges Dumézil, a man who allows his mind to change, who moves on when he finds a new thing to do. Unlike Dumézil, however, he does not usually care to look back, an odd quality in a historian, perhaps, but maybe not so odd in a Marxist historian. Dumézil constantly renounced and denounced his previous work; Bruce was willing to let it lie as it fell and simply go on moving forward—*avanti, avanti*.

But eventually I was able to prevail upon him to take another look at his old essays, and once he looked at them he came to terms with them in an entirely creative way. He tells us about this in his own Preface to this volume and in "The Two Paths," an essay which, by explaining why the Indo-European essays in the first section of the book are, in Bruce's view, frozen in amber, serves as his own epilogue to those essays. But this part of the book is, there-fore, all the more valuable for what it tells us about its subject, the author, over and above what it tells us about its object, Indo-European religion. It is a vivid documentary of the development of a brilliant young scholar, which shows us how, at first, he was attracted to a major field of investigation; then how he began to work in it and made his innovative contributions to it; and, finally, how he eventually became so critical both of his own work and of the work of other scholars in the field that he felt inclined to abandon it forever.

But when it came to preparing this book for the press, Bruce did not rest on these considerable laurels. He went on to write a number of entirely new chap-ters, extending the material both in time and in space, forging a complex link between his thinking then and his thinking now. The resulting volume com-bines previously published articles (many of them, however, published in Eu-ropean journals and obscure Festschrifts that American scholars too seldom know or use) with new, previously unpublished essays.

The second part of the book differs from the first both in method and in subject. Methodologically, it treats the Indo-European materials not by the comparative reconstructive method but, rather, by concentrating on one par-ticular group at a time. At the same time, its focus moves from death to the closely related but significantly different subject of killing. These essays deal with human sacrifice and war on two levels: some are published essays *about* war and rage, while others, on a level once removed, are new articles that express the author's own rage and engagement in intellectual wars. This level also prevails in the third section of the book, which returns to the author who inspired the methodology embodied in the first part—Georges Dumézil—but who now poses an explicit challenge to that methodology.

The metaphors of battle and sacrifice in these two final sections of the book (which I tend to think of as "Lincoln at War" or "Battling Bruce") might be made tripartite by the addition of a third, medical metaphor: for Bruce wields the knife primarily when he feels that academic surgery is of crucial impor-tance. But wield it he does; these essays are razor sharp, and have already drawn the blood of major academic controversy. The book itself, however, justifies the academic bloodshed, for it demonstrates why these issues *matter* to him as a scholar and as a human being. His is a deeply human, indeed humane, concern with the ways in which people treat one another, and more particularly with the ways in which they talk to one another and do (or do not) listen to one another. It is this human/e concern that lifts Bruce Lincoln's work high above the posturings of other scholars who are concerned merely with ideology, with rhetoric for rhetoric's sake, with the trendy deconstruction of social forms. Bruce has often been attacked for his feisty, passionate, no-respecter-of-persons battles over issues that engage both the scholar and the man—indeed, that demonstrate that it is naive to try to dissociate the scholar from the man. This book not only discusses but embodies the relationship between life and work, more precisely, between political life and academic work. In his moving preface, Bruce talks about the connection between the death of his grandfather and his attraction to the comforting mythology of the afterworld. So, too, he speaks of the sadness with which he came to believe in the ineluctable link between the work of Dumézil, which he so admired and to which he owed so much, and the life of Dumézil, which was politically flawed in ways that he could not ignore.

For me, Bruce Lincoln's writings have been essential, not only to my development as a scholar but deeply, often painfully, essential to my belated acceptance of the political dimensions of my own work, to my retarded transition from ostrich not, perhaps, to hawk, but at least to passionately committed dove. His friendship, too, has been a lifeline to me during this past decade in which, living parallel lives, we have watched our children grow up and our parents grow old, and have mourned together the death of colleagues dear to both of us, particularly Mircea Eliade. It seems to me to be proof of the magnanimity of both men that, despite their grave political differences, Mircea often said (in print, too), that Bruce was his most brilliant student, while Bruce's enduring affection and respect for Mircea, both as scholar and as friend, is reflected in the dedication of this book.

Wendy Doniger

PREFACE

This book would not exist were it not for Wendy Doniger's persistence and her kindness: rightfully I must begin by thanking her. For in a series of friendly letters and discussions, Wendy stressed to me that a set of articles I wrote between 1978 and 1980, treating the mythology of death and the geography of the otherworld as envisioned by the various Indo-European peoples, had some continuing interest and importance, which I in my dotage had either forgotten or come to overlook. She urged me to gather these essays together, perhaps with some newer materials, so that they could be more readily accessible to those who would benefit from them, and she generously offered not only to assist in the process, but to help persuade the University of Chicago Press that the project had merit. This book is the result of her initiative, her encouragement, her help, and her friendship, and I am deeply grateful to her.

Together we assembled a table of contents, which started with a general survey of Indo-European religions that was written in 1983 for a volume that never saw light of day, and then moved on to articles dealing with death, to which we added some other, more recent materials. Wendy then got me to sit down and reread the old stuff (Part I of this book), which I had not looked at for some time. Having now gone through it, I am struck by the differences which divide these materials from the kind of work that appears in Parts II and III. I still prefer these later pieces, I must admit—for reasons that I will spell out shortly—but I am forced to conclude that the older work has its value too.

Reading over the book as a whole, I see recurrent themes emerging, and I find it to be a book filled with my hopes and my terrors. It begins with a search to find meaning and consolation in the face of death, although the desperate nature of that search is masked by the scholarly diction in which it is couched and the philological rigor with which it was conducted. Still, I am struck by the fact that the first, brightest, and most hopeful essays—"On the Imagery of Paradise," "The Lord of the Dead," and "Waters of Memory, Waters of Forgetfulness," all of which end on a comforting, almost rhapsodic note—were written in the wake of my beloved grandfather's death (Frank William Lincoln, 11 January 1890–8 March 1977). In these studies and in that period, I now see I was struggling to recover the reassurance of myths that tell how the dead rest happy in a radiant land beyond suffering and cares, and that I took particular solace from a set of images that describes how the experiences and wisdom of the dead are not forever consigned to oblivion but flow back to the living in the form of memory.

Hope, reassurance, and consolation, however, proved difficult to sustain, and what began as a flight from the dread of nothingness and annihilation brought me face to face with nothingness again, as reflected in another set of mythic images more bleak and somber than those I'd studied before. The "Ferryman of the Dead" thus proved to be no ferryman, but senectitude personified in its most drear and menacing form, while the dwelling of the dead (the "House of Clay") proved to be nothing more than the grave. Ultimately, my project became unsustainable, in more ways than one, and further studies that I had eagerly projected—on the golden apples of the otherworld, for example, or on the women who beckon and greet one at the entry to the beyond—failed to hold my interest.[1] Having received a Guggenheim Fellowship in 1982–83 to write a book on "Death and the Otherworld in Indo-European Myth," I found myself blocked on a chapter that was to deal with representations of the two paths that lead different sorts of souls to different sorts of fates. In its original form, that essay was never finished, and I turned to other problems instead: those which led me to write *Myth, Cosmos, and Society.*[2] Thereafter, I never looked at the older pieces until Wendy's urgings forced me to do so, at which point I went back and completed the study of "The Two Paths" in a rather different form than that which I had originally anticipated, reflecting not only on the mythic materials themselves, but on the methodological and theoretic issues that have confronted me as I tried to make sense out of them. This piece is published here for the first time as Chapter 9.

A major break separates the studies that fall in Part I from those in Part II. I would observe, for instance, that the latter are more concerned with practices than beliefs, and more with killing than with dying. For the pieces of Part II, most of which were written between 1984 and 1988, deal with war and with sacrifice, the specialized lethal practices characteristic of warriors and priests respectively. Within these chapters, death is treated not so much as a natural event that comes ultimately to all but as something that in certain circumstances some human beings inflict on others. What is more—and this, for me, is the heart of the matter—by virtue of the positions that they occupy and beliefs that they hold, the killers are often able to do their work with a certain amount of confidence and a relatively clean conscience.

Such a shift of focus is obviously associated with a shift of tone and a shift of stance, for if the studies of death were marked by a general compassion prompted by the universal fact of human mortality, the studies of killing show a more politicized consciousness as I came to perceive significant differences in the lives led and fates suffered by different classes of human beings, and consequently felt compelled to intervene on the side of the victims. This intervention, however—in studies like "The Druids and Human Sacrifice," "On the Scythian Royal Burials," or "Homeric *lyssa:* 'Wolfish Rage'"—does not involve a simplistic and unproductive, if morally gratifying, denunciation of the killers. Rather, I have tried to give serious consideration to the images and arguments that persuaded the relevant actors that they had the right (or even the obligation) to kill, acknowledging that these constructs possessed (and continue to possess) very real and considerable persuasive power. My goal in studying these constructs is first to see how and why these discourses were so effective, and second to demystify them, revealing the consequences that they entail and rendering visible the social and material interests that they serve.

This project is carried furthest, perhaps, in the previously unpublished essay on "Sacrificial Ideology and Indo-European Society," which expands the notion of sacrifice beyond the practice of literal killing to encompass other situations in which religious discourses are systematically used to justify and perpetuate the subordination of some classes of people to others: warriors to priests, commoners to kings, women to men, youths to elders, or slaves to free. Often, these structures of domination are inscribed and legitimated in mythic narratives. Yet, as I see it, there is nothing necessarily oppressive about "myth" any more than there is anything necessarily liberating about "science": the politically significant questions are those of content and consequences, not those of genre. And that scientific discourse can be just as mystificatory and pernicious as that of myth, I try to make clear in the three final pieces of Part II that explore the ways in which ancient physiological "knowledge" implied and supported patterns of class, gender, and ethnic hierarchy.

Another aspect of the break between Part I and Part II is the move away from comparative studies to those more specifically grounded in time and space. For whereas all of the pieces in Part I are devoted to the recovery of an "Indo-European" or "Proto-Indo-European" content, those of Part II generally deal with peoples and texts that are known to us from history: Celtic Druids as reported by Caesar and others, or Iranian warriors as observed by Zarathustra, for example. Comparison still occurs, as in the essay on "War and Warriors: An Overview," but in general the kind of comparison that now interests me is one which explores common themes in different and discrete contexts: themes like the mapping of social hierarchy on the human body, animal metaphors and dehumanization in the experience of war, or the role of discourse in the formation of social borders.

In contrast, the kind of comparison which I earlier practiced, but now tend to eschew, is the reconstructive endeavor which constitutes as its object of study the posited beliefs and practices of a posited people who lived in a posited time and place, speaking a posited language. Each step of this chain has its pitfalls, and it seems to me there are several good reasons for avoiding them. The first of these is simple scholarly prudence. For if it is clear enough that the languages spoken by the ancient peoples of India, Iran, Anatolia, Armenia, and most of Europe are related to one another, it is by no means sure just what the nature of that relation is. Most specialists have assumed that these languages diverged from an unattested prototype to which they are all genetically related, much as the Romance languages are known to have derived from Latin. Yet others have argued that originally separate languages may just as well have influenced one another through processes of culture-contact and trade, and some have gone further to suggest that "Proto-Indo-European" may have been a constructed lingua franca, more on the order of Swahili or Tokpisin than that of Latin.[3] The attempt to locate an original community and an original homeland thus seems to me to be problematic from the start, and the latest round of debates among archaeologists does little to increase my confidence.[4]

Similar difficulties confront those who would attempt to reconstruct "Indo-European" myths, rituals, or religious beliefs, as if these belonged in some sense to Proto-people. Here, moreover, the situation is considerably more difficult than in the case of language, which itself is difficult enough. For as Cristiano Grottanelli has repeatedly shown, many of the same narrative patterns that some authors take to be classically "Indo-European" are also attested with equal clarity in the literatures of peoples who spoke very non-Indo-European languages.[5] One of the greatest pleasures for me in preparing this book was thus to find the record of my first conversation with Grottanelli, which took place in September 1979, after I had presented my paper on "Mithra(s) as Sun and Savior" (Chapter 6) at a conference in Rome. At that time, he opened the discussion by gently pointing out to me that a mythic theme which I had treated exclusively in terms of Indo-European traditions was also attested elsewhere, and others rose to pursue this line of argument. In response, I acknowledged that Indo-Europeans "hold no copyrights on any religious idea," but continued to insist that there were distinctive ways in which even the most broadly diffused ideas—the sun as psychopomp or the bonds of death—were articulated within Indo-European texts that set them apart from the articulation of these same ideas elsewhere. Since that time, Grottanelli and I have continued the discussion in person, in letters, and in print. Gradually, he has changed my mind. As he puts it in one of his articles that I value most highly, it is not common language or common descent that produces common myths, but common social structures and historic situations, for it is these which provide the problems that are addressed—but never resolved—within mythic narration.[6] And as he has also taught me over the years, it is much more interesting and more important to explore the nature of the relations that obtain between mythic discourses on the one hand and historico-social processes on the other than it is to recount and interpret the myths of any given people, real or reconstructed.

If myths tell stories about the long ago and far away for purposes of the place and moment in which these stories are told, the same may be observed regarding other forms of narrative, scholarship included. For even within the most disciplined and learned of academic discourses, the past enters the present for reasons of the present. This is not to say that scholarship differs in no way from myth, or that research produces only fictions. It is simply to assert that scholars are no different from other human beings. They exist within a time, a place, and a social situation, and their speech, thought, and interests originate in, reflect, and engage these givens of their own experience in some measure, although this is not all that they do. Still, the books and articles which scholars write and the lectures they give are not just descriptive accounts of something that unproblematically "is." Rather, these are synthetic constructions which partake in varying degrees of the people who are speaking, that of whom they speak, and those to whom their speech is addressed. Such processes can be extremely accurate, revealing, and enlightening; but they can never be perfectly neutral and distinterested, no matter how much those who are involved as speakers or hearers may sincerely take them to be so.[7]

Nowhere is this clearer than in the case of Indo-European studies. For it was the colonial encounter which first made Sanskrit available to European scholars, and following on their recognition of the affinities that exist between the ancient languages of India and Iran and those of Greece, Rome, and northern Europe, linguists and others rapidly came to contrast Indo-European (and especially Sanskrit) to Hebrew, which for reasons both theological and "scientific" had previously been viewed as the world's oldest language. Further, they systematically contrasted the speakers of these languages—Aryans and Semites, as they called them—to one another on grounds racial and spiritual, as well as linguistic, always to the benefit of the former and detriment of the latter group. The consequences of this construction, in which the interpretation of linguistic and other data was strongly inflected by nationalist and racist interests, are too well-known to need belaboring, but also too important ever to be ignored.[8]

Since 1945, other theories have been proposed, which show significant differences from those that fell into disrepute along with National Socialism. Scholars who speak of a Proto-Indo-European homeland now generally set it to the east, not the north, and the most recent accounts of an Indo-European expansion associate it with the gradual diffusion of agricultural practices, not with military conquest.[9] In part, these newer theories result from changes in scholars' attitudes and corollary changes in the kinds of evidence to which they give serious consideration (that of Anatolian and Soviet archaeology having risen in scholars' estimation, that of physical anthropology having fallen). Further, their attitudes and theories in part are formed in reaction against those of previous generations, and beyond this there are other sorts of interests that may be discerned within them. Some of these do not trouble me particularly, for all that they may give rise to specific interpretations with which one might quibble. I think of the strong feminist orientation which informs, and in some measure motivates, the work of Marija Gimbutas, for example.[10] Yet there are other interests and other theories about which I have come to have grave reservations, and this brings us to Part III of this book.

I was first asked by the editors of the *Times Literary Supplement* to review Georges Dumézil's *L'oubli de l'homme et l'honneur des dieux*[11] in early 1985, just as I was finishing work on *Myth, Cosmos, and Society*. At the time, I regarded Dumézil as the foremost scholar within the subdiscipline in which I was active: a man whose work was technically excellent, conceptually ground-breaking, and justly influential. Indeed, I felt that my own work had been deeply influenced by his, although our views differed in significant ways. At about the same time, I had just read the articles in which first Arnaldo Momigliano and then Carlo Ginzburg charged that Dumézil's early writings revealed fascist leanings, and although I was not persuaded by the cases which these eminent scholars made, I was troubled by them.[12] After brief consideration, I wrote back to the *TLS*, declined their invitation, and suggested several other people who might be able to take on the review in my stead.

Toward the end of 1985, however, I stumbled by chance across an extremely obscure article of Dumézil's. Published in the *Revue turque d'anthropologie* for 1927, it bore the title "De quelques faux massacres," and its contents were sufficiently disturbing to me—for reasons that I spell out in Chapter 21—that I felt the need to reconsider my opinions not only of Dumézil but of the connections between scholars' lives and their work. I thus went back and reread the critical pieces of Momigliano and Ginzburg, along with Dumézil's responses to them, and delved into many of Dumézil's other writings, while familiarizing myself with the history of the political right in France during the twentieth century. Further, I turned up a number of interviews with Dumézil that had appeared in right-wing French publications, wherein he regularly asserted, first, that the organization of society into three hierarchically differentiated "functions" was simply a fact of nature and, second, that among all peoples of the world, the Indo-Europeans alone had gained consciousness of this "natural" fact and formulated a proper conceptual model of it.[13] When I was finished, I had become convinced, first, that Dumézil had been significantly influenced in his youth by Charles Maurras, founder of the Action Française, and in his old age had flirted with the Nouvelle Droite of Alain de Benoist; second, that in his response to Momigliano, Dumézil had deliberately and strategically lied about the life and career of Pierre Gaxotte, out of loyalty to a deceased friend, no doubt, but also in order to disguise his own connections to the extreme right; and, third, that the royalist and corporate-statist views that Dumézil took from Maurras (*not* from any fascist source outside of France) had colored his selection and interpretation of data at numerous important points within his scholarly writings.

None of this was easy for me to swallow. I wrote back to the editors of the *TLS* and offered to prepare the review they had requested if they were still interested in my doing so. They were, and in June 1986 I submitted my finished manuscript to them, with every expectation that Dumézil would respond aggressively and that a fuller debate would ensue. On 3 October 1986 my review was published, all footnotes having been deleted from it in accordance with *TLS* style. One week later, Georges Dumézil died.

Naturally enough, the review—which appears here as Chapter 19, complete with the original notes—prompted considerable discussion, some of it quite critical, yet the posthumous publication of Dumézil's *Entretiens avec Didier Eribon* confirmed much of what I had deduced about Dumézil's early involvement with Maurras and his continuing commitment to many of Maurras's doctrines.[14] This revelation, which has provoked relatively little comment compared to that occasioned by similar discoveries regarding other luminaries, prompted me to go back and do further research on the connections between Dumézil's personal commitments and his scholarly writings. I offer the results of this research in Chapters 20 and 21, knowing that some will take me severely to task for continuing to criticize a dead man.

That charge I take seriously, and I wish that Dumézil were here to carry on the debate. Physically he is not, and yet in other ways he is, for in truth it is neither possible nor desirable to sever all connections with the deceased. Rather, the dead continue to speak to us, and inevitably we must speak of and to them, exploring in the process the nature and consequences of the influence that they continue to exercise in the land of the living. A healthy discipline, like any other group, continues to listen to its ancestors but also continues to cross-examine them. One day, I expect—with mixed hope and fear—that others may do the same for me.

It remains for me to thank the many people who provided suggestions and criticism on various of the pieces included within this book, to all of whom I am deeply grateful. I have already mentioned Wendy Doniger and Cristiano Grottanelli. To these, I should add Françoise Bader, Paul Bauschatz, Ugo Bianchi, Mary Boyce, Dominique Briquel, Walter Burkert, Ioan Culianu, Richard Dieterle, Ulf Drobin, Daniel Dubuisson, Erik af Edholm, Anne Enke, Paul Friedrich, Marija Gimbutas, Eric Hamp, Anders Hultgård, Åke Hultkranz, Stephanie Jamison, David Knipe, F. B. J. Kuiper, Per Kvaerne, William Malandra, Gregory Nagy, Tord Olsson, Juha Pentikäinen, Diego Poli, Edgar Polomé, Jaan Puhvel, James Redfield, Peter Schalk, John Scheid, Hanns-Peter Schmidt, Brian Smith, Pier Giorgio Solinas, Jørgen Podemann Sørensen, Jesper Svenbro, Tove Tybjerg, H. S. Versnel, and Margrit Warburg. Deepest thanks go also to Heidar Azodanloo, who compiled the indexes for this book.

My most profound gratitude is reserved for Louise Lincoln, whose encouragement, support, and criticism were all invaluable.

Notes

1. Earlier studies of these motifs are available. On the apples, see A. H. Krappe, "Avallon," *Speculum* 18 (1943): 303–22, and Th. Chotzen, "Emain Ablach—Ynys

Avallach—Insula Avallonis—Ile d'Avalon," *Études celtiques* 4 (1948): 255–74; on the summoners, Hermann Güntert, *Kalypso* (Halle: Max Niemeyer, 1919), written during and in the wake of the First World War, and *Kundry* (Heidelberg: Carl Winter, 1928).

2. Bruce Lincoln, *Myth, Cosmos, and Society: Indo-European Themes of Creation and Destruction* (Cambridge, Mass.: Harvard University Press, 1986).

3. For alternatives to and arguments against the so-called *Stammbaum* model, see N. S. Trubetzkoy, "Gedanken über das Indogermanenproblem," *Acta Linguistica* 1 (1939): 81–89; Franco Crevatin, *Ricerche di antichità indeuropee* (Trieste: Edizioni LINT, 1979); Ulf Drobin, "Indogermanische Religion und Kultur? Eine Analyse des Begriffes Indogermanisch," *Temenos* 16 (1980): 26–38; Jean-Paul DeMoule, "Les Indo-européens, ont-ils existés?" *L'Histoire* 28 (1980): 109–20; Bernfried Schlerath, *Die Indogermanen. Das Problem eines Volkes im Lichte seiner sozialen Struktur* (Innsbruck: Innsbrucker Beiträge zur Sprachwissenschaft, 1977); idem, "Ist ein Raum/Zeit Modell für eine rekonstruierte Sprache möglich?, *Zeitschrift für vergleichende Sprachforschung* 95 (1981): 175–202.

4. The "Kurgan culture" theory which Marija Gimbutas set forth in an influential series of articles has thus been significantly challenged by I. M. Diakonov, "On the Original Home of the Speakers of Indo-European," *Journal of Indo-European Studies* 13 (1985): 92–174, and Colin Renfrew, *Archaeology and Language: The Puzzle of Indo-European Origins* (New York: Cambridge University Press, 1987). It has also been defended by J. P. Mallory, *In Search of the Indo-Europeans: Language Archaeology and Myth* (London: Thames and Hudson, 1989). The relevant articles of Gimbutas are "The Indo-Europeans: Archaeological Problems," *American Anthropologist* 65 (1963): 815–36, "Proto-Indo-European Culture: The Kurgan Culture during the 5th to the 3rd Millennia B.C.," in G. Cardona, H. Hoenigswald, and A. Senn, eds., *Indo-European and Indo-Europeans* (Philadelphia: University of Pennsylvania Press, 1970), pp. 155–98; "The Beginning of the Bronze Age in Europe and the Indo-Europeans: 3500–2500 B.C.," *Journal of Indo-European Studies* 1 (1973): 163–214; "The First Wave of Eurasian Steppe Pastoralists into Copper Age Europe," *Journal of Indo-European Studies* 5 (1977): 277–338; "The Kurgan Wave Migration (c. 3400–3200 B.C.) into Europe and the Following Transformation of Culture," *Journal of Indo-European Studies* 8 (1980): 273–315; and "Primary and Secondary Homeland of the Indo-Europeans," *Journal of Indo-European Studies* 13 (1985): 185–202. I have spelled out my reservations regarding the contributions that archaeological evidence can make to the study of "Indo-European" civilization(s) in *Priests, Warriors, and Cattle: A Study in the Ecology of Religions* (Berkeley: University of California Press, 1981), pp. 179–84.

5. Cristiano Grottanelli, "Giuseppe nel pozzo, I. Un antico tema mitico in Genesi 37:12–24 e in RV I 105," *Oriens Antiquus* 17 (1978): 107–22; "Cosmogonia e sacrificio, I e II," *Studi Storico-Religiosi* 4 (1980): 207–35, and 5 (1981): 173–96; "L'Inno a Hermes e il Cantico di Deborah: due facce di un tema mitico," *Rivista degli Studi Orientali* 56 (1982): 27–37; "The King's Grace and the Helpless Woman: A Comparative Study of the Stories of Ruth, Charila, Sītā," *History of Religions* 22 (1982): 1–24; "Temi duméziliani fuori dal mondo indo-europeo," *Opus* 2 (1983): 365–89; and "Yoked Horses, Twins, and the Powerful Lady: India, Greece, Ireland and Elsewhere," *Journal of Indo-European Studies* 14 (1986): 125–52. See also the discussion

of "Trifunzionalismi bianchi e neri," in Grottanelli's forthcoming book, *Idealogie, miti, massacri: Gli indoeuropei di Dumézil* (Palermo: Sellerio).

6. Cristiano Grottanelli, "The King's Grace and the Helpless Woman," esp. p. 10.

7. With reference to scholarship on myth, for instance, see the discussion of Ivan Strenski, *Four Theories of Myth in Twentieth-Century History* (Iowa City: University of Iowa Press, 1987).

8. See, inter alia, Leon Poliakov, *The Aryan Myth: A History of Racist and Nationalist Ideas in Europe* (New York: Basic Books, 1974); Ruth Roemer, *Sprachwissenschaft und Rassenideologie in Deutschland* (Munich: Fink, 1985); Regina Pozzi, "Alle origini del razzismo contemporaneo. Il caso di Ernest Renan," *Rivista di Storia Contemporanea* 14 (1985): 497–520; Maurice Olender, *Les langues du paradis: Aryens et Sémites, un couple providentiel* (Paris: Gallimard, 1989); and Sheldon Pollock, "Deep Orientalism: Sanskrit and Power Beyond the Raj," in Peter van der Veer and Carol Breckenridge, eds., *The Post-Colonial Predicament* (Philadelphia: University of Pennsylvania Press, forthcoming).

9. Renfrew, *Archaeology and Language*.

10. In addition to the literature cited in note 4 above, see also Marija Gimbutas, *The Goddesses and Gods of Old Europe, 6500–3500 B.C.*, new and updated ed. (Berkeley: University of California Press, 1982); "Old Europe in the Fifth Millennium B.C.: The European Situation on the Arrival of the Indo-Europeans," in Edgar C. Polomé, ed., *The Indo-Europeans in the Fourth and Third Millennia* (Ann Arbor: Karoma Publishers, 1982), pp. 1–60; *The Language of the Goddess: Unearthing the Hidden Symbols of Western Civilization* (San Francisco: Harper & Row, 1989). Beyond the feminist dimension of Gimbutas's writings, there is another organizing subtext in which Baltic nationalism figures powerfully, as she champions the matrifocal peoples of "Old Europe" against the patriarchal invaders from the Russian steppes.

11. Actually, the invitation was to review either *La courtisane et les seigneurs colorés* (Paris: Gallimard, 1983) or *L'oubli de l'homme et l'honneur des dieux* (Paris: Gallimard, 1985). Ultimately, I chose to discuss the more recent volume.

12. Arnaldo Momigliano, "Premesse per una discussione su Georges Dumézil," *Opus* 2 (1983): 329–41; Carlo Ginzburg, "Mitologia Germanica e Nazismo: Su un vecchio libro di Georges Dumézil," *Quaderni Storici* 19 (1984): 857–82.

13. See, for instance, the interviews with Dumézil which appeared in *Nouvelle école* 10 (September 1969), p. 43, and *Le Figaro*, 20 April 1979, p. 20. Similar views are voiced in an interview published in the somewhat left-of-center *Nouvel observateur*, 14 January 1983, p. 21. Also of interest is Dumézil's discussion with Alain de Benoist in *Le Figaro Dimanche*, 29–30 April 1978, p. 19.

14. Georges Dumézil, *Entretiens avec Didier Eribon* (Paris: Gallimard, 1987), pp. 205–8.

ONE

INDO-EUROPEAN RELIGIONS: AN INTRODUCTION

Indo-Europeans and Proto-Indo-Europeans

It was not until the end of the eighteenth century—1786, to be exact—that modern researchers recognized the existence of a Proto-Indo-European language and posited, by extension, a Proto-Indo-European people who spoke that language. In that year, Sir William ("Oriental") Jones, delivering the Third Annual Lecture to the Royal Asiatic Society of Bengal, observed that close philological similarities exist between Greek, Latin, Sanskrit, and Persian, similarities so numerous and so precise as to preclude chance or simple borrowing as possible explanations. Going further, Jones suggested that Gothic and the Celtic languages might also be connected, and that all of these geographically and historically far-flung languages might be genetically related to one another, deriving from a common parent language much as the Romance languages (French, Italian, Spanish, Portuguese, and Rumanian) derive from Latin. The chief difficulty in this analogy is that, whereas Latin is attested and we know a good deal about the culture(s) in which Latin was spoken, Proto-Indo-European—the hypothetical parent language of Latin, Greek, Sanskrit, and the rest—is nowhere preserved either in spoken or written form, and thus comes to be known only through the painstaking work of linguistic reconstruction.

Later research has proved Jones's theory substantially correct, adding not only Germanic and Celtic firmly to the list of Indo-European languages, but also Baltic, Slavic, Armenian, Albanian, Anatolian (chiefly Hittite), and Tocharian (an obscure language found in western China and Turkestan) to the grouping. All of these languages are now designated "Indo-European," that is, they are the historically attested languages which can be shown to derive from a hypothetical "Proto-Indo-European" in both their vocabulary and grammatical form. Moreover, these languages provide the data from which we reconstruct our knowledge of "Proto-Indo-European," the parent language.

Such reconstruction involves the rigorous and systematic comparison of words from the attested Indo-European languages which are seen to correspond one to another in their phonetics and/or semantics.* To give a simple example, we might consider the word for "sheep," assembling a set of correspondences as follows:

* All translations in this and subsequent chapters are original, unless noted otherwise.

Phonetic form:	Sanskrit aviḥ	=	Latin ovis	=	Greek ois
Semantic meaning:	"sheep"		"sheep"		"sheep"

Armenian hov-iw	=	Old High German ouwi	=	English ewe
"shepherd"		"female sheep"		"female sheep"

From these correspondences, along with the knowledge of Indo-European and Proto-Indo-European phonetics gained from hundreds of other such sets, linguists can confidently reconstruct a P-I-E form * *owi-s* (the asterisk denotes a reconstructed term which is not attested in any written source) meaning "sheep." Sound rules specific to each of the separate Indo-European languages govern and explain the ways in which the proto-form has been transformed in each descendant language, and obvious semantic changes have taken place in Armenian (where the simple word for "sheep" is not derived from the P-I-E term, but a compound "shepherd" "protector of sheep," is built upon it) and Germanic, where another term (English *sheep*, et al.) has assumed the place of the generic term for the ovine family, leaving a specialized semantic range ("female sheep" for the old P-I-E term which was initially broader.

Other comparisons and reconstructions are less obvious. A classic example is the word which we reconstruct as * k^wek^wlo-s, meaning "wheel," based on such (apparently) disparate reflexes (i.e. examples encountered in the descendant I-E languages) as Sanskrit *cakra-ḥ* "wheel," Greek *kuklos* "circle," and English *wheel* (Old English *hwēol*, from Proto-Germanic **hweh(w)ula*). The details of such comparisons need not concern us here, although they are of crucial interest to linguists, but it is important to note a major methodological point: the reconstructed P-I-E form need not necessarily resemble all or even any of the I-E reflexes too closely, nor must the reflexes resemble one another in any specific example. *Wheel* and *cakra* are quite different from one another, and from *$*k^wek^wlo-s$* as well, yet the two former are certainly derived directly from the last, and the last is reconstructed from the two former, along with other reflexes also (Tokharian *kukäl*, Old Church Slavonic *kolo*, Lithuanian *kāklas*, etc.)

As is implicit in these two examples, one can move from the study of words to the study of culture with some facility. Given that the speakers of Proto-Indo-European possessed words for sheep and wheels, one can safely conclude that they had knowledge of, and in all probability possessed, sheep and wheels as well. Study of the full body of words which have been reconstructed (as listed in Pokorny 1959 or Buck 1949) thus leads to a picture of P-I-E civilization, via the method which is usually referred to as linguistic paleontology (see Schrader-Nehring 1917–23; Schrader 1890; Benveniste 1975).

The picture which emerges is one of a semi-settled pastoral people, whose wealth consisted of relatively large herds, including domesticated sheep, pigs, goats, and, most important of all, cattle. Horses were also highly important, especially when yoked to chariots and used in warfare, while cattle remained the normal draft animals for peaceful purposes, the source of most foods, and the measure of wealth. Some agriculture seems to have been practiced, although this was much less important and prestigious an activity than herding or war. The pursuit of warfare, especially the raiding of livestock from neighboring non-Indo-European peoples, was facilitated not only by use of chariots but also by an elaborate weaponry built on a single metal, most probably copper or bronze.

Such weaponry and martial mobility combined to give the Proto-Indo-Europeans military supremacy over most other peoples of prehistory. Their desire for ever larger herds and for more pastureland motivated war and raiding on ever larger scales, and ultimately led to the expansion of the Indo-European peoples from the original P-I-E homeland, until Indo-Europeans possessed and ruled over most of the territory from Iceland to India. In Europe, only the Finno-Ugrian peoples (Finns, Lapps, Estonians, Hungarians) and the Basques were not subjected to Indo-European conquest, while in Asia, the great civilizations of the Ancient Near East—Sumerians, Babylonians, Assyrians, and others—were able to resist for the most part, although certain Indo-European groups, most notably the Mitanni and the Kassites, were able to establish successful empires for a time.

The Mitanni Empire offers us a fairly clear picture of what most probably was the general nature of Indo-European conquest. Upon the successful completion of their penetration of a desired area, Indo-European warriors established themselves as a ruling aristocracy over the conquered indigenous population, imposing their language, religion, and values insofar as they were able to do so, while absorbing the indigenous population into the lower levels of their society. Indo-Europeanization, however, like any imperialism, was not simply a one-way process, for the conquerors not only absorbed certain aspects of the indigenous languages, religion, and cultural values themselves, but also had to adapt their own way of life and thought to the demands of their new ecology, economy, and society. In each place where Indo-Europeans entered, they experienced a complex synthesis with the indigenous populations (the so-called substrata). As a result of differing substratum influences, Indo-Europeans who settled in Italy came to differ significantly from Indo-Europeans who settled in the Balkans, or in Germany, or India, or Iran. For all that they share a common heritage *in part,* it is only in part, and each of the separate I-E peoples also possesses a heritage which is unrelated to any of the others and which sets it apart from them in significant ways.

Debates have long raged over the precise location of the homeland from which the Indo-Europeans dispersed (for a review of the controversy, see Mallory 1973). Over the last two decades, consideration of archaeological evidence has been of prime importance in this debate, as various scholars have sought to match the remains of various peoples of prehistory to what is posited for Proto-Indo-European civilization on the strength of linguistic paleontology. Of the arguments which have been advanced, those which have won the broadest acceptance are those of Marija Gimbutas, who has identified what she calls the "Kurgan Culture," dating to the middle of the fifth millennium B.C., and located in the southern Russian steppes, in the area stretching from the Urals to the land north of the Black Sea, including such groups as the Jamna culture of the Ural-Volga area north of the Caspian, and the Srednij Stog II culture north of the Black Sea (see Gimbutas 1963, 1970, 1973, and 1974; Mallory 1976–77; Thomas 1982). Here, Gimbutas has located a culture area which very closely parallels the known features of P-I-E society, and she has also suggested that the dispersion of Indo-Europeans into Europe and Anatolia occurred in three great waves of invasions during the fourth and third millennia B.C., through which they overthrew the civilizations which had earlier flourished there (Gimbutas 1977, 1980).

Social Organization and the Place of Priests

As we have already seen, Indo-European imperialist expansion introduced a class distinction between a victorious warrior aristocracy and a vanquished indigenous people. Yet already in the period before expansion, it would appear that the P-I-E warriors made up a well-defined social stratum within a society divided into three separate classes. Such a conclusion results from the comparison of texts describing the patterns of social organization among the Indian, Iranian, Celtic, and Germanic peoples, along with certain pieces of Greek and Roman evidence, all of which show a characteristic distinction between priests, warriors, and commoners (or food-producers), and sometimes a fourth class of servants, subjugated peoples, artisans, or the like (Dumézil 1930, 1958; Benveniste 1932, 1938, 1975, 227–38; Littleton 1982; see also now Polomé 1982).

While warriors occupy a privileged position within this hierarchy, being granted noble status, special training, and much of the wealth won by their conquests, they were never foremost in society. Always there remained something disquieting about their violence, which—while highly productive and quite necessary so long as it was directed against external enemies—threatened the stability and well-being of I-E society whenever it was asserted within that society itself (Dumézil 1970).

While warriors ever possessed the bulk of coercive force, political leadership was regularly vested in kings. Although born into the warrior class, and seemingly confirmed in their kingship by the full body of warriors, I-E kings were forced to pass through elaborate coronation ceremonies which had as their chief goal the creation of a new social identity for the future king, not as a warrior but as one who integrated within himself the essence of all three social classes (Dumézil 1959 and 1971; Ivanov 1960; Dubuisson 1978). It thus became the king's official responsibility to act on behalf of the society as a unified totality, *regulating* or setting *right*—both terms are related to the P-I-E royal title (**rēg'-s*)—the society, polity, and economy, the ideal characteristics of any king being, above all, truth and generosity: ideals that were only sometime, and even then only partially, met.

Technically, kings stand outside the social hierarchy, belonging to no class and to all classes, acting in the interests of the whole rather than any part. Yet, as Xazanov has rightly stressed with reference to Scythian kingship, which preserves the P-I-E pattern with great fidelity (Xazanov 1975, 335; see also Benveniste 1938, 534–35), this is decidedly an ideological smokescreen which served to rally populations around their kings and to imbue kings with an aura of legitimacy and affection, however much they might pursue their own interests and those of the class from which they came.

Again, technically the topmost position within the social hierarchy was occupied by the priests, who theoretically outranked even kings, as seen in the Indian ritual when the association of the king and his chief priest (the *purohita* or "chamberlain") is celebrated as a wedding, the priest playing the male (i.e. dominant) role to the king's female (subordinate). In some measure, this reflects the priority of sacred concerns—the priest's domain—over temporal ones, and it is also meant to establish that kings act only with the advice and consent of priests, which is to say that temporal actions were founded upon sacred principles. But once again, in large measure this must be regarded as an ideological smokescreen, whereby priests provided supernatural sanction and the prestige of the sacred for self-serving kingly policies.

There are other, less sinister grounds on which the priority of priests rested, however. Within a society not yet possessed of the art of writing, priests—who cultivated the art of memory with long years of training—were the chief repositories of all knowledge. Supported by the productive labor of the other classes, priests were able to devote their time to speculation on the most diverse topics, including much of what we would consider art and science rather than religion. One must also recognize that in a preliterate society, priestly speculation is much more directed toward contemplation of the cosmos than of sacred texts. Finally, priests were specialists in ritual, which in its most elaborate forms was directed toward the very maintenance of the cosmos, and the claim was regularly made that without proper—which is to say fully knowledgeable and technically perfect—performance of sacrifice, all existence would collapse. In this view, not only kings and warriors but gods and nature as well were dependent on and subordinate to the priestly class.

The Nature of the Gods

A number of general features of the P-I-E deities can be adduced from the vocabulary used with regard to them. The most common term used was P-I-E **deywo-s,* which most concretely means "celestial, luminous, radiant" (Hopkins 1932). It fixes the locus of the gods in the above, and places them in contrast to men, who are referred to—other terms are also used—as the "terrestrial, earthly" beings (Meillet 1907, 692–93). Yet another constrast between humans and deities is also explicitly stressed, for while the former are regularly designated as "mortals" (P-I-E *mṛto-), with equal frequency the latter are called "immortals" (*ṇmṛto-).

For the most part, the gods are felt to be benevolent, especially when rituals have been properly performed. They are thus called "givers of goods" (*dō-tores *weswām), and material wealth is seen as the result of their favor, itself being called "good," a term with an ethical as well as a material range of meaning (Schmitt 1967, 142–48; Buck 1949, 769). Thus, one who was morally good was believed to receive material wealth from the gods as the direct result and the tangible sign of his or her (but almost always his) goodness.

Within the P-I-E pantheon, a number of gods may be safely reconstructed on the grounds of linguistic evidence. Among these, the most important was a figure whose name was closely related to the "celestial" word: *Dyeus, who became *Zeus* among the Greeks, *Ju-piter* ("Celestial Father" or "Father Sky") among the Romans, and *Dyaus* among the Indians. Sometimes represented as a father (the Latin title preserves a P-I-E formulaic mode of address) and sometimes as a king, he was lofty, transcendent, sovereign, sometimes assertive and active, but more often tending toward otiosity (Eliade 1963, 82–86).

Of almost equal importance—to judge from archaeological remains, at any rate—was the personification of the sun, *Swel- (Sanskrit *Sūrya-*, Latin *Sōl*, etc.) who, like *Dyeus, was distant, powerful, radiant, and a source of goods. Also personified were the dawn (*Ausos, a goddess), fire (*Egni), water (*Nepto-no- "Lord of Water"), and the storm (several related formations from the verb *per- "to strike," on which see Nagy 1974), the last of these being extremely active, assertive, and occasionally aggressive, while fire and water played important roles as deities, cosmic elements, and items necessary for the functioning of any household (Schlerath 1977, 34–35; Boyce 1975, 1981).

Certain scholars, most notably Georges Dumézil, have sought to correlate the structure of the P-I-E pantheon with that of P-I-E society, seeing certain "sovereign" gods like the Germanic Odin and Tyr, the Roman Jupiter and Dius Fidius, or the Indic Varuṇa and Mitra, as the projections or representations of the sovereign (priestly) class, while others such as Germanic Thor, Roman Mars, and Indic Indra stand in the same relation to the warrior class; and others still, like the Germanic Njord, Freyr and Freyja (the grouping of twins plus a goddess is seen as prototypic), Roman Quirinus, and the Indic Aśvins are related to the class of commoners or producers (Dumézil 1952, 1977; Polomé 1980; Littleton, 1982). Yet it must be stressed that this system accounts for none of the gods for whom we can reconstruct P-I-E names—all of whom are personified natural phenomena—while reconstructible names exist for none of the deities included in the system (Schlerath 1977, 27 and

34). For this and for other reasons, I am inclined to reject the Dumézilian view of the pantheon.

This is not to say, however, that an important and explicit connection did not exist between society and religion, for among the Proto-Indo-Europeans— as indeed, everywhere—the two were intimately interwoven. Yet the connection was not forged in the theological structure of the pantheon—the gods, in truth, being a rather banal and relatively unimportant part of P-I-E religion— but in the myths of creation, especially those which recounted the deeds of the first human ancestors. Interest focused, not on the first primordium (that of the gods), as Eliade (1969) has put it, but on the second (that of the ancestors).

The Myths of Beginnings

At the beginning of time—so the P-I-E cosmogony held—there were two brothers, a priest whose name was "Man" (*Manu) and a king, whose name was "Twin" (*Yemo), who traveled together accompanied by an ox. For reasons that are not specified, they took it upon themselves to create the world, and toward that end the priest offered up his brother and the ox in what was to be the first ritual sacrifice. Dismembering their bodies, he used the various parts to create the material universe and human society as well, taking all three classes from the body of the first king who—as stated above—combined within himself the social totality.

As with the reconstruction of words, reconstruction of myths also depends on systematic and detailed comparison of numerous reflexes. And, again as with words, each reflex will differ in certain ways from every other, and from the reconstructed prototype as well. A thorough demonstration of how the P-I-E myth is reconstructed lies beyond the possibilities of a short discussion such as this, so only a few of the many variants which might be cited will be given here by way of illustration. To this end, we might cite an Indic, a Germanic, and an Old Russian version (for fuller discussion, see Lincoln 1981, 69–95; Puhvel 1975; Burkert 1962; and Güntert 1923, 315–94), each of which focuses on the division of the human victim.

> When they divided Purusha, how many pieces did they prepare?
> What was his mouth? What are his arms, thighs, and feet called?
> The priest was his mouth, the warrior was made from his arms;
> His thighs were the commoner, and the servant was born from
>   his feet.
> The moon was born of his mind; of his eye, the sun was born;
> From his mouth, Indra and fire; from his breath, wind was born;
> From his navel there was the atmosphere; from his head, heaven
>   was rolled together;
> From his feet, the earth; from his ears, the directions.
>
> Ṛg Veda 10.90.11–14

From Ymir's flesh   the earth was made
  and from his sweat, the sea;
Mountains from his bones,   trees from his hair,
  and heaven from his skull.
And from his brows   built the gentle gods
  Midgard for the sons of men;
And from his brain   shaped they all the clouds
  Which were hard in mood.

                  Grimnismal 40–41

Czars and Czarinas come into being
From the head of honest Adam.
Princes and heroes come into being
From the bones of honest Adam.
The orthodox peasants come into being
From the knee of holy Adam.

From the "Poem on the Dove King"

The P-I-E myth from which all of these reflexes derive was an enormously subtle and complex product of the social and religious imagination, in which numerous points were established. Among these we must note the following: (1) Society consists of vertically stratified classes, specifically priests (or sovereigns), warriors, and commoners; (2) the king embodies the totality of the social order and is willing to sacrifice himself for his people; (3) the priest has as his prime responsibility the performance of sacrifice, and sacrifice is the creative act par excellence; (4) the human organism is a microcosmic model (and indeed, the source) of the cosmos, while the cosmos is the macrocosmic projection of the human body.

This last point—the relation of man to cosmos as microcosm to macrocosm—was also expressed in another form, for the creation myth described not only the creation of the universe, but also the creation of man. One might cite here two reflexes, the first Old Frisian (Germanic) and the second Old Russian:

> God made the first man, that was Adam, from eight transformations: the bone from the stone, the flesh from the earth, the blood from the water, the heart from the wind, the thoughts from the clouds, the sweat from the dew, the locks of hair from the grass, the eyes from the sun, and then he blew in the holy breath. (From the *Code of Emsig*)

> And thus God made man's body out of eight parts. The first part is of the earth, which is the lowliest of all parts. The second is of the sea, which is blood and wisdom. The third is of the sun, which is beauty and eyes for him. The fourth is of the celestial clouds, which are thought and weakness. The fifth is of the wind—that is, air—which is breath and envy. The sixth is of stones, that is firm-

ness. The seventh is of the light of this world which is made into flesh, that is humility and sweetness. The eighth part is of the Holy Spirit, placed in men for all that is good, full of zeal—that is the foremost part. (From the *Discourse of the Three Saints*)

In these, and other like texts, we see the cosmogonic process reversed: the elements of the physical universe are converted into the constituent parts of a human body, as cosmogony becomes anthropogony. In truth, cosmogony and anthropogony can be—and were—regarded as separate moments in one continuous process of creation, in which physical matter eternally alternates between microcosmic and macrocosmic modes of existence, bones becoming stones becoming bones becoming stones becoming bones, ad infinitum. Matter and change are both eternal, while the body and the universe prove to be alloforms, alternate shapes, of one another. An important Indic text, *Aitareya Upaniṣad* 1.1–2.5, details the entire process of cosmogony and anthropogony, starting with the creation of the cosmos from the body of the first man (*Puruṣa*), who is dismembered by the first self (*ātman*) through the agency of ascetic heat (*tapas*).

> When [the man] was heated, his mouth broke off, like an egg. From the mouth there was speech; from speech, fire. His nostrils broke off. From the nostrils there was breath; from breath, wind. His eyes broke off. From the eyes there was vision; from vision, the sun. His ears broke off. From the ears there was hearing; from hearing, the four quarters. His skin broke off. From the skin there were hairs; from the hairs, plants and trees. His heart broke off. From the heart there was mind; from mind, the moon. His navel broke off. From the navel there was the downward [anal] breath; from the downward breath, death. His penis broke off. From the penis there was semen; from semen, the waters. (*Aitareya Upaniṣad* 1.4)

Once created, however, the elements of the universe experience hunger and ask that the man's body—from which they initially took their existence—be recreated, so that they may acquire the ability to eat and satisfy their craving for food. But just as the creation of the universe could come about only through the de-creation of the primordial man, so also the re-creation of man can come about only through the de-creation of the universe. All of the elements thus recombine to form a human body.

> Fire, having become speech, entered into the mouth. Wind, having become breath, entered into the nostrils. The sun, having become vision, entered into the eyes. The four quarters, having become hearing, entered into the ears. The plants and trees, having become hairs, entered into the skin. The moon, having become the mind, entered into the heart. Death, having become the downward breath, entered into the navel. The waters, having become semen, entered into the penis. (*Aitareya Upaniṣad* 2.4)

This passage suggests that the experience of hunger may be understood as nothing less than an anthropogonic urge, while eating—the process of nutrition—repeats the anthropogony, appropriating matter from elements of macrocosm (water and plants, for example) and converting them to their microcosmic alloforms. Similarly, simple respiration is an example of the complementary rhythms of cosmogony and anthropogony, creation and de-creation. As one exhales, breath (the microcosmic form) is converted into wind (the macrocosmic alloform), while inhalation changes wind back into breath. Each breath thus alternately de-creates the body while creating the world, then de-creates the world in order to re-create the body.

Speculation on the creation myth and the creative process seems to have been the special province of the priestly class, who read ever more subtle nuances into it, and constructed ever more elaborate rituals on the basis of it. Another myth, no less important than this, was of considerably greater interest to members of the warrior class. In this was told how the first warrior, whose name was "Third" (*Trito), conducted the first cattle raid (Lincoln 1981, 103–24; Ivanov and Toporov 1968). Here it is related that cattle originally belonging to the Indo-Europeans (in some versions to "Man" or "Twin," with whom "Third" is closely associated) were stolen by a monstrous three-headed serpent (his very name was "Serpent," *Ngʷhi-), who was a non-Indo-European, an aborigine living in land entered by I-E invaders. Following this theft, it fell to "Third" to recover the stolen cattle, and he began his quest by seeking the aid of a warrior deity to whom he offered libations of intoxicating drinks. Having won the god's assistance, and himself fortified by the same intoxicant, "Third" set forth, found the "Serpent," slew him, and released the cattle which had been imprisoned by the monster. An Indic, a Hittite, and a Roman version may conveniently be cited, although there are many more, including such Christianized favorites as St. George and the dragon or St. Patrick driving the snakes from Ireland.

> Trita, knowing the ancestral weapons and impelled by Indra [the
>   warrior god], did battle.
> Having killed the three headed, seven-bridled one,
>   Trita drove off his cattle.
> The mightly lord Indra struck down that conceited one who had
>   sought great power
> Driving forth the cattle of Viśvarūpa, he tore off those three
>   heads.
>
> *Ṛg Veda* 10.8.8–9

> When the Storm God and the Serpent came to blows in the city of
> Kishkillushsha, the Serpent defeated the Storm God, and the
> Storm God called out to all the gods: "Come to my aid."
>   The goddess Inara prepared a festival. She arranged all grandly:
> a vat of wine and vats of two other intoxicants. She filled the three
> vats to overflowing.

Now Inara went to the city Zigaratta and she encountered a man, Hupashiya. Inara said: "Look Hupashiya, I say such and such and such—you must hold yourself apart for me." Then Hupashiya said to Inara, "Hail! I will sleep with you. I will come to you. I will do as you desire." And he slept with her.

Inara led Hupashiya away and hid him. Inara adorned herself, and she beckoned the Serpent out of its cave. "Look, I am celebrating a festival. Come for the food and drink."

The Serpent came up with its children, and they ate and drank. They drank all the vats and became drunk. Then they could no longer go down into the cave.

Hupashiya came and bound the Serpent with a rope. The Storm God came and killed the Serpent there, and the gods were beside him. (KBo III 7 and KUB XVII 5)

In that season when Hercules bore off
The young oxen from your stalls, O Erythea,
He came to the Palatine hill
And himself being weary, he set down his cattle. . . .
But they did not remain safe with Cacus ["the Evil One"], a
    faithless host:
That one defiled Jove with theft.
Cacus was an aborigine, a robber from a dread cave,
Who spoke through three separate mouths.
He, in order that there be no clues to the theft,
Dragged the cattle backward into his cave—
But not unwitnessed by the god. The young oxen betrayed
    the thief by their lowing,
And wrath pulled down the rough doors of the thief.
Cacus lay dead, struck thrice by Hercules' club.

Propertius 4.9.1–20

The central concerns which are voiced in this myth are the eternal themes of power and wealth. To begin, it is asserted that cattle—which constituted the fundamental measure of wealth, means of production, and unit of exchange in I-E society (Schrader and Nehring 1917–23, 2:254–63)—properly belong to the Indo-European people, falling into non-I-E hands only as the result of theft. Theft is condemned here, as it consistently was in I-E law, primarily for its reliance on stealth and treachery, and it is set in straightforward contrast to raiding, which—far from being condemned—was heartily endorsed. Raiding is presented as a heroic action, sanctioned by divine approval, hedged with ritual, and open in its use of force to regain that which rightfully belongs to the Indo-European warrior and/or his people. Throughout Indo-European history, "Third" and his various reflexes ever remained the model for I-E warriors, who cast themselves in his image—raiding, plundering, and killing their non-I-E neighbors, convinced all the while that they were engaged in a sacred and rightful activity. This myth must be considered as one of, if not *the*, most historically important narratives in world history, for it provided the ideological impetus and justification for the Indo-European conquest of Europe and Asia: it is the imperialist's myth par excellence.

Myth and Ritual

What must be stressed in a study of these myths is that the personages who figure in them—"Man," "Twin," "Third," and "Serpent"—were not regarded as mere characters in a story but as paradigmatic models who established the proper mode of being and acting that would be followed forever after by members of specific social classes. Every priest, in order to be a proper priest, had the responsibility to act as "Man" acted, performing sacrifice to ensure the continuation of all creation. Every king was charged to act as "Twin" had acted, giving of himself for the good of all. Every warrior needed to act as "Third," fearlessly raiding on all foreign enemies—who were seen as thieves and subhuman monsters like "Serpent"—whom they killed or subjugated, and whose wealth they ruthlessly seized, secure in the belief that no livestock could ever rightfully have belonged to any non-Indo-Europeans but must have been stolen by them.

Each cattle raid was thus raised to the status of a ritual act. Gods were invoked for assistance, libations poured, ecstatic states of frenzy attained (Wikander 1938; Höfler 1934; Pryzluski 1940; Eliade 1972). Moreover, each young warrior had to pass through certain initiatory rituals before he attained full status as a member of the warrior class. Regularly, the first cattle raid figured as a rite of passage for the young warrior (Walcot 1979), and other initiations were consciously structured on the myth of "Third" and "Serpent" (Dumézil 1939, 91–106). In these, a monstrous dummy, complete with three heads, was constructed, and the initiand was forced to attack it. Were he able to summon up the necessary courage to do so, he discovered that his seemingly ferocious and formidable opponent was only a joke, with the implicit lesson that all of his future (non-I-E) enemies would be no more formidable than this dummy.

If the P-I-E warrior assumed the role of "Third" whenever he went raiding, the priest likewise assumed the role of "Man," whenever he performed sacrifice, which was always the most elaborate and self-consciously significant Indo-European ritual (Vendryes 1918; Koppers 1936; Mayrhofer-Passler 1953). What makes this so is that the sacrifice was held to be nothing less than a repetition of the cosmogony. In each sacrifice, the victim's body was dismembered and distributed to the cosmos, just as were the bodies of * Yemo and the primordial ox. Without the matter drawn from their bodies, all the items of the material world—sun, earth, water, air—would become exhausted, depleted, dead; it is only through their replenishment via sacrifice that continued existence is secured. An Indic manual of ritual practice provides instructions for the sacrificial dismemberment of an animal victim in terms drawn directly from the creation myth:

> Lay his feet down to the north. Cause his eye to go to the sun. Send forth his breath to the wind, his life-force to the atmosphere, his ears to the cardinal points, his flesh to the earth. Thus, the priest places the victim in these worlds. (*Aitareya Brāhmaṇa* 2.6)

Victims were most often domestic animals, and offerings drawn from plants or grains—cakes and the like—were also quite frequent, but these are generally described in the ritual texts as acceptable substitutes for the victim whose offering most perfectly repeats the cosmogonic sacrifice: man, and above all, the king (See Dumézil 1935; Rönnow 1929, 1943; Grottanelli 1980, 1981). Human sacrifice is attested by archaeological findings among the "Kurgan Culture" and also clearly survived among several of the Indo-European peoples. Among the most important accounts is that which Tacitus gives of the ritual of the Semnones, an ancient Germanic tribe:

> They say that the Semnones are the oldest and most noble of the Suebi. This belief is confirmed in a religious ceremony of ancient times. At a fixed time, all the people of the same blood come together by legations in a wood that is consecrated by the signs of their ancestors, and by an ancient dread. Barbaric rites celebrate the horrific origins, through the sacrificial dismemberment of a man for the public good. (*Germania* 39)

Further in this chapter, Tacitus tells us that the Semnones believed the first men to have emerged from the earth at the very spot where this gruesome sacrifice was regularly performed. And, as several scholars have pointed out, the "horrific origins" which were celebrated and the "ancient dread" which surrounds this rite most probably refers to the myth of creation through sacrificial dismemberment which is alluded to elsewhere in the *Germania* (Hammerich 1952; Ebenbauer 1974). Should this act not regularly be repeated, society and the very cosmos would crumble, and this is why the dismemberment of a man should be "for the public good."

Death and the Otherworld

Sacrifice is not the only means whereby matter is moved from the human microcosm to the universe in repetition of the cosmogonic myth. In death also—death being, in truth, a sort of sacrifice—the same thing occurs. Thus, within the most ancient Indian funeral hymn, the corpse is explicitly instructed that it must follow the mythic pattern and distribute itself throughout the cosmos:

> Your eye must go to the sun. Your soul must go to the wind. You
> must go to the sky and the earth, according to what is right.

Go to the waters, if you are placed there. You must establish the
plants with your flesh.

Ṛg Veda 10.16.3

This is not a final fate, however, for nothing within the cosmos is final,
given the basic tenets of P-I-E thought. And just as cosmogony alternates with
anthropogony, so also death alternates with resurrection (Lincoln 1977). The
matter which entered a cosmic form when one specific human body died and
fell into decay, will once again assume bodily form when that specific cosmos
dies and falls into decay, as will inevitably happen. P-I-E myth clearly looked
forward to an eschatological collapse, and beyond that to cosmic renovation
and collapse again, in an infinite cycle (Wikander 1960; Ström 1967; O'Brien
1976). The Iranian eschatologic accounts thus regularly depict the reconstruction of the body from its macrocosmic alloforms, and several of the most
important Presocratic philosophers—most notably Empedocles and Anaxago-
ras—presented a similar picture:

> [At the end of time] Ohrmazd summons the bone from the earth,
> the blood from the water, the hair from the plants, and the life
> from the wind. He mixes one with the other, and in this manner,
> he keeps on creating. (*Pahlavi Rivayat to the Dadestan i Denig*
> 48.98–107)

> When the elements are mixed into man or the race of wild animals
> or bushes or birds, that is called birth. And when the elements
> separate, that is "the evil-spirited fate" [i.e. death]. (Empedo-
> kles, Fragment 9 Diels-Kranz)

Behind these formulations, stand several very simple, yet very profound
principles: (1) matter is indestructible; (2) matter is infinitely transmutable;
(3) living organisms and the physical universe are composed of one and the
same material substance; (4) time is eternal. While change is thus constant, it
is also meaningless, for nothing that is essentially real is ever created or destroyed. Worlds come and go, as do individuals of whatever species, but
being—material being—is always there.

Such does not appear to have been true for the soul, however. Insofar as the
Proto-Indo-Europeans possessed any concept which one could equate with
that denoted by English *soul*, it seems only to have been identified with the
breath as the seat of life-force and vitality (*ṇsu-, on which see Güntert 1923,
101f.). Like the other parts of the body, the breath departed at death, turning
into the wind, its macrocosmic alloform.

Although an elaborate funerary geography clearly existed within P-I-E religion, whereby the soul's journey to the otherworld was traced across rivers in
a ferry, along pathways, past dogs and through gates, on close inspection all
this proves to be allegory and no more, for—as we have seen—there is no

soul to make the journey. The river, then, is nothing more than a mythopoetic representation of oblivion, the ferryman a personification of old age, and so forth (Schlerath 1954; see also chapters 2–8 below).

Among the most striking of these images is a female figure, sometimes presented as the goddess of the netherworld, sometimes merely as a maiden who greets the soul and guides it on its way. Her name is *Kolyo, "the Coverer," and as Hermann Güntert brilliantly demonstrated (Güntert 1919 and 1928), she is the personification of the grave, decomposition, and decay. She is not depicted in wholly negative terms, however, for when viewed from the front she appears young, appealing, and seductive in the extreme. Behind this attractive facade, however, she hides a back that is covered with serpents, worms, reptiles, and rot. Both the appeal and the horror of death fuse in this striking image: the longing for peace and the recoil from nothingness which all humans experience as their end draws near. That nothingness was the expectation is clear from the P-I-E formulaic description of the otherworld as a realm "without summer, without winter; without heat, without cold; without suffering, without labor; without hunger, without thirst; without illness, old age, or death." Though at first it all sounds quite enchanting, on further reflection one is forced to recognize that there is really nothing there.

Those who hoped for some continuation of their own individual, egotistical existence had only one recourse, summed up again in a poetic formula of P-I-E origin: "the fame that does not decay" (*ḱlewos *n̥dhgʷhitom, on which see Schmitt 1967, 61–102). In a universe where impersonal matter endured forever but the personal self was extinguished at death, the most which could survive of that self was a rumor, a reputation. For this, the person craving immortality—a condition proper only to the gods and antithetical to human existence—was totally reliant on poets and poetry. P-I-E warrior heroes—like their later I-E reflexes Siegfried, Achilles, Arjuna, and the like—desperately hoped to amass in their lifetimes a body of deeds so awesome as to move poets to sing of them forever. And while the poet was utterly dependent upon heroes to provide acts from which poems might be shaped, the hero was equally dependent on the poet to provide words in which heroic deeds might acquire a form which would endure for more than a moment.

The P-I-E warrior thus went out to battle as much in pursuit of fame as in pursuit of booty, and his pursuit of fame amounted to nothing less than a quest for immortality. Given such an ideological construct, it is little wonder that the Indo-Europeans proved so formidable militarily, and were able to expand from their homeland to India and Turkestan in the east and Iceland and Ireland in the west, subjugating their enemies and seizing their land and herds wherever they went. Yet in the process, countless would-be heroes died and countless others suffered—Indo-European and non-Indo-European alike—precious few of whom acquired the elusive "fame that does not decay."

References

Benveniste, Emile
　1932　"Les classes sociales dans la tradition avestique." *Journal asiatique* 221: 117–34.
　1938　"Traditions indo-iraniennes sur les classes sociales." *Journal asiatique* 230: 529–49.
　1975　*Indo-European Language and Society.* Coral Gables, Florida: University of Miami Press.
Boyce, Mary
　1975　"On Mithra, Lord of Fire." In *Monumentum H. S. Nyberg,* pp. 69–76. Liege: Bibliotheque Pahlavi.
　1981　"Varuṇa the Baga." In *Monumentum George Morgenstierne,* pp. 59–73. Leiden: E. J. Brill.
Buck, Carl Darling
　1949　*A Dictionary of Selected Synonyms in the Principal Indo-European Languages.* Chicago: University of Chicago Press.
Burkert, Walter
　1962　"Caesar und Romulus-Quirinus." *Historia* 11:356–76.
Dubuisson, Daniel
　1978　"Le roi indo-européen et la synthèse des trois fonctions." *Annales Économies Sociétés Civilisations* 33:21–34.
Dumézil, Georges
　1930　"La préhistoire indo-iranienne des castes. *Journal asiatique* 216:109–30.
　1935　*Flāmen-Brahman.* Paris: Annales du Musée Guimet.
　1939　*Mythes et dieux des Germains.* Paris: E. Leroux.
　1952　*Les dieux des indo-européens.* Paris: Presses Universitaires de France.
　1958　*L'ideologie tri-partie des indo-européens.* Brussels: Collection Latomus.
　1959　"Le Rex et les Flamines Maiores." In *La Regalità Sacra,* pp. 407–17. Leiden: E. J. Brill.
　1970　*The Destiny of the Warrior,* trans. Alf Hiltebeitel. Chicago: University of Chicago Press.
　1971　*The Destiny of the King,* trans. Alf Hiltebeitel. Chicago: University of Chicago Press.
　1977　*Les dieux souverains des Indo-Européens.* Paris: Gallimard.
Ebenbauer, Alfred
　1974　"Ursprungsglaube, Herrschergott und Menschenopfer. Beobachtungen zum Semnonenkult (Germania c. 39)." In *Antiquitates Indogermanicae: Gedenkschrift für Hermann Güntert,* pp. 233–49. Innsbruck: Innsbrucker Beiträge zur Sprachwissenschaft.
Eliade, Mircea
　1963　*Patterns in Comparative Religion.* New York: Meridian.
　1969　"Cosmogonic Myth and 'Sacred History.'" In *The Quest,* pp. 72–87. Chicago: University of Chicago Press.
　1972　"Dacians and Wolves." In *Zalmoxis: The Vanishing God,* pp. 1–20. Chicago: University of Chicago Press.

Gimbutas, Marija
1963   "The Indo-Europeans: Archaeological Problems." *American Anthropologist* 65:815–36.
1970   "Proto-Indo-European Culture: The Kurgan Culture during the Fifth, Fourth, and Third Millennia B.C." In *Indo-European and Indo-Europeans*, pp. 155–98. Philadelphia: University of Pennsylvania Press.
1973   "The Beginning of the Bronze Age in Europe and the Indo-Europeans: 3500–2500." *Journal of Indo-European Studies* 5:163–214.
1974   "An Archaeologist's View of PIE in 1975." *Journal of Indo-European Studies* 2:289–308.
1977   "The First Wave of Eurasian Steppe Pastoralists into Copper Age Europe." *Journal of Indo-European Studies* 5:277–338.
1980   "The Kurgan Wave #2 (c. 3400–3200 B.C.) into Europe and the Following Transformation of Culture." *Journal of Indo-European Studies* 8:273–316.
Grottanelli, Cristiano
1980   "Cosmogonia e Sacrificio, I. Problemi delle cosmogonie "rituali" nel RgVeda e nel Vicino Oriente Antico." *Studi Storico Religiosi* 4:207–35.
1981   "Cosmogonia e Sacrificio, II. Death as the Supreme God's Beloved Son and the Founding Myth of Human Sacrifice." *Studi Storico-Religiosi* 5:173–96.
Güntert, Hermann
1919   *Kalypso.* Halle: Max Niemeyer.
1923   *Der arische Weltkönig und Heiland.* Halle: Max Niemeyer.
1928   *Kundry.* Heidelberg: Carl Winter.
Hammerich, L. L.
1952   "Horrenda Primordia: Zur 'Germania' c. 39." *Germanische-Romanische Monatsschrift* 33:228–33.
Höfler, Otto
1934   *Kultische Geheimbünde der Germanen.* Frankfurt: Moritz Diesterweg.
Hopkins, Grace Sturtevant
1932   *Indo-European *Deiwos and Related Words.* Philadelphia: Linguistic Society of America.
Ivanov, V. V.
1960   "L'organisation sociale des tribus indo-européens d'après les données linguistiques." *Cahiers d'histoire mondiale* 5:789–800.
Ivanov, Vyatcheslav, and Toporov, Vladimir
1968   "Le mythe indoeuropéen du dieu de l'orage poursuivant le serpent: Reconstruction du schéma." In *Échanges et communications: Mélanges offerts à Claude Lévi-Strauss*, pp. 1180–1206. The Hague: Mouton.
Koppers, Wilhelm
1936   "Pferdeopfer und Pferdekult der Indogermanen." *Wiener Beiträge zur Kulturkunde und Linguistik* 4:279–411.
Lincoln, Bruce
1977   "Death and Resurrection in Indo-European Thought." *Journal of Indo-European Studies* 5:247–64.
1981   *Priests, Warriors, and Cattle: A Study in the Ecology of Religions.* Berkeley and Los Angeles: University of California Press.

Littleton, C. Scott
1982   *The New Comparative Mythology*, 3d ed. Berkeley and Los Angeles: University of California Press.

Mallory, James
1973   "A Short History of the Indo-European Problem." *Journal of Indo-European Studies* 1:21–65.
1976–77   "The Chronology of the Early Kurgan Tradition." *Journal of Indo-European Studies* 4:257–94 and 5:339–68.

Mayrhofer-Passler, E.
1953   "Haustieropfer bei den Indo-iraniern und den anderen indogermanischen Völkern." *Archiv Orientalni* 21:182–205.

Meillet, Antoine
1907   "La religion indo-européenne." *La Revue des idées* 4:689–99.

Nagy, Gregory
1974   "Perkū́nas and Perunь." In *Antiquitates Indogermanicae: Gedenkschrift für Hermann Güntert*, pp. 113–31. Innsbruck: Innsbrucker Beiträge zur Sprachwissenschaft.

O'Brien, Steven
1976   "Indo-European Eschatology: A Model." *Journal of Indo-European Studies* 4:295–320.
1980   "Social Organization in Western Indo-European." *Journal of Indo-European Studies* 8:123–64.

Pokorny, Julius
1959   *Indogermanisches etymologisches Wörterbuch*. Bern: Francke Verlag.

Polomé, Edgar
1980   "The Gods of the Indo-Europeans." *The Mankind Quarterly* 21:151–64.
1982   "Indo-European Culture, with Special Attention to Religion." In *The Indo-Europeans in the Fourth and Third Millennia*, pp. 156–72. Ann Arbor: Karoma.

Pryzluski, Jean
1940   "Les confréries de loups-garous dans les sociétés indo-européennes." *Revue de l'histoire des religions* 121:128–45.

Puhvel, Jaan
1975   "Remus et Frater." *History of Religions* 15:146–57.

Rönnow, Kasten
1929   "Zur Erklärung des Pravargya, des Agnicayana und der Sautrāmaṇī." *Le Monde Oriental* 23:113–73.
1943   "Zagreus och Dionysos." *Religion och Bibel* 2:14–48.

Schlerath, Bernfried
1954   "Der Hund bei den Indogermanen." *Paideuma* 6:25–40.
1977   *Die Indogermanen. Das Problem der Expansion eines Volkes im Lichte seiner sozialen Struktur*. Innsbruck: Innsbrucker Beiträge zur Sprachwissenschaft.

Schmitt, Rüdiger
1967   *Dichtung und Dichtersprache in indogermanischer Zeit*. Wiesbaden: Otto Harrassowitz.

Schrader, Otto
1890   *Prehistoric Antiquities of the Aryan Peoples.* London: Charles Griffin.
Schrader, Otto, and Nehring, A.
1917–23   *Reallexikon der indogermanischen Altertumskunde.* Strassburg: Otto Harrassowitz.
Ström, Åke V.
1967   "Indogermanisches in der Völuspa." *Numen* 14:167–208.
Thomas, Homer L.
1982   "Archaeological Evidence for the Migrations of the Indo-Europeans." In *The Indo-Europeans in the Fourth and Third Millennia,* pp. 61–86. Ann Arbor: Karoma.
Vendryes, Joseph
1918   "Les correspondances de vocabulaire entre l'indo-iranien et l'italo-celtique." *Mémoires de la société de linguistique de Paris* 20:265–85.
Walcot, Peter
1979   "Cattle Raiding, Heroic Tradition, and Ritual: The Greek Evidence." *History of Religions* 18:326–51.
Wikander, Stig
1938   *Der arische Männerbund.* Lund: C. W. K. Gleerup.
1960   "Från Bravalla til Kurukshetra." *Arkiv för Nordisk Filologi* 75:183–93.
Xazanov, A. M.
1975   *Sošial'naja Istorija Skifov.* Moscow.

PART ONE

DEATH AND FUNERARY GEOGRAPHY
IN INDO-EUROPEAN MYTH

TWO

ON THE IMAGERY OF PARADISE

Alongside the gloomy picture of Hades common in Greek poetry from Homer onward, there exists another set of descriptions of a quite different other-world, a paradisal realm reserved for specially favored souls. Three classic texts are particularly noteworthy:

> It is not ordained by the gods for you, O Menelaos, beloved of
> 　　Zeus,
> To die in the Argive fields and reach your fate,
> But the immortals will lead you to the Elysian field
> At the ends of the earth, where fair-haired Rhadamanthys
> 　　dwells,
> And where life is most free from care for men;
> There is neither snow, nor much of cold, nor rain,
> But always Okeanos rouses blasts
> Of the whistling-breathed Zephyr to cool men;
> For you possess Helen, and to the gods are a son-in-law of Zeus.
>
> 　　　　　　　　　　　　　　Homer, *Odyssey* 4.561–69

> And for the other group of men [in contrast to those who died at
> 　　Troy], Father Zeus, son of Kronos,
> Set down a life and a country of their own at the ends of the
> 　　earth,
> Far from the immortals. Kronos holds sway over them.[1]
> And they abide without cares of spirit
> In the Isles of the Blessed beside deep-swirling Okeanos.
> Fortunate are these heroes; the grain-giving earth
> Bears them luxuriant honey-sweet fruit three times over.
>
> 　　　　　　　　　　　　Hesiod, *Works and Days*, 167–73

> Ever possessing the sun—in nights
> As much as in days—
> The good receive a life most devoid of trouble. They do not stir
> 　　up the earth with the strength of their hand,
> Nor the sea water
> For a barren living. Rather, beside those who are honored
> 　　among the gods
> They who have been faithful to their oaths rejoice: they possess
> Life without tears, and the rest endure unbearable pain.[2]
>
> 　　　　　　　　　　　Pindar, *Olympian Ode* 2:61–67

For all their differences, there are some clear similarities among these three texts. Two of them place paradise at the ends of the earth (*peirata gaiēs*) beside Okeanos. Two of them emphasize the rich productivity of the soil, which bears fruit without requiring any labor of the blessed souls. Two of them dwell on the wonders of the climate: eternal sunshine, lack of precipitation, the dreamland of any tourist. Yet of all these similarities, the most important is that paradise is described almost entirely in terms of a negative sort. It is a realm without cares (*rhēistē*—Odyssey 4.565; *akēdeos*—*Works and Days* 170); without tears (*adakrus*—Olympia 2:66); without cold, snow, or rain (*Odyssey* 4.566); without labor (*Works and Days,* 172f.; *Olympia* 2:63–5); and without darkness (*Olympia* 2:61f.). It is, as Pindar tautologically put it, a place in which life is "most without trouble" of any sort (*aponesteron*— *Olympia* 2:62). So common is the use of words with privative prefixes (*a*- or *an*- < P-I-E *ṇ-) that Homer can play on the sound associations of this prefix in line 568, using three consecutive words that begin with an *an*- element, none of which however, have a privative sense: *Ōkeanos aniēsin anapsykhein anthrōpous.*

This poetic device, whereby paradise is defined more by *what it is not* than by what it is, is also quite common in texts describing paradise in the literatures of other Indo-European peoples. Clearly, the common Celtic and Germanic theme of the inexhaustible banquet, the food and drink of which are provided by magical cauldrons or animals[3] can be taken in this light, for the otherworld is here marked not so much by the *presence* of comestibles as by the *absence* of want. More specifically, a Celtic text such as the *Voyage of Bran,* stanzas 9–10, is remarkably similar in language and ideology to the Greek sources cited above:

> Not known is wailing, nor treachery
> In the well-known cultivated land.
> There is nothing rough or harsh,
> But only melodious music striking the ear.
> Without sorrow, without gloom, without death,
> Without any sickness, without debility:
> That is the mark by which Emain[4] is known.
> Not common is an equal wonder.
>
> *Imram Bráin* 9–10

While the precise imagery is quite unlike that of Homer, Hesiod, and Pindar—only the phrase "without grief, without sorrow" (*cen brón, cen duba*) may be directly compared—the general negative thrust of these verses is quite in keeping with that of the Greeks. Here, attention is paid to emotional and ethical categories ("Not known is wailing, nor treachery"—*Ní gnáth écóiniud na mrath*), and to aesthetic ones as well ("nothing rough or harsh"—*ní bii nach gargg fri crúais*), but the culminating vision is the absence of the physical changes which mark the human life-cycle: death, disease, and infirmity (*cen bás cen nach n-galar cen indgás*).

Certain specific images found in the Greek texts are encountered in another important Celtic description of paradise, contained within an eighth-century Christianized Imrara ("Voyage") tale,[5] where the *Terra Repromissionis Sanctorum*, "the land promised to the Saints"[6] is described.

> Having passed almost an hour, a vast light surrounded us, and a land appeared—spacious and grassy and extremely fruitful. . . . We saw no plant without flowers, or trees without fruit. Even the stones themselves were of the precious variety. . . .
>
> [Shortly after landing, the travelers encounter an angel, whose name they ask, to which he replies:] "Why ask me where I come from or what I am called? Why not ask me about this island? Just as you see it, thus it remains from the beginning of the world. Do you have need of any food, drink, or clothing? You have been in this island a year, and have not tasted food or drink. Never have you been oppressed by sleep, nor has night covered you, for it is always day without shadows. Our Lord Jesus Christ is himself the light." (*Navigatio Sancti Brendani*, chap. 1)

The Christian influence could not be clearer in the figure of the angel and in the last line, but that overlay notwithstanding, the imagery is pure Indo-European. The realm of the blessed is seen as an island at the outer limits of the world; light is omnipresent to the extent that no shadows appear;[7] the earth brings forth abundant fruit with no evidence of agricultural labor being required—all this is familiar from the Greek materials. The *Navigatio Brendani* goes further, however, to make several new and striking points. First, it is stated that "even the stones themselves were of the precious variety" (*Lapides enim ipsius preciosi generis sunt*), which is to say that in paradise there is no gross matter, no physicality of the lower kind. Further, it is implied that time as we know it does not exist, for what seemed only a few hours to the travelers proves to have been an entire year.[8] Finally, it is stated that none of the normal processes needed to sustain life in this world are necessary—no sleep, no food, no drink. While the liberation from the need to eat would seem to contradict the theme of the island's rich fruitfulness, both images have their origin in the same basic principle: paradise as the negation of all that is unpleasant in the normal terrestrial world.

Celtic descriptions of the otherworld are numerous, rich, and varied, but for all their differences most preserve this basic negative definition.[9] Consider, for instance, this description of the Isle of Glass, a common designation of the otherworld,[10] ruled over by Maheloas, whose name means "Prince of Death."[11] The text is taken from one of the earliest Grail romances, composed in the late twelfth century:

Among those whom you hear me name
Is Maheloas, highly regarded by us,
The Lord of the Isle of Glass.
In this isle there is no thunder,
No lightning strikes, nor storm;
No toad or serpent there remains;
It is not too hot, nor is there winter.

Chrétien de Troyes, *Erec* 1933–39

Much like Homer, Chrétien dwells on the climate of paradise or, to put it more precisely, the *lack* of a climate in paradise. At a semantic level, the terms are almost exactly the same: no heat, no cold, no storms. Beyond this, however, the French romancer adds a new dimension to the negative definition: in paradise, he tells us, there are no noxious creatures, serpent and toad being appropriately singled out for mention, as the serpent was identified with treachery, hostility, and violence in Indo-European mythic thought.[12]

The later Germanic saga literature also contains accounts of paradise which are remarkably close to those presented above. Perhaps the most important of these is the description of Ódáinsakr, the "field of the Immortals,"[13] said to be the name given by heathen men to that realm which Christians call "the land of living men, or Paradise" (*jǫrð lifandi manna eðr Paradísum*).[14]

Guðmund is the name of the ruler of Jǫtunheim ["Giant-home"]. His dwelling is at Grund ["Field"] in the district of Glasisvellier ["Shining meadow"].[15] He was a powerful man and wise, and he and all his men were so old that they outlived many generations. Therefore, heathen men believed that Ódáinsakr must be in his kingdom, the place in which sickness and old age depart from every man who comes there, and where no one is permitted to die. (*Hervararsaga,* chap. 1)

The figure of Guðmund is extremely mysterious, and seems to have displaced Old Norse Ýmir (< P-I-E *Yemo-) in the role of ruler of paradise, as I have argued elsewhere.[16] Similarly, the name Ódáinsakr—which appears nowhere in the earlier literature—may be a new coining, its etymology still being insufficiently clear to permit conclusive judgment.[17] But the description of this realm as "the place . . . in which sickness and old age depart and where no one is permitted to die" (*sa staðr . . . hverfr sótt ok elli, ok má engi deyja*) tallies so closely with those we have considered, particularly with stanza 10 of the *Imram Bráin,* that it must be considered an authentic German reflex of a Proto-Indo-European idea.

Equally close is the description of Yima's realm as given in numerous Avestan texts, such as *Yašt* 9.9–10, 15.16–17, 17.29–30, and 19.32–33. According to *Vīdēvdāt* 2.5, when accepting the kingship from Ahura Mazdā,

Yima pledged: "In my realm there will be no cold wind, nor heat, nor disease, nor death." In one of the more extensive descriptions, this list is extended:

> . . . And to Vivanhant a son was born, who was shining Yima of the beautiful herds, most possessed of $x^v aranah$ ["solar radiance"] of all those who have been born, whose appearance was like the sun among men, and in his realm he made it that the cattle and men were immortal, water and plants did not dry up, and edible food was undiminishing.
>
> During the region of swift Yima, there was no cold nor heat; there was no old age, nor death, nor envy created by the *daēvas*. . . . (*Yasna* 9.4–5)

To be sure, Yima is not here depicted as a ruler of the dead, but rather, as Christensen so elegantly demonstrated, as the first man and the first king of Iranian legend.[18] The descriptions given do not apply to a *post mortem* realm, but to a primordial paradise in which all people lived until the moment at which Yima first sinned and death came into the world.[19] Still, given that the Indian Yama—who directly corresponds to the Iranian Yima—*is* presented not only as first man and first king, but also as the first to die[20] and thereafter the ruler of the otherworld,[21] it has often been suggested that this last aspect of Yama's career was detached from the career of his Iranian counterpart after the latter was denounced by Zarathustra.[22] In my opinion, this analysis is a sound one, and the Indo-Iranian *Yama must be seen as having been regarded as ruler of the otherworld, the features of which were projected back into Yima's primordial realm.

If the Iranian Yima lost part of his original role under the impact of the Zarathustrian reform, he also acquired at least one new role by way of compensation: builder of the enclosure (*vara-*) in which chosen people, animals, and plants will survive winters of destruction, and from which they will issue forth to repopulate the world.[23] The origins of this legend are obscure, and it has been argued that it represents an Iranian version of the Mesopotamian flood saga,[24] of the P-I-E eschatological drama,[25] or is simply a mythic account of the seasonal alternations fundamental to the life of a pastoral people.[26] The story is recounted in *Vīdēvdāt* 2.20–43, and one verse in particular requires our attention:

> Here there was not one who has a hump in front [i.e., a malformed sternum?],[27] nor a humpback, nor a eunuch, nor madness, nor blemish, nor *daiwi* [?], nor *kasvi* [?], nor deviance, nor those whose teeth are decayed, nor a leper whose body is overcome, nor any other marks which are the mark of Aŋra Mainyu ["the Evil Spirit"] set down upon mortals. (*Vīdēvdāt* 2.37)

Despite its obscurities of language, this verse is clear in its general intent. It directly follows other verses spelling out how Yima permitted only those who were "biggest, best, and most beautiful" (*mazištaca vahištaca sraēštaca*) in his enclosure, and the specifications of this passage thus serve to amplify the more general point that the enclosure was reserved for the best and the brightest. This amplification, however, is voiced in entirely negative terms, stating that no disease or deformity is permitted, for these are the brands of shame placed by the Evil Spriit on those beings whom he has contaminated. The enclosure, as a paradisal realm, is free from all such evil, and the important Pahlavi gloss to *Vidēvdāt* 2.41 describes it clearly as a paradise in familiar negative terms: "It is said that they live a hundred and fifty years (in Yima's enclosure); that they live an existence which is most beautiful in soul; and that they never die."

This negative pattern of imagery is also found in Indian descriptions of the otherworld, as for instance, the following Vedic verse:

> Where the light is inexhaustible, in the world where heaven is
>   established,
> Place me there, Pavāmana, in the endless, deathless world!

Ṛg Veda 9.11.7

Two of these images are quite familiar by now: absence of darkness, here expressed as inexhaustible light (*jyótir ájasraṃ*), and absence of death (*amŕta-*) to which is added a new negative image: absence of end (*ákṣita-*) to the realm, an endlessness that must be understood as both spatial and temporal. Underlying all is a broader point, namely that paradise knows none of the limits which characterize mundane existence.

More detailed than this brief verse, and more striking in many ways is the epic description of Yama's palace, which has often been compared to Yima's enclosure.[28]

> Narada said:
> "Listen, Yudhiṣṭhira, I will tell you about the divine hall
> Which Viśvakarman made for the sake of [Yama], Vivasvat's
>   son.
> This hall is splendid, O King, being a hundred spans [250–900
>   miles]
> In length and width, or even more, O Pandava,
> Sparkling, bright as the sun, moving at pleasure in every
>   direction.
> It is not excessively cold, nor excessively hot, but gladdening in
>   spirit;
> There is no pain nor old age there, no hunger, thirst, nor
>   anything disagreeable;
> There is no misery or fatigue, nor any perversity.

All desires are fulfilled there, those which are divine and those
which are human.
The food and drink are flavorful and abundant, O Tamer of
foes!"

Mahābhārata 2.8.1–5

On the strength of these examples, we may safely reconstruct the broad out-
lines of the Proto-Indo-European poetic description of paradise: a realm without heat or cold, snow or rain; without cares or suffering, tears or pain; a
realm without darkness, sickness, old age, or death; a realm where labor and
want are equally unknown. In short, it is a realm in which appear none of
those things which make this world unpleasant in the slightest degree.

The point of this is not simply to sing the wonders of paradise—indeed, no
wonders are mentioned. Nor is it to paint the next world as a sphere of absolute nonbeing, for were it so, surely the description would include the lack of
light rather than the lack of darkness, to name but one example. In the last
analysis, it would seem that the intent of this negative definition is to emphasize the radical otherness of the Otherworld. In truth, nothing positive is said
of paradise for the reason that it is so totally unlike our own mortal sphere that
our very language and normal set of images are thoroughly inadequate for the
task of describing it.

Of the otherworld, all that can be said is that things there are totally *other*,
completely opposed to all of this earth. The logic which supports the negative
definition is thus much like that which undergirds the view of the next world as
a topsy-turvy kingdom, where people walk on their hands, trees chop down
woodsmen, and the like.[29] But unlike the poet or seer who tells of such a land,
the one who employs the negative definition of paradise displays also a charm-
ing and profound reticence, daring not to speak of that which he knows not,
venturing only to say that it is unlike anything he knows.

Notes

1. Line 169 appears in only two manuscripts of the *Works and Days*, and has thus
been rejected as spurious by some editors, following the lead of such ancients as Proclus. In my opinion, however, it is more likely that the striking content of this line—
that the fallen Kronos was made ruler of paradise by Zeus—led to its suppression in
the majority of copies. On the principle of *lectior difficilior*, here applied to mythological questions, it ought certainly be retained.

2. One should note that this is not the only paradisal realm described in the Second
Olympian Ode, for Pindar goes on to deal with the "Isle of the Blessed" (*nāsos
makarōn*) in the lines which follow those cited here.

3. As, for instance, *Grimnismál* 25; *Gylfaginning* 39; *The Spoils of Annwn; The
Conquest of the Sid;* et al. Note particularly the texts collected by Wolfgang Krause,
Die Kelten (Tübingen, J. C. B. Mohr, 1929), pp. 28ff.

4. This place name is usually left untranslated, but ought to be compared to the well-known Emain Macha, "field of the twins." As it is no doubt short for the fuller designation Emain Ablach, so often used for the Celtic paradise, one might then translate it "the twin of the apple orchard."

5. The *Navigatio Sancti Brendani* has been treated thus by, inter alia, Eleanor Hull, "The Development of the Idea of Hades in Celtic Literature," *Folklore* 18 (1907): 156ff.; Roger Sherman Loomis, *The Grail: From Celtic Myth to Christian Symbol* (New York: Columbia University Press, 1963), pp. 127–29; and Alwyn and Brinley Rees, *Celtic Heritage* (London: Thames and Hudson, 1961), pp. 323–25.

6. The translation of *terra repromissionis* most literally is "the land of the counterpromise," which is to say that the land is promised to the saints in return for their service to the faith.

7. On the imagery of paradise as filled with light, see especially Willy Krogmann, "Neorxna wang und Iðavǫllr," *Archiv für das Studium der neueren Sprachen und Literaturen* 191 (1954): 30–43, and the wealth of evidence assembled by Jacob Grimm, *Teutonic Mythology*, trans. James Stallybrass (London: George Bell, 1883), pp. 823 and 1444.

8. On this theme, see Marie-Louise Sjoestedt, *Gods and Heroes of the Celts*, trans. Myles Dillon (London: Methuen, 1949), p. 50f.

9. In addition to the sources quoted, see for instance *Echtra Condla* 1f.; *Conquest of the Síd;* or the Welsh poem cited in Loomis, p. 126, said to be older than the *Mabinogion.* The bard Taliesin is speaking: "Perfect is my seat in the Faery Fortress (*Caer Síddi*); / Neither plague nor age harms him who dwells therein."

10. See A. H. Krappe, "Avallon," *Speculum* 18 (1943): 307–11; John Rhys, *Studies in the Arthurian Legend* (Oxford: Clarendon Press 1891), pp. 328–47; and Rudolf Much, "Balder," *Zeitschrift für deutsches Altertum* 61 (1924): 101–4.

11. As demonstrated by Ferdinand Lot, "Celtica: VI. Melvas, Roi des morts, et l'ile de verre," *Romania* 24 (1895): 327–35. The etymology offered is *Maheloas* < *Melvas* (cf. the parallel figures of Geoffrey of Monmouth's *Malvasius* and David ab Gwilym's *Melwas*) < **Mael-bās*, "Prince of the Dead" or "Prince of Death."

12. See Bruce Lincoln, "The Indo-European Cattle-Raiding Myth," *History of Religions* 16 (1976): 42–65. In this light, perhaps the legend of St. Patrick having driven the snakes out of Ireland ought to be interpreted as expressing the belief that he thereby transformed the island into a paradisal realm.

13. On which, see Grimm, p. 823n.; Rudolf Much, "Undensakre—Untersberg," *Zeitschrift für deutsches Altertum,* 47 (1904): 67–72; and Jan de Vries, *Altgermanische Religionsgeschichte* (Berlin: Walter de Gruyter 1970), pp. 2,284f.

14. *Eiriks saga viðfǫrla*, chapter 1, in Valdimar Asmundarson, ed. *Fornaldarsögur Nordlanda* (Reykjavik: Sigurdur Kristjanssen, 1889), pp. 3, 517.

15. Glasisvellir, also written Glæsisvellir in some manuscripts, is certainly to be connected with the Glasislundr which appears as the dwelling of King Hjǫrvarðr in the Helgakviða Hjorvarðssonar of the Elder Edda, and with the grove (*lundr*) named Glasir which is said to lie in front of the door of Valhalla according to *Skaldskaparmál* 34. It has also been suggested that it ought to be connected with the "amber islands" named *Glēsiae* in Pliny, *Natural History* 4.103, on which see Krappe, "Avallon," p. 308; Much, "Balder," p. 101; and Franz Rolt Schröder, "Der Ursprung der Hamletsage," *Germanisch-Romanische Monatsschrift* 26 (1938): 102.

16. See Chapter 3, "The Lord of the Dead."

17. Grimm, for instance, p. 823n., suggested that *Ódáinsakr* replaced an older *Óðinsakr* (= Valhalla).

18. Arthur Christensen, *Le premier homme et premier roi dans la tradition legendaire iranienne*, vol. 2; *Yima* (Uppsala: Archives d'études orientales 1923). See also my brief summary, "Yima," in Carsten Colpe, ed., *Wörterbuch der Mythologie: Altiranische und zoroastrische Mythologie* (Stuttgart: Klett Verlag, 1974–1982), pp. 469–73.

19. See such sources as *Yašt* 19.33 f.; *Aogəmadaēca* 94–7; *Dādēstān ī Dēnīg* 39.16.

20. *Atharva Veda* 18.3.13; *Ṛg Veda* 10.14.1 f., and 10.13.4, noting also *Ṛg Veda* 10.10.3, where he is called the "only mortal" (*ékasya . . . mártasya*).

21. *Ṛg Veda* 9.113.8, 10.14.1 and 7, 10.16.9; *Atharva Veda* 18.2.25 and 46.

22. Zarathustra clearly denounces Yima in *Yasna* 32.8, the only verse in which the prophet mentions him. On the results of this denunciation with regard to Yima's presumed pre-Zoroastrian role as lord of the dead, see Christensen, *Le premier homme*, p. 45f.; Friedrich Spiegel, *Arische Periode und ihre Zustände* (Leipzig: Wilhelm Friedrich, 1887), p. 244f.; Georges Dumézil, *The Destiny of a King*, trans. Alf Hiltebeitel (Chicago: University of Chicago Press, 1971), p. 6; and Hermann Collitz, "König Yima und Saturn," *Oriental Studies in Honour of Pavry* (London: Oxford University Press, 1933), pp. 88–92. See also Mary Boyce, *A History of Zoroastrianism*, vol. 1 (Leiden: E. J. Brill, 1978), pp. 83–84.

23. The exit from the enclosure is never mentioned in the Avesta, but is described with clearly eschatological tones in *Dādēstān ī Dēnīg* 37.94 f. and *Mēnōg ī Xrād* 27.27–31. Note also a Persian paraphrase of the *Bahman Yašt* cited by Christensen, *Le Premier homme*, p. 63.

24. Thus, Bruno Lindner, "Die iranische Flutsage," in *Festgruss an Rudolf von Roth* (Stuttgart: W. Kohlhammer 1893), pp. 213–16.

25. Christensen, *Le premier homme*, pp. 56–59.

26. Marijan Molé, "La guerre des geants d'apres le Sutkar Nask," *Indo-Iranian Journal* 3 (1959): 291–94.

27. I owe this suggestion to W. W. Malandra.

28. Christensen, *Le premier homme*, p. 42; A. V. Williams Jackson, "On Maha-Bharata iii. 142. 35–45, an echo of an old Hindu-Persian legend," *Journal of the American Oriental Society* 17 (1896): 186; Georges Dumézil, "La sabha de Yama," *Journal asiatique* 253 (1965): 162–64. Descriptions of paradise couched in wholly negative terms are also common in the Upaniṣads, as for instance, *Śvetāśvatara Upaniṣad* 2,12; *Katha Upaniṣad* 1,12; *Chandogya Upaniṣad* 8,4.1–2 *Bṛhadāraṇyaka Upaniṣad* 5,10.

29. To cite but two examples of this theme, see Herman Lommel, "Bhṛgu im Jenseits," *Paideuma* 4 (1950): 93–109; Roger Sherman Loomis, "King Arthur in the Antipodes," *Wales and the Arthurian Legend* (Cardiff: University of Wales Press 1956), pp. 61–76.

THREE

THE LORD OF THE DEAD

Several years ago, writing on the cosmogonic myth of the Proto-Indo-Europeans, I argued that the world was depicted as resulting from a primordial act of sacrifice in which the first priest, whose name was *Manu ("Man"), sacrificed his twin brother, the first king, whose name was *Yemo ("Twin"), along with the first member of the bovine species.[1] These findings have since received support from the research of Jaan Puhvel on the Roman reflexes of the myth,[2] and in two succeeding articles I have indicated the signal importance of the cosmogonic myth for some other aspects of Proto-Indo-European (P-I-E) religion.[3] Most recently, the argument for this reconstruction of the P-I-E cosmogony—notwithstanding the gracious demurral of Georges Dumézil[4]—has been further strengthened by the recognition of two closely related Celtic reflexes of the myth in the conclusion of the *Táin Bó Cúalnge* and the prefatory tale to the Táin entitled *"De Chophur in da Muccida."*[5]

As with all cosmogonic myths, the wealth and importance of this tale were enormous, and we are only beginning to recognize the full range of its significances. It established an etiology for the physical world, a system of macrocosmic and microcosmic homologies, a charter for the organization of society, a foundation for the central ritual action, and a depiction of the proper interrelation of the human, animal, and physical worlds. I strongly suspect that, in years to come, we will recognize still further implications of the P-I-E cosmogony, one of which provides the topic for this article. For it can now be shown, as was suspected by Hermann Güntert more than fifty years ago,[6] that the career of *Yemo did not end with his sacrificial immolation, death being the end to but one chapter of his mythos, for thereafter he went on to establish the realm of the dead, where he ruled as king forever after.

Indic Yama

The clearest example of this formulation is Yama as he is presented in Vedic literature. Said to be the first mortal,[7] he chose death freely;[8] and although the precise nature of his death is not spelled out in Indian texts, it is clear from comparison with Iranian and other evidence that it was a sacrificial death at the hands of his brother (or half-brother)[9] Manu.[10] Within the Vedas, Yama is never called a god, bearing the title of king instead,[11] a title which refers to his status prior to death and after death as well, for he is said to be king in heaven,[12] where he reigns over the souls of the departed.[13] Most of these points are summarized in the first two verses in the longest hymn addressed to Yama in the corpus of the *Ṛg Veda:*

> We bring gifts with libation to King Yama, gatherer of mankind,
>   son of Vivasvat,
> Who went forth to the great heights, who showed the path to
>   many.
> Yama first found the way for us; this cattle pasture is not to be
>   borne away from us;
> Where our fathers of old [have gone], by this path those who are
>   born after, themselves should go.

RV 10.14.1–2

The path of Yama is, of course, death,[14] a path established by Yama's demise. As all mortals thereafter also perish, so they follow his example, treading his path. The term "path of Yama" (*pathā́ yamásya*), however, ought not be dismissed as metaphor only, for his realm does have a concrete side to it as well.[15] Frequently it is said to be in the highest heaven,[16] but it is also often set in the southern world region,[17] with entry to it from the southeast.[18]

In epic and Puranic literature, Yama is regularly portrayed in a horrific, even ghoulish, manner, although a notable exception is the description of his paradisal palace in the *Mahābhārata* (2.8).[19] A hint of his fearsome aspect is found in so early a source as *Ṛg Veda* 10.97.16, where the "foot fetter of Yama" (*yamásya pā́ḍbīśa-*) is mentioned, an image derived from the older Indo-European theme of the "bonds of death." Originally, however, these bonds had no association with the ruler of the dead, belonging to Death herself, personified as a Goddess.[20] Originally, there seems to have been nothing terrifying about Yama, as most scholars have agreed,[21] and his realm is presented in the Vedas as one primarily characterized by feasting, light, beauty, and happiness.[22]

Celtic and Germanic Correspondences

This picture of Yama as first king, first mortal, first of the dead, so clearly delineated in India, has occasionally been compared with an important datum for the study of Celtic religion, a single sentence from Caesar's *De bello Gallico* (6.18), in which it is stated: "All the Gauls proclaim themselves to be born from Father Dis, and they say this is revealed by the Druids." Chief among the difficulties in interpreting this testimony is the use, as was common with all Roman authors, of the Latin name of a Roman deity who corresponded more or less closely to that of the Gallic deity being discussed. Thus, it is not clear just whom Caesar was referring to by the phrase *Dis pater,* a common name for the Roman god of the underworld. It is significant, however, that he chose this name rather than Pluto, for it includes the specification *pater* ("father"), and it is this deity's absolute fatherhood that he emphasizes, stating that within Druidic teachings the primordial father was also regarded as lord of the dead—precisely the ideology we encountered in Indian sources.

This shred torn from Caesar need not stand alone, however, for there is considerable evidence in the literature of the insular Celts to support these conclusions. Irish literature in particular is quite rich in descriptions of the otherworld, although—as several scholars have noted—the Irish otherworld is rarely depicted as a realm of the dead, being more usually described as a paradisal faeryland.[23] There is one striking exception to this general tendency, however, which has been recognized as an Irish *Totenreich* by even the most skeptical authorities: an island to the southwest of Ireland known since antiquity as *Tech Duinn,* "the house of Donn."[24] The island takes its name from an incident in the history of the "Sons of Mil," as told in book 8 of the *Lebor Gabála Érenn* ("The Book of the Taking of Ireland"), Mil being the ancestral hero of all the Irish and his sons the first humans to inhabit Ireland. Of Mil's eight sons, two stand foremost: Donn, the eldest, identified as the king (*rí*), and Amairgen, poet and judge (*filid*) among them,[25] but it is Donn who is our chief interest.

The sons of Mil made two landings on Irish soil. After the first, they defeated the Tuatha Dé Danaan, the gods who previously inhabited the island, and thereby established their claim to the realm. The Tuatha Dé, however, used magic powers to force the sons of Mil back beyond the ninth wave offshore, where they had to remain for a total of three days. When trying to regain the shore, according to the *Metrical Dindsenchas* (4.311), Donn climbed the mast of the ship, where he bore the brunt of a curse launched by the Tuatha Dé, died and fell into the sea, whereupon Amairgen declared Donn's folk would forever after travel to his last resting place. According to the poet Maél Muru of Othan (died A.D. 887), it was Donn himself who set down the decree:

> A stone cairn was raised across the broad sea for his people,
> A long-standing ancient house, which is named the House of
> Donn after him.
> And this was his mighty testament for his hundredfold offspring:
> "You shall all come to me, to my house, after your death."[26]

Donn is thus one of a set of brothers, most clearly related to Amairgen, with whom he stands in the relation of king to priest. Moreover, he is the first king of myth, having won the realm of Ireland upon his first landing. First king, he is also first to die, and upon his death he established the realm of the dead to which all his descendants venture when their time comes. In all this, he is strikingly similar to the Indian Yama and to Caesar's Dis pater.

There is also another Donn who merits our attention: Donn Cúalnge, "the dark [bull] of Cooley," the prize so eagerly sought in the *Táin*. The conclusion of this epic tale is a duel between Donn and his rival, Findbennach Aí, the "White-horned [bull] of Aí," in which Donn literally tears his opponent limb from limb, creating the Irish landscape from the fragments of his body.[27] As I have shown elsewhere, this constitutes an Irish reflex of the P-I-E creation myth,[28] yet if this is so, then Donn occupies the place of the sacrificer (*Manu) and not that of the sacrificed who becomes lord of the dead (*Yemo). This shift demands explanation.

Such a transformation may be understood, I believe, if we perceive the way in which the Irish reinterpreted the P-I-E cosmogonic materials they inherited. Thus, it is crucial to see that what was originally a myth of creation *through sacrifice* became for them a myth of creation *through combat*. Within the context of sacrifice, the figure who stands out as most admirable is the victim— he who permits the ritual to be enacted upon his body for the sake of the world that comes into being as a result. Within the context of combat, however, the vanquished attains no such eminence, and it is the victor alone whose stature is noble. If one of the two is to be further elevated after death, it must be the conqueror, not the conquered, and the myth is adjusted accordingly. Thus, we are told that Donn died shortly after the Findbennach Aí, suffering a broken heart and giving his body also to create the Irish landscape.[29] Donn thus comes to play the role of *Yemo as well as that of *Manu. With regard to the P-I-E myth, he occupies the position of sacrificer and sacrificed alike, while within the Irish myth he is only the victor. Insofar as he assumes *Yemo's role, however, and insofar as he is infinitely more admirable than the fallen Findbennach Aí, it is he who becomes lord of the dead.

The name *Donn* is particularly appropriate for a lord of the dead, literally meaning "the dusky, the dark one," and being derived from P-I-E *dhus-no,* like Welsh *dwnn,* Old English *dunn,* and Latin *fus-cus.*[30] In Christian sources, it is a frequent epithet for Satan,[31] which leads one to wonder whether it is simply a descriptive term which has replaced an older proper name. If this is so, the name we might expect is Emon, "Twin," the old Irish reflex of P-I-E *Yemo.[32]

Although there is no personage bearing such a name in Irish lore, this expectation finds striking confirmation in a rather unexpected source. Among the most celebrated island paradises described in the Old Irish *Imrama* ("Voyage") tales is one named Emain or, more fully, Emain Ablach.[33] Most often the name is left untranslated, although there is no reason to do so. *Ablach* means "having apple trees," being derived from Old Irish *aball,* "apple,"[34] and *Emain* is an alternative form of the singular nominative of *emon,* which can mean either "a twin" or "a pair of twins."[35] This same form is found in another important Irish place-name, *Emain Macha,* "the twins of Macha," where Macha gave birth to twin boys.[36] As most have recognized, Emain Ablach is a paradisal realm, an otherwordly island,[37] and its name may be interpreted as meaning "the twin of the apple orchard,"[38] apples being a particularly prominent feature of the Celtic and Germanic otherworlds.[39] The twin in question is the lord of that island, renamed Donn within the mainstream of the Celtic tradition, but ultimately derived from P-I-E *Yemo.

Germanic sources also provide valuable evidence that corresponds to the pattern we have encountered in Indic and Celtic texts. Most important is a passage from the first chapter of the *Hervararsaga,* in which the realm of King Guðmund is described:

> It is written in old books that to the north of Gandvik ["Magic Bay"] was called Jǫtunheim ["Giant home"], and Ymisland ["Ymir's land"] was in the south in the middle of Halogoland ["Holy land" (?)]. Before the Turks and men of Asia came to the Northland, giants and some demi-giants inhabited the northern regions. Then there was a great intermingling of peoples. The giants seized for themselves women from Mannheim ["Man's Home"], and some gave their daughters thither. Guðmund ["Protected by the God"] is the name of the ruler of Jǫtunheim. His dwelling is at Grund ["Field"] in the district of Glasisvellir ["Shining meadow"]. He was a powerful man and wise, and he and all his men were so old that they outlived many generations. Therefore, heathen men believed that Ódáinsakr ["Field of Immortals," "Southeastern Field," or "Field of the Underworld"][40] must be in his kingdom, the place in which sickness and old age depart from every man who comes there, and [where] no one is permitted to die. After the death of Guðmund, men sacrificed to him and called him their god.[41]

As has been generally recognized, this description of Ódáinsakr is a description of paradise,[42] and elsewhere in the Old Norse sagas it is explicitly referred to as "that place which heathen men call 'Ódáinsakr' and Christian men call 'the land of living men' or 'Paradise.'"[43] What has not been recognized, however, is that, far from establishing the location of Ódáinsakr in Guðmund's realm, the text cited above refutes any such view. For it explicitly states that in Ódáinsakr "no one is permitted to die" (*má engi deyja*), while making reference to Guðmund's death in the very next sentence. Upon closer inspection, we note that the text does not state that Ódáinsakr was in Jǫtunheim, where Guðmund ruled, only that "heathen men believed" (*trúðu heiðnir menn*) it to be there; clearly they were mistaken, however, given the evidence of Guðmund's death.

Now, it may be argued that this is only the means for a Christian author to express his doubt about heathen superstitions, but I believe there is more at stake here, as is shown when we consider some other evidence. Jǫtunheim, we are told—and this is consistent with other accounts[44]—is located in the north, and if Ódáinsakr is found there, it too is in the north. But in the second chapter of *Eireks saga viðfǫrla,* we are provided with nothing less than a set of directions for reaching this fabled realm. The saga concerns the quest of Eirik to find Ódáinsakr. Leaving his native Norway, he travels south, first to Denmark, then to Constantinople (*Myklagard*), where he confers with the king. In part, their discussion is as follows:

> Eirik asked: "What is beyond the earth?"
> The king said: "A great sea called Ocean."
> Eirik asked: "Where is the outermost land in the southern hemisphere?"
> The king answered: "We say that India is at the end of the lands in that hemisphere."
> Eirik asked: "Where is the place which is called Ódáinsakr?"
> The king said: "We call this 'Paradise,' or 'the land of the living.'"
> Eirik asked: "Where is this place?"
> The king said: "In the east is this land, furthest from India." [45]

Following these directions, Eirik goes southeast beyond India, ultimately reaching Ódáinsakr, although the Christian author hastens to add that paradise itself lies still farther beyond Ódáinsakr. Contrary to what "heathen men believe" according to the *Hervararsaga,* it is thus not in the far north; like Yama's realm and Tech Duinn, it is in the south. [46] Having recognized this, it is interesting to return to our text from the *Hervararsaga,* where we are given some important information regarding the southern world quarter. Paralleling Jǫtunheim, the chief land of the north, there is a chief land of the south: Ymisland, "Ymir's land." And Ymir, whose name literally means "twin," like *emon* and *Yama,* being derived from **Yemo,* [47] is the sacrificial victim from whose body the earth was made in the Norse cosmogonic account, which closely adheres to the ancient Indo-European pattern. [48] If the conclusions we have drawn are correct, it is thus not Guðmund who is king of paradise, but Ymir, "the Twin," first to die and first of the dead.

Special Cases: Iranian

In Iran, there is yet another figure whose names derives from P-I-E **Yemo:* Yima, the mythology of whom is extraordinarily complex. Originally the first man and first king, he was displaced to make room for two non-Indo-European figures drawn from local Iranian mythology, but he remained the greatest king, king of the golden age, and king for the lion's share (616 1/2 years) of the first millennium in world history. [49] Overthrown by a usurper, he went into hiding, then was caught after a hundred years and killed by his own brother, who cut his body in two. [50] Thus far, the story of Yima wholly reflects the events of the P-I-E cosmogony, [51] but of his fate after death we are told nothing. Nowhere in Iran is there explicit mention of Yima as lord of the dead.

This is not surprising, however, given the absolute monotheism of Zarathustra's doctrine. For the prophet, there could be no lord in heaven but Ahura Mazdā ("the Wise Lord"), and any pre-Zoroastrian figure who played this role would have to give way.[52] Moreover, Yima himself was explicitly condemned by Zarathustra for having introduced the eating of meat[53] and was relegated to a position considerably inferior to that which he enjoyed prior to the prophet's reform.[54]

It is thus a reasonable hypothesis that Yima was stripped of his role as lord of paradise, which was accorded Ahura Mazdā alone. This theory finds support in the account of Yima's paradisal realm, the famous "enclosure of Yima," as related in *Vīdēvdāt* 2.20–43. The story—which in large measure is influenced by the Mesopotamian flood legend[55]—begins by telling how Ahura Mazdā and Yima held parallel gatherings at the center of the earth, in Airyaṇam Vaējah ("the homeland of Aryas"), the former assembling deities and the latter the best of mortals. When all were present, Ahura Mazdā spoke to Yima, warning him of destructive winters to come and urging him to build an enclosure in which the best of men, animals, plants, and fires would survive.[56] The lord's directions are quite precise, and when Yima asks how he is to construct such an enclosure, he tells him: "Stamp the earth apart with your heels, squeeze it apart with your hands, as men now separate earth when it is fluid." As this method—with its reference to the potter's art—implies, the haven made by Yima was carved out of the earth. Given three sections— "upper" (fratəməm), "middle" (maδəmō), and "lower" (nitəmō)—the enclosure is a cavern, as Christensen and Lommel recognized[57] and as Pahlavi texts such as *Mēnōg ī Xrād* 62.15–19 confirm: "The enclosure made by Yima was in the home of the Aryas *below the earth* (*azēr zamīg*) and the genus and species of every creature and creation of Ohrmazd the lord, the best and most choice of men and horses and cattle and birds, each was brought there. And every forty years a child was born to one man and one woman of that place. And their lives were 300 years long, and their pain and misfortune were very slight" (emphasis added).

Yima's enclosure is an underworld, a world of perfection, a world without cares—in many ways, a paradise. The passage from the *Mēnōg ī Xrād* states that the occupants lived to an enormous old age, a testimony which is supported by the important Pahlavi gloss to *Vīdēvdāt* 2.41, in which various popular ideas concerning Yima's enclosure are collected. One of these goes well beyond the testimony of the *Mēnōg ī Xrād*, however, and describes the enclosure as a land without death: "It is said that they live 150 years [in Yima's enclosure]; that they live an existence which is most beautiful in soul; *that they never die*" (*Kū hagurz bē nē mirēnd*).

Significantly, Yima is nowhere said to rule over those who inhabit his enclosure; he was responsible for its construction, nothing more. Rule within the enclosure falls to two people, Zarathustra and his son Urvatat.nara, something which is self-evidently a Zoroastrian innovation. Clearly, another mythological figure played this role prior to the career of Zarathustra.[58] On the basis of logic, as well as comparative evidence, I contend that that personage was he who built the realm, Yima.[59]

Special Cases: Greek

The question of locating reflexes of the P-I-E lord of the dead within Greek mythology is perhaps even more complex. The initial difficulty lies in the absence of a prominent first-man figure within the corpus of Greek myths. While there are a number of founding heroes who figure as the first man for specific cities—Kadmos for Thebes, Kekrops for Athens, etc.—these are usually local heroes, unrelated to the Indo-European heritage. Moreover, in Hesiod's *Theogony,* humans go almost unmentioned, all the action taking place on the divine plane, and most of the primordial beings are female, Gaia and Nyx standing foremost. In the generation of Titans, however, two males do stand out—Ouranos and Kronos—and in the latter's castration of the former we may see a much-transformed reflex of the P-I-E myth of creation by a sacrificial dismemberment,[60] noting that, as with Ymir, Puruṣa, and the like, the dismembered portions of Ouranos's body became significant parts of the cosmos, his blood producing the Furies, and his phallus Aphrodite.[61]

It is thus quite stunning when we recall that in Hesiod (*Works and Days* 169) and Pindar (*Olympia* 2.70), Kronos appears as ruler of the Isle(s) of the Blessed, the paradisal realm reserved for specially favored heroes, located at the ends of the earth.[62] Given the above analysis, however, we might expect that Ouranos would have assumed this role, being the first king and first victim, suffering overthrow by dismemberment, if not death itself.[63] Instead, Ouranos retreats into the heavens, a move dictated by the meaning of his name ("Sky") and by another dimension of the myth, for, by castrating Ouranos, Kronos effectively separated Sky (Ouranos) and Earth (Gaia), who up to this moment were locked in unceasing sexual embrace.[64] Severed from his mate, Sky withdraws into the distance, becoming an otiose deity, according to a pattern well established in the history of religions.[65] Kronos thus replaces him as lord of the dead, the dismemberer substituting for the dismembered and victor for vanquished, just as the Donn Cúailnge assumes the role which might have been expected to go to the Findbennach Aí in Irish myth.[66] The argument is suggestive, if not conclusive on all points.

Also suggestive are Homer's remarks on the ruler of the Elysian field, as contained in the *Odyssey*, where Proteus prophesies to Menelaos:

> It is not ordained by the gods for you, O Menelaos, beloved of
>   Zeus,
> To die in the Argive fields and reach your fate,
> But the immortals will lead you to the Elysian field

> At the ends of the earth, where fair-haired Rhadamanthys dwells
> And where life is most free from care for men.
> There is neither snow, nor much of cold, nor rain,
> But always Okeanos rouses blasts
> Of the whistling-breathed Zephyr to cool men,
> For you possess Helen, and to the gods are a son-in-law of Zeus.

Odyssey 4.561–69

Two mortals are thus said to inhabit this paradisal field: Rhadamanthys and Menelaos. The association of the former with the otherworld is quite common in Greek lore,[67] while that of the latter is more unusual, calling for the explanation on Homer's part that it is a husband of the divine Helen that Menelaos merits his place in Elysium.[68] But whatever their differences, the two have several features in common. Both are kings, both are primordial culture heroes, and both are twins, although this last point is open to some debate. For his part, Rhadamanthys is born of the union of Zeus with Europa, along with Minos—whose name has been compared with that of Manu[69]—and, according to some accounts, Sarpedon.[70] Since Zeus mated with Europa only once, it is clear that Rhadamanthys must be one of a set of twins or triplets, depending on whether or not the third brother is included. As for Menelaos, he is most frequently treated as the younger brother of Agamemnon, but an important passage from Aeschylus (*Agamemnon* 40–46) points to another conclusion:

> This is the tenth year since Priam's
> Great adversary,
> Menelaos the king and Agamemnon—
> Twin-throned and twin-sceptered, by Zeus' grace,
> Firm in their fame, the twin Atreides—
> Put forth from these lands
> A thousand Argive ships.

This testimony alone is not enough to afford certainty, and the Greek evidence in general has been much transformed as a result of the rich synthesis among Indo-European, Old European, and Near Eastern mythologies, but there is clearly enough evidence for one to suspect that Kronos, Rhadamanthys, and Menelaos alike may have all succeeded to the position of the earlier Indo-European lord of the dead, whose name was *Yemo, "the twin."

Conclusions

Some of the comparisons offered above are hardly new, although to the best of my knowledge some are novel, and the full set has never been assembled in its totality. But Yima has been compared with Guðmund[71] and Yama with Rhadamanthys,[72] and other resemblances have been noted. Among the most successful is the masterful article of Kuno Meyer, "Der irische Totengott und die

Toteninsel," in which he compared Yama with Donn and Dis pater, drawing the totally justified conclusion that all derived from a P-I-E figure regarded as *both* the first man and the ruler of the dead, having established the land of the dead and the path to that land through his original, exemplary death.[73]

The most brilliant reconstruction, however, remains that of Hermann Güntert, who argued on the strength of Indo-Iranian evidence, amplified by the Greek example of Rhadamanthys, that this first man, first of the dead, was * Yemo, who offered himself as victim in the first, cosmogonic, sacrifice.[74] On the strength of Celtic and Germanic evidence, plus several Greek examples untreated by Güntert, we have now confirmed this insight, the implications of which we may begin to assess.

* Yemo's death was no ordinary death; as the first, it was a paradigmatic death which established a model for all deaths to follow. Furthermore, it was a sacrificial, and thus a creative, act as a result of which the world came into being.[75] Not only was this world created, but the realm of the dead was also established, and we may thus observe that the otherworld does not stand outside the cosmos but is an integral part of it, having been created at the same time and in the same manner as the rest of the universe. The world of the dead and the world of the living are thus intimately connected, being parts of the same world—a world that is nothing more than the extension of * Yemo's body.

As * Yemo was the first king, so is he also the last king, ruling over the souls of the departed, whom he greets as they arrive. In this, he acts not only as king but also as father, for he is the primordial father of all humanity, and the final meeting with him is, in effect, a reunion with the totality of one's lineage.[76] It is a meeting in which time turns backwards on itself, the end being the same as the beginning of all things.

* Yemo's realm is a happy one, a paradise where sickness, cares, death, and extremities of climate are all unknown.[77] With the exception of the later Indian texts, all evidence points in this direction. That the Indo-Europeans also knew the realm of the dead as a fearful, dreary place, dark and sorrowful or filled with serpents and other terrifying creatures, is clear from other sources, such as Homer's description of Hades, Old Norse accounts of Hel, or the picture of Dušox ("Evil Existence") presented in the *Arda Wirāz Namāg,* but whether this is a separate otherworld or the same realm viewed from a totally different perspective[78] cannot be ascertained at present.

Above all, we may conclude that * Yemo's life did not end unhappily. As a sacrifice, it was a creative act, and it led him into a totally new mode of being, lived in a paradisal realm which he founded for himself and his descendants through this act of self-sacrifice. Insofar as each individual's death is a repetition and an imitation of * Yemo's, it too is a sacrifice which renews the world he created,[79] and which leads the deceased into his paradisal realm, a realm which is also re-created by each death and each act of sacrifice.

There is one final detail which may be posited for the P-I-E otherworld. On the strength of Indic, Celtic, and Germanic testimony, we may conclude it was located in the distant south, Yama's realm being so placed, Tech Duinn being in the southwest (relative to Ireland), and Ódáinsakr in the southeast. That it was not in the distant above or below, as are so many otherworlds in various mythologies, would indicate that it was felt to be an integral part, however, remote, of the same world as that in which humanity dwells while living. This same point is also clear from the fact that the otherworld is ruled by one who was originally a mortal, and not a divine or demonic being.[80]

These observations, however, do not resolve the question of why paradise was set in the south rather than in some other direction, west being particularly appropriate due to its association with sunset and thus with death. To this question no definitive answer can be offered, for the texts themselves are silent. It is perhaps not irrelevant, however, to recall that the Proto-Indo-Europeans, whether we place their homeland in the Kurgan culture of the Russian steppes, as most now urge,[81] or in any of the other possible homelands which are given serious consideration,[82] dwelt well within the northern hemisphere. For them, the south was thus that region from which light is constant, a region whose warmth stands in marked contrast to the wintry north. Such associations of light and warmth are appropriate for a paradisal realm, and such climatic considerations may well have had some part in the formation of P-I-E cosmology.

Notes

1. Bruce Lincoln, "The Indo-European Myth of Creation," *History of Religions* 15 (1975): 121–45.

2. Jaan Puhvel, "Remus et Frater," *History of Religions* 15 (1975): 146–57.

3. Bruce Lincoln, "Death and Resurrection in Indo-European Thought," *Journal of Indo-European Studies* 5 (1977): 247–64, and "Treatment of Hair and Fingernails among the Indo-Europeans," *History of Religions* 16 (1977): 351–62.

4. Georges Dumézil, *Les Dieux souverains des indo-européens* (Paris: Gallimard, 1977), p. 207.

5. Bruce Lincoln, *Priests, Warriors, and Cattle: A Study in the Ecology of Religions* (Berkeley and Los Angeles: University of California Press, 1981), pp. 87–92.

6. Hermann Güntert, *Der arische Weltkönig und Heiland* (Halle: Max Niemeyer, 1923), pp. 370–95.

7. *Ṛg Veda* 10.10.3; *Atharva Veda* 18.3.13.

8. RV 10.13.4; AV 18.3.41.

9. Both Yama and Manu are designated Vaivasvata, "son of Vivasvant," but, as no mother is specified for either, later sources, particularly *Bṛhaddevata* 6.162–7.7, invented different mothers for them.

10. See Lincoln, *Priests, Warriors, and Cattle*, pp. 80–82. The argument regarding Indian evidence hinges on seeing the Puruṣa of RV 10.90 as a replacement for the Yama of RV 10.13.4, as suggested by Güntert, *Arische Weltkönig*, pp. 386–90, and

R. N. Dandekar, "Yama in the Veda," *B.C. Law Volume* (Calcutta: Indian Research Institute, 1945), 1: 194–209.

11. A. A. Macdonnell, *Vedic Mythology* (Strassburg: Karl Trübner, 1897), p. 171.

12. RV 9.113.8.

13. RV 10.14.1; AV 18.2.25, 46.

14. RV 10.14.1, 1.38.5.

15. Similarly, when the P-I-E image of the psychopompic ferryman is plainly an allegorical figure (on whom, see Chapter 5 below) he was also felt to have physical reality, as shown, for instance, by the Greek custom of burying the dead with coins to pay Charon's fare.

16. RV 1.35.6, 9.113.8, 10.123.6.

17. This is not expressly stated in the *Ṛg Veda* but follows inexorably from two other facts: (1) Yama rules over the realm of the Fathers (*pitaráḥ:* RV 10.14.7–9, AV 18.2.25 and 46); and (2) the realm of the Fathers is in the south (RV 10.15.6, 10.17.9). Yama's realm is explicitly said to be in the south in *Taittirīya Saṃhitā* 1.8.7, *Bṛhadāranyaka Upaniṣad* 3.9.21, and *Mahābhārata* 3.42.16, to name but a few. On its southern location, see Willibald Kirfel, *Die Kosmographie der Inder* (Bonn: Kurt Schroeder, 1920), pp. 7–8, 95, 121, 157; and Hermann Oldenberg, *Die Religion des Veda,* 4th ed. (Stuttgart: J. G. Cotta, 1923), p. 544 n. 4, who sees this as dating to the Indo-Iranian period.

18. *Śatapatha Brāhmaṇa,* 13.8.1.5.

19. See Chapter 2 above, "On the Imagery of Paradise." Others who have treated this passage include Güntert, *Arische Weltkönig,* p. 390, A. V. Williams Jackson, "On Mahā-Bhārata iii.142.35–45, an Echo of an old Hindu-Persian Legend," *Journal of the American Oriental Society* 17 (1896): 186; Arthur Christensen, *Le premier homme et premier roi dans la tradition legendaire iranienne,* vol. 2, *Yima* (Uppsala: Archives d'études orientales, 1923), p. 42; and Georges Dumézil, "La sabhā de Yama," *Journal asiatique* 253 (1965): 162–64.

20. On this theme, see Chapter 6 below, "Mithras(s) as Sun and Savior."

21. Güntert, *Arische Weltkönig,* pp. 318, 390–91; Macdonnell, *Vedic Mythology,* p. 172; Dandekar, "Yama in the Veda," p. 195; Oldenberg, *Religion des Veda,* pp. 537ff.; A. B. Keith, *Religion and Philosophy of the Veda and Upanishads* (Cambridge: Harvard University Press, 1925), p. 408, and Jan Gonda, *Die Religionen Indiens,* vol. 1, *Veda und älterer Hinduismus* (Stuttgart: W. Kohlhammer, 1960), p. 228.

22. RV 10.14.9, 10.135.1; AV 18.4.31–32.

23. Eleanor Hull, "The Development of the Idea of Hades in Celtic Literature," *Folklore* 18 (1907): 121–65; Alfred Nutt, "The Happy Otherworld," appendix to Kuno Meyer, ed. and trans., *The Voyage of Bran* (London: David Nutt, 1895) 1: 105–331; Roger Sherman Loomis, *Wales and the Arthurian Legend* (Cardiff: University of Wales Press, 1956), pp. 141–45; and Kuno Meyer, "Der irische Totengott und die Toteninsel," *Situzungsberichte der preussisches Akademie der Wissenschaften* (1919): 544–46.

24. Meyer, "Der irische Totengott," pp. 537–46. See also Wolfgang Krause, *Die Kelten* (Tübingen: J. C. B. Mohr, 1929), p. 10; Jan de Vries, *Keltische Religion* (Stuttgart: W. Kohlhammer, 1961), p. 257, Alwyn and Brinley Rees, *Celtic Heritage* (London: Thames and Hudson, 1961), p. 97.

25. See *Lebor Gabála Érenn* 8.385, where Mil's sons are listed, among them:

"Donn the king, Amairgen the poet" (*Donn in rí, Amargen in file*). Donn's title also applies to his status after death, when he became king of Tech Duinn, as shown by the description of the island in a ninth-century poem cited by Meyer, "Der irische Totengott," p. 541:

> The house of Donn, who has a large following . . .
> The fort of the king by the full, smooth sea . . .
>
> Tech Duinn dámaig . . .
> ráith ríg fri lán lir féthaighthe . . .

The use of the term *ráth,* here translated "fort," should also be noted. Most literally, it describes a fortification surrounded by earthenworks, and in this regard should be compared to the enclosure of Yima, also made of stamped earth, as described in *Vīdēvdāt* 2.31.

26. Text in Meyer, "*Der irische Totengott,*" p. 538.

27. For an English translation, see Cecile O'Rahilly, ed. and trans., *Táin Bó Cúalnge from the Book of Leinster* (Dublin: Institute for Advanced Studies, 1967), pp. 270–72.

28. Lincoln, *Priests, Warriors, and Cattle,* pp. 87–90.

29. O'Rahilly, *Táin Bó Cúalnge* p. 272. A fuller version is found in other manuscripts and appears in English translation in *The Ancient Irish Epic Tale Táin Bó Cúalnge* (London: David Nutt, 1914), p. 368.

30. Meyer, "Der irische Totengott," p. 543; Julius Pokorny, *Indogermanisches etymologisches Wörterbuch* (Bern: Francke, 1959), p. 270–71.

31. Meyer, "Der irische Totengott," p. 542 and n. 4.

32. Pokorny, *Indogermanisches etymologisches Wörterbuch,* p. 505.

33. Osborn Bergin, general ed., *Dictionary of the Irish Language,* fasc. 2, E (Dublin: Royal Irish Academy, 1932), p. 119. The most prominent appearance of the name Emain for the paradisal isle is in the *Voyage of Bran,* stanzas 3, 10, 19, and 60, where it alternates with the form *Emne.*

34. Bergin, fasc. 1, A (1964), p. 11.

35. Ibid., fasc. 2, E, p. 119.

36. For the story of Macha's twins, see Rees and Rees, p. 58.

37. Nutt, pp. 229ff.; Krause, pp. 10–11; Rees and Rees, esp. pp. 315, 325.

38. Contra Julius Pokorny, "Zur Urgeschichte der Kelten und Illyrier," *Zeitschrift für celtische Philologie* 21 (1938): 127, I interpret *Ablach* as the plural genitive of *ablach* on the analogy of other o-stem nouns ending in -ch, such as *enech* and *étach,* on which see Rudolf Thurneysen, *A Grammar of Old Irish* (Dublin: Institute for Advanced Studies, 1946), p. 178.

39. See especially Th. M. Th. Chotzen, "Emain Ablach—Ynys Avallach—Insula Avallonis—Ile d'Avalon," *Études celtiques* 4 (1948): 255–74; A. H. Krappe, "Avallon," *Speculum* 18 (1943): 303–22; Jacob Grimm, *Teutonic Mythology* (London: George Bell, 1883–88), 319–20.

40. The first etymology is the one most frequently offered. The second was suggested by Axel Olrik, *Kilderne til Sakses Oldhistorie* (Copenhagen: G.E.C. Gad, 1892–94) 2:158–59, and the third by Rudolf Much, "Undensakre—Unterberg," *Zeitschrift für deutsches Altertum* 47 (1904): 67–72, but the evidence for none of these is fully convincing.

41. Text in Christopher Tolkien, ed., *The Saga of King Heidrek the Wise* (London: Nelson, 1960), p. 66.

42. Grimm, p. 2:823n.; Much, "Undensakre—Untersberg," p. 68, "Balder," *Zeitschrift für deutsches Altertum* 61 (1924): 99–100; Krappe, "Avallon," pp. 307–8, Willy Krogmann, "Neorxna wang und Íðavǫllr," *Archiv für das Studium der neueren Sprachen und Literaturen* 191 (1954): 36; E. O. G. Turville-Petre, *Myth and Religion of the Ancient North* (New York: Holt, Winston, and Rinehart, 1964), p. 32; Jan de Vries, *Altergermanische Religionsgeschichte* (Berlin: Walter de Gruyter, 1970) 2: 284–85; Åke Ström, *Germanische Religion* (Stuttgart: W. Kohlhammer, 1975), pp. 192–93.

43. *Eireks saga viðfǫrla*, chap. 1.

44. See E. Mogk, "Jotunheimar," in *Reallexikon der germanischen Altertumskunde*, 4 vols., ed. Johannes Hoops (Strassburg: Karl Trübner, 1911–19) 2:617.

45. Text in *Fornaldar Sögur*, 3 vols. (Reykjavík: S. Kristjánsson, 1886–91), 3:521.

46. Saxo Grammaticus (8.240–46) also deals with Guðmund's realm, although he never places Odáinsakr there (in fact, the one time he does mention Undensakre [4.9.1], he states that it "is unknown to our people" [*nostris ignotum populis*]). Saxo's account is particularly interesting for two details, however. First, he gives his Guthmundus (= Old Norse Guðmundr) a brother, Geruthus (= Old Norse Geirrǫð), whose realm is distinctly infernal, directly paralleling aspects of Snorri's description of Hel. Second, Guthmundus's realm is positioned such that it is both northern *and* southern at the same time, being located in the far north, but to the south of Geruthus's kingdom.

47. First established by Güntert, *Arische Weltkönig*, p. 337. See now Pokorny, p. 505; Jan de Vries, *Altnordisches etymologisches Wörterbuch* (Leiden: E. J. Brill, 1961), p. 678.

48. See Lincoln, *Priests, Warriors, and Cattle*, pp. 73–76. The chief primary sources are *Gylfaginning* 7, *Vafþrúðnismál* 35, and *Grímnismál* 40.

49. Güntert, *Arische Weltkönig*, p. 376; Christensen, *Premier homme*, 2:35–36 (see n. 20 above).

50. *Yašt* 13.46, on which see Güntert, *Arische Weltkönig*, p. 378; Lincoln, *Priests, Warriors, and Cattle*, pp. 79, 83; and Friedrich von Spiegel; *Die arische Period und ihre Zustände* (Leipzig: W. Friedrich, 1887), p. 253.

51. Lincoln, "The Indo-European Myth of Creation," pp. 129–32, 135–36 (see n. 1 above).

52. Note, e.g., the drastic changes in the mythology of Vayu as psychopomp wrought by the Zoroastrian reform, as studied by Stig Wikander, *Vayu* (Uppsala: A. B. Lundquist, 1941).

53. *Yasna* 32.8, on the significance of which, see Lincoln, *Priests, Warriors, and Cattle*, pp. 76, 155.

54. Christensen, *Premier homme*, 2:49–50; Herman Lommel, *Die Religion Zarathustras* (Tübingen: J. C. B. Mohr, 1930), pp. 138–39, 249; James Moulton, *Early Zoroastrianism* (London: Willims and Norgate, 1913), pp. 148–49; Geo Widengren, *Die Religionen Irans* (Stuttgart: W. Kohlhammer, 1965), pp. 52–53.

55. Bruno Lindner, "Die iranische Flutsage," in *Festgruss an Rudolf von Roth* (Stuttgart: W. Kohlhammer, 1893), pp. 213–16, which remains convincing despite the critical remarks of Christensen, *Premier homme*, 2:58–59.

56. *Vidēvdāt* 2.20–30.

57. Christensen, *Premier homme,* 2:56; Herman Lommel, *Die Yašts des Awesta* (Göttingen: Vandenhoeck & Ruprecht, 1927), pp. 200–201. Güntert, *Arische Weltkönig,* p. 372, argued that the way in which the enclosure was constructed indicated that it was a *pairi.daēza-,* a walled garden. This Iranian term entered Greek as the loanword παράδεισος in the writings of Xenophon, after which it was used for the "garden" of Eden in the Septuagint, and for heavenly realms more generally, English *paradise* being thus ultimately derived from Iranian *pairi.daēza-.* Since this word does not appear in the second chapter of the *Vidēvdāt,* however, the argument does not really rest on solid ground.

58. *Vidēvdāt* 2.43, on which see Güntert, *Arische Weltkönig,* pp. 373–74.

59. Note the extremely interesting myth recounted in *Dēnkart* 3.227, where Yima wins immortality for his people by confounding the demons (dēws) in debate, which should be compared to RV 1.83.5: "We sacrifice to the immortality born of Yama" (*yamásya jātám amŕtám yajāmahe*), which is, of course, the immortality that Yama won for all humanity through his own death and subsequent founding of the otherworld.

60. Hesiod *Theogony* 170ff. This story has been treated as a reflex of the "Kingship in Heaven" theme by Stig Wikander, "Hethitiska myter has greker och perser," *Vetenskaps-societen i Lund Årsbok* (1951), pp. 35–36; idem, "Histoire des Ouranides," *Cahiers du sud* 36 (1952): 8–17; and C. Scott Littleton, "Is the 'Kingship in Heaven' Theme Indo-European?," in Henry Hoenigswald et al., eds., *Indo-European and Indo-Europeans* (Philadelphia: University of Pennsylvania Press, 1970), pp. 383–404; idem, "The Kingship in Heaven Theme," in Jaan Puhvel, ed., *Myth and Law among the Indo-Europeans* (Berkeley: University of California Press, 1970), pp. 83–122.

61. *Theogony* 182–200.

62. Line 169 appears in two manuscripts only of the *Works and Days,* and has been rejected as spurious by some editors, following the lead of such ancients as Proclus. Whether or not the line is authentic, however, is irrelevant for our purposes, since it is clear that there was a body of opinion among the Greeks which made Kronos ruler in the Isle(s) of the Blessed, given the evidence of Pindar, *Olympia* 2.70–72, who states that those souls who have lived through three perfect lives

> Travel the path of Zeus to the tower of Kronos, where round the Isle of
>   the Blessed
> Ocean breezes blow and flowers of gold blaze forth . . .

63. His status as an immortal, of course, rules out the possibility of his death.

64. *Theogony* 126–27, 155ff.

65. See Mircea Eliade, *Patterns in Comparative Religion* (Cleveland: Meridian, 1963), pp. 240–42.

66. See discussion above in the section on Celtic and Germanic correspondences.

67. As in Plato *Gorgias* 523e; Pindar *Olympia* 2.75 and 83, and *Pythia* 2.73; Apollodorus *Bibliotheca* 2.70, 3.6; Diodorus Siculus 5.79.1–2. The classic treatment of Rhadamanthys is Ludolf Malten, "Elysion und Rhadamanthys," *Jahrbuch des kaiserlich deutschen archäologischen Instituts* 28 (1913): 35–51, which has been disputed on a number of points by Güntert, *Arische Weltkönig,* pp. 380–81, and Paul Capelle,

"Elysium und Inseln der Seligen," *Archiv für Religionswissenschaft* 26 (1928): 17ff. The chief point of contention is how much importance ought be accorded the *-nthus* suffix in Rhadamanthys's name, which is normally associated with pre-Greek words. The pre-Greek origin is taken as a certainty by Hjalmar Frisk, *Griechisches etymologisches Wörterbuch* (Heidelberg: Carl Winter, 1973) 2:637. In light of this, I see Rhadamanthys as a pre-Greek name which has replaced a Proto-Greek name derived from *Yemo, as part of the merger of the Indo-European and Old European religious systems.

68. For other examples of mythic heroes who have gained entry to paradise as a result of their kinship to the gods—Akhilles, Kadmos, etc.—see Capelle, p. 259 n.2.

69. The phonetics of this comparison are extremely strained, and the early attempts to establish its validity, such as that by Adalbert Kuhn, "Sprachvergleichung und Urgeschichte der indo-germanische Völker," *Zeitschrift für vergleichende Sprachforschungen* 4 (1855): 90–94, were quite ill-founded. More recently, Güntert, pp. 381–84, and Albert Carnoy, *Dictionare étymologique de la mythologie gréco-romaine* (Louvain: Editions Universitas, 1957), p. 129, have attempted to put it on a firmer ground.

70. Apollodorus *Bibliotheca* 3.1.1; Hesiod, Fragment 30 (in *Hesiodus Carmina*, ed. A. Rzach, [Stuttgart: B. G. Teubner, 1958], p. 143). Homer, however, makes Sarpedon the son of Zeus and Laodamia (*Iliad* 6.198–99), Minos and Rhadamanthyus alone being the children of Zeus and Europa (*Iliad* 14.321–22).

71. Nutt, "The Happy Otherworld," pp. 305ff.; Viktor Rydberg, *Teutonic Mythology* (London: Norroena Society, 1906), pp. 379ff.

72. Christensen, *Premier homme*, 2:40–41; Fr. Windischmann, "Ursagen der arischen Völker," *Abhandlungen der philosophischen-philologischen Classe der königlich bayerischen Akademie der Wissenschaften* 7(1855): 11–20.

73. Meyer, "Der irische Totengott," pp. 542–45 (see n. 25 above).

74. Güntert, *Arische Weltkönig*, pp. 370–95.

75. Lincoln, "The Indo-European Myth of Creation," pp. 139–45.

76. On the theme of the reunion with one's ancestors in Indo-European funerary lore, see Paul Thieme, *Studien zur indogermanischen Wortkunde und Religionsgeschichte* (Berlin: Akademie, 1952), pp. 35–55, Jaan Puhvel, "Hittite annaš šiwaz," *Zeitschrift für vergleichende Sprachforschungen* 83 (1969): 59–63.

77. See Chapter 2, "On the Imagery of Paradise."

78. The latter has been argued with regard to Celtic materials, e.g., by Marie-Louise Sjoestedt, *Gods and Heroes of the Celts* (London: Methuen, 1949), p. 49.

79. Lincoln, "Death and Resurrection in Indo-European Thought," pp. 263–64.

80. This is true for Yama, Donn, Guðmund, Yima, Menelaos, and Rhadamanthys, i.e., all of the figures we have considered except Dis pater (whom Caesar may have misunderstood), Ymir (a giant), and Kronos (a titan). Our earlier assessment of *Yemo in "The Indo-European Myth of Creation" led also to the conclusion that he was a primordial human ancestor, not a deity.

81. As argued by Marija Gimbutas, "The Indo-Europeans: Archaeological Problems," *American Anthropologist* 65 (1963): 815–36, idem, "Proto-Indo-European Culture: The Kurgan Culture during the 5th, 4th, and 3rd Millennia B.C.," in *Indo-European and Indo-Europeans*, pp. 155–98, idem, "An Archaeologist's View of PIE

in 1975," *Journal of Indo-European Studies* 2 (1974): 289–308.

82. For presentations of the argument for a P-I-E homeland in the Neolithic cultures of central Europe, see Pedro Bosch-Gimpera, *Les Indo-européens: problèmes archéologiques* (Paris: Payot, 1961), and Giacomo Devoto, *Origini Indeuropee* (Florence: Sansoni, 1962). For the older theory of a homeland on the Baltic, see Paul Thieme, *Die Heimat der indogermanischen Gemeinsprache* (Wiesbaden: Akademie der Wissenschaften und der Literatur, 1953).

FOUR

WATERS OF MEMORY,
WATERS OF FORGETFULNESS

While texts describing the otherworld abound in the various Indo-European literatures, the data do not seem to permit confident reconstruction of a single specific locale for the realm of the dead. Some texts indicate a celestial otherworld, reached by ascending through the sphere of stars, moon, and sun.[1] Others point to a subterranean region reached by a *descensus ad inferos*.[2] The most frequent depiction, however, is that in which the next world is found beyond a body of water: ocean,[3] bay,[4] or most often a river which is crossed variously by ferry,[5] bridge,[6] or act of wading.[7] Given that there is independent evidence for all of these concepts in two, three, or even more of the Indo-European families, there is little ground for assuming the priority of one over the others. Rather, I am inclined to believe either that the Proto-Indo-Europeans accepted a cosmology including numerous different otherworlds, or that the location of the (single) otherworld was a topic still open to debate in the Proto-Indo-European period, with the result that there were several competing sets of speculation.

The image of the river of the otherworld is thus only one item out of a complex funerary geography, and yet it is a very fascinating one, subtle and richly elaborate in its imagery. Perhaps the most famous of all the rivers associated with the otherworld is the Greek *Lēthē*. This stream is mentioned in numerous sources,[8] but the fullest account is that given by Plato in the *Republic* 621, within the framework of his celebrated myth of Er—the Pamphylian soldier taken for dead who returned after twelve days to relate what he had seen in the otherworld.[9] The relevant passage reads as follows:

> He went to the throne of Necessity, and when he and the others had passed through, they all crossed to the Plain of Forgetfulness [*Lēthēs pedion*] through fearful stifling heat, for that plain is void of trees and all that the earth brings forth. When evening fell, they encamped beside the river Without Memory [*Amēleta potamon*], whose water no vessel can contain. Then it was compulsory for all to drink some measure of that water, and men do not understand that which would save them, but drink that [full] measure, and those who drink are caused to forget everything forever.
>
> And after they were asleep, in the middle of the night, there

was thunder and an earthquake, and suddenly they were borne up
thence this way and that to [their next] birth, like shooting stars.

Now Er himself was prevented from drinking of that water.
How, and by what means he arrived at his body, he did not see.
But suddenly, upon opening his eyes, he saw himself lying upon
the funeral pyre at dawn.

And thus, O Glaukon, the story was preserved and not lost, and
it will save us if we trust in it, and we will cross over that River
of Forgetfulness [*Lēthēs potamon*], and we will not sully our
soul. . . .

Now this passage comes at the very culmination of the *Republic,* and its
position within the dialogue plus the urgent exhortation to Glaukon in the final
paragraph indicate the importance which Plato attached to it. In truth, like the
myths of the otherworld presented in other dialogues,[10] it plays a crucial role
in Plato's whole theory of recollection (*anamnēsis*). Briefly, Plato maintained
that one can only learn that which one already knew before. Such knowledge
he believed to have been received during the time after death and before rebirth while the soul was in the otherworld. This realm he saw as the locus
of all the forms (*ideas*), perfect archetypes of everything that exists in imperfect form within this world.[11] The experience of Er thus acquired great importance for Plato because it demonstrated that although the normal fate of men is
to forget what they have seen in the otherworld, it is possible to preserve some
knowledge of what was seen in that realm.[12]

The critical step in preserving this knowledge is the exercise of restraint at
the river that stands at the border between this world and the other. All souls
must drink from this river before rebirth, however, and the thirst produced by
their journey across a hot and arid plain makes such restraint exceedingly
difficult. Only if one is self-disciplined in the extreme, and knowledgeable
with regard to the river's pernicious effect, will one be able to master the
temptation to drink deeply. For Plato, it is only the philosopher who has such
knowledge and self-control, and as a result of these qualities he is able to bring a
deep understanding of the fundamental nature of things back from that world
into this.

That understanding comes as a result of the philosopher's triumph over the
river, a river which bears two synonymous names in this text—*Amelēta,*
"without memory" (from *melō*), and *Lēthē,* "forgetfulness" (from *lanthano,*
lēthō).[13] The river is true to its name, for contact with it—here in the form of
drinking—wipes away memories, eradicates the past. But certain highly
gifted individuals are able to reverse, or at least minimize, the river's effect
and carry knowledge of tremendous importance back from the otherworld.

A similar idea is found in another Greek text that has often been compared
to the passage cited above from the *Republic.*[14] This is the famous inscription
on gold plate discovered in a grave in Petelia, southern Italy, and most likely

dating to the fourth or third century B.C.[15] The thin plate was rolled into a cylinder, inserted in a sheath, and hung around the neck of the deceased. The verses written there are generally considered to be Orphic in origin, and given their nature and their placement on the very body of the deceased, there can be little doubt that they were meant to be instructions for his *post mortem* journey.[16] The text reads as follows:

> You will find a spring to the left of the house of Hades,
> And standing beside that [spring] is a white cypress.
> Do not approach close to the spring.
> You will find another, flowing cold water
> From the pool of Memory (*Mnēmosunēs . . . limnēs*), and
> before it there are guards.
> Say [to them]: "I am a child of Earth and starry Heaven,
> But my lineage is heavenly [alone]. You must see this
> yourselves.
> I perish and am withered with thirst. Give [me] quickly
> The cold water flowing from the pool of Memory."
> And they themselves will give you to drink from the divine
> spring,
> And thereafter you shall reign among the other heroes.[17]

The content of this funerary tablet is strikingly similar to that of *Republic* 621 in a great many ways, especially if one makes the assumption that the reason for avoiding the first spring is that its waters produce the opposite effect of those from the second. Both texts speak of memory and forgetfulness, and both relate those categories to the effect of certain bodies of water in the otherworld. Both suggest that most mortals are stripped of their memory at the border to the otherworld. And both also indicate that certain highly gifted and favored individuals—Plato's philosophers or the Orphic initiates who know the proper ritual formulae—can overcome this fate and preserve their wisdom more or less intact.

The resemblance of these two documents is so strong that many scholars have been tempted to see Plato's account as relying on the same Orphic materials that served as a base for the Petalia tablet.[18] There are, however, certain differences of detail which must be noted and which have importance for any reconstructive effort with an eye toward comparisons within the broader Indo-European realm. In the first place, there is the matter of in which direction the soul is traveling when it comes to the waters of the otherworld. In Plato's account, the soul has finished its thousand-year sojourn in the world beyond, and is on its way back to earth. The *Lēthē* is the last hurdle prior to rebirth. But from the context of the Petelia tablet, it is clear that the deceased is on his way into Hades, and he reaches the twin springs just before coming to Hades' dwelling (*Aidao domōn*). On the strength of these two examples alone, one could not possibly decide which of the versions presents the older view, but given the inventive use Plato makes of the myth as a buttress for his theory of *anamnēsis,* I am inclined to believe he revised or modified a traditional story in order to make his own didactic point, and this suspicion is borne out when Indian materials are compared.

A second divergence is the specific nature of the body/bodies of water. Plato describes a river; the Petelia tablet, two springs. Third, there is a difference of opinion on how these waters produce their respective effects. For Plato, forgetfulness is the result of drinking and memory results from abstinence, while the Orphic text relates both effects to drinking alone. The picture of souls drinking from the river in Plato's *Republic* is particularly strange, for as Nilsson noted, Greeks almost never drank from rivers, preferring always to drink from wells or springs.[19]

Again, there is not really enough evidence in these two examples to permit secure reconstruction on their strength alone, but a recognition of Plato's tendentious use of traditional materials may help us to formulate hypotheses that can be confirmed or disproved by further comparative evidence. In this regard, I would point to his insistence on the virtue of abstemiousness on the part of the philosopher. Thus, he attributes the superior retention of memory to the philosopher's ability to overcome the temptation to drink despite the withering heat, and he makes the drink somewhat distasteful: it comes from a river and produces an undesirable effect. In no way is Plato willing to admit that drinking may have a desirable effect, and he thus eliminates the second spring of the Petelia tablet, the pool of memory (*Mnēmosunēs . . . limnēs*). In light of this, I would suggest that this second body of water, a pool or spring from which one drinks in order to acquire memory is most likely an authentic part of the cosmologem.[20] Two questions thus remain: was the first body of water a spring or a river, and were the souls of the dead believed to drink from it? Evidence from other Indo-European families is sufficient to resolve the first question in favor of the river, Plato having retained this faithfully and the tablet having transformed the original in order to more neatly mirror the pool of memory.[21] But the answer to the second question is a bit more surprising, for in no other version than these two Greek accounts is there ever the suggestion that the souls of the dead might drink from the first body of water.

The first variant from another Indo-European culture which we might consider comes from India, a passage from *Kauṣitaki Upaniṣad* 1.4, where the *post mortem* journey of the soul is once again the topic.[22]

> Five hundred celestial nymphs [*apsarasās*] go to him [the deceased]. . . . They decorate him with Brahma-decorations. Decorated with Brahma-decorations, knowing Brahma, he approaches Brahma. He comes to the pond Āra.[23] He crosses it by mind. Those who know only the obvious drown when they come to this [pond]. He comes to the moments Yeṣṭiha. They run away from

him. He comes to the river "Apart from Old Age" [*Vijarā*]. He crosses it by mind. Then he shakes off his good deeds and bad deeds. Truly, his dear relatives receive his good deeds, and those who are not dear his bad deeds. Just as one who drives a chariot looks down on the two chariot wheels, so he looks down on night and day, good and bad deeds, and all dualities. Without good deeds, without bad deeds, knowing Brahma, he approaches Brahma.

Primary attention is here focused upon the river in the otherworld, and it remains to be seen in what way it is comparable to Plato's *Lēthē*. For where Plato spoke of a river that annihilated memories, this Upaniṣad points to the annihilation of good and bad deeds. It seems to me, however, that there is no unbridgeable gulf between these two notions, and that the latter is best understood as a specifically Indian transformation of a Proto-Indo-European cosmologem under the influence of the theme of *karman*, "deeds, actions," which rises to a position of importance in Indian speculative thought beginning with the Upaniṣads.[24] In brief, the *karman* ideology as laid out in such texts as *Bṛhadāraṇyaka Upaniṣad* 4.4.5, *Kaṭha Upaniṣad* 5.7, or *Śvetāśvatara Upaniṣad* 5.11, has it that one's deeds (*karman*) in this world determine one's next rebirth—the good deeds leading to a higher rebirth in the scale of beings, and the evil ones to a lower. But in any event, deeds of either sort will lead one into rebirth after rebirth in an endless chain which offers no final salvation. Moreover, given an infinite succession of births, *all* births ultimately become meaningless. The goal thus becomes total release from the cycle of rebirths, something that can be accomplished only by doing away with the root cause of rebirth, which is to say with deeds (*karman*). This is usually done by means of renunciation and ascetic exercise, but in the text cited above it is the river *Vijarā* that wipes away all deeds and makes it possible for one to enter a heavenly realm beyond the cycle of rebirth. In effect, the river eradicates the accumulation of the past, the residue of one's previous existence, just as does Plato's *Lēthē*. The only difference between the two in this regard is that the accumulated past is understood as memory in one case and as deeds in the other.

It is important for us to note, however, that the river does not *destroy* those deeds and their karmic power to affect rebirths. What becomes of them is carefully described in the text. The dead person's good deeds are said to go to the favored relatives, whom they help to better rebirths, and the evil deeds go to those less favored, who will receive worse rebirths as a result. Thus, a mechanism exists whereby those deeds lost at the river make their way back to the world, just as—according to Plato—there is a path whereby memories may return to this world, and a means whereby memories may be preserved, according to the Petelia tablet.

A number of similar ideas are preserved in an important Norse text, Snorri Sturluson's description of Mimir's Spring[25] from *Gylfaginning* 15:

> And under that root [of the world-tree Yggdrasill] which turns toward the frost-giants is Mímir's Spring, in which knowledge and understanding are hidden. He who owns that spring is called Mímir, and he is full of wisdom, because he drinks from that spring out of the Gjallarhorn.

At first sight, it is perhaps difficult to see the relation of this text to those we have already discussed, even when it is acknowledged that a position underneath the roots of the cosmic tree implies a location in the underworld. The chief problem is the apparent lack of a river that governs forgetfulness, and yet the lack is only apparent, coming as a result of the radical shift of emphasis in the Norse version from the obliterative power of the river to the inspirational power of the spring. This may be due to the belief—attested in other texts—that Mímir's Spring contained mead,[26] which, in Germanic ideology, undoubtedly called to mind the role of intoxicants as a source of inspiration.[27] This mead-spring of wisdom thus became a topic for rich speculation at the expense of the river to which it was earlier closely linked.

While hidden, the river has not completely disappeared, however. It still may be perceived in the specification that Mímir drinks from his spring with the Gjallarhorn. This word is a compound, its second member, *-horn,* meaning here "drinking vessel," [28] and its first member, *Gjallar-* is the regular genitive form of the proper noun *Gjǫll,* the name of a river. Nor is it just any river; rather, it is named as one of the major rivers of the otherworld. According to *Grímnismál* 28, it falls close to men, and thence to Hel, the realm of those dead who have not fallen in battle.[29] Again, in *Gylfaginning* 4 where Snorri names the rivers that flow from the spring *Hvergelmir* ("the roaring kettle") in Hel, the *Gjǫll* appears and is said to be "next to the gates of Hel" (*Gjǫll er næst Helgrindum*).

We are thus told, on the one hand, that the *Gjǫll* terminates in a spring, which is named *Hvergelmir,* and, on the other, that a spring called Mímir's Spring exists, from which Mímir drinks with "the horn of the river *Gjǫll.*" In both instances, the spring and the river are located in the underworld. On the basis of this information, I am inclined to conclude that the two wells are one and the same, albeit referred to under different names.[30]

The etymology of the name *Mímir* most widely accepted also affords valuable material for comparison, although there are serious difficulties that make ready acceptance impossible. It has been suggested that *Mímir* is best seen as a reduplicated form of the P-I-E verb **(s)mer-,* "to think, recall, reflect, worry over" (>Sanskrit *smárati;* Avestan *hi-šmaraiti;* Greek *mermaírō;* Gothic *maúrnan;* etc.).[31] As a nominal form, its sense would best be rendered as "memory," and the personified being Mímir, a wise giant, patron of memory, might thus be compared to the Celtic goddess *Rosmerta,* patroness of memory, whose name is also derived from P-I-E *(s)mer-*.[32]

Interpreting Mímir's Spring as "Spring of Memory" is, of course, most attractive in terms of the semantic correspondence to the "Pool of Memory" of the Petelia tablet that would then result. But there are several phonological problems that must give us pause. Initial *s-* is usually preserved in Germanic from a P-I-E *sm-* cluster; the long *-i-* in the first syllable ought to be short; and the final *-r* is only the case-ending and not part of a verbal root. Until these difficulties are accounted for, it would be premature to accept an interpretation of *Mímir* as "memory," however much comparative mythology points in favor of such a reading.[33]

Fortunately, the weight of my argument does not rest on this etymology alone. Etymology is a tool of tremendous importance for the study of Indo-European myth, but is not the only one, and correspondence of content must be considered along with lexemes and phonemes. In this regard I note that: (1) Mímir's Spring is located in the otherworld; (2) drinking from it gives supernatural knowledge; (3) it is connected with a river; and (4) that river flows in the otherworld. In all these points it can be shown to be derived from a Proto-Indo-European original, from which Greek, Indic, and Celtic variants were also derived.

In one other respect, the story of Mímir's Spring closely resembles the other accounts we have considered and will consider: only a very few, specially favored, individuals are able to drink from it and derive the benefit it bestows. Besides Mímir himself, only one being is said to have tasted of the spring. This is Óðinn, the lord of the gods, who—as we are told in *Vǫluspá* 28—tasted it but once, and paid for the privilege with the loss of one eye.[34]

As I noted above, the Norse texts have little to say about the effect of the river, given their greater interest in the spring as source of intoxication and inspiration. Two points, however, might be ventured. The first is that the river feeds the spring, an arrangement that makes a great deal of sense symbolically if we are to understand the river as governing forgetfulness and the spring as governing memory, for the act of forgetting is similar to a flowing away, and that of remembering to a bubbling up from some invisible source. The second point is something of an argument *e silentio,* but worth noting nonetheless. In neither the Norse nor the Indian reflex is drinking from the river mentioned: this is something found only in the Greek versions, and secure reconstruction cannot proceed on the basis of these alone.

Actually, a correspondence may be drawn between the Indic and Celtic versions of the cosmologem that will resolve this problem. In the Indian version, the deeds of the deceased are seen to pass away as he crosses over the river *Vijarā,* a crossing that is made in typically Indian fashion: "by mind" (*manasā*). This psychic passage notwithstanding, the important point is that the deeds—and in an earlier version, memories—are lost while making the passage. Now, if we consider the transitus "by mind" as a specifically Indian transformation of an earlier version, then we must ask how the river was crossed in such a version. Several means are possible: bridge, boat, wading, or swimming. In the first two, however, there is nothing that would indicate why crossing the river should cause one's memories to drift away. But if one actually made physical contact with the river's water by wading or swimming across, and if the river's waters were turbulent—as those of the *Gjǫll,* for instance, must have been, given the meaning of its name as "resounding" [35]— then the action of the water might tend to cleanse or purify the individual, washing away his memories like so much dirt that clings to a traveler in the course of a long and arduous journey.

A Celtic legend provides support for this hypothesis, and must be considered as another reflex of the cosmologem we are considering. Here, two bodies of water related to the otherworld are encountered, although neither one is a river or a spring. But the first washes something away, and a drink from the second restores that which was lost in addition to giving supernatural wisdom. The story is but one of the three versions of the tale of how the hero Finn Mac Cumhaill gained his wisdom, as presented in the *Feis Tighe Chonáin.* [36] I quote here O'Rahilly's summary of the legend:

> Finn, after bathing in a lake at Sliab Cuilinn [Slieve Gullion, County Armagh], found himself transformed into a feeble old man. The warrior band led by Finn thereupon laid siege to the neighboring *síd* [burial mound, one locus of the Celtic otherworld, and the dwelling-place of spirits originally associated with the otherworld]. [37] Cuilenn, the lord of the *síd,* came forth, bearing a golden cup, and when Finn had drunk from it his former strength and appearance returned to him. Finn then handed the cup to Mac Reithe, who likewise drank from it; but the cup then sprang out of Mac Reithe's hand and disappeared into the earth. By drinking from Cuilenn's cup Finn and Mac Reithe acquired supernatural knowledge. [38]

The river of the underworld has here become a lake, in order to conform with details of the geography of Slieve Gullion. [39] And, in another transformation, the water of the lake is described as having the power to wash away youth and strength—virtues dearest to Finn as a hero—rather than memory. But the story betrays that these were not the original entities taken away by the waters, for when Cuilenn, the lord of the *síd* (which is to say, the ruler of the underworld) relents and gives Finn a drink—presumably from the water that robbed him of his strength—it is not just strength that is returned to him, but strength *and wisdom.* This point is underscored when Mac Reithe gains wisdom alone from the draught, with no reference to strength. Finally, we must note that the origin of this water in the otherworld is firmly established when the cup miraculously returns to the subterannean realm before any others can drink from it.

There is, of course, considerable divergence of detail in the materials I have presented above. The various texts usually mention two bodies of water, but sometimes only one. They are usually located on the way to the otherworld, but sometimes on the way back or on the surface of this world. The first body of water is described as a river, a pool, or a lake; the other, a pond, a spring, or a drink from a golden cup. Sometimes the first body of water has the power to rob one of memory; sometimes one's deeds, youth, or strength are lost, and this effect is said to be caused either by drinking the water, crossing over it, or bathing in it. The effect of the second body of water usually comes as a result of drinking from it—although Plato omits the second body entirely, and transfers its effect to abstention from the waters of the first. Finally, although the Indian reflex is aberrant, the other versions consistently state that the second body of water bestows memory or supernatural wisdom on those who drink from it. The sources are also fairly consistent in maintaining that only a privileged few receive the benefits of the second body of water, but they do not agree about who those beneficiaries are—philosophers, initiates, dear relatives, gods, giants, and heroes all are mentioned.

All of these variations are of interest and importance, and none should be prematurely minimized or argued away. On the other hand, their importance ought not be overemphasized, and I believe they can best be understood as the ways in which different branches of the Indo-European family reinterpreted and transformed certain inherited materials which were Proto-Indo-European in origin. When the various texts are systematically compared, their correspondences culled, their differences analyzed and explained, it is possible to reconstruct from them a P-I-E cosmologem from which all were derived.

The picture that emerges is as follows. On the way to the otherworld, souls of the dead had to cross a river, the waters of which washed away all of their memories. These memories were not destroyed, however, but were carried by the river's water to a spring, where they bubbled up and were drunk by certain highly favored individuals, who became inspired and infused with supernatural wisdom as a result of the drink.

Many points can be made about the nature of Indo-European religion on the basis of this cosmologem; for instance, the view of water as a purifier, drink as a source of inspiration, and wisdom as something to which only a privileged few are entitled. To my mind, however, the most interesting point is the basic symmetry in the relations between this world and the next. For on the one hand, the otherworld is quite often cut off from this one; the soul making the passage must leave behind all his memories, all the history he has accumulated during his life. But on the other, this world is not cut off from the next in the same sense, for those memories constantly flow back and become a source of the deepest wisdom and most profound inspiration.

Ultimately, this cosmologem is not just a piece of funerary geography, but conveys basic truths about the nature of human existence. It relates that the dead have no need of their memories, having passed beyond the realm in which those memories are of value. But the memories of the departed are not without value for those who are yet living. The accumulated memories of the dead comprise the totality of human history. Preserved and appreciated, they are the source of true wisdom, the wisdom that is based on the full sweep of human experience rather than just the idiosyncratic events of one human life. In the last analysis, the present depends upon the past, the living upon the dead, and this world upon the other.[40] Those who die do not just pass on but continue to contribute to the sustenance of this world,[41] as the world of the living draws strength, meaning, and wisdom from the world of the dead, much as one draws water from a spring.

Notes

1. See *Arda Wirāz Nāmag* 7–9, and the Russian lament recorded in Elsa Mahler, *Die russiche Totenklage* (Leipzig: Otto Harrassowitz, 1935), p. 88.

2. See, inter alia, *Vafþrúdnismál* 43; Vergil *Aeneid* 6; Hesiod *Theogony* 455, Homer *Odyssey* 11.

3. Most often this image occurs in stories of a hero's journey to the otherworld, as in Herakles' quest for the Apples of the Hesperides (Apollodorus, *Bibliotheca* 2.5.11a, et al.); the voyage of Odysseus to the isle of Kalypso (as interpreted by Hermann Güntert, *Kalypso* [Halle: Max Niemeyer, 1919]); or the voyages of Bran, Connla, and Oisin (for a collection of the relevant texts, see Wolfgang Krause, *Die Kelten* [Tubingen: J. C. B. Mohr, 1929], pp. 10–28).

4. Procopius, *De Bello Gothico*, 4.48ff.; *Frá dauða Sinfjǫtla*, paragraph 2.

5. Pausanias 10.28.2 (the earliest mention of *Charon*); Mahler, p. 285; *Frá dauða Sinfjǫtla*, paragraph 2 (although here the ferry crosses a bay rather than a river; see also the German folktale cited by Jacob Grimm, *Teutonic Mythology*, vol. 2, trans. James Stallybrass [London: George Bell, 1883], p. 832).

6. Most notably the *Gjallarbrú* of Norse mythology (*Gylfaginning* 49, et al.), and the *Cinvat* Bridge of Iranian (*Yasna* 46.10–11, 51.13; although it is not specified there that this bridge crosses a river). On the latter, see my article "Cinvat.pərətu," in *Mythologische Wörterbuch: Altiranische und zoroastrische Mythologie*, Carsten Colpe, ed. (Stuttgart: Klett Verlag, 1974–82), pp. 315–16.

7. Thus *Vǫluspá* 39 and the Pahlavi accounts of an eschatological ordeal in a river of molten metal, as in *Bundahišn* 30.20, et al. This comparison was first drawn by Åke V. Ström, "Indogermanisches in der Völuspa," *Numen* 14 (1967): 190. The Iranian idea is already presented in the Gāthic Avesta: *Yasna* 51.9, 30.7, and 32.7.

8. For references, see *Pauly Wissowa Realencyclopädie der classischen Altertumswissenschaft* (Munich: A. Druckenmüller, 1925), 24:2141–43.

9. The full myth of Er includes a good deal more than just the account of the river. It is found in *Republic* 614 B–621 D.

10. As in *Meno* 81 A–E, *Phaidros* 248 C–249 D, *Gorgias* 521 ff.

11. On the importance of myth for the theory of *anamnēsis*, see Paul Friedländer, *Plato*, 3 vols. (New York: Pantheon, 1958), 1:180–82, 195–96; and Walter Hirsch, *Platons Weg zum Mythos* (Berlin: Walter de Gruyter, 1971), pp. 330–35. Although

this has been known since Louis Couturat, *De Platonicis mythis* (Paris: 1896), the usual trend in philosophy has been to minimize the importance of Plato's use of myth, as in Ernesto Grassi, *Il Problema della Metafisica Platonica* (Bari: G. Laterza, 1932), pp. 88f., 94–123.

12. Hirsch, pp. 330f., 334 f.

13. On *Lēthē*, Hjalmar Frisk, *Grieschisches etymologisches Wörterbuch*, 2 vols. (Heidelberg: Carl Winter, 1973), 2:81; on *Amelēta*, Henry George Liddell and Robert Scott, *A Greek-English Lexicon* (Oxford: Oxford University Press, 1968), p. 80f.

14. Albrecht Dieterich, *Nekyia*, 2d ed. (Leipzig: 1913), pp. 122ff.; J. A. Stewart, *The Myths of Plato*, 2d ed. (Carbondale: Southern Illinois University Press, 1960), pp. 161–63; W. K. C. Guthrie, *Orpheus and Greek Religion*, 2d ed. (London: Methuen, 1952), pp. 171ff.; idem. *The Greeks and Their Gods* (Boston: Beacon, 1954), pp. 230, 322–23; Karl Kerenyi, "Mnemosyne—Lesmosyne. Über die Quellen "Erinnerung" und "Vergessenheit" in der griechischen Mythologie," in *Die Geburt der Helena* (Zurich: Rhein Verlag, 1945), pp. 99–101; H. J. Rose, *Handbook of Greek Mythology* (New York: E. P. Dutton, 1959), p. 88f.; M. P. Nilsson, "Die quellen der Lethe und der Mnemosyne," in *Opuscula Selecta*, 3 vols (Lund: C. W. K. Gleerup, 1960), 3:85–92.

15. Guthrie, *Orpheus and Greek Religion*, p. 172; Rose, *Handbook*, p. 89.

16. Stewart, *Myths of Plato*, p. 161; Guthrie, *Orpheus and Greek Religion*, p. 172.

17. Text from Otto Kern, *Orphicorum Fragmenta*, 2d ed. (Berlin: Weidmann, 1953), Fragment 32a, pp. 104–5.

18. Thus, Rose, p. 88; Dieterich, p. 122; Guthrie, *Orpheus and Greek Religion*, p. 171.

19. Nilsson, "Die quellen," p. 86.

20. I am not inclined to call the idea of the waters of the otherworld a myth because it lacks both a narrative structure and a setting in the primordial past, elements I take as necessary in myth. Rather, this idea is a piece of geography or cosmology, thus a "cosmologem."

21. In later reflexes of the cosmologem, this tendency to level the difference between the two bodies of water, is quite pronounced. An alternation is apparent, however, between those versions that focus primary attention on the act of forgetting and thus present two rivers—Dante, *Purgatorio* 33, on the Lethe and the Eunoe, for instance—and those that focus on memory and present two springs—thus, e.g., Higden's *Polychronicon* 1:197: "There be over ij welles also, of whom oon induce the memory, that other oblivion" (trans. John de Trevisa [1387]).

22. The importance of this text for the reconstruction of Indo-Iranian and Indo-European ideas of the otherworld was first recognized by Stig Wikander, *Vayu* (Uppsala: A. B. Lundquist, 1941), p. 47ff.

23. The initial long ā notwithstanding, I am inclined to see this pond Āra as identical to and perhaps derived from the sea Ara described in *Chāndogya Upaniṣad* 8.5.3–4; "Now, what is called 'the retreat to the forest' [*aranya-ayana*, the third stage of life], that is really just studentship [*brahmacārya*, the first stage of life]. For truly, Ara and Nya are the two seas in the Brahma-world, the third heaven from here. There is the lake Airammadīya; there the fig tree 'Soma-pressing' [*Somasavana*]; there the walled city of Brahma 'Unconquerable' [*Aparājitā*], and the golden hall of the lord. One may discover these two seas Ara and Nya only by studentship. Only for those

[who have done studentship] is there the Brahma-world. Those ones can move freely in all the worlds" The names Ara and Nya here are certainly back-formations from the term *aranya*, "forest," given the virtual impossibility of any Sanskrit word beginning with ṇ-. They have been inserted here to make a point about studentship and the retreat to the forest as means of attaining the heavenly realm of Brahma. One might speculate that they have replaced older names for the twin seas, and that those twin seas might ultimately be derived from the Indo-European cosmologem reconstructed in this article, but given the paucity of information provided in the text about these seas, this can only remain guesswork.

24. On this, see, inter alia, R. E. Hume, *The Thirteen Principal Upanishads* (London: Oxford University Press, 1921), pp. 54–57; Surendranath Das Gupta, *A History of Indian Philosophy* (Cambridge: Cambridge University Press, 1922), 1:53–57; and Paul Deussen, *Philosophy of the Upanishads*, A. S. Geden, trans. (Edinburgh: T. Clark, 1906), pp. 313–38.

25. On the specific nature of the Old Norse *brunnr* as a spring, whose source has been located and isolated by shaft-like walls to create a natural gushing fountain, see Paul C. Bauschatz, "Urth's Well," *Journal of Indo-European Studies* 3 (1975): 70–72.

26. The most important text is *Vǫluspá* 28, where it is said, with reference to the spring, that "Mímir drinks mead each morning" (*Drekkr mjǫð Mímir morgin hverjan*). On this passage and on the nature of Mímir's Spring as filled with mead, see especially Robert Höckert, *Vǫluspá och Vanakulten*, 2 vols (Uppsala: Almquist and Wiksells, 1926–30), 1:49–55.

27. On which, see Renate Doht, *Der Rauschtrank im germanischen Mythos* (Vienna: Karl M. Halosar, 1974).

28. Richard Cleasby and Gudbrand Vigfusson, *An Icelandic-English Dictionary*, 2d ed. (Oxford: Clarendon Press, 1957), p. 279, entry III. The Gjallarhorn also appears in a very different context in *Vǫluspá* 45, where it is said to be the trumpet that Heimdallr sounds at the beginning of the Ragnarǫk. This is another legitimate sense of *-horn* (Cleasby-Vigfusson, p. 279, entry IV), but it is hard to see why this instrument should be specified as "of the river Gjǫll." In light of this, I am inclined to take Snorri's meaning as original.

29. On Hel, See Güntert, *Kalypso* pp. 35ff.; Gustav Neckel, *Walhall* (Dortmund: W. Ruhfus, 1913), pp. 51ff.

30. This is also the opinion of Bauschatz, p. 77, E. O. G. Turville-Petre, *Myth and Religion of the North* (New York: Holt, Rinehart & Winston, 1964), p. 279; and Åke V. Ström, *Germanische Religion* (Stuttgart: W. Kohlhammer, 1975), p. 118, all of whom would also equate these springs with that of Ur in *Vǫluspá* 19, *Hávamál* 111, and *Gylfaginning* 16.

31. Jan de Vries, *Altnordisches etymologisches Wörterbuch* (Leiden: E J Brill, 1962), p. 387; Julius Pokorny, *Indogermanisches etymologisches Wörterbuch* (Bern: Francke, 1959), p. 969; Sigmund Feist, *Etymologisches Wörterbuch der gotischen Sprache* (Halle: Max Niemeyer, 1923), p. 265; Alois Walde, *Lateinisches etymologisches Wörterbuch*, 3d ed. revised by J. B. Hofmann, 2 vols. (Heidelberg: Carl Winter, 1938–39), 2:67f.; all following C. C. Uhlenbeck, "Etymologica," *Zeitschrift für vergleichende Sprachforschung* 40 (1907): 558.

32. Joseph Vendryes, 'Variétés Étymologiques," *Études Celtiques* 2 (1937): 134f.

33. I am grateful to Jaan Puhvel and Edgar Polomé for emphasizing to me the difficulties of deriving *Mímir* from *(s)mer-.

34. For interpretation of this fascinating stanza, see A. G. van Hamel, "Voluspá 27–29," *Arkiv för Nordisk Filologi* 37 (1925): 293–305.

35. de Vries, *Altnordisches etymologisches Wörterbuch*, p. 171.

36. On the three versions, see T. F. O'Rahilly, *Early Irish History and Mythology* (Dublin: Institute for Advanced Studies, 1946), pp. 318–23; Alwyn and Brinley Rees, *Celtic Heritage* (London: Thames and Hudson, 1961), pp. 161, 311–12; and Patrick K. Ford, "The Well of Nechtan and 'La Gloire Lumineuse,'" in G. J. Larson, ed., *Myth in Indo-European Antiquity* (Los Angeles: University of California Press, 1974), pp. 67–74. All of these authors make the comparison to Mímir's Spring, and Ford further attempts to relate the Celtic materials to the ideology reconstructed by Georges Dumézil, *Mythe et Epopée*, 3 vols (Paris: Gallimard, 1968–73), 3:21–89.

37. On the *síd* and the *áes síde*, "people of the *síd*," see Joseph Vendryes, *La Religion des Celtes* (Paris: Presses Universitaires de France, 1948), p. 307f.; Jan de Vries, *Keltische Religion* (Stuttgart: W. Kohlhammer, 1961), p. 255f.; and Maartje Draak, *Áes Síde* (Amsterdam: J. M. Neulenhoff, 1949).

38. O'Rahilly, p. 327, parenthetical glosses mine. For the full text and a rather dated translation, see Nicholas O'Kearney, ed., *Feis Tighe Chonáin Chinn-Sheibhe*, Transactions of the Ossianic Society, vol. 2 (Dublin: John O'Daly, 1855), pp. 168–75.

39. O'Kearney, p. 168 n. 2, states that the lake of Slieve Gullion was in his day still believed to have the power to turn men's hair gray.

40. Cf. the conclusions reached by Bauschatz, "Urth's Well."

41. A similar dependence of the realm of the living on that of the dead may be noted in P-I-E ideas of the fate of the body after death, on which see my "Death and Resurrection in Indo-European Thought," *Journal of Indo-European Studies* 5(1977): 244–64.

FIVE

THE FERRYMAN OF THE DEAD

Even to the Greeks, the origins of Charon, the ferryman of souls across the river Styx, were something of a mystery. Diodorus Siculus, for instance, considered him to be of Egyptian origin,[1] and although this idea is now generally dismissed as just another case of Greek "Egyptomania,"[2] no clear and convincing thesis has emerged to take its place. In general, two factors have militated against any solution to the problem: the lack of a convincing etymology for the name *Kharōn*,[3] and the great frequency with which similar figures are encountered in cultures completely unrelated to Greece,[4] something which must give pause to the comparatist who wishes to establish correspondences leading to historical reconstruction.

Notwithstanding these difficulties, it is my intention to assert a Proto-Indo-European origin for Charon. To be sure, the soul's passage over a river is a well-established part of Indo-European funerary belief,[5] and it stands to reason that a ferryman may have been believed to conduct it across, but reconstruction cannot proceed on the grounds of mere probability. Nor can it rest simply on the ground that there are vaguely similar figures—ferrymen of souls—in Norse, Celtic, or Indian mythology. Rather, if we are to conclude that Charon derives from a P-I-E prototype, it is necessary for us to point out specific and detailed correspondences that assure us of the genetic relation of the figures being compared. I believe we can find such a significant detail if we focus on the issue of Charon's old age.

The earliest text in which Charon is mentioned, the *Minyas* as cited by Pausanias, 10.28.2, is extremely brief and tells us very little, but it does establish one thing with certainty: Charon was seen as a very old man. The text, in which Pausanias is discussing some paintings by Polygnotus depicting the underworld, reads as follows:

> It seems to me that Polygnotus followed the poem *Minyas,* for truly in the *Minyas* there is a passage about Theseus and Peirithous: "There, truly, is the ship in which the corpses embark, whose aged ferryman [*geraios porthmeus*] is Charon, but they did not find it in the harbor." And truly, Polygnotus painted that old man [*geronta*] Charon as high in age.

The description of Charon as an old man (*gerōn*) is consistently encountered in other Greek sources, such as Aristophanes, *Frogs* 139f., where he is called "an old man, a sailor" (*anēr gerōn nautēs*), or Euripides, *Alcestis* 441, where he appears as "the old man, conductor of corpses" (*gerōn nekropom-*

pos). It is the satirist Lucian, however, who makes most striking use of the theme of Charon's old age, saying of an extremely ancient character that he is "almost as old as the ferryman," much as we might say that a person is "old as Methusaleh." [6]

In the dialogue entitled *Charon,* Lucian describes the ferryman as working in partnership with Death (*Thanatos*),[7] and this image is also found in Latin literature most notably in Seneca's *Oedipus* 164–70, where Charon's old age is also mentioned:

> Black Death opens its greedy, gaping
> Mouth and spreads its wings.
> And he who watches over the troubled
> Waters with his broad ship—
> a sailor strong in his rough old age [*durus senio navita crudo*]—
> Can scarcely pull back his arms,
> Exhausted by the constant poling,
> Weary from conveying the new mob.[8]

The locus classicus for Charon in Latin literature, however, is the *Aeneid* 6.298–304, where Vergil also dwells on the boatman's age, calling particular attention to one aspect of his senectitude: his whitened hair and beard.

> A dreadful harbormaster watches over these streams and waters
> In terrible filth: Charon, most of whose gray-white hair
> Lies disarrayed upon his chin, while his eyes stand in flame.
> His squalid clothing hangs from his shoulders by a knot.
> He himself propels his vessel with a pole and he tends to the
>   sails
> As he hauls the bodies in his rusty skiff.
> Already he is old [*senior*], but the old age [*senectus*] of a god is
>   raw and green!

This theme of Charon's old age and his white hair persists in later European literature. Thus, Dante refers to him as an old man "with wooly cheeks," [9] and Racine dubs him "le vieux nocher sur la rive infernale," [10] while it is possible for T. S. Eliot to evoke Charon with the brief and poignant epigraph to "The Hollow Men," "A penny for the Old Guy." [11] In that these all ultimately derive from the Greco-Roman tradition, however, they are not terribly useful for the work of reconstruction, and we must turn to independent testimonies of other Indo-European civilizations.

One of the clearest instances of a ferryman of the dead occurs within Germanic myth in the story of Sinfjǫtli's death, as related in the *Vǫlsunga Saga,* chapter 10, and in the second paragraph of the prose account of the Elder Edda, *Fra dauða Sinfjǫtla.* The latter tells that after Sinfjǫtli's death by poison, his brother Sigmund picked up his corpse.

> Sigmund bore him a long way in his arms, and he came to a fjord
> that was at once long and narrow. There was a small ship there,

and a man in it. He offered Sigmund passage over the fjord, yet when Sigmund bore the corpse out to the ship the boat was laden full [with the body]. The man said that Sigmund should proceed to the head of the fjord. Then the man pushed off the ship and disappeared straightaway.

The unnamed boatman is intentionally left a figure of mystery, and most scholars who have commented on the passage have believed that hearers were meant to understand him as the god Oðinn in one of his many disguises, receiving the body of a fallen warrior.[12] For my part, I am inclined to agree with these suspicions, but, while interesting, they are quite unnecessary for the argument at hand. Of much greater importance for our purposes is a linguistic detail, namely the fact that the boatman is called a *karl*.

In Old Norse, *karl* is one of several terms which may simply denote a man as opposed to a woman. When used in a more specific sense, it most often means a free man of the lower class, as do its cognates Old High German *karal* and Anglo-Saxon *ceorl* (from which we have English *churl*, "a country bumpkin, a rustic dolt"), although it may also indicate a married man or an old man.[13] It is the last of these meanings, however, which is the oldest, for Old Norse *karl* is derived from the Proto-Indo-European verb *ǵer- "to age, mature, ripen," or in its oldest sense "to rub away, erode, become worn down."[14] It is this very same verb which gives rise in Greek to the term *gerōn* "old man," which we saw was consistently applied to Charon.[15] The only difference is that whereas Gk. *gerōn* is a present participle of the verb (thus "one who is aging," "one who is being worn down"), ON *karl* has an -l- suffix, like Old Church Slavonic *zьrělъ* "ripe" (< *zьrěti* "to ripen").[16] Originally, then, *karl* meant "old man."

There is another ferryman of Germanic myth who is referred to as a *karl*. This is Hárbarðr, the central figure of the *Hárbarðsljóð* of the Elder Edda, a lay which begins when the god Thorr is returning to Asgard (the realm inhabited by the gods) after an expedition against hostile giants in Jotunheim. The two realms are separated by a body of water, and Thorr asks passage from a ferryman who is described as a *ferjukarl*, a "ferry-churl," or etymologically more exactly an "old ferryman." Surprisingly, however, the ferryman refuses and exchanges taunts with the mightiest of the gods. Finally Thorr is forced to walk around the bay, being unable to force the ferryman to convey him.

On the identity of this ferryman there can be no debate. He is undoubtedly Oðinn, as is clear from a number of data. First, no other personage could successfully defy Thorr. Second, the *Harbarðsljod* is placed between four lays devoted to Oðinn and four devoted to Thorr in the *Codex Regius,* and thus is an intermediate poem in which both gods figure with equal importance. Third, and most important, the name of the ferryman—which is not given until extremely late in the poem—is listed as one of the by-names of Oðinn in *Grímnismál* 49 and in a well-known *lausavísa* of Ulfr Uggason.[17] That the ferryman is Óðinn is useful information, for alone of the Norse gods he is consistently depicted as an old man[18] and a long beard is a regular feature of his many disguises,[19] but the name he takes when he appears as ferryman between different worlds is most interesting of all, for the name *Hárbarðr* means "he whose beard is hoary white."[20]

Now Hárbarðr is not a ferryman of the dead in any sense, but he is a ferryman between different worlds, plying his boat from one cosmic region to another. As such, I submit, he represents a Germanic transformation of an older P-I-E figure who carried souls of the dead from this world to the next. Why such a transformation took place is hard to say, although it may be due to the fact that in Germanic ship burials the craft to which the corpse was consigned was usually without a steersman.[21] As a result of this detail of practice, the mythic image of the ferryman may have become obsolete, may have disappeared from its original context, and been preserved in other stories of boats and boatmen. One cannot be certain. But given the specification of this ferryman as a *karl* with a white beard, one can safely draw a correspondence between him and Charon.

There is yet another Old Norse boatman designated as a *karl* who merits our attention. This is Hymir, central figure of the *Hymiskviða,* a giant who lives at the ends of the earth, and who rows Thorr out to the utmost limits of the sea in order to fish for the world-encircling Midgard serpent. The story preserves some extremely ancient features of Proto-Indo-European myth, as I have shown elsewhere,[22] but for our purposes the most important portion is an otherwise insignificant verse, stanza 10, in which Hymir's entrance before the fishing expedition is described.

> The woe-shaper came late
> Home from the hunt—Hymir, hard in councils.
> [As] he came into the hall, the icicles rattled;
> Frosty was the beard of the *karl* who entered.

Here the detail of the white beard is no longer connotative of age but has been turned into a striking piece of poetic description. As one who is bearded and lives in the frosty north, I can testify that on the coldest days of winter icicles do indeed form in one's beard from the condensation of water vapor in one's breath. But the question is not whether this description corresponds to any physical reality, but what the source is from which it derives. Given the existence of other ferrymen in Greek, Roman, and Germanic myth who are described as white of beard and are identified by terms derived from a verb meaning "to age, grow old," I take the description of Hymir's beard more seriously and view him also as a transformed reflex of the P-I-E ferryman of the dead, a ferryman consistently said to be white of beard.

Celtic evidence lends support to this hypothesis, for there too the ferryman of the dead is well attested.[23] The most interesting of these figures is Barinthus, who first appears in the *Navigatio Sancti Brendani*, chapter 1, where he tells St. Brendan of his trip across the sea to the paradisal *Terra Repromissionis Sanctorum*, "the land promised to the saints," thus stimulating St. Brendan to go in quest of that marvelous realm. Despite its Christian content, the *Navigatio Brendani* has been recognized as preserving the form and content of ancient Celtic *Imrama* ("Voyages") tales,[24] and of the Barinthus episode it has been said, "[it] is useless for the narrative, and obscure and incoherent in itself. It must be a survival of something, almost certainly therefore of some Celtic tradition." [25]

The nature of this Celtic tradition becomes a little clearer when we consider the other major text in which Barinthus appears, Geoffrey of Monmouth's *Vita Merlini*, lines 908–40, which describes the events after the battle of Camlann, in which Arthur was mortally wounded.

> They call the Isle of Apples *Fortunata,*
> And it has that name because it brings forth [fruit] by itself
>   alone.
> There is no work of farmers plowing the fields,
> And no cultivation at all, except that which nature provides.
> Moreover, it produces fruitful fields and vines,
> And apples are born, springing forth from the grass of its
>   forests.
> All the soil gives birth abundantly, moreover, not just the grass,
> And people live a hundred years or more there.
> There, nine sisters give the laws in a pleasant manner
> To those who come from our realms to them.
> The foremost of them is more learned in the healing art
> And her beauty exceeds that of her sisters.
> Morgen is her name; she has learned what there is of use
> In all the grasses in order that she may care for weakened
>   bodies.
> . . . .
> We dragged Arthur there, with Barinthus as guide,
> He to whom the seas and stars of heaven are known.
> With this steersman of the raft, we arrived there with the prince,
> And Morgen received us with such honor as was fitting.
> She placed the king upon a golden couch in her chamber,
> Uncovered his wound with her honorable hand,
> And examined it for a long while. At last she said
> It was possible to restore health to him, if he remained with her
> For a long time and would be willing to take her drug.
> Rejoicing accordingly, we entrusted the king to her
> And gave up our sails to favorable winds for our return.

The promise of Arthur's cure notwithstanding, there can be no doubt that the island *Fortunata* is an isle of the dead. Apples, gold, and a group of nine women are regular features of the Celtic otherworld,[26] and Morgen's name is best explained as derived from that of the Old Irish *Morrígain*, goddess of war and death.[27] While British, and perhaps Welsh, national hopes required that Arthur not die, and ever looked forward to his predicted return, harsher realities underlie the story, and Barinthus is, as Henri Martin recognized as early as 1857, the ferryman of the dead, "le Caron gaulois, qui passe les âmes." [28] What is most interesting about Barinthus, however, is his name, for as Heinrich Zimmer demonstrated, it is a latinization of an older Irish form. According to his reconstruction, that form is *Barrfind*, which literally means "white hair." [29]

Time and again we encounter the same recurrent image: the ferryman of the dead is himself an old man, white of hair and white of beard, conveying souls to Death (*Thanatos, Mors, Morrígain*). And the image is not an idle or a whimsical one, a mere poetic flight of fancy, for beneath it lies a profound and disturbing observation. In truth, the ferryman we have reconstructed is not so much a person as a personification. He is old age incarnate, and it is old age that carries us inexorably to death.[30]

At this point, it must be recognized that the sources we have considered, drawn from Greek, Roman, Germanic, and Celtic mythology, all come from the Centum division within the Proto-Indo-European grouping. If we are truly to consider this mythic image and the underlying ideology to be Proto-Indo-European, supporting evidence will have to be found from one or more of the Satəm peoples, and this is not a simple matter.

It is not that ferrymen of the dead are unknown among the Balts, Slavs, Indians, or Iranians: such is hardly the case, although the position of some of these peoples away from any large bodies of water produced certain changes in the nature of the image. Thus, for instance, in Russian laments for the dead, which are among our best evidence for Slavic funerary beliefs, souls of the departed make passage across a river, but the passage is described as more a fording than a ferry ride. One representative song reads as follows:

> A river runs here, a fiery river,
> From east to west,
> From west to north.
> Over that river, the fiery river,
> Drives the Archangel Michael, the light.
> He transports souls, the souls of the righteous.
> The righteous souls, the souls rejoice.
> They sing a cherubic song;
> Their voices are heard, seraphic.
> But the twisted, sinful souls remain.[31]

This text is noteworthy, not only for its similarities to the other sources we have considered, but also for its differences. We have already noted one, the lack of a boat, but we must also note that St. Michael, unlike Charon, Hárbarðr, Barinthus, or the others, is regularly depicted as extremely young, his clean shaven face being a particular sign of his youth.[32] Also, unlike our other sources, the psychopomp here does not conduct all the dead to the other side, but only certain chosen souls while others less deserving are abandoned to a crueller fate.

This same notion—that only certain souls can make the final crossing—is also found within the Indian tradition. To appreciate this, it is helpful to begin with a very straightforward statement of the ferryman theme from the *Śatapatha Brāhmaṇa* 2.3.3.15:

> Truly, the heaven-bound boat is the Agnihotra sacrifice. The two sides of that heaven-bound boat are the Āhavanīya and the Gārhapatya altars.[33] Truly, the steersman of the boat is the milk-pouring priest.

Given the tremendous importance accorded the performance of sacrificial ritual in the *Brāhamaṇas,* such a formulation is hardly surprising. Just as the priest is he who conducts the sacrifice, so is he the steersman of the heaven-bound boat (*nauḥ svargyā*) which the sacrifice is said to be. Such a view has certain consequences, however, as was laid out in *Śatapatha Brāhmaṇa* 4.2.5.10.

> Truly, the Bahiṣpavamāna praise-verse is the heaven-bound boat. The priests are truly the spars and oars which convey one to the heavenly world. Even one [priest] who is blameworthy would sink that [boat]. He sinks it just as one who mounts into a full [boat] sinks that one. Truly, every sacrifice is a heaven-bound boat. Therefore, one should try to exclude a blameworthy [priest] from every sacrifice.

The conclusion is plainly drawn. If the sacrifice is the heaven-bound boat, it only reaches its destination when properly performed. Any ritual error or any moral shortcoming on the part of a priest is sufficient to cause disaster. It is not primarily the priest who will suffer, however, but the patron of the rite, who had hoped to win salvation by its fulfillment. The danger is particularly great because most sacrifices of any size require numerous priests to perform them, and a failing on the part of any one of these officiants is enough to cause disaster. One is thus urged in the strongest possible terms to be aware of all the priests, not just the presiding priest, and this is why the priests are described as the "spars and oars" (*sphyāś cāritrāś ca*) of the sacrifice, and not its steersman (*nāvājas*). There can be only one steersman, but there are multiple priests, and a text which stresses the importance of attention to all priests cannot reduce their multiplicity to unity, even in the service of an ancient metaphor or homology. Thus, a new equation had to be forged, one which would do justice to the large number of priests involved in a sacrifice, acknowledge their importance, and show the dangers should any one of them be faulty. "Spars and oars" is just such an equation.

Later Indian texts came to reject the valuation of sacrificial action as that which is most important in life and crucial for one's salvation, advancing claims for other types of endeavor. Thus the *Śvetāśvatara Upaniṣad* 2.8 regards yogic discipline in this light and accordingly terms it the "raft of *Brahman*" by which one who knows may cross over all fear-inducing streams. Although the ferryman per se goes unmentioned, the implication is clear. It is the knowledge of absolute reality (*Brahman*) won through yoga which makes passage possible beyond the confines of this world of suffering. Such knowledge is the ferryman. This line of thought is further pursued by the heterodox religious movements in India. For the Buddhists, the doctrine which helps one to win salvation is a vehicle, a "ferry-boat" (*yāna*) and the two largest doctrinal groups are the "big ferryboat" (*Mahāyāna*) and the "little ferryboat" (*Hīnayāna*). For the Jains, salvation is a fording (*tirtha*) of a dangerous river, and the saints who establish the models of salvation are "makers of the fording" (*Tirthaṅkāras*).[34]

The Iranian evidence is extremely complex, but here—as with the Russian lament we examined—the idea of separation of the righteous from the unrighteous at the final crossing stands out clearly. Within Iranian myth the crossing is not made by boat but by bridge, and the very name of the bridge emphasizes this point—the Cinvat Bridge, "Bridge of the Separation,"[35] over which only the souls of the righteous (*ašavan-*) may cross. Descriptions of the bridge vary widely. Sometimes it is said to be enormously wide when a righteous soul walks upon it, narrowing to a razor's breadth when an unrighteous (*drəgvant-*) soul steps on it.[36] Elsewhere it is the scene of a furious battle between gods and demons for possession of the soul.[37] In such instances the soul is usually without a psychopomp, but other texts specify one, although again these vary widely. Sometimes the conductor—whom I trust we may safely see as having taken the place of the P-I-E ferryman—is the god Sraoša ("Obedience" or "Discipline" of a religious nature);[38] sometimes, a person's good thoughts, words, and deeds;[39] or sometimes (as in the Middle English morality play *Everyman*) one's good deeds alone.[40] Most often, the guide across the perilous Cinvat Bridge is a maiden who is the personification of one's own religion (*daēnā-*),[41] being beautiful, fragrant, stately, and virtuous if one's religion is all it should be, and repulsive, putrid, knock-kneed, and whorish if it is not.[42] Needless to say, it is only the beautiful Daēnā-maiden who assists one over the bridge into heaven, while her hideous counterparts drags the soul down into torment.

These are the most frequent statements within the Avesta and the Pahlavi texts on the topic of who assists the soul over the Cinvat Bridge. In addition, there is one rather unusual observation found in *Dēnkart* 3.182, which states: "Now there are six things most beneficial to men and the world. . . . One is for pupils to take up the character of [their] good teacher-priest [*hērbed*] in order that they cross the [Cinvat] Bridge well."[43] Apparently, one is meant to internalize the virtues of an exemplary priest, and insofar as one is able to do so, that priest assists one over the bridge. Although this may be a novel piece of Iranian speculation, it is also possible that it is a transformed version of an older Indo-Iranian idea, in which the priest is the psychopomp. That notwithstanding, in all the sources we have considered from the Satəm peoples, nowhere is there a hint of the ferryman as an old man or as the personification of old age.

It will be noticed, however, that while our Satəm examples do not adhere to the Centum pattern, they do possess a certain order of their own. Some of them present the psychopomp as a religious leader, a priest or a saint. Others present him as an important aspect of religion: discipline, knowledge, sacrifice, good works, doctrine, or the like. Still others, most notably in Iran, present her (the sex change being due to the feminine gender of the noun *daēnā*) as the personification of religion itself. But in all these instances, the conductor is seen as religion in one of its guises, a fact which coincides with another important divergence from the Centum pattern. Whereas the Centum texts described the ferryboat's destination only as death, the Satəm texts consistently state that the boat (or ford or bridge) leads to heaven, to a transcendent beatific realm. Furthermore, whereas the Centum ideology permitted all souls to make the passage, that of the Satəm peoples excluded those who were undeserving, either through moral or ritual failing. Only the righteous might enter the heavenly regions while those less deserving are either left at the river or fall to a considerably less pleasant afterlife.

In truth, we are able to reconstruct two different mythic images, one for the Centum grouping and one for the Satəm. In the former, the ferryman of the dead is the personification of old age—that which carries souls off to death. In the latter, the ferryman is the personification of religion—that which carries them up to heaven. What is more, this is not just a question of two different images, but of completely different religious *Weltanschauungen,* the one soteriological, the other emphatically not. The blunt, this-worldly, stoical Centum view contents itself with an image of mundane reality. Things wear down, and the human body is no exception to the universal law of erosion and entropy. What value there is lies in life, exuberance, energy, and action. Senescence and death are the fate of us all. In contrast, the exuberant, hopeful, otherworldly Satəm view extends the hope of salvation, of escape from the limitations of this life to the glories of a transcendent, thoroughly different mode of being. Such an escape is made possible by religion, or through religious knowledge, faith, sacrifice, righteousness, and the like. That which man does in this world is not an end in itself but only a means of conveyance to something far better and more meaningful.

Inevitably, the question must arise—which of these formulations and which of these styles of religious thought was the original Proto-Indo-European? On the strength of the evidence presented thus far, such a question is impossible to answer, although my general sense is that Proto-Indo-European religion tended to be nonsoteriological in nature, much more concerned with questions of winning a good life in the here and now than with the question of salvation in the hereafter. Such a suspicion may be confirmed, however, with consideration of two additional texts, one from India and one from Iran.

The first of these is *Muṇḍaka Upaniṣad* 1.2.7, a passage in which the older Brāhmaṇic ideas of salvation through sacrifice are soundly rejected in favor of salvation through esoteric knowledge. The text reads as follows:

> Truly, unsteady ships are those which take the form of sacrifice:
> The eighteen [older sacred texts][44] in which the lesser [form of]
> action is stated.
> Those fools who praise this [doctrine] as better [than that which
> is revealed here],
> Truly they go again to old age and death [*jarāmṛtyum*].

The key to this text is the compound *jarāmṛtyu-*, "death and old age," in the last line, which is presented as the destination of those foolish individuals who have placed their faith in a fallacious and/or outmoded means of salvation. Death and old age are parallel terms here, both unpleasant, distressing fates. But in earlier Indian texts, *jarā-* and *-mṛtyu-* were not seen thus, and in the *Atharva Veda*, the compound *jarāmṛtyu-* means, not "death and old age," but "one whose death is of old age," and what is more, to be a *jarāmṛtyu-* is considered a very desirable thing. Repeatedly, the wish is expressed to be a *jarāmṛtyu-* rather than one whose death is from accident, violence, or disease in youth.[45] The author of the Upaniṣad has thus taken this old term and drastically altered its meaning. Whereas old age and death were seen as a fitting and proper end to a long and rich life, they are twin terrors in his eyes, for he sees a hope beyond old age and death, a hope of salvation. But the old view remains in the Vedic *jarāmṛtyu-*, and, needless to say, Sanskrit *jarā-* is derived from P-I-E *ǵer-*, like Greek *gerōn* and Old Norse *karl*.[46] Once again we have the view that old age is the ferryman, old age is that which conducts one to death.

The second text which I take as conclusive for this reconstruction is a verse of the Gāthic Avesta, *Yasna* 46.10, one of the oldest mentions of the Cinvat Bridge in all Iranian literature, in which Zarathustra expresses the opinion that it is he himself who will conduct the souls of the righteous across the bridge.

> Whoever, male or female, O Mazdā Ahura,
> Gives to me that which you know to be best in life,
> [Give them] a reward for [their] righteousness: dominion by
> virtue of good mind.
> And those whom I will drive to praise of those like you,
> With all of them may I cross over the Bridge of Separation!

Here, Zarathustra puts himself in the place of the psychopomp, taking the mythic role earlier played by the ferryman of the dead, and his claim is as audacious as it is striking. It is only natural that we might ask what suggested this bold move to him, and in order to answer that question it is helpful to consider the prophet's name. All authorities are in agreement that the name is best analyzed as Zaraθ–uštra, with -θ- replacing earlier -t- for reasons that have not yet been fully clarified.[47] Further, Bailey's ingenious suggestions notwithstanding,[48] the best explanation of the name is "he whose camels are old," zarat- being the past participle of the verb zar- "to age, grow old," cognate to Sanskrit járant-, Ossetic zärond "old," and Greek gerōn "old man,"[49] the most common word applied to Charon, and the term with which we began our investigation.

In light of this, I would hypothesize that Zarathustra's insertion of himself into the ferryman's role was suggested by the similarity in their names, and that the Proto-Indo-European ferryman of the dead was known as *Ǵer-ont-, "the Old Man." Habitually, he was described with the hallmarks of old age— white hair and a white beard—and perhaps other details were mentioned as well, although our sources do not permit their reconstruction. The Old Man was a personification, a poetic expression of the fact that life is a process of wearing away, that time erodes the body, and that old age leads ineluctably to death. In this there is nothing soteriological in nature, nor hope of a finer existence beyond. Such hopes are the innovation of the Satəm peoples, whose religion assumed a strong soteriological coloring at some later point in time. The Centum peoples, however, remained more faithful to the nonsoteriological outlook of their P-I-E ancestors, comfortable with the realities of this world, free from illusions of any other, and fully prepared for their final meeting with the ferryman.

Notes

1. Diodorus Siculus 1.92.2 and 1.96.8.

2. The phrase and the verdict are from Otto Waser, *Charon, Charun, Charos* (Berlin: Weidmann, 1898), p. 12f.

3. See the summary of various attempts in Hjalmar Frisk, *Greichisches etymologisches Wörterbuch* (Heidelberg: Carl Winter, 1973), 2:1075f.

4. The image is encountered frequently in Melanesia, Polynesia, West Africa, etc., and even in such unlikely sources as Broadway musical comedies, as for instance the closing song in Frank Loesser's *Guys and Dolls,* a popular production of the mid-1950s, which begins, "I dreamed last night I got on a boat to heaven." Heinrich Schurtz, quoted by Waser, p. 3, was of the opinion that "wohl kein grösserer Teil der bewohnten Erde nachweisbar, wo nicht der Glaube an ein Totenschiff oder doch Spuren der Sage vorhanden waren."

5. See above, Chapter 4, "Waters of Memory, Waters of Forgetfulness,"

6. *Dialogues of the Dead* 27.9. The prominence of the theme of Charon's old age was noted by Waser, p. 22f., and by Francis A. Sullivan, "Charon, the Ferryman of the Dead," *Classical Journal* 46 (1950): 12.

7. *Charon* 8, where a particular wrestler is said to be thrown by Thanatos, then taken to the boat by Charon.

8. See also Seneca's description of Charon in *Hercules Furens* 764–68.

9. *Inferno* 3.97 "le lanose gote."

10. Prologue to *Iphigénie*.

11. As usual, Eliot does not content himself with a single allusion here, but fuses Charon with Guy Fawkes. That Charon is part of the image is made certain by the second stanza of Section 4 of the poem: In this last of meeting places/ We grope together/ And avoid speech/ Gathered on this beach of the tumid river.

12. Thus Hugo Gering, *Kommentar zu den Liedern der Edda* (Halle: Max Niemeyer, 1927), 2:138; Lee M. Hollander, *The Poetic Edda* (Austin: University of Texas Press, 1962), p. 203.

13. Richard Cleasby and Gudbrand Vigfusson, *An Icelandic-English Dictionary* (Oxford: Clarendon Press, 1957), p. 331.

14. Jan de Vries, *Altnordisches etymologisches Wörterbuch* (Leiden: E. J. Brill, 1962), p. 301; Julius Pokorny, *Indogermanisches etymologisches Wörterbuch* (Bern: Francke, 1959), p. 390f. The original sense of the verb is perhaps best preserved in the beautiful imagery of RV 1.92.10: "The ancient goddess [Dawn] who is born again and again, shining forth in the same color,/ wears away the length of a mortal's life as an active gambler wears away his eroding dice."

15. Frisk, 1:301f.

16. Pokorny, 391.

17. For the identification of Hárbarðr as Oðinn, see: Gering, 1:240; Jan de Vries, *Altgermanische Religionsgeschichte* (Berlin: Walter de Gruyter, 1970), 2:80; Jacob Grimm, *Teutonic Mythology*, trans. James Stallybrass (London: George Bell, 1883), 1:147; E. O. G. Turville-Petre, *Myth and Religion of the Ancient North* (New York: Holt, Rinehart, and Winston, 1962), p. 11; Folke Ström, *Nordisk Hedendom* (Göteborg: Akademiforlaget, 1967), p. 129; following lines pioneered by R. von Liliencron, "Das Harbardslied," *Zeitschrift für deutsches Altertum* 19 (1856): 181; and Felix Niedner, "Das Harbardsljod," *Zeitschrift für deutsches Altertum* 31 (1887): 218. The *lausavísa* of Ulfr Uggason is found in Finnur Jonsson, *Den Norskislandiske Skjaldedigtning* (Copenhagen: Gyldendanske, 1912), 1:138.

18. Grimm, 1:147.

19. de Vries, *Altgermanische Religionsgeschichte*, 2:80.

20. Contra de Vries, *Altnordisches etymologisches Wörterbuch*, p. 210, who interprets the name as meaning "high beard," from Old Norse *hár* "high," ignoring the fact that the final *-r*, which is only the sign of the nominative, is dropped in all compounds having *hár* as the first element, which are listed in Cleaby-Vigfusson, p. 244.

21. See Grimm, 2:830f.; de Vries, *Altergermanische Religionsgeschichte*, 1:153–55; Hilda Ellis (-Davidson), *The Road to Hel* (Cambridge: The University Press, 1943), pp. 16–19, 39–50; and the primary sources cited therein.

22. Bruce Lincoln, *Priests, Warriors, and Cattle* (Berkeley: University of California Press, 1980), pp. 115–18.

23. The most famous text is Procopius, *De Bello Gothico* 4.20. 49–58, which closely resembles the eighteenth-century report recorded in Grimm, 2:832, both of which show myth stripped of its specific features slipping into folk history and imagination.

24. Thus, Eleanor Hull, "The Development of the Idea of Hades in Celtic Literature," *Folklore* 18 (1907): 156ff.; Roger Sherman Loomis, *The Grail: From Celtic Myth to Christian Symbol* (New York: Columbia University Press, 1963), pp. 127–29; and Alwyn and Brinley Rees, *Celtic Heritage* (London: Thames and Hudson, 1961), pp. 323–25.

25. Arthur C. L. Brown, "Barintus," *Revue Celtique* 22 (1901): 339f.

26. On apples, see A. H. Krappe, "Avallon," *Speculum* 18 (1943): 303–22; Th. Chotzen, "Avalon—Avallach—Emhain Abhlach," *Etudes Celtiques* 4 (1948): 255–74. On gold, see Roger Sherman Loomis, *Wales and the Arthurian Legend* (Cardiff: University of Wales Press, 1956), p. 196; F. M. Warren, "The Island of Avalon," *Modern Language Notes* 14 (1899): 93–95. On the nine women, compare stanza 2, line 4 of *The Spoils of Annwn* and Pomponius Mela 3.6.9.

27. The derivation of *Morgen* is much disputed, and the most important possibilities are listed in Basil Clarke, ed., *Life of Merlin* (Cardiff: University of Wales Press, 1973), pp. 203–6, that from Old Irish *Morrígain* having been championed by Lucy Allen Paton, *Studies in the Fairy Mythology of Arthurian Romance*, 2d ed. (New York: Brut Franklin, 1960), pp. 148–66, accepted for the most part by R. S. Loomis, "Morgain la Fée and the Celtic Goddesses," in *Wales and the Arthurian Legend*, pp. 105–30, esp. pp. 116–19. For other possibilities, see, however, John Rhys, *Studies in the Arthurian Legend* (Oxford: Clarendon Press, 1896), p. 348f., and Ferdinand Lot, "Morgue la Fée et Morgan Tud," *Romania* 28 (1899): 321–28.

As for the etymology of *Morrígain,* it is universally seen as a compound, the second element of which is *-rígain,* "queen." The first element is thus *mor-*, which has best been explained by Whitley Stokes, "The Second Battle of Moytura," *Revue Celtique* 12 (1891): 128, as cognate to Old High German and Old Norse *mara*, Anglo-Saxon *maere*, German *Nicht-mahr*, French *cauche-mar*, and English *night-mare*. She is thus the nightmare queen, a fitting title for a goddess of war and death, whose name is glossed by *lamia, monstrum in femine figure* (J. Strachan, *Thesaurus Paleohibernicus* [Cambridge: University Press, 1901]; 1:2). For a fuller discussion, see E. G. Quinn, general ed., *Contributions to a Dictionary of the Irish Language: M* (Dublin: Royal Irish Academy, 1966), p. 173. Interpretation as "great queen" (*Mórrígain*) is probably to be rejected, for the long *-o-* is only found in Middle Irish sources, as the result of folk etymologizing (Quinn, p. 173).

28. Henri Martin, *Histoire de France*, 4th ed. (Paris: Furne, Jouvet, [1857]), 1: 73 n. 2.

29. H. Zimmer, "Keltische Beiträge: II. Brendans Meerfahrt," *Zeitschrift für deutsches Altertum* 33 (1889): 312–14, noting also the alternative form *Findbarr,* which relates to *Barrfind* as a *tatpuruṣa* compound to a *bahuvrīhi*. In the *Lebor Brec, Findbarr* is glossed *folt find bui fair,* "white hair is upon him," as noted by Zimmer, "Keltische Studien," *Zeitschrift für vergleichende Sprachforschung* 32 (1893): 159.

30. A similar personification is to be found in the P-I-E imagery of the infernal waters, on which see Chapter 4, "Waters of Memory, Waters of Forgetfulness."

31. Text from Elsa Mahler, *Die russische Totenklage* (Leipzig: Otto Harrassowitz, 1935), p. 286.

32. See, for instance, the examples in the Metropolitan Museum of Art, *Catalogue of Russian Icons* (New York: Metropolitan Museum, 1931), plate 58; A. I. Anisimov, et al., *Masterpieces of Russian Painting* (London: A. Zwemmer, n.d.), plate 15; or

Manolis Chatzidakis and Vojislav Djuric, *Les icônes dans les collections suisses* (Geneva: Musée Rath, 1968), plate 141.

33. That is, the eastern and western altars. The boat is thus seen to be moving either in a northerly direction, which would carry it to the home of the gods, or in a southerly one, which would take it to the realm of the dead.

34. See, for instance, the discussion in Heinrich Zimmer, *Philosophies of India* (Princeton: Princeton University Press, 1951), pp. 474ff.

35. Translation contra the badly misguided argument of R. C. Zaehner, "Postscript to Zurvan," *Bulletin of the School of Oriental and African Studies* 17 (1955): 246f., which is based upon a single text from the *Pahlavi Rivayat to the Dādestān ī Dēnīg* best explained as a simple scribal error undeserving of Zaehner's baroque treatment.

36. *Dādestān ī Dēnīg* 21.1–7; *Mēnōg ī Xrad* 2.123; *Dēnkart* (Sanjana) 9.20.3.

37. *Mēnōg ī Xrad* 2.115 ff.

38. *Mēnōg ī Xrad* 2.124; *Sad Dar* 58.5.

39. *Dādestān ī Dēnīg* 20.3, 24.6; *Dēnkart* 3.98.

40. *Dādestān ī Dēnīg* 34.3.

41. *Vīdēvdāt* 19.30; *Hadoxt Nask* 2.7 ff.; *Dādestān ī Dēnīg* 21.6.

42. *Hadoxt Nask* 3.7 ff.; *Arda Wirāz Nāmāg* 17.10 ff.

43. Text from M. J. Dresden, *Dēnkart* (Wiesbaden: Otto Harrassowitz, 1966), p. 151, lines 12 and 16–18.

44. The identity of these texts—the four Vedas, each with a Saṃhita, Brāhmaṇa, and Sūtra, plus the six Vedāngas—is established in *Muṇḍaka Upaniṣad* 1.1.5.

45. As in AV 2.13.2 or 2.28.1–2, noting also RV 8.67.20 and 10.18.6 Perhaps most interesting of all is *Hiraṇyagarbha Sūtra* 1.4.2, which is an exact repetition of AV 2.13.2, with the exception that *jarāmṛtyum*, which was no longer understood as an adjective expressing a desirable state of being, is replaced by *śatāyuṣam*, "one whose life is a hundred (years long)."

46. Manfred Mayrhofer, *Kurgefasstes etymologisches Wörterbuch des Altindischen* (Heidelberg: Carl Winter, 1956), 1:421.

47. Bartholomae, *Grundriss der iranische Philologie*, 1.1.82, collected several other Gathic instances of -t > -θ at the end of a syllable and followed by a vowel, but the reasons for this shift are still inadequately understood. The -d- in the Pahlavi form of the prophet's name, however—*zrdrwšt*—assures us of an original -t- in *Zaraθuštra*.

48. H. W. Bailey, "Indo-Iranian Studies," *Transactions of the Philological Society* (1953): 40–42. Essentially, I see two important arguments against this attempt to derive the name from a verb *zar-* "to move." First, the Old Iranian evidence for such a verb is very slim, and none of the forms cited require an underlying sense of movement, as for instance, *zrvān-* "time," which might equally well be derived from *zar-* "to age," or a number of other verbal roots. Second, the interpretation of *zaraθ-uštra* as "he who drives camels" is quite inappropriate for a priest, while "he whose camels are old" might well befit a priest who confesses himself to be impoverished, as in *Yasna* 44.18 and 46.2.

49. As proposed by Christian Bartholomae, *Altiranisches Wörterbuch* (Berlin: Walter de Gruyter, 1904), p. 1676. This remains the most widely accepted explanation.

SIX

MITHRA(S) AS SUN AND SAVIOR

If there is any specific reason for the revival of interest in Mithraic studies I believe it must be sought in the issue of change and continuity through history. There is virtually no deity of the ancient world whose worship we can follow over a greater span of time and space: from India and central Asia to North Africa and the British Isles, from the Proto-Indo-Iranian period (ca. 2000 B.C.) or even Proto-Indo-European (Third, Fourth, or Fifth Millennium B.C.)[1] to the fall of the Roman Empire and even beyond. Throughout this tremendous spatio-temporal expanse, certain features of the god remain much the same, while others experience radical transformation and still others seem to disappear or to appear almost from nowhere. Sorting out the ways in which the figure of Mithra(s) is adapted to different locales and periods in history thus ought to form the bulk of Mithraic studies, in my opinion, and from this process we may learn much about the relative tenacity and flexibility of the religious imagination in general.

Traditionally, this concern has been formulated in terms of the relative contributions of Iran and the Greco-Roman world to the ideology and iconography of the Mithraic mysteries. All sides of the question have been argued at one time or another, from the insistence of Franz Cumont and his followers on the Zoroastrian background for virtually all the mysteries' contents,[2] to the view of Stig Wikander and others that Iran contributed little more than the god's name.[3] Recently, however, certain studies have shown an awareness that a more complex synthesis took place in the formation of the Mithraic mysteries, whereby Iranian, not necessarily Zoroastrian, materials were reinterpreted, reformulated, and thoroughly adapted to fit the requirements of worshipers in Asia Minor, Rome, and other parts of the Roman Empire.

One important case in point is the tauroctony scene which formed the focal point of innumerable Mithraea, as interpreted by John Hinnells.[4] Rejecting, on the one hand, Cumont's view that the scene of Mithras as bull-slayer reflects a transformation of a Zoroastrian myth in which Mithra kills the bull and acts as creator (in place of Ahriman, who performs this deed in the celebrated Chapter 4 of the Greater Bundahišn)[5] and, on the other hand, that of those who would deny any Iranian content,[6] Hinnells traces the scene to Iranian sacrificial ideology, to which important astrological and soteriological materials have been added. Summing up, he writes: "The thesis of this paper is that the Roman Mithraic beliefs depict the divine sacrifice which gives life to men, a concept which ultimately derived from Iran but which was expressed in terms meaningful to people living in the Greco-Roman world."[7] One could pursue Hinnells's analysis even farther, however, for the ideology of the primordial sacrifice of a bull does not originate in Iran but with the Proto-Indo-Europeans, as I have shown elsewhere.[8] This Indo-European construct was then adapted and reinterpreted by the Iranians along several different lines,[9] one of which was then further adapted and reinterpreted within the Mithraic mysteries.

The example of Mithras Tauroctonos is instructive, for it is one of the places within the mysteries where the Iranian component is most readily visible. Two other points of Mithraic doctrine are perhaps equally worthy of our attention for the opposite reason, i.e., they seem most thoroughly rooted in the West: the association of Mithras with the sun[10] and his role as savior or conductor of the soul.[11] It is my intention in this chapter to show first, that these two ideas are not separate, but intimately related to one another, and second, that the origin of the relation between these two ideas lies in Iran, although it is much more richly elaborated in Asia Minor and the West.

In order to appreciate the role of Mithras as sun in assisting the liberation of the *post mortem* soul from the bonds of this world, it is helpful to begin with the most important Western texts touching on Mithraic soteriology. Origen, for instance, relates (*Contra Celsum*, 22) that within the Mithraic mysteries, the path of the soul was seen as an ascent through the planetary spheres, each of which is represented by a rung of a ladder made of a different metal, the first, of lead, representing Saturn; the second, of tin, Venus; and so forth. The seventh and highest rung is made of gold, and represents the sun. Salvation is thus seen as an exit through the solar gate into the boundless heavens.[12]

Again, Porphyry, having argued that souls ascend to the heavens through the celestial winter solstice and descend to earth again through the summer solstice, states that Mithras is assigned a place on the equinoctial circle (*De Antro Nympharum*, 24). The god thus exists with the sun at the ends of the universe, assisting human souls in their transit from one world to the other.

Two passages in the writings of the emperor Julian are also worthy of note. The first is the concluding advice he maintains was given to him by Hermes, related at the end of *The Caesars*, 336 C:

> "And to you," Hermes said to me, "I have granted the discovery of father Mithras. Keep his commands, [thus] preparing a steadfast haven and anchorage for yourself in life, and with good hope establishing that god as your guide when it is necessary to depart from this world."

Here Mithras is clearly presented as psychopomp and savior. In Julian's fifth *Oration*, 172 D, this is again the case, and there Mithras is referred to as "the seven-rayed god" (*heptaktina theon*), a reference to his solar nature.[13] The context of this passage is, in fact, a longer discussion of the sun's saving powers. Having established that the sun may lead souls upward, just as it leads matter upward through the process of evaporation, Julian goes on to say:

> And if I should touch on the ineffable Mysteries which the Chaldaean frenziedly celebrated concerning the seven-rayed god, leading souls upward through that [deity], I would be telling things that are not to be known, indeed things that are most not-to-be-known for the rabble, [but] which are [already] well-known to the blessed performers of divine works. Therefore, I will keep silence about these things for now.

Let me be quick to emphasize that I do not see these texts as all presenting the same basic idea, nor are they simply variants on a common theme. Each is idiosyncratic in a different way, and each presents its own difficulties for interpretation. All that I want to point out is that Origen, Porphyry, and Julian each in his own way fused Mithras's association with the sun and his role as savior or psychopomp. Rather than being two separate aspects of the god, according to these sources they are intimately connected.[14] Moreover, as I hope to show, that connection is considerably older than these sources.

In order to appreciate this, it is necessary to step back and consider an important theme in Indo-European mythology that is on first glance quite unrelated to our present concern: the theme of the bonds of death.[15] The Proto-Indo-Europeans saw death as a goddess, at the same time beautiful and hideous, fatally attractive in the literal sense of the expression.[16] Her name, as reconstructed by Hermann Güntert, was *Kolyo, "the coverer," a name which is preserved in the name of the old Norse Goddess *Hel* (English *Hell*), that of the Greek *Kalypso,* and that of the Indian God *Śarva* (= Avestan *Saurva*).[17] Her domain is underground, and she physically conveys her victims thence by fixing a snare or noose on their bodies and dragging them down. Her bonds regularly fall upon the neck or the foot of the victim, the same places where domestic animals are fettered. The deceased are thus led away like animals by Death, in whose bonds they may struggle, but which they cannot escape, caught in her snares and dragged under. The Indian Thugs' strangulation of their victims derives from this mythic theme,[18] as does execution by hanging among Germanic peoples,[19] and the following texts will attest the survival of the ideology in Greek, Roman, Norse, Indian, and Iranian mythology.

> And then they heard much uproar around the cattle
> While they were sitting idly in front of the speaking-place. At
>   once mounting
> Behind their high-stepping horses, they went in pursuit and
>   straightaway were off.
> And standing, they did battle beside the banks of the river,
> And cast at one another with bronze-tipped spears.

And Strife and Confusion joined the battle there, and baneful
    Death [*Kēr*] was there;
Holding one live man who was freshly wounded, another still
    unwounded,
She dragged off another, a dead man, down from the battle by
    his feet.
And the garment across her shoulders was red with the blood
    of men.

> *Iliad* 18.530–38 (a scene from the Shield of Akhilles)

[You who are] richer than the unrifled
Treasuries of the Arabs, and the wealth of India—
    You may fill all the Tyrrhenian
And the Apulian sea with the foundations [for your villa],
    [But] if grim Necessity drives
Her adamantine nails in the highest heavens,
    You'll not free your soul from fear,
Nor your head from the snares of Death [*mortis laqueis*].

> Horace, *Ode* 3.24, lines 1–8

The ropes of Hel
Came swiftly;
They swung at my sides.
I wanted to break them,
But they were tough.
Light it is to fare when free!

> *Sólarljóð* 37

That cord which the goddess Nirṛti ["Dissolution, Death"]
    bound to your neck, which was unloosenable,
That I remove from you, for [your] long life, energy, [and]
    strength. Being born [again], eat the food which does not
    cause inconvenience [*adomadam*—?].
Praise to you, Nirṛti, you whose splendor is scorching. Untie the
    fetters made of iron!
Truly, Yama gave you back to me.
    Praise to that Yama; [praise to] Death!
You [i.e. the sacrificial patron] were bound here to a pillar made
    of iron, harnessed by deaths which were thousandfold.
United with Yama and the fathers, raise this [man] to the highest
    heaven!

> *Atharva Veda* 6.63.1–3

Now truly, that deed which is most important for a man to do
for himself is that which no one else will do for him, and which
no one else is able to do for him, to wit, preventing the cord of
Astwihād ["the Binder of the Body"] from coming around the

soul, by protecting from sin and not abandoning works of virtue. Thus, when Astwihād bears the body to another place at death and he kills it, he may not pass the fetter around the soul whereby he would drag the soul to hell and thus impede the Renovation of the world. He may torture the body, causing it most extraordinary pain and sorrow, and he may kill it; but the soul, he will free. It strides up to immortality itself, along with the Righteous, where it rests and prays in the highest peace and happiness. *Dēnkart* 3.358 (Dresden edition, p. 263, lines 1–9)

While each of the individual Indo-European civilizations developed this theme differently to a certain extent, as is evidenced by the variances in the above texts, still they resemble one another sufficiently to permit the conclusion they all derived from a single Proto-Indo-European idea. One of the more important differences, however, arises with regard to the theme of salvation from Death's bonds. For while the Indian and Iranian texts cited above are primarily concerned with being freed from those bonds, the European sources make no mention of this possibility, focusing only on the harshness and ineluctability of the bonds.[20] In my research I have only come across one European text which speaks of the possibility of salvation from Death's bonds, and while it may preserve authentic Indo-European ideas, it seems more likely that it incorporated Christian themes at this point, given the mention of St. Peter, Rome, and the presence of loan-words from the Christian liturgy such as *postoli,* "apostle," and *djǫfull,* "devil."

> Hrafn the Red was chased into a river. There, he seemed to see the torments of Hell below, and it seemed to him that devils would drag him down and Hrafn said, "Thy hound has run to Rome twice [referring to his earlier pilgrimages], O Apostle Peter, and would run a third time, if you permit it." Then the devils let him loose, and he came across the river.[21] *Njal's Saga,* chap. 157

Within the general Indo-European theme of Death's bonds, one may thus perceive a specifically Indo-Iranian concern for learning the means of salvation from those bonds, something perfectly consistent with the strong soteriological thrust of Indo-Iranian religions. At this point, however, there is still further divergence, for the means that are described to free one's self from the snares of Nirṛti,[22] Mṛtyu (Death personified),[23] or Yama[24] as described in Indian texts differ from those described for extricating one's self from the bonds of Astō.vīδatu ("the binder of the body")[25] or Vīzarəša ("he who drags away")[26] in the Iranian sources.

For the most part, in India it is the sacrificial priest who frees his patron, as in the passage from the *Atharva Veda* quoted above. It is his knowledge and his proper performance of the sacrifice that unbinds the knots and allows him to triumphantly claim "The cord which the goddess Nirṛti bound to your neck, which was unloosenable, that I remove from you," adding elsewhere that this victory is won by means of the priest's "divine speech" (*daivyā vacā*).[27] Such claims are plentiful, particularly in the *Atharva Veda*,[28] and are amplified in the later ritual texts, which detail the ritual gestures whereby the bonds of Nirṛti are overcome. Thus, for instance:

> He places [the offerings] upon a sling. Truly, a snare is con-
> nected to Nirṛti. Thus, before one's eyes the [the sacrificer] frees
> this [man] from the snares of Nirṛti. (*Taittirīya Saṃhitā* 5.2.4.3)

> Now he casts down the stool, sling, golden snare, and the two
> pads on the far side. Truly, a snare is connected to Nirṛti. Thus, he
> is freed from Nirṛti's snare, [as the priest says:] "That snare which
> the goddess Nirṛti bound on your neck, which is unloosenable"—
> truly it is unloosenable for him who knows not thus—"that I
> remove from you, as [from one in] the midst of a long life."
> (*Śatapatha Brāhmaṇa* 7.2.1.15)

In Iran, however, rather than ritual action being the means for escaping the binder, it is usually ethical action that is expected to produce this result. *Dēnkart* 3.358, cited above, stresses that one must free oneself from Astwihād's cord (< Avestan *Astō.vīδātu-*) "by protecting from sin and not abandoning works of virtue." It further emphasizes that one must do this for one's self, because no one else—a priest, for example—can do it for one. The Pahlavi translation of *Vīdēvdāt* 19.29 expresses the same general point of view and goes on to state that the effect of ethical actions in life is to produce an automatic escape from death's bonds: the demon's noose will of its own slip away from the neck of a righteous man. The text reads as follows:

> Wizarš [Avestan *Vīzarəša-*] is the demon named, O Spitāma
> Zarathustra, who carries away the bound soul of the followers of
> the Lie, of demon-worshippers, of men whose lives are quick like
> gazelles. This noose falls around the neck of every person when
> he dies; when it is a righteous person, it falls from his throat;
> when it is a person who is a follower of the Lie, they drag him to
> hell with that same noose.

This ethical view is the mainstream opinion in Iran on the topic of salvation from death's bonds. It is perfectly in keeping with the Zoroastrian view of life as a constant struggle between the forces of good and evil, acted out at the human level between the righteous (*ašavan-*) and the followers of the Lie (*dragvant-*). Good words, good thoughts, and good deeds are required of the righteous man, through which he aids in the purification or renovation of the cosmos and wins the salvation of his own soul.

There is, however, another opinion current in Iran, attested in some of the oldest texts of the Younger Avesta. Thus, in *Yašt* 10.93, the poet invokes the assistance of Mithra to overcome "the Binder," Vīδātu, whose name is a shortened form of Astō.vīδātu.[29]

> In both existences,
> Protect us in both existences,
> O Mithra, Lord of Wide Pastures;
> This existence which is bodily,
> And that which is spiritual
>   [i.e., before and after death][30]
> [Protect us] from Death, a follower of the Lie,
> From Furor, a follower of the Lie,
> From the hordes, followers of the Lie,
> Who would hoist up the bloody banner of Furor,
> From the assaults of Furor
> Which malignant Furor sets in motion
> Together with the Binder [Vīδātu], created by the daēvas.

The prayer is a warrior's prayer, in which he turns to Mithra, protector of the righteous and punisher of those who violate treaties, contracts, friendship, and other ties that ought to bind men together. He seeks the god's assistance against the enemy hordes (*haēna*—a daēvic term)[31] who are characterized by their murderous furor (*aēšma-*).[32] But the things he fears most are those which he lists first and last: death (*mahrka*—another daēvic term)[33] and the Binder (Vīδātu-), and to save him from these he calls on the god Mithra.

The importance of this passage can hardly be overestimated. Here we confront a figure that is very familiar in Western Mithraism, but very unfamiliar in Iran: Mithra(s) as savior. Yet the text is the *Mihr Yašt,* the oldest and best source for the worship of Mithra in Iran.

Another text is of almost equal importance, although the same claims cannot be made for its antiquity. This is *Vīdēvdāt* 19.28–29, a portion of one of the classic discussions of the fate of the soul (Vd. 19.27–33). Here, immediately after Zarathustra has asked the Wise Lord where it is that a righteous man will reap the rewards he has earned by his good deeds, the Creator responds:

> Then spoke Ahura Mazdā: "After a man has deceased, after a man has come to an end, after the demons, followers of the Lie, evil in thought, split him open completely, at dawn on the third night [after death], the radiant goddess [Dawn] lights up and shines, and Mithra, whose weapons are good, shining like the sun, rises up and ascends the mountains which possess the bliss of Aša.
>
> Vīzarəša ["He who drags away"] is the demon named, O Spitāma Zarathustra, who leads the bound soul of the mortals who are followers of the Lie, worshippers of the demons, to a life of . ? [The soul] goes along the paths created by time, which are for the followers of the Lie and for the Righteous, to the Cinvat

Bridge, created by Mazdā, [where] the consciousness and the soul request a portion of the possessions which were given [them] in bodily life.[34] (Verses 30–33 go on to describe the ascent of the soul to the heavenly throne.)

The content of this passage is striking, and of the greatest import for the question at hand. Here it is stated that on the third day after death, the soul of the righteous man is rescued from Vīzarəša and the other demons who assault his body, whereafter the soul's ascent into the heavenly realms becomes possible. Furthermore, it is stated that this victory, this salvation from death's bonds, depends on the appearance of Mithra, who rises with (or perhaps even *as*) the sun on that third morning. In this Avestan text, we encounter a picture of Mithra identified with the sun and acting as savior of the soul, precisely that which we noted in Origen's, Porphyry's, and Julian's accounts of the western Mithraic mysteries.

If the content of the passage is striking, some of the grammatical details are of no less interest, for they furnish a clue as to who the author may have been, and how he arrived at this highly original conception. Thus, the shoddy grammar has been taken as a sign of the text's late redaction by someone with an imperfect knowledge of Avestan.[35] Given that it is written in prose,[36] and is part of the heavily legalistic *Vīdēvdāt*, it is thus a logical conclusion that the author of Vd. 19.28–29 was a member of the west Iranian priesthood, i.e., a Magus.[37]

Of the grammatical lapses, perhaps the most interesting is the use of the accusative case for the subject of the last clause in verse 28 (*miθram*). While this is occasionally found in the Younger Avesta, it is almost never so when the verb precedes the subject, as is true here.[38] Given this highly anomalous occurrence, one must ask what might possibly motivate it, and to date no satisfactory answers have been forthcoming.[39] The problem may be solved, however, when we note that the noun *miθra-* occurs as the subject of the same verb (*āsnaoiti*) in another passage, *Yašt* 10.12–13, and there it properly is in the accusative case. The topic of that passage is Mithra's association with the rising sun:

> We sacrifice to Mithra [*mithrəm . . . yazamaide*] protector of
> wide pastures,
>
> . . . .
> Who first of the spiritial deities
> Rises across Mount Hara [*yō . . . harąm āsnaoiti*]
> Before the immortal
> Sun, whose horses are swift;
> Who first grasps
> The beautiful, gold-adorned heights
> And then looks over all
> The dwelling place of the Aryas, he who is most powerful.

This conjunction of *miθrəm* as subject with *ās(ə)naoiti* as verb in both texts clearly indicates that the author of Vd. 19.28 had Yt. 10.13 in mind as he wrote. In addition, it seems to me that he also drew upon two other Avestan passages: *Hadoxt Nask* 2.7, in which the ascent of the soul on the third morning after death is described,[40] and *Yašt* 10.93, in which Mithra is implored to save one from the bonds of death. Linguistically inept perhaps, but theologically astute and creative, the author has woven together these three strands, placing Mithra at the center of the drama and homologizing his role in assisting the ascent of the soul—one is reminded of Kuiper's analysis of him as the progressive, liberating force of the otherworld[41]—with his role in assisting the ascent of the sun.

The picture of Mithra as sun *and* savior as found in the mysteries thus has its origin in this passage from the *Vīdēvdāt,* most likely written by a Median Magus some time during the Hellenistic era. It is not enough just to indicate a point of origin in Iran, however, and baldly affirm that this idea made its way into the West. One must also be prepared to trace the path of transmission. This, fortunately, we are able to do by means of two intermediate testimonies, in which Mithra(s) once again appears as sun and savior. The first of these comes from the writings of the Armenian historian, Elišē Vardapet:

> The chief-executioner said: "I swear by the god Mihr, you speak more stubbornly than your teachers. It is clear that you are even more criminal. So it is not right for you to escape death unless you worship the sun and perform what our religion demands."[42]

Here, swearing by the god Mithra and adoring the sun seem to be synonymous—one recalls the testimony of Strabo 15.3.13 that the Persians call the sun (Greek *Hēlios*) Mithra[43]—and it is this action which sustains one after death. But the *locus classicus* for the identification of Mithra with the Greek god of the sun is the inscription of Antiochus I of Commagene at Nimrud Dagh.[44] The crucial position of Commagene, and also Pontus, between the Persian and Roman empires inevitably made them a meeting ground for religious forms, and their importance in the transmission of Mithraic worship to the west has been emphasized by both Geo Widengren and Carsten Colpe.[45]

On the strength of several pieces of evidence, it has seemed clear to most scholars that Antiochus paid special reverence to Mithra above the other gods he mentions.[46] Thus, Mithra alone has a special priest attached to him;[47] the king took the by-name *dikaios,* "righteous, just," a title also carried by Mithra;[48] he celebrated his own birthday on the sixteenth day of the month, the day sacred to Mithra;[49] a dexiosis scene is inscribed at Arsameia with Antiochus standing at the right hand of Mithra, who wears the national costume of the royal family of Commagene—something unprecedented in other Commagenian dexiosis scenes—as token of his role as royal and national patron.[50] But in all this, it is not just Mithra who appears, but rather a syncretistic association of four deities, whose names appear in differing order on various Commagenian inscriptions, that of the Nimrud Dagh text being: Apollo-Mithras-Helios-Hermes.[51]

The reason for Mithra's association with Apollo and Helios is immediately clear: all are solar deities, although it must be continually emphasized that such is *not* Mithra's primary role in the Avestan tradition.[52] The reason for Hermes's inclusion is a bit less obvious, however, although from the preceding line of argument, it should pose no great mystery. Hermes, like Mithra, is a psychopomp, a conductor of souls, as was first suggested by D. Dittenberger in 1903.[53]

At this point, another aspect of the inscription at Nimrud Dagh stands out more boldly, and the religion of Antiochus becomes more clear. For whatever its legal, political, ritualistic, and cultic implications, the inscription also has a strong soteriological thrust. It is set at Antiochus' burial place, and there he had written:

> And then I conceived to establish the foundation of this mausoleum, unravaged by the outrages of time, and in closest proximity to the heavenly throne [it is set at the highest point in Commagene], in which the outward form of my body, having existed to an enviable old age, will sleep in boundless eternity, and my soul, beloved of the gods, will be led to the heavenly throne of Zeus Oromasdes. (lines 36–44)

Even the hyperskeptical Heinrich Dörrie has had to acknowledge the Iranian origins of this idea of the soul's ascent to the heavenly throne,[54] and the specific language of the passage leads to questions that reinforce this conclusion. Thus, Antiochus states that his soul (*psykhē*) will be led (*pro-pempō-*) to the heavens, but he does not say by whom. Who is the psychopomp (<*psykhē* + *pempō-*) for his soul? To any Greek-speaker of the first century B.C., the answer could only be Hermes, who appears here as Apollo-Mithras-Helios-Hermes. It is thus the Commagenian Mithras, Antiochus' special patron, identified as sun and savior, who will lead the king's soul to its reward. And it is this same picture of Mithra(s) as sun and savior that we have traced from Iran to Asia Minor to the Mithraic mysteries of the Roman Empire.

The chain is a long one. Beginning with an Indo-European theme, the bonds of death, there follows an Indo-Iranian concern: how can one escape those bonds. Within Iran, there develop different answers to this problem. In addition to the mainstream Zoroastrian opinion that ethical actions are sufficient to win the soul's release, there is also the view that the aid of Mithra is needed, an opinion voiced in a warrior's prayer that dates at least to the fifth century B.C.[55] Next, in a late Avestan text, most probably authored by one of the Magi, Mithra's role as savior is homologized to his association with the rising sun. It is this concept which finds its way to Armenia and Commagene, most probably carried there by wandering Magi.[56] Finally, the same idea turns up in the Western mysteries, where it forms the core of Mithraic soteriology, and it must here be noted that according to Plutarch, *Pompey* 24, Romans first encountered the Mithraic mysteries with Pompey's conquest of the Cilician Pirates (67 B.C.), who practiced these rites, and many of whom originally came from Commagene and Pontus.[57]

At every step of the way there is a change, and at every step there is continuity, although there are precious few similarities between the starting point and the end. It is quite striking, however, when a fairly late text (fourth century A.D.) contains strong echoes of the ancient Proto-Indo-European theme with which the chain of development began. The text describes initiation into the Mithraic mysteries, to which the author is thoroughly hostile. Certain details are very difficult to explain, notably the use of chicken intestines. But given the standard Indo-European imagery of the journey to the otherworld as a journey across a body of water,[58] the relation of this description to the theme of the bonds of death and the idea of Mithras as savior becomes abundantly clear:

> Others, their hands bound with the intestines of a chicken, are thrown across pits filled with water. [Then] someone approaches with a sword and breaks into the intestines, wherefore he calls himself liberator. (Pseudo-Augustine, *Quaestiones veteris et novi testamenti, 114*)

Change within continuity, continuity within change: thus it always seems to be in the development of Mithra(s), and thus, I suspect, it always is with any important religious idea.

Discussion

CRISTIANO GROTTANELLI (University of Rome): The theme of the Sun as a psychopomp is also present, of course, in religions that are not Indo-European (e.g. Shapash, the sun goddess, at Ugarit and her relationship with the Rephaim. Secondly, Professor Lincoln said that he knows of only one European case of the bonds of death being broken. There is another such case. In the Celtic tradition about Cuchulainn, in the *Tain Bó Cúailnge* or somewhere else, at a certain point, just as happens with Hrafn the Red, Cuchulainn is fighting in a river, at a ford, and his feminine enemy, the Morrigan, comes to make things difficult for him. She takes on the form of a water snake, I think, or an eel, and binds his legs. And what is interesting is that he is saved in the end. So this is another European example, and maybe it is an element in favor of the idea that the European example quoted by Professor Lincoln is not of Christian origin but is probably of more ancient, let us say "pagan," tradition.

LINCOLN: Thank you, Professor Grottanelli, the example you have provided me is extremely interesting and I will certainly look into it.

As regards the question of non-Indo-European solar deities who are also psychopomps, of course there are many. To say that an idea is Indo-European is never to say it is exclusively Indo-European. To my knowledge they hold no copyrights on any religious idea, and that such an idea could occur in other civilizations is of course to be expected, but your point is well taken.

H. S. VERSNEL (University of Leiden): May I show how much I enjoyed your exciting contribution by making one or two remarks? First a minor point. You were a little surprised about the prominent position of Hermes in Commagene. In order to explain this I would not refer to his function of psychopomp, at least not in the traditional meaning of that word, but rather to the fact that in this period Hermes has become an *Angelos,* a mediator between the Gods and the human world, and as Angelos he has become great in Hermetic circles, but also elsewhere. I am convinced this might explain his prominence in the Commagene pantheon too.

I have, however, a more fundamental comment to make. During your lecture you have been touching upon the eternal problems concerning polygenesis and diffusion on the one hand, and evolution on the other, and as to your theory of Mithra(s) as Sun and Savior you have definitely chosen an explanation by diffusion. Yet you run the risk of tracing back the theme of the escape from death as a liberation from chains or fetters perhaps too easily to a general and common Indo-European origin. You even quote Horace in this context, whereas particularly in this instance it is practically certain that the hammer and nails of *Anankè (Necessitas)* are not of Indo-European origin but have come from the Near East, probably via Etruria. So, as far as it is at all permitted to reason along evolutionary lines it is necessary to realize that various civilizations, although of Indo-European origin, have undergone radical influences from other cultures, as in fact you suppose yourself to have taken place in the case of the saving actions of Mithra, where you explain the imagery of the freeing from fetters as a borrowing from Iranian material in the West. In this connection you speak of a "chain."

I would certainly not exclude the possibility, but I do think another possibility should be considered at least as seriously. May I quote from one of the Isis hymns? In the Isis hymn v. 97 the goddess says *desmon egō katelusa,* and in 144–45 *desmoon d'aekousan anagkan anluō.* Greater specialists than I can affirm that this is a liberation from the bonds of death. It is very improbable that this is either a relic of Indo-European thought or a derivation from Iranian ideals. It is just Egyptian or Greek, where, in both civilizations, examples abound where the liberation from death is metaphorically expressed in the way described. So I would opt for the possibility that this symbolism is a general imagery used by all sorts of cultures when speaking of the victory over death, illness, and distress, and I would like to have your opinion on this suggestion.

LINCOLN: Thank you. Let me address first the citation from Horace, and the question of the reconstruction of the Indo-European theme of the bonds of death. Certainly I would agree that, whenever you have similarities, multiple explanations are possible. Similar phenomena can be connected historically, by culture-contact, dissemination, and so forth, or they can be totally independent. For me, what is conclusive is when the details are sufficiently similar and sufficiently tight to posit common origin. By positing the notion of death's bonds as an Indo-European idea, I do not mean to say that the idea doesn't occur elsewhere; certainly it does. Scheftelowitz cites numerous examples from Melanesia, for instance, where fishing nets figure as death's bonds, and these are certainly not Indo-European in origin. For me the conclusive point is that, consistently within the Indo-European texts, the bonds fall upon the neck, as they do in Horace, or upon the foot, as in *Rg Veda* 10.97.16, that is, on those places where animals are bound. The Indo-Europeans, being a pastoral society, dependent on the herding of livestock, were very familiar with these methods, and it seems to me the imagery here is that of leading a tamed beast away, perhaps to slaughter. That for me is conclusive for the Horatian citation. Certainly you were right that the nails come from elsewhere; I do not mean to claim that Horace did nothing but transmit Indo-European traditions. He is a poet and a creative genius, who draws on many sources, but in that line, "you will not free your head from death's snares," it seems to me this is Indo-European in origin, and that is why I would argue for common origin and genetic connection.

Second is your citation from the Isis text, and again I am sure there are many texts from many cultures where salvation is described in terms of being freed from the bondage of death or fate or necessity. What for me is conclusive is this concatenation of details: sun, ascension, liberation from bonds; Isis is not a solar deity, she does not carry the name "Mithras," which is an Iranian name, and it seems to me that when you have Mithras as sun, Mithras as savior, Mithras as aiding in the ascent of the soul, and Mithras as liberating from bonds, that is too much to assume to be invented independently by western Mithraicists and Iranians. That is a very complex cluster of ideas. I would consider it highly unlikely that such a cluster evolved independently in Rome, Commagene, Armenia, and Iran, and in all places came to be associated with the very same deity sheerly by chance.

JUHA PENTIKÄINEN (University of Helsinki): My comments also deal with the existence of the idea of God as sun and savior. Professor Lincoln writes that the Proto-Indo-Europeans saw death as a goddess, at the same time beautiful and heartless, attractive and so on. On the basis of my experience, among most of the so-called "primitive" religions and cultures in the North, e.g., Finno-Ugrians and other Arctic peoples, the idea seems to be the very truth there, too. We are dealing with one of the universals of the religions of mankind. Because these ideas exist in many regions and areas, it is not so very clear what is primary and what is secondary. As far as the Finno-Ugrians cultures are concerned, we could possibly assume that we have the same idea because of certain historical contacts in the past; i.e., someone has taken something from another culture. I, however, think that the answer is not so clear. This idea, having the combination of God as sun and savior as its depth structure, seems to be almost as universal as the fact of death and dying. From that point of view we could, of course, in historical analysis come to certain historical chains and links, but these links could be confused as well on the basis of the materials which do not belong to the culture which we are now studying. So, to conclude, we could either deal with the topic as a historical matter, as you have done so well, but also as a universal problem, and then in more structural and phenomenological ways.

LINCOLN: I tend to agree, although I am skeptical when talk turns to "universals." When you find the same sorts of ideas in cultures that are not related in linguistic and historical ways, I would certainly vote for independent invention and for phenomenological study and I would not relate Indo-European and Finno-Ugric mythic constructions in most instances. It seems to me, however, when you are dealing with the Indo-Europeans alone, there is such an overwhelming mass of evidence that we are entitled to do so when it comes to myth, ritual, cosmology, and so forth. This method seems to me well established in the work of many scholars over the last century.

Notes

1. The issue of whether or not an Indo-Iranian *Mitra- can be seen as derived from an Indo-European *Meitro- depends on whether or not convincing correspondences can be adduced from European sources. To date, the leading candidate is Russian *mir*, "peace, commune," as argued by V. N. Toporov, "Parallels to Ancient Indo-Iranian Social and Mythological Concepts," in *Pratidānam: Indian, Iranian, and Indo-European Studies Presented to F. B. J. Kuiper* (The Hague: Mouton, 1968), pp. 108–13. For my part, I do not find the impersonal concept of "peace" sufficient to permit reconstruction of a personified deity, but would agree that it most probably indicates the existence of a P-I-E abstract, most probably neuter, expressing the idea "that which binds together." The god, however, who incarnates this abstract idea, I take to be an Indo-Iranian innovation, being unconvinced by the typological comparisons adduced by Georges Dumézil, *Mitra-Varuna*, 4th ed. (Paris: Gallimard, 1948), or Jaan Puhvel, "Mitra as an Indo-European Divinity," in *Études Mithriaques* (Leiden: E. J. Brill, 1978), pp. 339–40.

2. The classic source is, of course, Franz Cumont, *Textes et monuments figurés relatifs aux mystères de Mitha*, 2 vols. (Brussels: H. Lamartin, 1896–99). Cumont has been followed, most notably, by M. J. Vermaseren in his numerous publications.

3. Stig Wikander, *Études sur les mystères de Mithras* (Lund: Årsbok, 1951). More recently, see such works as R. L. Gordon, "Franz Cumont and the Doctrines of Mithraism," in John R. Hinnells, ed. *Mithraic Studies* (Manchester: Manchester University Press, 1975), pp. 215–48.

4. John R. Hinnells, "Reflections on the Bull-Slaying Scene," in *Mithraic Studies*, pp. 290–312.

5. Cumont, *Textes et Monuments*, 1:186f. The most detailed and influential attempt to demonstrate an Indo-Iranian tradition of Mithras as bull-slayer is that of Herman Lommel, "Mithra und das Stieropfer," *Paideuma* 3 (1949): 207–18.

6. Wikander, *Études sur les Mystères de Mithras*, p. 46.

7. Hinnells, p. 309.

8. Bruce Lincoln, "The Indo-European Myth of Creation," *History of Religions* 15 (1975): 121–45.

9. In the Proto-Indo-European version, the primordial ox is slain by *Manu ("Man"), the first man and the first priest. With the rejection of cattle sacrifice by Zarathustra, however, *Manu disappears in Iran. His role in the myth is then taken, according to the mainstream Zoroastrian tradition, by the arch-demon Ahriman, as in Greater Bundahišn 4, reflecting the opinion that such a sacrifice, however beneficial it may be, is still a demonic act. The version which appears in the Mithraic mysteries seems to indicate another variant of the tradition that is unattested in the native Iranian sources which have come down to us, whereby the god Mithra takes the place formerly occupied by *Manu.

10. As attested by the countless inscriptions to *deo Soli invicto Mithrae* and similar formulae, for which see the listing in M. J. Vermaseren, *Corpus Inscriptionem et Monumentorum Religionis Mithriacae*, 2 vols. (The Hague: Martinus Nijhoff, 1956–60), 1:347f., 349f., and 2:422f., 425. The most important discussions to date of the connection between Mithra(s) and the sun are: I. Scheftelowitz, "Die Mithra-Religion der Indoskythen und ihre Beziehung zum Saura- and Mithras-Kult," *Acta Orientalia* II (1933): 293–333; Herman Lommel, "Die Sonne das Schlechteste?" *Oriens* 15 (1962): 360–73; and Ilya Gershevitch, "Die Sonne das Beste," in *Mithraic Studies*, pp. 68–90. Briefly, Scheftelowitz argues for the Indo-Scythian origin for this connection, Lommel for the Indo-Iranian, and Gershevitch for the Manichaean.

11. As attested in the sources discussed below (Origen, Porphyry, Julian), and certain inscriptions such as Vermaseren, *Corpus Inscriptionum et Monumentorum*, numbers 72, 171, 333, 348, 658, and the problematic 463. An interesting discussion of Mithra's role as savior in Iran and the West is Geo Widengren, "Salvation in Iranian Religion," in Eric Sharpe and John Hinnells, eds., *Man and His Salvation: Studies in Memory of S. G. F. Brandon* (Manchester: Manchester University Press, 1973), pp. 315–26.

12. Classically, this text has been correlated with the seven grades of initiation in the Mithraic mysteries, as reported by St. Jerome, *Epistle* 107, and has also been used to show Babylonian influence on the mysteries, the seven-storied universe here being seen as the Babylonian system which replaced an Iranian three-storied universe (for this older view, see D. W. Bousset, "Die Himmelsreise der Seele," *Archiv für Religionswissenchaft* 4 (1901): 165–69, 234–49). More recently, however, it is the influences of western Gnosticism on Celsus that have been stressed, as reported by Origen, who in turn is something less than an impartial reporter. See Carsten Colpe, "Die Mithramysterien und die Kirchenväter," in W. den Boer et al., eds., *Romanitas et Christianitas: Studia J. H. Waszink* (Amsterdam: North Holland, 1973), p. 34f.; and Ugo Bianchi, "Mithraism and Gnosticism," in *Mithraic Studies*, p. 463f.

13. As in Proclus, *Ad Timaeus* 33.21 (ed. Festugière).

14. Along these lines, I am led to wonder what is the true significance of the title Sol Invictus. It is possible that Invictus ought to be understood as a soteriological title—not just "undefeated," but also "undefeatable," with specific reference to the struggle for the *post mortem* soul.

15. Previous treatments of this theme are: Isidor Scheftelowitz, *Das Schlingen- und Netzmotiv im Glauben und Brauch der Völker* (Giessen: Alfred Töpelmann, 1912), pp. 5–10; Hermann Güntert, *Der arische Weltkönig und Heiland* (Halle: Max Niemayer, 1923), p. 125f.; Richard Broxton Onians, *The Origins of European Thought* (Cambridge: Cambridge University Press, 1951), pp. 310–31; and, most important, Mircea Eliade, "Le 'dieu lieur' et le symbolisme des noeuds," *Revue de l'histoire des religions* 134 (1948): 15–20.

16. See especially, Hermann Güntert, *Kundry* (Heidelberg: Carl Winter, 1928).

17. Hermann Güntert, *Kalypso* (Halle: Max Niemayer, 1919).

18. Güntert, *Der arische Weltkönig*, p. 125.

19. The sacral origin of hanging has been argued by Karl von Amira, *Die germanischen Todesstrafen: Untersuchungen zur Rechts und Religionsgeschichte* (Munich: Bayerische Akademie der Wissenschaften, 1922), pp. 87–105, 201–4; and Dag Strömbäck, "Hade de germanska dödsstraffen sakralt ursprung?" *Saga och sed* (1942), p. 64ff.; and disputed by Folke Ström, *On the Sacral Origin of the Germanic Death Penalties* (Stockholm: Wahström & Widstrand, 1942), pp. 115–61. My argument is rather different from that of Amira, however. Whereas he saw hanging as a sacrifice to Oðinn, I view it as a literal acting out of the mythic construct whereby Death—represented among the Germans by the goddess Hel, or one of the Disir, choosers of the slain rather like (but significantly different from) the Valkyries—carries off her victims by means of a noose or other bonds. I would thus emphasize such evidence as the Middle High German name for the noose, *helsing* (for *helle-sling?*), "Hell's sling," and the description of a hanging in *Ynglingatál* 10, lines 3–4:

Then Logi's Dis   Hove the nobleman
Up to the sky   With her golden necklace.

20. *Aogəmadaēca* 57–58, however, is an Iranian text that follows the European pattern: "Then spoke Ahura Mazda: The Binder of the Body (*Astō.vīδātu*), who is created demonically, . ? . , is inescapable: no one can save mortal men from him."

Given this correspondence, I would see the European pattern—horror at the ineluctability of death's bonds—as faithfully preserving the Proto-Indo-European ideology, while the soteriological concern is a specifically Indo-Iranian development.

21. In the course of the discussion, Cristiano Grottanelli was kind enough to point out to me another text which may indicate a soteriological thrust within European treatments of the "Bonds of Death" theme. This is the account of Cúchulainn's struggle with the Morrígain ("Nightmare queen"), one of the important Celtic goddesses of war and death. In the *Táin Bó Cúailnge* as related in the *Book of Leinster*, lines 1997–2000 (Cecille O'Rahilly, ed., *Táin Bó Cúalnge from the Book of Leinster* (Dublin: Institute for Advanced Studies, 1967), text p. 54, English trans. p. 194), it is told that while Cúchulainn was doing battle in a ford, the Morrígain attacked him in the shape of an eel, wrapping herself around his leg. He was able to free himself, however, with a mighty blow to her ribs. The episode is set within the context of three assaults the Morrígain made upon him, one in the form of an eel, one in the form of a she-wolf,

and one in the form of a heifer, all of which are unsuccessful. The story is also told in the *Táin Bó Regamma*. In many ways it is quite similar to the text from *Njal's Saga*, and one must thus hold open the possibility that they both derive from a common pre-Christian substratum, although direct derivation of one from the other is also possible.

22. The bonds of Nirṛti appear in such passages as: *Atharva Veda* 1.31.2, 6.84.3, 8.1.3, 19.44.4, and *Kauṣika Sūtra* 46.19.

23. *mṛtyupāśā-* appears in *Atharva Veda* 8.2.2 and 8.8.16; *mṛtyoḥ pāśā-* in *Atharva Veda* 3.6.5 and *Aitareya Brāhmaṇa* 3.14; *mṛtyoḥ paḍbīśa-* in *Atharva Veda* 8.1.4 and 16.8.27. Semantically, Mṛtyu is closer to the Proto-Indo-European **Kolyo*, while Nirṛti is closer in gender.

24. The earliest text mentioning the bonds of death refers to the *paḍbīśa-*, literally "foot-fetter," of Yama (*Ṛg Veda* 10.97.16), which is also mentioned in *Atharva Veda* 6.96.2 and 7.112.2. Bonds are also placed in the hands of Yama's messengers, as in *Atharva Veda* 8.8.10–11. By way of early reflexes of the Indo-European idea, one might also note the "bonds of the lie" (*druhaḥ pāśā*) of *Ṛg Veda* 7.59.8.

25. For the etymology, see Herman Lommel, "Awestische Einzelstudien: 3. Astō.vīδōtus," *Zeitschrift für Indologie und Iranstik* 2 (1923): 253f. In the Avesta, Astō.vīδātu appears in *Vīdēvdāt* 5.8f. and 4.49; and *Aogəmadaēca* 57f. In the Pahlavi literature, *Dadestān ī Dēnīg* 23.3 and 37.11; *Indian Bundahišn* 3.21; *Dēnkart* (Sanjana) 9.16.2. In Sanskrit translations, he is identified with Yama as *astigvahādayamaḥ* (Christian Bartholomae, *Altiranisches Wörterbuch* [Berlin: Walter de Gruyter, 1904], p. 214). Astō.vīδātu's name also appears in the simplified form Viδātu ("the Binder") in *Yašt* 10.93 and *Yasna* 57.25, which should be regarded as a metrical variant of the longer form.

26. Vīzarəša appears in *Vīdēvdāt* 19.29, and in such Pahlavi texts as *Indian Bundahišn* 28.18. In the opinion of Arthur Christensen, *Essai sur la démonologie iranienne* (Copenhagen: Einar Munksgaard, 1941), p. 32, Vizarəša and Astō.vīδātu ought to be grouped closely together, along with Nasu, the demon of corpses and putrefaction (= Greek *nekus*, "corpse").

27. *Atharva Veda* 8.1.3.

28. As, for instance, in *Atharva Veda* 8.2.2, 8.7.28; *Aitareya Brāhmaṇa* 3.14.

29. Thus Bartholomae, p. 1443f.; Lommel, "Awestische Einzelstudien," p. 235f.; Christensen, *Démonologie*, p. 32; and all other authorities who have commented on this name. The form *Vīδātu-* also occurs as the name of this demon in *Yasna* 57.25, a close variant of *Yašt* 10.93, where Sraoša replaces Mithra; and as a common noun in *Yašt* 13.11, 22, and 28.

30. Thus Herman Lommel, *Die Religion Zarathustras* (Tübingen: J. C. B. Mohr, 1930), p. 105.

31. This term always refers to enemy armies, never one's own, in the Avesta and in the Old Persian inscriptions. See Hermann Güntert, *Über die ahurischen und daevischen Ausdrücke im Awesta* (Heidelberg: Carl Winter, 1914), p. 29.

32. On *aēšma-*, see Stig Wikander, *Der arische Männerbund* (Lund: Gleerupska, 1938), pp. 57–60; Lommel, *Die Religion Zarathustras*, p. 78f.; Güntert, *Über die ahurischen und daevischen Ausdrücke*, p. 12; Adalbert Bezzenberger, "Homerische Etymologien," *Beiträge zur Kunde der indo-germanischen Sprachen* 4 (1878): 334.

33. Güntert, *Über die ahurischen und daevischen Ausdrücke*, p. 7. Since the speaker invoking Mithra is assumed to be a righteous man (*ašavan-*), his death would

properly be described with the ahuric term *para.iristi-*. Being righteous, he cannot possibly suffer *mahrka-*, the death reserved for the followers of the Lie (*drəgvant-*), and his salvation is thus assured.

34. Given the numerous peculiarities of this passage, let me offer the following notes on the translation.

Verse 28: *para.iristahe-* this is the Ahuric term for death, thus it is assured that the deceased of whom the passage speaks is to be considered a righteous (*ašavan-*) man.

θrityå̊ xšapō . . . bāmya- parallel to *Hadoxt Nask* 2.7: *θritya xšapō θraošta vyusą saδayeiti*, "At the end of the third night, one sees [the dawn] light up." I am inclined to see the construction of the *Hadoxt Nask* phrasing as more natural and, in all probability, older, Vd. 19.28 being modelled after it in part, although F. B. J. Kuiper, "Indoiranica," *Acta Orientalia* 17 (1938): 54–57, argued to the opposite conclusion.

uši—absolute locative.

bāmya—contra Ilya Gershevitch, *The Avestan Hymn to Mithra* (Cambridge: Cambridge University Press, 1959), p. 290f.

aša.xᵛaθranąm—on this as referring to the realm of the otherworld, F. B. J. Kuiper, "The Bliss of Aša," *Indo-Iranian Journal* 7 (1964): 96–129.

āsənaoiti—accepting the readings of manuscripts K1 and L4, and following the etymology proposed by Gert Klingenschmitt, "Avestisch āsnaoiti," *Münchener Studien zur Sprachwissenschaft* 28 (1970): 71–74. This interpretation is phonologically preferable to that offered by Lommel, "Awestische Einzelstudien," *Zeitschrift für Indologie und Iranistik* 3 (1925): 177, and Gershevitch, *Avestan Hymn to Mithra*, p. 171, and also semantically, in that it demonstrates the consistent usage of this verb (*san-* "to rise up," contra Bartholomae, *Alitranisches Wörterbuch*, p. 1755), to describe the rising of the sun, as attested in Pahlavi *xwarāsān;* Manichaean Middle Persian *xwr's'n;* New Persian *xwarāsān*, "East"; all of which are derived from **huwar-āsāna-*, "sunrise."

miθrəm huzaēnəm hvarəxšaētəm —all published translations have, to my knowledge, separated this phrase into two units, associating *miθrəm huzaēnəm* with the verb *āsənāoiti* and *hvarəxšaētəm* with *uzyoraiti*, a move for which there is no justification. Rather, *huzaēnəm* and *hvarəxšaetəm* must both be taken as adjectives modifying *miθrəm*, which in turn is the subject of both verbs, *āsənaoiti* and *uyoraiti*. That this must be so is shown by the specific use of *āsənaoiti* to describe the rising of the sun, as demonstrated by Klingenschmitt, a usage which only makes sense in this passage if *miθrəm* is associated with, rather than held separate from, *hvarəxšaētəm*.

Verse 29: *mərəzujītīm*—no convincing explanation has ever been offered for *mərəzu-*. The Pahlavi translation has *āhūg-zīwišnān*, "whose lives are quick like gazelles."

paθąm—plural genitive, root noun, as indicated by the modifier.

zrvō.datanąm—I am not inclined to see this as evidence for Zurvān as a deity, as did H. S. Nyberg, "Questions de Cosmogonie et de Cosmologie Mazdéenes, II," *Journal Asiatique* 219 (1931): 124f., and R. C. Zaehner, *Zurvān: A Zoroastrian Dilemma* (London: Oxford University Press, 1955), p. 87. Rather, it seems perfectly natural that the path of death should be said to have been created by (impersonal) time. Note, however, that the Pahlavi translation replaces *zrvō.dātanąm* with *zamāndād*, to remove any possible suspicion of heterodoxy.

35. Thus, for instance, Stig Wikander, *Vayu* (Uppsala: A. B. Lundquist, 1941), p. 27.

36. Contra the attempts of Lommel, "Awestische Einzelstudien," (1925): 177; idem, "Untersuchungen über die Metrik des Jüngeren Awesta," *Zeitschrift für Indologie und Iranistik* 5 (1927): 67; and Nyberg, "Questions de Cosmogonie et de Cosmologie," pp. 119–21, to show the opposite.

37. This is the general opinion on the composition of the *Vīdēvdāt*, first argued by James Hope Moulton, *Early Zoroastrianism* (London: Williams and Norgate, 1913), pp. 101f., 152, 183, 202f., 301, and 322, an opinion supported by H. S. Nyberg, *Die Religionen des alten Iran* (Leipzig: J. C. Hinrichs, 1938), pp. 337ff.; R. C. Zaehner, *Dawn and Twilight of Zoroastrianism* (New York: G. P. Putnam, 1961), p. 162; and Geo Widengren, "Holy Book and Holy Tradition in Iran: The Problem of the Sassanid Avesta," in F. F. Bruce and E. G. Rupp, eds., *Holy Book and Holy Tradition* (Manchester: Manchester University Press, 1968), p. 41.

38. H. Reichelt, *Awestisches Elementarbuch* (Heidelberg: Carl Winter, 1909), p. 225f.

39. The only serious attempt to address this question is that of Lommel, "Awestische Einzelstudien," (1925): 177, who sees it as necessitated by metric concerns. Gershevitch, *Avestan Hymn to Mithra*, p. 290f. takes the anomalous use of the accusative here as so bizarre as to give license to his interpretation of the locative *uši* as the subject of the same verse!

40. For the similarities in language, see above, note 38, gloss on θrityā̊ xšapō . . . *bāmya*.

41. F. B. J. Kuiper, "Remarks on the Avestan Hymn to Mithra," *Indo-Iranian Journal* 4 (1961): 46.

42. Robert W. Thomson, trans., Elishē, History of Vardan and the Armenian War (Cambridge, Mass.: Harvard University Press, 1982), p. 231. Cf. p. 213, where the sun is explicitly identified with the god Mihr.

43. On which, see Emile Benveniste, *The Persian Religion according to the Chief Greek Texts* (Paris: Paul Geuthner, 1929), pp. 53–56.

44. The full text has most recently appeared in Helmut Waldmann, *Die Kommagenischen Kultreformen unter König Mithradates I Kallinikos und seinem Sohne Antiochos I* (Leiden: E. J. Brill, 1973), pp. 63–71.

45. Geo Widengren, "The Mithraic Mysteries in the Greco-Roman World with Special Regard to Their Iranian Background," in *La Persia e il mondo greco-romano* (Rome: Accademia Nazionale dei Lincei, 1966), p. 435f.; Carsten Colpe, "Mithra-Verehrung, Mithras-Kult, und die Existenz iranischer Mysterien," in *Mithraic Studies*, pp. 389ff.

46. Thus Waldmann, pp. 166–69; F. K. Dörner, in *Arsameia am Nymphaios* (Berlin: G. Mann, 1963), pp. 142–44; idem, "Mithras in Kommagene," in *Études Mithraiques*, pp. 123–33; Elmar Schwertheim, "Monumente des Mithraskultes in Kommagene," *Antike Welt* 6 (1975): 63–68; and Jacques Duchesne-Guillemin, "Iran and Greece in Commagene," in *Études Mithraiques*, p. 199.

47. Schwertheim, p. 64f.; Duchesne-Guillemin, p. 199; Dörner, "Mithras in Kommagene," p. 125. Text in Waldmann, p. 78ff.

48. Waldmann, p. 166; Schwertheim, p. 66; Duchesne-Guillemin, p. 199, following K. Humann and O. Puchstein, *Reisen in Kleinasien und Nordsyrien* (Berlin: D. Reimer, 1890), pp. 341–43.

49. Schwertheim, p. 66; Dörner, *Arsameia am Nymphaios*, p. 67f.; Waldmann, p. 170.

50. Waldmann, p. 166, following Humann and Puchstein, p. 324. See the illustrations in Waldmann, pp. 118, and Dörner, "Mithras in Kommagene," plate V.

51. For the variants, see Waldmann, p. 121f. The Nimrud Dagh order must be taken as the original one, as argued by Duchesne-Guillemin, pp. 196–99.

52. Note the opinion of Richard N. Frye, "Mithra in Iranian History," in *Mithraic Studies*, p. 65. While allowing that the identification may have had pre-Achaemenid roots in Iran, he stresses that the emphasis on such an identification at Commagene is primarily a development of Hellenistic symbolism. Similarly, Ilya Gershevitch remarked in the first plenary session of the Manchester conference, published in *Mithraic Studies*, p. 132, that this association of Mithra and Helios at Commagene was "from the narrowly Iranian point of view, surprising."

53. Wilhelm Dittenberger, *Orientis Graecae Inscriptionis Selectae*, 2 vols. (Leipzig: S. Hirzel, 1903), 1:599.

54. Heinrich Dörrie, *Der Königskult des Antiochos von Kommagene im Lichte neuer Inschriften und Funde* (Göttingen: Vandenhoeck and Ruprecht, 1964), p. 190.

55. Dated to the second half of the fifth century B.C. by Gershevitch, *Avestan Hymn to Mithra*, p. 3; and considerably earlier by others, such as Widengren and Wikander.

56. It should be noted that according to the Nimrud Dagh inscription, lines 71–72, the priests of the cult established by Antiochus were dressed in Persian garb, and it is reported by Lucian, a native of Commagene in the second century A.D., that the Iranian language survived in the worship of Mithras at that time. See *Deorum concilium* 9, *Jupiter tragoedus* 8 and 13.

57. A fact emphasized by Colpe, "Mithra-Verehrung, Mithras-Kult und die Existenz iranischer Mysterien," p. 398; Widengren, "The Mithraic Mysteries in the Greco-Roman World," p. 436. On the limitations to the value of Plutarch's testimony, however, see E. D. Francis, "Plutarch's Mithraic Pirates," in *Mithraic Studies*, pp. 207–10.

58. See Chapters 4, "Waters of Memory, Waters of Forgetfulness," and 5, "The Ferryman of the Dead."

SEVEN

THE HELLHOUND

One of the few correspondences adduced by the comparative mythologists of the nineteenth century which continues to have its defenders, and which is still listed in standard lexicons, is the equation of Greek *Kerberos*, the proper name of Hades' hound, with the Sanskrit adjective *śabála-*, "spotted, vari-colored," used of the two dogs of Yama, who guard the pathway into the next world,[1] a comparison requiring the reduction of a whole set of Sanskrit adjectives similar in meaning to *śabála-—karabará-, kambara-, karburá-, karbu-,* and *śárvara-*—to a single Proto-Indic form, **śárbara-*, in order to posit a Proto-Indo-European **kérbero-*, "spotted."[2] While phonetically possible, such an argument faces certain difficulties. On the one hand there are problems in the manipulation of the Indic evidence,[3] and on the other we are left with a P-I-E **-b-* in the posited proto-form, something most unlikely. Further, while some scholars have attempted to adduce correspondences in other linguistic stocks, most notably Slavic *sobolь*, "sable,"[4] and Old Irish *corbaim*, "soiled, stained," these remain distant from a semantic point of view.[5]

In truth, the chief justification for retaining such a reconstruction is not any linguistic evidence but the numerous mythological references to a hellhound not only in Greek[6] and Indic texts,[7] but also in Celtic,[8] Germanic,[9] Latin,[10] Armenian,[11] and Iranian sources.[12] This mass of evidence was subjected to the most penetrating analysis by Bernfried Schlerath, some twenty-five years ago, in an article that stands as a model for research into P-I-E myth.[13] One point which has not been sufficiently appreciated, however, is that while Schlerath's discussion makes absolutely certain the existence of a mythic hellhound, at the same time it deals a death blow to any view of **Kérbero-*, "the spotted one," as that animal's name.

The core of Schlerath's argument is that the Proto-Indo-Europeans did not believe in just one otherworldly dog but accepted the existence of two such beasts, as is attested in Indic, Iranian, Armenian, and certain Celtic and Germanic texts.[14] Moreover, in the reconstructed P-I-E version, these dogs are clearly differentiated, one being the dog of life and the other the dog of death, the latter serving to carry off one about to die, while the former can restore him or her to life.[15] This pattern is most clearly preserved in the Armenian tradition, where the hound of life is named Spitak, "the White," and the hound of death, Siaw, "the Black."[16] In light of this evidence and Schlerath's skillful reconstruction, one can only conclude that Bloomfield was right many years ago when he argued that the use of *śabálau* (dual) for Yama's dogs was merely a way of expressing that there were two dogs of different color, one dark and one light.[17] There is thus no evidence for *śabála-* meaning "spotted" in the earliest Vedic text,[18] nor does *Kerberos* ever appear with this sense.[19] Accordingly, there are no semantic grounds for reconstructing P-I-E **kérbero-*, "spotted," and there was thus no hellhound named "Spot."

We are left with a difficult problem. Having decided that there was a P-I-E hellhound (i.e., Schlerath's black dog of death), we have gone on to reject the most commonly accepted reconstruction of that beast's name. It is, of course, entirely possible that he had no name, but it may be worth considering certain other possibilities before we accept that conclusion.

In this regard, Germanic evidence is particularly helpful, as it provides several different descriptions of the hellhound. Perhaps the most vivid is that of *Baldrs draumar* 2–3, in which Oðinn's descent to the underworld is described:

> Up rose Oðinn,   the ancient Goth,
> And he on Sleipnir   the saddle laid.
> Rode he down from thence   to Misty Hel.
> He met a whelp   who came from Hel.
> That one was bloody   about his chest;
> At the father of charms   barked he long.
> Forth rode Oðinn,   the Earth-way roared,
> Till he came to the high   house of Hel.

While the hellhound of this passage goes unnamed, most scholars have agreed that he is to be identified with Garmr, the monstrous, ravening dog bound in front of the peak of Hel, whose release is one of the cardinal signs of the Ragnarǫk.[20] Two aspects of the beast stand out in the text: his bark, also stressed in other mentions of Garmr,[21] and his appetite, implied by his blood-stained chest, befouled in the course of his grisly feasting.[22] As for the name, Old Norse *garmr* simply means "dog" (compare Faroese *garmur* "dog"), applied to the hellhound as a proper name.[23] Derivation is from P-I-E **gher-*, an onomatopoetic formation typically used for rough, hoarse sounds (including animal noises), represented in Germanic, *inter alia*, by Old English *gierman*, "to roar, howl," and *grimetan*, "to rage, roar," used for lions, bears, and boars.[24]

The most interesting Germanic description of the hellhound from a comparative point of view, however, is found in *Fjǫlsvinnsmál* 19–24, a text which recounts a *descensus ad inferos* under the folkloric guise of a quest for a beautiful maiden in a forbidden realm.[25]

> [Svipdag said:] "Tell me, Fjǫlsvið, that which I ask you,
>   For I will know
> What the dogs [*garmar*] are called who roam in front of the yard
>   With wily temper."

[Fjǫlsviđ said:] "One is called Gífr and the other Geri,
   If you'll know that.
Guardians strong, they keep watch
   Until the gods are broken."
[Svipdag said:] "Tell me, Fjǫlsviđ, that which I ask you,
   For I will know
Whether there is any one who can come in
   While those [dogs] bold in attack sleep."
[Fjǫlsviđ said:] "Strange are their sleeping habits in the extreme
   Since their watch was assigned them.
One sleeps at night, and the other by day,
   So no one gets through."
[Svipdag said:] "Tell me, Fjǫlsviđ, that which I ask you,
   For I will know
Whether there is any meat men can give them
   And leap inside while they eat."
[Fjǫlsviđ said:] "The raw flesh of two wings lie in the limbs of
   Viđofnir [a mythical bird],
   If you'll know that.
That alone is the meat men can give them
   And leap inside while they eat."

A number of close resemblances to the Greek, Roman, and Indo-Iranian hellhounds(s) are immediately evident. First, there are two dogs here, a fact which contributed significantly to Schlerath's reconstruction.[26] Second, they are specified as sleepless guardians,[27] watchers of the path or entrance, as are Yama's dogs, Kerberos, and the Iranian dogs.[28] Third, they may be overcome by offering them choice morsels, just as one can win passage past Yama's dogs by steady offering of the Agnihotra sacrifice[29] or by giving them the kidneys from a sacrificial victim,[30] and just as one can distract Kerberos or his Latin equivalent, Cerberus, with a honey-soaked sop.[31]

The names of the dogs in the *Fjǫlsvinnsmál* text are also noteworthy. As a noun, *Gífr* means "the greedy one," and as an adjective, "greedy, rapacious," being cognate to Old English *gīfre*, "rapacious, lustful," and closely related to the OE noun *gīfer,* "devourer."[32] In this light, one should also note the Old Norse compound *hræ-gífr,* "greedy for raw meat."[33] *Geri* is quite similar in meaning. As a common noun, it can mean "wolf," "dog," or "raven," being formed as a substantive from the adjectival *gerr,* "greedy, hungry," a term which corresponds to Old High German *ger~ker,* "desirous, rapacious, lustful" (verbal *gerōn,* "to covet") and Old Saxon *gerag* (= OHG *girig*), "greedy."[34]

Geri also appears in *Gylfaginning* 38 and *Grímnismál* 19, alongside another animal named Freki ("greedy, voracious" < ON adj. *frekr*), where he is described as one of the hounds or wolves of Ođinn.[35] The latter text states that they are fed by Ođinn himself, and *Helgakviđa Hundingsbana I,* verse 13, specifies the nature of their hunger, calling them "greedy for (the corpses of) those fallen in battle" (*valgjǫrn*).

The three names given for these dogs—*Geri*, *Gífr*, and *Freki*—share a basic meaning, "greedy," and it is helpful to consider the Germanic terms cognate to English *greed* at this point. Of the older Germanic languages, only Gothic preserves a verbal formation from the term "greed," and this furnishes a convenient starting point. There, the verb *grēdon* occurs as the translation of Greek *peináō*, which has as its primary meaning "to be hungry" and which only rarely refers by extension to needs or desires other than that for food.[36] Similarly, the Gothic adjective *grēdags*, cognate to Old Norse *gráðugr*, Old English *grǣdig* (English *greedy*), Old Saxon *grādag*, and Old High German *grātag*, translates Greek *peinōn*, the present particle of *peinaō*, thus "hungry, one who is hungering."[37] In Old Norse, too, it is literal hunger that is denoted, the term *gráðugr* being used to describe the cravings of, *inter alia*, a glutton, a belly, and wolves, being applied by extension to such hungers as that of devouring fire and all-consuming ambition.[38] The situation in the other stocks is quite similar. As for abstract nouns signifying "greed"—Gothic *grēdus*, Old Norse *gráðr*, and Old English *grǣd*—they too apply first and foremost to hunger, the Gothic being a translation of Greek *limós*, "hunger, famine,"[39] and the Old English being glossed by Latin *fames* ("hunger") as well as *aviditas* ("greed").[40]

These terms are all derived from P-I-E **gh(e)-rēdh-*, an extension in *-dh-* from the root **gher-*, the same root which lies behind Old Norse *Garmr*.[41] Now, no basic meaning can really be established for **gher-*. Rather, like the closely related roots **ger-* and **ker*, it is purely onomatopoetic, being used to express rough, hoarse noises of all sorts, but most particularly animal cries.[42] From these roots are built numerous verbs for the grunting of swine (OHG *grunzen*, OE *grunettan;* Gk. *grulizō*, *gromphazō;* Lat. *grundiō*); the growling or howling of dogs and wolves (ON *hrjóta;* Lat. *hirrīre;*[43] Alb. *ngurónj;* Skt. *gárjati*); the croaking of frogs[44] or ravens (ON *krúnka*, OE *cracettan;* Gk. *krazō*, *krozō;* Lat. *crōciō;* note also the phonologically parallel but historically unrelated forms in Balto-Slavic: Lith. *krankiù*, *krañkti;* Russ. and OCS *kraču*, *krakati*, Pol. *kraczę*, *krakać*, etc.); the cackling of geese or hens (Lat. *gingriō*, *gracillō;* parallel formations: Czech *krákorati*, Serb. *krakoriti*); the cawing of crows (OHG *crāen*, OE *crāwan*, Goth *hrukjan*); and others. Similarly, a great many animals derive their names from the sounds they make, expressed in formations from the P-I-E roots in which a velar, **k-*, **g-*, or **gh-*, is combined with an *e*-vowel and an *-r-*, which may be abbreviated **Ger-*, where **G-* represents any velar. Birds' names tend to take this form: crow (OE *crāwe*, ON *kráka;* Gk. *korōnē;* Lat. *cornix*, Umbr. *curnāco* (Sing. Acc.); MIr. *crú;* Alb. *sorrë*); rook (OE *hrōc*, Goth *hrūk*, ON *hrókr*, OHG *hruoh*); raven (OHG *(h)raben*, OE *hræfn*, ON *hrafn* [Runic *HrabnaR*]; Gk. *korax;* Lat. *corvus;* parallel formations: Bulg. *krókon*, Slovene *krēk*); heron

(OE *hrāgra*, ON *hegri*, OHG *heigaro;* Welsh *crychydd*, OBret. *corcid;* Skt. *śarāri;* parallel formations: Lith. *garnȳs*, Lett. *gārns*); crane (OHG *kranuh*, OE *cranoc* ~ *cornuc;* Gk. *geranos;* Lat. *grus;* Arm. *krunk;* Bret. *garan*, Irish *corr*, Gallic inscr. *-garanos;* Lett. *dzerve;* Russ-OCS *žerauь;* parallel formation: Skt. *karāyikā-*); jackdaw (Lat. *graculus*); rooster (Gk. *kerkos;* parallel formation: Av. *kahrkatāt*); starling (Arm. *sareak*); and others. **Ger-* also appears in the names of other, non-avian animals: pigs (Gk. *grisōn*, *grūlos;* MIr. *cráin;* parallel formation: Lett. *krĩna*); frogs: (OPruss *crupeyle*, Lett. *krupis*); insects (Gk. *kornops;* Lat. *grillus;* parallel formation: Skt. *ghurghurī-*); dogs (ON *garmr*, Eng. *cur*); and a number of mythological beasts (Gk. *Geryonēs*, *Gorgō;* OE *Grendel;* and perhaps Skt. *śarku-;* with metathesis, one might also include here Lat. *Orcus*).[45]

Another class of words built upon the root **Ger-* may be described as sub-verbal utterances: sounds commonly made by people, none of which constitute actual words. Among these would be shrieks (ON *hrína*, OHG *scrīan;* Gk. *kraugē*, OIr *scret*, Welsh *cre;* Skt. *króśati;* Av. *xraosaiti;* parallel formation: OCS *krikъ*, *kričati*); calls or cries (Gk. *gērus;* OIr *gáir*); laments (ON *gráta*, OE *grǣtan*, Goth. *grētan*, Skt. *krpate*); snoring (ON *hrjóta*, OE *hrūtan*, OHG *hrūzzan*, OFris. *hrūta;* compare Gk. *koruza*, "to sniff"); spitting (ON *hrǣkja*, OE *hrǣcan*); and hoarseness or clearing one's throat (OHG *hrāchisōn*, Gk. *kérkhnos;* Welsh *cryg;* parallel formations: Lith. *krankščiu*, *krañksti*, Lett. *krecêt*).

Returning to the starting point for this excursus, we may conclude that implicit in the Germanic terms for "greed" is an understanding of greed as that characteristic whereby a human being is reduced to the level of a hungry beast: growling, ravenous, and inarticulate. The mark of greed is, in fact, a twofold growl issuing simultaneously from the belly and the throat of a starving animal, and one can hear that fierce growl in the harsh sound of the word itself (English *growl* and *greed* being themselves derivates of P-I-E **Ger-*).[46]

A similar interpretation was advanced for the name *Kerberos* by Wilamowitz almost fifty years ago, when he wrote "in it one hears the snarl of a vicious mongrel," going on to compare Kerberos to the bloody whelp of *Baldrs draumar*.[47] What Wilamowitz did not recognize, however, is that the two can be etymologically connected, *Kerberos*, *śabála-*, *Garmr*, and *Geri* all coming from P-I-E **Ger-*, the first two from the form **ker-*, and the last two from **gher-*.

The Indo-European hellhound, then, had a name which was drawn from the sound of his snarl or growl. To a certain extent, this may be due to the role of dogs as devourers of corpses, noted so often in the literature of the various Indo-European peoples,[48] something which naturally gave them strong funerary associations.[49] Further, the growl may be seen as the voice of the hellhound's greed, the greed of none other than all-devouring death.

Beyond these interpretive ventures, a still deeper point may be made regarding the hellhound's name, one that is congruent with many other features of his symbolism. As Schlerath and others have made abundantly clear, the essence of the hellhound is his intermediary position—at the border of this world and the next, between life and death, hope and fear, and also (given its pairing with the dog of life) between good and evil.[50] For this role, the dog is perfectly suited, being the domestic species par excellence, the tamed carnivore who stands midway between animal and human, savagery and civilization, nature and culture.

The growl of the hellhound is yet another expression of this liminal position, for the growl is a halfway station between articulate speech and silence. It is a speech filled with emotion and power, but utterly lacking in reason. Like death itself, the hellhound speaks, but does not listen; acts, but never reflects or reconsiders. Driven by hunger and greed, he is insatiable and his growl is eternal in duration. In the last analysis, the hellhound is the moment of death, the great crossing over, the ultimate turning point.

Notes

1. First suggested by Friedrich Max Müller, *Chips from a German Workshop*, vol. 2 (London: Longmans Green, 1894, first published: 1848) p. 182, followed quickly by Albrecht Weber, *Indische Studien*, vol. 2 (Berlin: F. Dümmler, 1852), pp. 295–98, and Adalbert Kuhn, "Namen der Milchstrasse und des Höllenhunds," *Zeitschrift für vergleichende Sprachforschung* 5 (1856): 148–49. Accepted, *inter alia*, by Alois Walde, *Vergleichende Wörterbuch der indogermanischen Sprache*, ed. J. Pokorny (Berlin: W. de Gruyter, 1927), 1:425; Wilhelm Schulze, *Kleine Schriften* (Göttingen: Vandenhoeck & Ruprecht, 1933), p. 125; Franz Specht, *Der Ursprung der indogermanische Deklination* (Göttingen: Vandenhoeck & Ruprecht, 1947), pp. 119 and 262; Julius Pokorny, *Indogermanische etymologische Wörterbuch* (Bern: Franke, 1969), p. 578. While accepting the validity of the correspondence, Vittore Pisani, "Indo-iranica," *Rivista degli Studi Orientali* 18 (1939): 91–92, attempted to trace it to an Indo-Mediterranean origin rather than Indo-European.

2. On these various forms and the possibility of their relation to one another, see Manfred Mayrhofer, *Kurzgefasstes etymologische Wörterbuch des Altindisches* (Heidelberg: Carl Winter, 1956–76) 1:175 and 3:297–98.

3. Chief among these are the question of whether the *ś*- and *k*- of the various forms can be equated, and the shift in accent. The loss of the first -r- in *śabála-* can be explained as a dissimulation from the -r- of the second syllable by reduction. On -v- for -b-, see Jacob Wackernagel, *Altindische Grammatik, I. Lautlehre* (Göttingen: Vandenhoeck & Ruprecht, 1957), pp. 183–84. F. B. J. Kuiper, "Indoiranica," *Acta Orientalia* 16 (1937): 306, argued for an Austroasiatic origin of the Sanskrit terms, and his view has been tentatively endorsed by Mayrhofer, 1:175.

4. Max Vasmer, *Russisches etymologisches Wörterbuch* (Heidelberg: Carl Winter, 1958): 2:685.

5. Pokorny, p. 578.

6. Homer knows the hellhound but does not name him in the two passages where he

mentions him (*Iliad* 8.368 and *Odyssey* 11.623–25), probably due to metric considerations. The name *Kerberos* appears first in Hesiod, *Theogony* 311, and the dog is treated in lines 310–12 and 767–73. Other important Greek sources are Bacchilides 5.60–62, Sophocles, *Oedipus at Colonnus* 1568–78, *Women of Trachis* 1098–99; Euripides, *Herakles* 21–25, Apollodorus, *Bibliotheca* 2.122ff., Lucian, *Nekyomanteia* 14, *Kataplous* 28; and Diodorus Siculus 4.25–26.

7. The most important Indic texts are: *Ṛg Veda* 10.14.10–12; *Atharva Veda* 8.1.9; and *Jaiminīya Brāhmaṇa* 1.6. For one of the more interesting treatments, see Ernst Arbman, "Tod und Unsterblichkeit im vedischen Glauben," *Archiv für Religionswissenschaft* 26 (1928): 217–20.

8. See Hans Hartmann, *Die Totenkult in Irland* (Heidelberg: Carl Winter, 1952), p. 145; Anatole Le Braz, *La légende de la mort chez les bretons armoricains* (Paris: Honoré Champion, 1902), 1:90–92, incorrectly cited by Schlerath as 1:107ff.

9. The chief texts are discussed below. They are: *Baldrs draumar* 2–3; *Vǫluspá* 44, 49, 58; *Gylfaginning* 51; *Fjǫlsvinnsmál* 19–24; and *Grímnismál* 19. Otherworldly guard dogs also appear in *Skírnismál* 10–12.

10. Vergil, *Aeneid* 6.417–23; Horace, *Carmina* 2.12.33–35, 3.11.13–20; Ovid, *Metamorphoses* 7.408–17.

11. See the summary provided in Bernfried Schlerath, "Der Hund bei den Indogermanen," *Paideuma* 6 (1954): 39.

12. *Vīdēvdāt* 13.8f. and 19.30.

13. Schlerath, "Der Hund," pp. 25–40.

14. The most important Germanic text for this reconstruction is *Fjǫlsvinnsmál* 19–24, and the chief Celtic source is Le Braz 1:90–92. Schlerath, p. 32, has speculated that the representation of Cerberus with two heads in Attic vase painting may derive from an originally dual hellhound, as may the ambiguous portrait of the hound in the *Theogony* 767ff. A similar argument might be advanced for the ambivalent Germanic attitude toward Garmr, who is normally despised but is called the best of dogs in *Grímnismál* 44.

15. Schlerath, p. 31 et passim.

16. Ibid., p. 39.

17. Maurice Bloomfield, *Cerberus, the Dog of Hades* (Chicago: Open Court, 1904), p. 31, supported by Schlerath, p. 36.

18. Pisani, p. 91n., argued that there was nothing in the *Ṛg Veda* to suggest the meaning "spotted" for *śábala-*, and felt it possible that this was an old proper name reinterpreted as an adjective.

19. See the listing in Henry George Liddell and Robert Scott, *A Greek-English Lexicon* (Oxford: Clarendon Press, 1968), p. 942. Etymological discussion in Frisk, *Griechisches etymologisches Wörterbuch* 1:828–29.

20. Jacob Grimm, *Teutonic Mythology*, trans. J. Stallybrass (London: George Bell, 1883) 2:814n.; Elard Hugo Meyer, *Germanische mythologie* (Berlin: Mayer & Müller, 1891), p. 108; Paul Herrman, *Nordische Mythologie* (Leipzig: W. Engelmann, 1903), p. 584; Richard H. Meyer, *Altgermanische Religionsgeschichte* (Leipzig: Quelle & Meyer, 1910), pp. 466–68; Julius von Negelein, *Germanische Mythologie* (Leipzig: B. G. Teubner, 1912), p. 32.

21. *Vǫluspá* 44, 49, 58: "Now Garmr howls loudly before the peak of Hel" (*Geyr nú Garmr mjǫk fyr Gnipahelli*).

It is particularly interesting to note that the howl of the hellhound is carefully preserved in the chief Avestan description (*Vīdēvdāt* 13.8–9), but is transformed into a salvific noise made by the two dogs of the Daēnā-maiden (the personification of one's religion) on behalf of a righteous soul. This transformation is fully in keeping with the unambiguously positive valuation placed upon these dogs, and on dogs in general, within the Zoroastrian tradition. The text reads as follows:

> He who kills one among these—herding dogs, watch dogs, bloodhounds, or entertainment dogs—his soul goes forth from us to its future existence crying and lamenting more than the wolf laments when trapped in the deepest pit. No other soul aids his dead soul with crying and lamentation for his [future] existence, nor do the two dogs who protect the bridge aid his dead soul with crying and lamentation for his (future) existence.

The crucial point in interpreting this passage is the recognition that any soul needs the assistance of the dogs to successfully pass over the bridge which connects this world to the heavens, assistance which they render by howling laments for the deceased. Their refusal to perform this service (as here, for those who have sinned against the canine species) is thus tantamount to condemning the deceased to hell.

22. Thus Hermann Güntert, *Kalypso* (Halle: Max Niemeyer, 1919), pp. 55–57, followed by Arbman, p. 220, n. 3; Schlerath, p. 32; and Gering, 1:340.

23. Jan de Vries, *Altnordisches etymologisches Wörterbuch*, 2d ed. (Leiden: E. J. Brill, 1977), p. 157.

24. de Vries, p. 157. On **gher-*, see Pokorny, p. 439; on *gierman* and *grimetan* see Joseph Bosworth, *An Anglo-Saxon Dictionary*, ed. T. N. Toller (Oxford: Oxford University Press, 1973), pp. 489 and 495.

25. For numerous examples and general discussion of this folkloric recasting of the mythic theme of the descent, see A. H. Krappe, "Lancelot et Guinièvre," *Revue celtique* 48 (1931): 94–123.

26. Schlerath, p. 31.

27. Compare the specification of Yama's dogs as "four-eyed" (*caturakṣáu*) in RV 10.14.10f. and elsewhere, expressive of their eternal vigilance and watchfulness in all directions (thus Hermann Oldenberg, *Die Religion des Veda* [Stuttgart: J. G. Cotta, 1923], p. 471, n. 7; Abel Bergaigne, *La religion védique*, reprint ed. [Paris: Maisonneuve, 1963] 1:93). The Iranian tradition also knows of a four-eyed dog (Avestan *spānəm . . . caθru.cašməm*) in a funerary context, but in light of the unambiguously positive valuation placed on the dog within Zoroastrianism, this dog has been given the role of protecting the corpse from the assaults of Nasu, the demon of decomposition and putrefaction. The very glance of this dog is supposed to ward off Nasu, whence the naming of the ceremony in which the dog keeps vigil over the corpse as *Sag-did*, "the dog's glance." Aspects of the *Sag-did* are mentioned in *Vīdēvdāt* 8.14–18, and it is discussed in Herman Lommel, *Die Religion Zarathustras* (Tübingen: J. C. B. Mohr, 1930), p. 191.

28. Compare Vedic *rakṣitárau . . . pathirákṣī*, "the two protectors protecting the path" (RV 10.14.11); Avestan *pəšu.pāna*, "the two protectors of the bridge" (Vd. 13.9), and the description of Cerberus in the *Theogony*, lines 767–69:

> In front stands the resounding dwelling of the Chthonian god—
> Of valiant Hades and dread Persephone—
> And a fearsome dog stands guard in front . . .

29. *Jaiminīya Brāhmaṇa* 1.6; *Kauṣitaki Brāhmaṇa* 2.9.

30. See Willem Caland, "Altindische Toten- und Bestattungsgebrauche," *Verhandelingen der Koninklijke Akademie van Wetenschappen te Amsterdam: Afdeeling Letterkunde* 1/6 (1896), p. 54.

31. The Greek practice of burying the dead with honey cakes for Kerberos is attested in only a few sources, most notably, a scholium to Aristophanes, *Lysistrata* 601, and the entry in the *Suida* under *melitoutta*. More interesting is the classic passage, Vergil, *Aeneid* 6.417–23, where the same aspects of the hellhound are stressed as in *Baldrs draumar:* his howl and his appetite:

> Huge Cerberus fills these realms with the baying
> Of his triple throats; enormous, he crouches before the cave.
> The seer, observing his neck bristle with serpents,
> Tossed him a sleep-inducing sop containing honey
> And enchanting fruits. Extending his three ravenous throats, he
> Seized that which was offered, relaxed his immense body,
> And sprawled upon the ground. Enormous, he stretched through the
>   whole cave.

In truth, the Greco-Roman tradition reports three different means of overcoming the hellhound: force (Herakles), food (Aeneas), and song (Orpheus). The latter two methods are of particular interest, for they speak to the signal characteristics of the hellhound, food assuaging his hunger and music quieting his growl.

32. de Vries, p. 166.

33. Richard Cleasby and Gudbrand Vigfusson, *An Icelandic-English Dictionary,* 2d ed. (Oxford: Clarendon Press, 1957), p. 289.

34. de Vries, p. 164.

35. Snorri, *Gylfaginning* 38, describes them as wolves (*ii úlfum*), but it is not clear whether he has a source for this or whether he is venturing his own interpretation. The source which he does quote (*Grímnismál* 19) leaves the precise species of the canines unspecified.

36. Sigmund Feist, *Vergleichendes Wörterbuch der gotischen Sprache,* 3d ed. (Leiden: E. J. Brill, 1939), p. 220. For the occurrences of *peinao* in the New Testament text, see Walter Bauer, *A Greek-English Lexicon of the New Testament,* trans. W. F. Arndt and F. W. Gingrich, 2d ed. (Chicago: University of Chicago Press, 1979), p. 640.

37. Feist, p. 220; Bauer, p. 540.

38. See the occurrences listed in Cleasby-Vigfusson, p. 212.

39. Feist, p. 220; Bauer, p. 475.

40. C. W. M. Grin, *Sprachschatz der angelsächsischen Dichter,* 2d ed. by J. J. Köhler (Heidelberg: Carl Winter, 1912), p. 273. The adjectival form is glossed by *avidus, cupidus,* and *vorax* according to the same source, but in Arthur S. Napier, *Old English Glosses* (Oxford: Clarendon Press, 1900), one notes also *lurcont,* "gluttonizing" (p. 20), *rabidus* (p. 40), and *lascivus* (p. 89) as glosses for *grædig.* See also the discussion in Toller, p. 483. Several texts are noteworthy, esp. the description of hell as *grædige* and *gifre* (*Caedmon,* ed. Benjamin Thorpe, p. 49, line 16), and Blickling's Homilies 211.1: *Da fynd heora grípende wæron swá swá grædig wulf,* "The fiends were gripping them like a greedy wolf."

41. Feist, p. 220; de Vries *Altnordisches etymologisches Wörterbuch,* p. 183f. Pokorny, p. 441, however, prefers to list these as derived from a P-I-E root *ǵher-,

although he offers this suggestion only tentatively ("*vielleicht*"). There is also some debate as to whether the Germanic forms ought be compared to Sanskrit *gŕdhyati,* "to desire," *gŕdhra-* adj. "greedy," masc. subst. "vulture," *gardha-* "desire," and Avestan *gərəδa-* "greedy" (*hapax legomenon* occurring as an epithet of the psychopompic god Vayu ["Wind"] in *Yašt* 15.47), or whether the Indo-Iranian forms are better grouped with Slavic *žъldĕti* "to desire" (Old Bulgarian *žlĭditi,* Old Church Slavonic *žlъdĕti,* Serbo-Croatian *žúdjeti,* etc.). The former position has been defended by Feist, p. 220, and de Vries, *Altnordisches etymologisches Wörterbuch,* p. 183, following Ernst Zupitza, "Die germanische Gutturale," *Schriften zur germanischen Philologie* 8 (1896): 176, and H. Grassman, "Ueber das ursprüngliche vorhandsein von wurzeln, deren anlaut und auslaut eine aspirate enthielt," *Zeitschrift für vergleichende Sprachforschung* 12 (1863): 130. The latter position is preferred by Mayrhofer, 1:329 and 343, and Pokorny, p. 434 (positing a root **gheldh-* "to covet, desire," attested only in Slavic and Indo-Iranian), following Johannes Schmidt, "Zwei arische a-laute und die Palatalen," *Zeitschrift für vergleichende Sprachforschung* 25 (1881): 73. Most recently, this position has received significant support from Oswald Szemerényi, "Slavic Etymologies in Relation to the Indo-European Background," *Welt der Slaven* 12 (1967): 274, who modifies the P-I-E root to **gʷel-dh-.* In any event, the Germanic forms should be grouped with Old Irish *goirt* "hungry," *gortae* "hunger, famine," noting the extremely significant usage in Ernst Windisch, *Irische Texte,* vol. 1 (Leipzig: S. Hirzel, 1880), p. 41 line 9: *Do luid cú goirt elscothach isin tech* "a greedy, hungry dog came into the house,' where hunger (adj. *goirt*) is clearly differentiated from more general greed (adj. *elscothach* < *elscoth, elscud* "intense heat," and by extension "ardent longing").

42. On these roots, see Pokorny, pp. 383–85, 439, and 567–71.

43. The gloss of Paulus, Festus 101 is of particular interest, for he specified *garrire* (= *hirrire*) as the sound made by a rabid dog (*genus vocis . . . canis rabiosae*).

44. In addition to the forms cited, one should also note the song of the frogs in Aristophanes, *Frogs,* lines 209–10 et al.:

> *Brekekekèx koàx koàx*
> *Brekekekèx koàx koàx*

45. For other suggestions on the etymology of *Orcus,* see Hermann Osthoff, "Griechische und lateinische Wortdeutungen," *Indogermanische Forschungen* 8 (1898): 54–56; A. Bezzenberger, "Etymologien," *Beiträge zur Kunde der indogermanischen Sprachen* 26 (1901): 166; H. Wagenvoort, *Studies in Roman Literature, Culture, and Religion* (Leiden: E. J. Brill, 1956), pp. 102–31; and the summary in A. Walde, *Lateinisches etymologisches Wörterbuch,* 4th ed., revised by J. B. Hofmann (Heidelberg: Carl Winter, 1965), 2:221.

46. English is extremely rich in words derived from the **Ger-* roots, both as a Germanic language, and from Latin via French. Among the many examples which could be cited are: *gargle, garrulous, grackle, grebe, groan, grouse, growl, grudge, grumble, grunt; crake, crane, creak, crepitate, croak, croup, crow, crunch, cry, cur,* and if one also recognizes forms with an initial *s-* as derived from the same root, *screak, scream, screech, scrunch, shrew, shriek, shrike,* and *shrill.*

47. Ulrich von Wilamowitz-Moellendorff, *Der Glaube der Hellenen* (Berlin: Weidmann, 1932) 1:314 n.

48. See, for instance, *Iliad* 1.4–5, 13.831–32, 17.127, 22.354, etc.; *Vīdēvdāt* 6.45–46, 7.29–30; and the formulaic curse of the Old Norse sagas: "dogs shall gnaw you in Hel." Note also the specification of Cerberus as "devourer of raw flesh" (*omēstēn*) in *Theogony*, 311.

49. Note the interpretation of Albrecht Dieterich, *Nekyia*, 3d ed. (Stuttgart: B. G. Teubner, 1969), p. 49, who saw the hellhound as "the devouring depths of the earth (presented) in the form of a fearful hound."

50. Schlerath, p. 36f.; see also, Manfred Lurker, "Hund und Wolf in ihrer Beziehung zum Tode," *Antaios* 10 (1969): 199–216, esp. pp. 199 and 215.

EIGHT

THE HOUSE OF CLAY

Dying of thirst, the Vedic seer Vasiṣṭha calls out to Varuṇa in *Ṛg Veda* 7.89, the first stanza of which contains a curious locution:

> May I not now go to the house of clay, King Varuṇa! Be gracious,
> you whose sovereignty is good, be gracious!

The phrase in question is *mṛnmáyam gṛhám* (Sing. Acc.), "house made of clay or earth."[1] But what is the "house of clay"? What is its place in the complex funerary geography of the Vedic Indians? These questions are thorny ones, for nowhere else in Vedic texts is the "house of clay" mentioned.[2] As a result, Geldner was inclined to see it as a metaphoric expression for the funerary urn in which the bones of a deceased were buried after cremation,[3] while Zimmer compared *mṛnmáya- gṛhá-* to *bhūmigṛha-* of the *Atharva Veda*, a description of the deceased as "one whose house is the earth."[4] Alternatively, one might simply consider the "house of clay" as a rare name for the otherworld, much as the mortally stricken Enkidu refers to his destination as "the house of dust" in the Babylonian *Gilgamesh Epic*.[5] That the Vedic verse cited above is concerned with issues of death and dying cannot be doubted, given the context of the hymn (Vasiṣṭha's thirst) and its poetic assonance. With regard to the latter, we must note that terms with the form *mṛD- (where -D- represents any dental) appear three times within a total of eleven words— *mṛdmáyam, mṛḍā*, and *mṛḍáya*—conjuring up the presence of a fourth such form: *mṛtá-*, "dead."

One problem in arriving at an understanding of what is signified by the "house of clay" is our tendency toward the fallacy of misplaced concreteness as we conjure up a clearer vision than is actually conveyed by the words themselves. Thus, *mṛdmáya-* can mean either "made of earth" or "made of clay."[6] The meaning of *gṛhá-*, normally rendered "house," admits even more possibilities. Derived from a Proto-Indo-European form *ghordho-, gṛhá- denotes nothing more than an enclosure, a space surrounded by some sort of a wall, being built upon a P-I-E verbal root *gherd-, "to surround, enclose, gird, hedge in." It is thus comparable to such nouns as Avestan *gərəδa-*, "cave"; Albanian *garth, -dhi*, "hedge"; Phrygian *-gordum*, "city"; Old Saxon *gard*, "fenced piece of land"; Lithuanian *gaȓdas*, "fold, pen"; and Russian *ogoród*, "fence enclosure, kitchen garden," *górod*, "city," as well as to Gothic *gards*, "house."[7] "House" is but one of the many possible meanings, and while it was clearly the prevalent sense of the Sanskrit term, *gṛhá-* could be used to denote other kinds of bounded space.[8]

Two other Sanskrit terms serve to describe the otherworld as an enclosure having earthen walls. Thus, in *Atharva Veda* 18.1.54 and 18.4.63, the departed Fathers (*pitárah*) are said to travel from this world to the next *pathíbhih pūryáṇair,* "by the paths leading to the fortress."[9] The otherworld is thus seen as a *púr-,* a fortified stronghold having ramparts most often made of hardened earth,[10] such ramparts being designated *dehí-* in two Vedic verses,[11] a term to which we shall return below.

Again, in the Upaniṣads,[12] the heavenly realms are said to have a *sétu-,* a "boundary wall," the noun being derived from the verb *si- syáti,* "to bind, tie, fetter."[13] Although *sétu-* can also mean "bridge, causeway" in later texts (as, for instance, the great bridge from India to Śrī Lanka in the *Rāmāyana*), this sense does not occur in the earliest texts,[14] and is less appropriate for the Upaniṣadic usages than that of "boundary wall," already attested in the Ṛg Veda.[15] A *sétu-* is most properly "that which binds," not "that which connects," as is seen from its cognates in European languages: Old Norse *seiðr* (masc.), "bond," Old English *sāda,* Old High German *seito,* Lithuanian *saītas, siētas,* and Lettish *saīte,* all of which mean "cord, bond," as well as those terms which have taken on the specialized sense of "magic, binding force": Welsh and Breton *hud,* and Old Norse *seið* (fem.).[16] Perhaps the most instructive text is *Chandogya Upaniṣad* 8.4.1–2:

> Now, the soul is the dividing boundary wall [*setu-*] for the separation of these worlds. Day and Night do not cross the boundary wall, nor old age, nor death, nor pain, nor good deeds, nor bad deeds. All evils turn back from it, for truly the Brahma-world is free of evil.
>
> Therefore, a blind man, having crossed that boundary wall becomes non-blind; a wounded man, having crossed that boundary wall becomes non-wounded; a feverish man, having crossed that boundary wall becomes non-feverish. Therefore, having crossed that boundary wall, night appears as day, for truly the Brahma-world is forever radiant.

The picture is one of paradise, described in familiar Indo-European imagery as devoid of all ills.[17] But what is of greatest interest to us is that paradise is radically separated from this mortal sphere, set apart by a boundary wall (*setu-*). The new, Upaniṣadic teaching is that the self (*ātman*) constitutes that boundary wall and that when one appreciates the true nature of this self, one has crossed over the boundary which confines him to this earthly and bodily prison; but the imagery of the heavenly boundary wall on which the text builds is an extremely ancient one.

At the very least, the image must ascend to the Proto-Indo-Iranian period, for an Avestan cognate, *haētu-,* also denotes the wall surrounding paradise in one of the most important funerary texts of the Avesta, and assures a parent term *saitu- for Proto-Indo-Iranian.[18] The text reads as follows:

> That beautiful maiden [the daēnā-maiden, personification of the deceased's religious life], bold and shapely, comes forth, having two dogs, having [nivavaiti], having a diadem, having powers, having excellence. She drags the evil soul of the followers of the Lie down into darkness. She brings the soul of the righteous man over Hara Bərəzaiti [the cosmic mountain], she conducts it over the Bridge of Separation within the boundary wall (haētu-) of the spiritual deities. (Vd. 19.30)

Sanskrit gṛhá- also has an Avestan cognate which appears within a funerary context. This is gərəδa-, which occurs three times with the meaning of "cave," always being described as the dwelling place of demonic beings.[19] Clearest is Vīdēvdāt 3.7, where Zarathustra asks Ahura Mazdā what is the most unpleasant place on earth, and the Wise Lord answers as follows:

> There, Spitāma Zarathustra, where the scruff of the neck of Arəzūra is, where the demons [daēvas] gather together from the cave of the Lie [drujō . . . gərəδāt].

On the face of it, this hardly seems connected to death or the underworld, but several important factors concerning the Zoroastrian transformation of Indo-Iranian religion must be considered. First, alone among the Indo-European peoples, the Iranians rejected burial, which they regarded as desecration of the earth, in favor of exposure of corpses to beasts and birds of prey.[20] As a result, the tomb or burial place lost all of its symbolic significance, and such significance as it had was largely reinterpreted. Second, Zoroastrianism is marked by an abhorrence of death and the pollution associated with all things dead. In large measure, the extensive Avestan demonology consists of figures that personify death and decomposition: Nasu, "corpse" (=Gk. nekus), Astō.vīδātu, "the binder of the body," Vīzarəša "who drags away (the deceased)," Aoša, "destruction," Maršavan, "decrepitude," Vayu, the psychopompic wind, and so forth.[21] The mountain Arəzūra is the consistent gathering place of these demons,[22] the most demonic and most deadly place on earth. What is more, the mountain is personified, described as the skull of the demon Arəzūra or the scruff of his neck,[23] Arəzūra being the son of Aŋra Mainyu, the "Evil Spirit," and the first demon ever to be slain, according to a myth preserved in one Pahlavi source.[24] The "cave of the Lie" on Mount Arəzūra, whence all demons issue, is thus that subterranean enclosure most contaminated with death, corruption, and putrefaction, and gərəδa- is the term used to describe it.

Two other Avestan terms merit our attention. The first of these is vara-, "enclosure," used of the dwelling of Aŋra Mainyu once,[25] and more regularly of the enormous subterranean refuge built by Yima for the preservation of humanity and animals from an all-destroying winter.[26] Yima, as I have shown elsewhere, is the Iranian reflex of a crucial figure in Indo-European mythology: the first king, first sacrificial victim, and lord of the dead forever after.[27] While Yima was rejected by Zarathustra and lost much of his importance in Zoroastrian myth, he still could not be suppressed altogether, and details in the description of his *vara-* show that it is a transformed image of his paradisal *post mortem* realm.[28] What is most interesting for us at present, however, are the details of its construction, for we are told that the *vara-* was *made of earth*. Ahura Mazdā himself gives the instructions, saying:

> Yima, beautiful son of Vivahvant, stamp the earth apart with your heels, squeeze it apart with your hands, as men now separate earth when it is fluid [i.e., clay]. (*Vīdēvdāt* 2.31)

Like the *mṛnmáya- gṛhá-,* Yima's *vara-* was an enclosure made of earth, and in pre-Zoroastrian times was understood as the home of the dead. One more Avestan term needs to concern us: *pairi.daēza-,* the word from which Greek *paradeisos,* English *paradise* are ultimately derived.[29] *Pairi.daēza-* occurs only once in the entire Avestan corpus, but that occurrence is an extremely significant one, coming in a passage which treats the question of what is to become of the man who is an attendant of corpses (*iristō.kaša-*) and thus most contaminated of all mortals with the pollution of death.[30] It is stated that he is to be taken to that place which is "most waterless of the earth, most devoid of plants, where the earth is most purified of death" and most distant from sacred entities of any sort: animals, the fire, the *barəsman* twigs, and righteous humans (Vd. 3.15). In this desolate region, the worshippers of Mazdā are said to have "enclosed enclosures out of this earth" *ainhå zəmō pairidaēząn pairi.daēzayąn,* Vd. 3.18, where the corpse-bearer is kept until he grows old and dies. At death, his body is delivered to the vultures, and in his last moments he gains release by renouncing his evil thoughts, words, and deeds (Vd. 3.20–21). We thus meet another earthen enclosure, described as the dwelling place of those intimately associated with death. The word used for that enclosure is *pairi.daēza-.*

Etymologically, *pairi.daēza-* is of some interest, being related to one term we have already encountered and one which will concern us shortly. It is a compound formed from the preposition *pairi-* (=Skt. *pári-,* Gk. *peri-,* etc.), "around," and **daēza-,* "heap, pile," the latter stemming from the verbal root *daēz-,* "to heap or pile up," cognate to Sanskrit *dih-,* "to anoint, smear, plaster."[31] The nominal form which corresponds to **daēza-* in Sanskrit is *deha-,* which from an original meaning of "that which has been shaped, heaped up, formed" has come to denote most usually the human body. Occurrences of this term are rather late, however, beginning only with the Āraṇyakas.[32] The original sense is better preserved in the feminine form, *dehī-,* which occurs already in the *Ṛg Veda,* as we saw above, denoting the ramparts or defensive walls that surround a *púr-*. In considering the Indo-Iranian connections of *daēza-*, one must also note Old Persian *didā-* (< *dizā-*), Pahlavi and New Persian *diz*, and Yidγa *lizo*, all of which mean "fort"; also, *MAΛZO* (< *ham-ā-dizā-*), "enclosure," of the Kaniṣka Inscription, and—most interestingly—Yidγa *dizəm, dizdəm* (< *han-diz-*), "to bury."[33]

The Indo-Iranian verb *dhaiźh-* thus originally meant "to construct out of earth," and the noun *dhaiźha-*, "that which has been built out of earth," both terms being capable of modification by prepositions to specify the type or shape of the construction being described. The noun, in turn, can be derived from Proto-Indo-European *dhoiǵho-s* (masc.), from which are also Greek *toikhos* "wall, esp. of a house," Gothic *daigs* "dough, paste," and perhaps, with metathesis, Old Church Slavonic *zidŭ, zĭdŭ*, "wall."[34]

Greek *teikhos* (neuter) is also interesting, since it occurs in the earliest Greek passage describing the walls of the underworld, Hesiod's *Theogony* 726–33, where the Titans' imprisonment in Tartaros is being discussed:

> A bronze bulwark [*herkos*] is driven round it, and night is spread in triple rows about its throat, while upward push the roots of earth and barren sea.
> There the Titans, gods, are buried below the misty darkness, according to the plan of cloud-gathering Zeus, in a dank region at the ends of monstrous earth. For these there is no way out, and Poseidon has fitted doors of bronze, while a wall [*teikhos*] is set all about.

Once again we confront the image of the otherworld[35] as an enclosure, a fortified space surrounded by formidable walls. While the walls here are said to be bronze, this is only an updating of the inherited tradition in order to keep pace with improved technology, much as the walls of the Welsh otherworld became castle walls, Annwn being repeatedly described as a *caer*, a "castle," in *Preiddeu Annwn*, "The Spoils of Annwn," from the *Book of Taliesin*.[36] But from certain references in the *Iliad*, we can be fairly certain that a *teikhos* consisted mainly of earth, placed over a framework of beams and stones.[37]

Teikhos also occurs in an extremely interesting text describing, not the Greek realm of the dead, but that of the continental Celts. The source is Procopius, *De Bello Gothico* 4.20.42–46, in which he describes Brittia, the island to which he states souls of the dead are ferried (4.20.49–58).

> In the island of Brittia, long ago men built a great wall [*teikhos*], cutting the island into two large parts. On each side of this wall, the air and the earth, and all else are not alike. For to the east of that wall, the air is good, changing with the seasons, moderately warm in summer and cool in winter. And many men dwell there, living alongside other men, and the trees blossom in the proper seasons, bearing fruit, and the grain sprouts no worse than among

other peoples. Furthermore, that place appears to pride itself on its ample water. To the west, all is the opposite of that. Thus, truly, it is not possible for a man to live there for half an hour, while vipers and serpents, and countless other beasts of every sort have been allotted to that place. The people of that country say that the most extraordinary thing is that if any man crosses the wall, going to the other side, he dies immediately, being unable to bear the pestilential airs of that place. As for animals who go there, death straightaway meets and receives them.

While this wall has been compared to Hadrian's Wall,[38] this suggestion seems ill-founded. The wall described by Procopius divides Brittia along a north-south axis, not east-west, as does Hadrian's. What is more, it does not separate the Empire from unconquered territory, but the land of the living from the land of the dead, although both formulations may express in different ways the division between chaos and cosmos. But the wall of Brittia is a mythic wall, a wall of the imagination, that separates being and nonbeing, light and shadow. Life, correlated to the rising sun (the term used for "east" is *aniokhonta hēlion*) is cut off from death, correlated to the setting sun (*duonta*) by that wall, and on the side of death only vipers and serpents—the mythic magnifications of necrophagous worms[39]—are said to survive.

An Old Irish poem dating to the ninth century also makes mention of a similar wall surrounding the realm of the dead. Here, the poet Mael Muru (died 887) describes the "House of Donn," the island home to which all go upon death.[40]

> The House of Donn [*Tech Duinn*], who has a large following,
>   fortress [*dun*] of battle.
> Remarkable rock, red and keen;
> The battlement [*ráth*] of the king by the full, smooth sea,
> Place of a boar, nest of a high-ranking griffin.[41]

Three very precise words are used here which permit a clear description of Donn's Totenreich. These are: *dun* (line 1), a fortress complex made up of two parts, a *ráth* or earthen rampart (line 3) inside of which is a *tech,* a house (line 1), here said to be made of stone (line 2).[42]

Of these three, it is *ráth* which corresponds most closely to the examples adduced above. A *ráth* was almost always made of earth, and served as a defensive wall surrounding a king's residence.[43] This word is used in Irish texts to describe the fortifications surrounding Troy and the Greek camp, where *teîkhos* is used by Homer.[44] While its etymology is insecure, the basic notion underlying *ráth* would seem to be the piling up of earth in a mound, as is evident from the highly significant related terms in other Celtic languages: Middle Welsh *bed-rawt* and Modern Welsh *bedd-rodd,* "burial mound, grave," and Breton *bez-ret,* "burial place, cemetery."[45] Further, *ráth* itself is used on occasion to denote a grave mound or a burial area,[46] and in another poem by Mael Muru the House of Donn is described as a stone cairn across the sea.[47]

Consideration of Germanic evidence brings us full circle, for there the term used for the walls of Hel is directly related to the Sanskrit word with which we began, *garðr* and *grhá-*, both stemming from P-I-E *ghordho-s*.[48] For his part, Snorri tells that in the underworld (*Niflheim*), the goddess of death, Hel, "has a great lair, her walls [*garðar*] are remarkably high, and her gate remarkably huge" (*Gylfaginning* 34). Elsewhere, we are told that the gates are so high that the divine steed Sleipnir had to leap mightily to clear them.[49] But the most striking correspondence of all to the Vedic *mrnmáya- grhá-* is to be found in the *Fjǫlsvinnsmál*, a poetic-mnemonic map of the otherworld, which recounts a *descensus ad inferos* in the folkloric guise of Svipdag's quest for a beautiful maiden in a forbidden realm.[50] The description of that realm's defensive wall (*garðr*) appears in verses 11–12.

> [Svipdag said:] "Tell me, Fjǫlsvið, that which I'll ask you,
> For I would know
> What that wall is called, a more dangerous spot than which
> Men saw not among the gods."
> [Fjǫlsvið said:] "Gastropnir it is called and I built it
> Out of Clay-flood's limbs.
> I have so propped it that it will stand
> As long as this age lives."

The specification that this enclosing wall is built "out of Clay-flood's limbs" (*ór Leirbrimis limum*) is, as Hugo Gering recognized, a kenning which expresses the fact that the wall was made of clay, as the "name" *Leirbrimir* appears nowhere else in Norse mythology.[51] For its part, *Gastropnir*, the name of the wall, seems to mean "guest-squeezer," perhaps encoding a mythology in which those seeking unauthorized entrance became entrapped in the clay of the walls,[52] a fact which might help explain the name of the mysterious maiden who guards the bridge on the path to Hel, *Muðguðr*, literally "Slime-god, Mud-god."[53]

Certain definite conclusions emerge from this mass of data, itself occasionally sticky as clay. First, given the correspondence of Indic, Iranian, Greek, Roman, Celtic, and Germanic materials, we can state with confidence that the Proto-Indo-European otherworld was believed to have surrounding walls. Second, we can reconstruct two words that were used to denote those walls: *ghordho-s* (comparing Skt. *grhá-*, Av. *gərəδa-*, and ON *garðr*) and *dhᵉ/oįgho-s* (Av. *pairi.daēza-*, Gr. *teikhos*). In the separate Indo-European languages, other terms were later used for these otherworldly walls, and among them we have observed Indo-Iranian *saitu-*, Skt. *púr*, Av. *vara-*, Gk. *herkos*, Lat. *moenia* and *murus*, and OIr. *ráth*. None of these, it should be noted, are technical terms, but they are words that could be used of enclosing walls more generally, or of spaces encircled by such walls.[54]

In this image of the walls of the otherworld, there is nothing that is terribly rich or surprising, the walls serving to express the homely truth that the world of the dead is radically separated from the world of the living. One does not gradually slide from one realm to the other: a formidable threshold must be crossed. The statement may be profound, but it is not difficult to interpret.

What poses more difficulty for interpretation is the specification that these walls were made of earth, a point we can reconstruct from the correspondence of the *mṛnmáya- gṛhá-* of RV 7.89.1, the *garðr . . . ór Leirbrimis limum* of *Fjǫlsvinnsmál* 12, the *aiŋhā̊ zəmō pairi.daēzan* of Vd. 3.18, the description of Yima's *vara-* in Vd. 2.31, and the normal usage of such terms as Latin *moenia* and Old Irish *ráth*. The simplest view would be that this accurately reflects P-I-E building methods, but such a view is unsatisfactory for two reasons. First, archaeological evidence now indicates that P-I-E fortifications were made of stone, not earth, as had earlier been believed.[55] Second, if it could be shown that earthen walls were the norm, there would have been no need to semantically mark the otherworldly walls as themselves being made of earth: a P-I-E audience would automatically have made that assumption, and only walls which departed from the norm in some way would need semantic marking.

I thus reject the suggestion that, by stressing the earthen nature of the otherworld's walls, Proto-Indo-European priests, seers, or poets were implicitly comparing them to the normal walls of this world. Rather, I suspect that they had a very different comparison in mind, to another typically Indo-European construction made of earth and one particularly well suited to speculation on funerary geography: the kurgan or burial mound, the earthen walls of which served to separate the dead from the living forever after.[56]

The otherworld's walls are thus seen to be nothing more than the burial mound writ large; the otherworld, nothing more than the grave. Such was already suggested with regard to the Old Norse Hel by Gustav Neckel almost seventy years ago,[57] and almost a century ago by Abel Bergaigne, who, in considering RV 7.89.1—the text with which we began our inquiry—glossed "la maison de terre" (*mṛnmáya- gṛhá-*) as "la tombe."[58]

Notes

1. Manfred Mayrhofer, *Kurzgefasstes etymologisches Wörterbuch des Altindischen*, 3 vols. (Heidelberg: Carl Winter, 1956–76), 3:781.

2. Unless one accepts the suggestion of Karl Friedrich Geldner, *Der Rigveda*, 4 vols. (Cambridge: Harvard University Press, 1951), 1:253, and H. W. Bailey, "Hyaona," in H. Pilch and J. Thurow, eds., *Indo-Celtica: Gedächtnisschrift für Alf*

Sommerfelt (Munich: Hueber, 1972), that *duryoṇé . . . mṛdhí* of RV 1.124.7 ought to be emended to read *duryoṇé . . . mṛdí.*

3. Geldner, 2:260; idem, *Der Rigveda in Auswahl. 2. Kommentar* (Stuttgart: W. Kohlhammer, 1909), p. 115, where he cites RV 10.18.10–11 in support of this view.

4. Heinrich Zimmer, *Altindisches Leben* (Berlin: J. Weidmann, 1879), p. 407.

5. Tablet 7, Column 4, line 40. See the translations of Alexander Heidel, *The Gilgamesh Epic* (Chicago: University of Chicago Press, 1949), p. 60, or E. A. Speiser, in James Pritchard, ed., *Ancient Near Eastern Texts*, 3d ed. (Princeton: Princeton University Press, 1969), p. 87.

6. Mayrhofer, 2:675f., 3:781.

7. Mayrhofer, 1:344; Julius Pokorny, *Indogermanisches etymologisches Wörterbuch* (Bern: Francke, 1969). Comparison to Latin *urbs* (< *hurbs* < *ghordhos*), "city," has also been suggested by V. Georgiev, "Lat. urbs und orbis," *Indogermanische Forschungen* 56 (1938): 198–200.

8. Sir Monier Monier-Williams, *Sanskrit-English Dictionary* (Oxford: Oxford University Press, 1899), p. 361.

9. AV 18.1.54 is a repetition of RV 10.14.7, with only one significant alteration: for the *pathíbhiḥ pūrvyébhir*, "ancient paths" of the latter, *pathíbhiḥ pūryā́nair*, "paths leading to the fortress" is substituted. This substitution thus introduces a new term for the otherworld into Indic lore, but not a new idea, given the other evidence assembled here.

10. On *púr-*, see: Pokorny, p. 799; A. B. Keith and A. A. Macdonnell, *Vedic Index of Names and Subjects* (London: John Murray, 1912), 1:538–40; Carl Darling Buck, *A Dictionary of Selected Synonyms in the Principal Indo-European Languages* (Chicago: University of Chicago Press, 1949), p. 1308; and Emile Benveniste, *Le vocabulaire des institutions indo-européennes* (Paris: Minuit, 1969), 1:367. Comparison to Lithuanian *pilìs*, "castle, fortress" and Greek *polis*, which still shows the sense of "fortress" in *akro-polis* (see Thucydides 2.15), establishes the fundamental meaning as a fortified enclosure and not a city. The prevalence of earthen walls is noted by Keith and Macdonell, 1:539.

11. RV 6.47.2, 7.6.5.

12. E.g., *Śvetāśvatara Upaniṣad* 6.19, *Bṛhadāraṇyaka Upaniṣad* 4.4.22, *Muṇḍaka Upaniṣad* 2.2.5.

13. Mayrhofer, 3:501.

14. *sétu* occurs five times in the Ṛg Veda, for which Hermann Grassmann, *Wörterbuch zum Rigveda* (Leipzig: F. A. Brockhaus, 1873), p. 1578, lists three different meanings: (1) "Band, Fessel" for 8.67.8; (2) "Eine aus Stricken gebildete Vorrichtung zum Festhalten der Menschen oder Thiere" for 7.65.3, 9.73.4, and 10.67.4; and (3) "Brücke" for 9.41.2. There is nothing in the last passage to necessitate translation by "bridge," however, "boundary wall" being equally appropriate. Thus:

We think of the good passage over the boundary wall (*sétu-*) that is difficult to approach. . . .

15. In addition to RV 9.41.2, see 7.65.3, 10.67.4, both of which use the same formula: *ánṛtasya sétu-*, "the boundary wall of unright."

16. Pokorny, p. 892.

17. See Chapter 2 above, "On the Imagery of Paradise."

18. As noted by Geo Widengren, *Die Religionen Irans* (Stuttgart: W. Kohlhammer, 1965), p. 40.

19. Vd. 3.10 and 3.22 (*aŋro.mainyava- gərδa-*); Vd. 3.7 (*drujō gərδδa-*).

20. See, for instance, Strabo 11.11.3. On Iranian and Zoroastrian funerary customs, see Widengren, pp. 35–37; Mary Boyce, *A History of Zoroastrianism*, vol. 1 (Leiden: E. J. Brill, 1975), pp. 109–14.

21. See Arthur Christensen, *Essai sur la démonologie iranienne* (Copenhagen: Einar Munksgaard, 1941), pp. 32–33; A. V. Williams Jackson, *Zoroastrian Studies* (New York: Columbia University Press, 1928), pp. 91–101; Herman Lommel, *Die Religion Zarathustras* (Tübingen: J. C. B. Mohr, 1930), pp. 116–18.

22. Vd. 3.7, 19.44–45; *Greater Bundahišn* 9.10; *Dādestān ī Dēnīg* 33.5; *Šāyast nē Šāyast* 13.19. See my article "Arəzūra" in Carsten Colpe, ed., *Wörterbuch der Mythologie: Altiranische und zoroastrische Mythologie* (Stuttgart: Klett Verlag, 1974–82), pp. 287–88.

23. Vd. 19.44–45, 3.7, respectively.

24. *Mēnōg ī Xrad* 27.15.

25. *Aogəmadaēca* 28.

26. Vd. 2.20–42.

27. Chapter 3 above, "The Lord of the Dead."

28. Chapter 2, "On the Imagery of Paradise."

29. The development of the loanword in Greek is, ironically, quite unrelated to what we know of the Avestan term. It first appears in Xenophon's accounts of the Persian court to denote walled parks or pleasure gardens (*Cyropaedia* 1.3.14; *Anabasis* 1.2.7, 2.4.14; and most significantly, *Hellenica* 4.1.15). Later, the Septuagint uses *paradeisos* for the Garden of Eden, as in *Genesis* 2.8, and in the New Testament it is used for the abode of the blessed *paradeisos tou theou* [*Luke* 23.42], *paradeisos tōn dikaiōn* [Second Cor. 12.14]).

30. *Vīdēvdāt* 3.15–21. Note that *irista-* is the Ahuric term for "deceased," which indicates that the corpse-bearer in question handles only the bodies of the righteous. By contrast, when mention is made of his head, the daēvic term, *kamərəδa-* is used, designating him as an evil or polluted individual.

31. Mayrhofer, 2:62.

32. See the occurrences listed in Monier-Williams, p. 496.

33. I am grateful to W. W. Malandra for having called these data to my attention.

34. Pokorny, p. 244f.; Buck, p. 472; Hjalmar Frisk, *Griechisches etymologisches Wörterbuch* (Heidelberg: Carl Winter, 1973), 2:865f. Note also the related verbal forms of the nasal class, such as Latin *fingō*, etc., on which see Alois Walde, *Lateinisches etymologisches Wörterbuch*, ed. J. Hofmann (Heidelberg: Carl Winter, 1965), 1:50–52.

35. Hades is, of course, the usual Greek underworld. Here, Tartaros figures as the underworld beneath the underworld (see *Iliad* 8.13–16), and thus the most fitting place for the greatest of outcasts, the Titans. The imagery of the walls and gates, however, is taken from descriptions of Hades, whose gates are mentioned in *Iliad* 5.646, 8.367, 13.415, 23.71, and *Odyssey* 11.277. In general, on the Greco-Roman theme of the gates of death, see Hermann Usener, *Kleine Schriften* (Stuttgart: B. G. Teubner, 1912), 2:226–28.

36. Thus, Annwn is called *Kaer Siddi*, "the Faery Fortress," *Kaer Veddwit*, "the fortress of carousal," and *Kaer Wydyr*, "fortress of glass." See the discussion in Roger Sherman Loomis, *Wales and the Arthurian Legend* (Cardiff: University of Wales Press, 1956), pp. 131–78, esp. pp. 148, 164, and 165f.

Vergil also updates the construction of the walls of the underworld, adding iron towers, although one of the terms he uses to denote those walls (*moenia*) is usually used for walls built of earth and stone (*Aeneid* 6.548–54):

Aeneas looked back, and suddenly, under the cliff on the left
He saw broad battlements [*moenia*], triple surrounding walls [*muro*].
A devouring river surrounds them with boiling flames,
Tartarean Phlegethon; it sends the sonorous rocks flying.
A huge gate was opposite, with solid, adamantine columns.
No men have the strength, nor the celestials themselves, to raze it
    in war.
An iron tower rises to the heavens.

37. Thus, note *Iliad* 20.145, where *teikhos* is modified by *amphikhuton*, "poured round, heaped up," with reference to earthen construction. *Iliad* 12.28–29 mentions the framework of wood and stones (*themeilia . . . phitrōn kai laōn*) within the Greek defensive wall, but the frequent association of that wall (*teikhos*) to the ditch (*taphros*) built at the same time (8.177–79, 9.67, 12.4–6, 15.344–45, and 18.215, and esp. 7.435–40) strongly suggests that the earth excavated from the ditch was used to build up the wall. Note that a burial mound of earth (*tumbon . . . poieon exagogontes akriton ek pediou* 7.435–36) was erected at the same time as the ditch and wall, a coincidence which may be more than fortuitous.

38. Arthur C. L. Brown, *The Origin of the Grail Legend* (Cambridge: Harvard University Press, 1943), p. 341.

39. As suggested with regard to the serpents of Hel by Gustav Neckel, *Walhall* (Dortmund: Wilhelm Ruhfus, 1913), p. 52.

40. On Donn and Tech Duinn, see Kuno Meyer, "Der irische Totengott und die Toteninsel," *Sitzungsberichte der preussischen Akademie der Wissenschaften* (1919): 537–46, and Chapter 3 above, "The Lord of the Dead."

41. Text in Meyer, p. 539.

42. Osborn Bergin, general ed., *Dictionary of the Irish Language* (Dublin: Royal Irish Academy, 1913–76), vol. D, p. 449.

43. Ibid., vol. R, p. 17.

44. *Togail Troi*, 197 and 1271.

45. Pokorny, p. 843f. His tentative derivation from a P-I-E verbal form **pra-*, "to bend, to bow," rests only on comparison with the semantically distant Latin *prāvus* and *prātum*, and must thus be rejected.

46. *Scél Baili Binnbérlaig*, ed., Kuno Meyer, in *Révue Celtique* 13 (1892): p. 222, line 27 and 36; *Lebor na hUidre* 2833; *Metrical Dindshenchas* 3.130.28.

47. The reference is specifically to the stone house (*tech*) within the earthen rampart (*ráth*). The text is cited above in Chapter 3.

48. Pokorny, p. 444; Jan de Vries, *Altnordisches etymologisches Wörterbuch* (Leiden: E. J. Brill, 1961), p. 156.

49. *Gylfaginning* 49.

50. For another instance where the *Fjǫlsvinnsmál* preserves the Proto-Indo-European mythology of the otherworld more faithfully than any other Germanic text, see Chapter 7 above, "The Hellhound."

51. Hugo Gering, *Kommentar zu den Liedern der Edda* (Leipzig: Waisenhaus, 1927), p. 411.

52. Ibid., following the argument of F. Detter and R. Heinzel, *Saemundar Edda* (Leipzig: G. Wigard, 1903), 2:642.

53. *Gylfaginning* 49.

54. See the discussion in Buck, pp. 462–63, 472–73, 1403–4.

55. See Marija Gimbutas, "Proto-Indo-European Culture," in G. Cardona, H. M. Hoenigswald, and A. Senn, eds., *Indo-European and Indo-Europeans* (Philadelphia: University of Pennsylvania Press, 1970), pp. 164–68, contra the opinion of, for example, Otto Schrader, *Reallexikon der indogermanischen Altertumskunde,* 2d ed. by A. Nehring (Berlin: de Gruyter, 1929), 2:46–50, who followed lines laid out by Rudolf Meringer for the most part.

56. On the Kurgan, see Marija Gimbutas, "An Archaeologist's View of PIE in 1975," *Journal of Indo-European Studies* 2 (1974): 293–94.

57. Neckel, *Walhall,* p. 52.

58. Abel Bergaigne, *La religion védique* (Paris: Honoré Champion, 1878–83), 3:155.

THE TWO PATHS

Between 1977 and 1982, much of my time was given over to the set of researches in which I considered certain details of myth that crop up repeatedly in accounts of the otherworld that are written in the various Indo-European languages, ranging from the ancient hymns of the Ṛg Veda (1200 B.C.?) to Russian folksongs collected as recently as the nineteenth century of our era. In this undertaking, my general intent was to reconstruct in piecemeal fashion the presumably common antecedent beliefs that informed and were preserved in these recurrent images of funerary geography: beliefs regarding the nature of life and death, time and mortality, being and nonbeing.

At first these researches unfolded happily, resulting in the publication of those articles which, thanks to the efforts of Wendy Doniger, have been brought together in Chapters 2–8 of this book. Such difficulties as I encountered tended to be difficulties of detail, and most of these ultimately yielded to fairly conventional methods of analysis. The case was different, however, when I turned to what would be the last of my inquiries along these lines, in which I examined a mythic motif that is extremely well known and well attested. This is the image of the path which the dead travel from this world into the beyond, or—to put it more precisely—the two paths, for it is regularly told that the path reaches a critical bifurcation, from which two alternate routes diverge.[1] One of these, characterized as well lit, straight, and easy to travel, ascends to a pleasant celestial otherworld, where one dwells happily, feasting in the company of the gods. The other path, predictably enough, contrasts to the first in its particulars, being depicted as dark, dreary, twisting, and treacherous, as it descends to a gloomy underworld marked by tedium, suffering, filth, and bad food.[2]

This is the picture one finds, for example, in descriptions of the "God-way" (goðvegr) and "Hell-way" (helvegr) of the Eddas, which nineteenth-century scholars rightly compared to the "Path of the Gods" (devayána) and "Path of the Fathers" (pitryána) of the Vedas and Upaniṣads,[3] and to these, other data may easily be added. Zoroastrian eschatology gives a prominent position to the "Bridge of Separation" (cinvatō pərətu-), to which all the deceased journey, and over which the righteous ascend to the "Best Existence" or "House of the Song," while liars are cast down to the "Worst Existence" or the "House of the Lie."[4] Similarly, Plato tells of a "crossroads from which extend two paths, one to the Isles of the Blessed and one to Tartaros,"[5] and a like pattern is evident in the "Orphic" tablets of the Fourth century B.C., in which initiates are provided with the responses they must give to guardians in the below in order that they may gain access to the favored of two paths.[6] Other Greek sources, including Parmenides' Proem[7] and the celebrated parable of "Herakles at the Crossroads,"[8] contain the same mythic image in slightly altered form, and should Vergil, *Aeneid* 6.540–43, preserve anything in the way of old Italic traditions, that text ought also be taken into account.

The documentation of this pattern is thus abundant, and its concrete details are fairly clear. What is *not* clear, however, is what it all means. For as consistent as the sources are in their description of these two paths, they are equally inconsistent in their description of the principles that determine which of the dead come to travel the preferable path and enjoy the preferable *post-mortem* fate, while others are consigned to an alternate route and destination.

Normally in such circumstances, one looks for shared traits in the various sources—"correspondences"—on the strength of which a prototype may be posited. That prototype is then taken to be both logically and historically anterior to the attested data, among which some exemplars or "reflexes" are seen to derive more faithfully and others with ever greater transformations of the prototypical pattern. In this case, however, the data resist any simple and straightforward application of this method and serve ultimately to call its theoretical presuppositions into question.

Several texts identify ethical criteria as the basis on which the dead are set on one path or the other, but these consistently bear the mark of religious reform or novel lines of speculation. Such is the case, for instance, in the passage mentioned above where Plato describes the crossroads from which those who have passed their lives "justly and piously" (*dikaiōs . . . kai hosiōs*) proceed to the Isles of the Blessed, while those who lived "unjustly and in ungodly fashion" (*adikōs kai atheōs*) wend their way to Tartaros.[9] In constructing this picture, Plato drew consciously upon and alluded openly to several sources that would have been familiar to his audience, all of which presented rationales quite different from that which he articulated, for nowhere prior to the fifth century is there evident any consideration of moral issues in eschatological discourses. Rather, the older texts generally place only the greatest of heroes, i.e., those distinguished by their noble lineages and their deeds in war, in the preferred otherworldly realm. What is more, the oldest text of all sets in the paradisal Elysian Fields those who are connected by kinship to the gods, even when (as in the case of Menelaos), that kinship was established only through marriage.[10] Moreover, Plato acknowledged the innovative nature of his views by inscribing them within an account of how it was that moral criteria were introduced as a radical departure from an earlier system of judging the dead. For in the primordial reign of Kronos, as he whimsically relates, the dead came to their place of judgment fully clothed, and since the living at that time had foreknowledge of their death, many were able to present themselves in such elaborate, luxurious, and impressive attire as to secure themselves a favorable afterlife on the strength of their appearance alone. This state of affairs, however, was set to rights with the onset of Zeus's reign, so that humans no longer know when they will die, and the deceased approach naked to their last judgment.[11]

Similarly innovative is a passage from Snorri Sturluson's *Prose Edda,* in which moral criteria are made the basis for assignment of the dead to one realm or the other:

> It was the greatest deed when he [sc. Óðinn] made a man and gave him a soul, which shall live and never perish, although the corpse will rot into earth or burn into ashes. And all men who were upright and well-mannered live there with him, in that place called Gimlé or Vingólf, while wicked men fare to Hel and thence to Mist-hel, which is below it and is the ninth realm. (*Gylfaginning* 3)

That the ideas expressed in this text reflect the conversion of Iceland to Christianity some two centuries prior to its composition is evident, not only from the neat congruence of its contents with Christian doctrine, but also from a strategic detail of Snorri's discourse. For not only did he use the relatively rare name *Gimlé* in this passage, a term which could easily be associated to that employed for the Christian heaven (*himill* ~ *himinn,* of which *Gimlé* is an old frozen dative),[12] but in so doing he also avoided the usual name given to Óðinn's paradise: *Valhalla.*

This is particularly important, for that name itself presents an alternative ideology considerably older than the ethically based eschatology we have been considering. Thus, *Val-halla* denotes heaven as the "hall of the battle-slain," a view attested in the *Poetic Edda,* and which Snorri acknowledges elsewhere, saying "all the men who have fallen in battle since the beginning of the world have now come to Óðinn in Valhalla."[13] Moreover, this realm—to which one ascends via the God-way—was set in the starkest contrast to Niflhel or Niflheim ("Mist-realm"), the underworld ruled by the dark goddess Hel, to whom are brought, via the Hel-way, "those men who die of disease and those who die of old age" (*Gylfaginning* 34). In this cosmology, then, it was the mode of death—specifically the question of whether or not one died a proper warrior's death—that made all the difference.

In Snorri as in Plato, when ethical criteria appear as the basis for division of the dead, we encounter an innovative ideology rather than one which derives in both places from a common ancestral tradition. The same could be said of Zoroastrian texts in which like ideas follow from the prophet's reform. Somewhat more useful for reconstructive research, but not without its problems, is a set of texts in which discrimination among the dead is based upon their relative states of knowledge and ignorance. Consider *Yasna* 31.6ab:

> The Best shall be for him, the knower who speaks to me
> The right formula, which is of truth, wholeness, and
>   immortality.

Here, "the Best"—a techical term for the heavenly realms[14]—is reserved for "the knower" (Av. *vīdvā̊*, singular nominative of *vīdvah-*), a term that recurs in Parmenides' Proem, where, after describing his celestial ascent via a bifurcated path, the author speaks of himself as "a knower," using the Greek term *eidota*,[15] singular accusative of *eidōs*, which corresponds precisely to Avestan *vīdvah-* and other cognate terms (Sanskrit *vidvás-*, Gothic *weitwōþs* [= Greek *martys*]), on the strength of which may be posited P-I-E *weyd-wōt-s-*, a perfect participle formed from the verb *weyd-* "to know, to comprehend, to see."[16] Yet this lexical congruence notwithstanding, there is a significant difference between the kinds of knowledge that are at issue in Parmenides and in the Gāthic Avesta, for whereas the former text refers to abstract knowledge, particularly in the realm of ontology and epistemology, the latter refers to technical mastery of sacred speech, which permits its possessor to "speak the right formula, which is of truth, wholeness, and immortality" (*vaocat haiθīm mąθrəm yim haurvatātō ašahyā amərətātascā*).[17] Further, such Indic evidence as can be adduced makes things more complicated still. For while one finds mention of "the knower of the god-way paths" (*vidvā́n pathá. . . devayā́nān*) in *Ṛg Veda* 10.98.11c, where the same term for "knower" is once again used (Skt. *vidvā́n*, singular nominative from *vidvás*), this phrase refers not to some paragon of humanity on his way to heaven, but rather to the god Agni, who is invoked to lead a distinctly *nonknowing* human to that place among the gods which he deserves, not by virtue of knowledge, but as the result of having performed sacrifice on an absolutely massive scale. The verse in full reads as follows:

> Present these ninety thousand [cattle?] to Indra the bull as his portion, O Agni.
> As a right knower of the god-way paths, you must place Aulāna [sc. the patron of the sacrifice] in heaven among the gods.

Further, that humans are *incapable* of knowing the heavenly paths, and are thus forced to rely on Agni as the god who knows, is asserted in RV 10.2.3:

> We have trod the path of the gods [*devā́nām . . . pánthām*] as far as we are able to advance.
> Agni, the knower [*vidvā́n*], should sacrifice. He truly is the presiding priest: he should arrange the ceremonies and sacred occasions.

Later Indic sources, particularly the Upaniṣads, dispute this view of things and argue that "he who knows thus" (*ya ittham viduḥ, yo evam veda*) is indeed capable of winning the "Path of the Gods" by virtue of his knowledge. But the knowledge in question is once more quite different from any that appears in the other texts we have considered. For according to the Upaniṣads, it is knowledge of the self (*vidyayātmānam* [*Praśna Upaniṣad* 1.10]) and the ascetic discipline through which such knowledge may be gained that is so valorized, while the sacrificial practice favored by earlier texts is here denigrated as leading to the lesser "Path of the Fathers," which brings rebirth, not liberation or immortality.[18]

The problem, as my training and past experience led me to pose it, was how to reconstruct a prototype that could account for myths that grant the better afterworld to those who in life had variously performed sacrifice, spoken sacred formulae (or simply the truth), gained knowledge of the self through ascetic endeavors, died heroically in battle, received initiation, or enjoyed kinship relations with the gods. In frustration, after producing a sixty-eight-page manuscript filled with idiocies and contradictions, I finally abandoned the project, and turned to other, less maddening endeavors. In recent years, however, I have come to see that the problem lies less in the nature of these specific data than in the theory and method which I brought to them. In particular, it now strikes me that the attempt to reconstruct a prototypical ("Proto-Indo-European") form from which all attested variants can ultimately be derived may actually obscure much of what is most fascinating and important in myth. For while this stance acknowledges that the contents of a given myth will vary as it is recounted by different persons over time and across space, such variation is treated as a problem—or better, *the* problem—to be undone by scholarly research: research that takes as its task the restoration of some hypothetical "original". Such research thus aims, in effect, to reverse historic processes and to recapture a primordial (and ahistoric) moment of unity, harmony, and univocal perfection. In its very presuppositions, such research—it now seems to me—is itself a species of myth and ritual, based upon a romantic "nostalgia for paradise," to cite Mircea Eliade's famous formulation.[19]

Since abandoning my work on funerary geography, I have come to think of myth in rather different ways than I did previously, and have sought to define it as an authoritative mode of narrative discourse that may be instrumental in the ongoing construction of social borders and hierarchies, which is to say, in the construction of society itself. As such, myth has tremendous importance and is often a site of contestation between groups and individuals whose differing versions of social ideals and reality are inscribed within the rival versions of the myths they recount.[20]

Returning to the theme of the two paths, I would now stress that this mythic image is, in effect, nothing other than an idealized representation of human hierarchies as if these contingent systems were grounded in the nature of a cosmos whose structure and operations are depicted in such a way as to endorse and reward the values characteristic of particular social groups or strata. This is clear, for instance, in those Greek texts which grant the Isles of the Blessed to heroes and the Old Norse sources that make death in battle the sine qua non for admission to Valhalla, variants which assert and help to construct a privileged position for warriors.[21] No less tendentious, however, are those texts that reserve heavenly rewards for "knowers" of whatever sort, insofar as knowledge was the prerogative of priests just as death in battle was that of warriors, to judge from priestly titles built upon the verb "to know" (e.g., Old Irish *druí* [< **dru-wid-*]; Old Prussian *waidelotte*),[22] as well as those which identify priests as "makers of the [heavenly] path" (Latin *ponti-fex*, Sanskrit *pathi-kṛt-*).[23]

In the confrontation of these two ideologies—salvation by battle-death and salvation by knowledge—we may thus perceive not regional variation or temporal change, but arguments advanced on behalf of rival social groups which competed for privilege and position not only in this world but also in the beyond, their competition over that beyond being a part of their competition in the here and now. In addition to these arguments, others were also possible, as for instance arguments about precisely what kind of knowledge was most salvific, or arguments that claimed preferential this-and-otherworldly status for those of noble families who could successfully assert their kinship with the gods, or for those of whatever social station who could afford to commit their time, wealth, and energy to sacrificial practice, ascetic endeavors, the gaining of specialized initiation, or "simple" ethical conduct. And for all that it may be a historically innovative line of argument, the last of these, as my quotation marks signal, is hardly so simple as it seeks to appear, for that which is "ethical" is not just *given* by nature or revelation but is constituted through discourses such as those of Plato, Snorri, and Zarathustra, in which specific and contingent human preferences are represented as normative, transcendent, and even salvific.

Studies of myth, I am now convinced, ought be attentive to the multiple competing voices that find expression in differing variants, and to the struggles they wage in and through mythic discourse, a position that derives more from Gramsci than from Lévi-Strauss. Beyond this, I believe one must relate any discourse to the tensions characteristic of that society in which it circulates. In the case at hand, this means that one does better to travel the lower path of inquiry into the social and material world in which eschatological, soteriological, and cosmological beliefs operate than to follow the supposedly higher path that remains within the heavenly worlds these beliefs describe. As a result of these changes in my perspective, I am less happy with the chapters which make up the first part of this book than I once was, and have agreed to their republication only at Wendy Doniger's urging. In them, I hear my voice of the past: a voice which a valued friend and an accomplished scholar assures me still has real value, but a voice with which my voice of the present—better represented in the chapters that follow—is in conflict. Of these competing voices and different paths, let the reader make what he or she will.

Notes

1. This point is variously referred to as a place of crisis (Greek *krisis*, Plato *Gorgias* 524A), one of separation (Greek *skhisis*, Plato *Phaedo* 107E, Avestan *cinvat-*), a turning point (Sanskrit *vyâvartanam, Chandogya Upaniṣad* 5.3.2), or a crossroads (Greek *triodos, Phaedo* 107E, *Gorgias* 524A).

2. For the miserable fare served in the underworld, which contrasts to the perpetual banquets of the above, note *Yasna* 31.20 and 53.6, where "evil food" (*duš.x*ᵛ*arəθa-*) is said to await liars in the beyond, and the specification of *Gylfaginning* 34 that "Hunger is the dish of Hel" (*Hungr diskr hennar* [sc. *Heljar*]).

3. The *helvegr* is mentioned in *Vǫluspá* 47 and 52, and described in detail in *Gylfaginning* 49, whereas the *goðvegr* is named in *Hyndluljóð* 5 and described (without being named) in *Helgakviða Hundingsbana* II 49. Vedic texts in which the *devayána* and *pitṛyána* are mentioned include *Ṛg Veda* 10.2.3 and 7, 10.88.15, and *Atharva Veda* 15.12.5. Relevant for the *devayána* are also RV 1.46.11, 1.162.21, 3.54.5, 7.76.2, 10.98.11; for the *pitṛyána*, RV 10.14.1–2 and 7–10.

4. The most important texts from the Gāthic Avesta are *Yasna* 46.10–11, 51.13–15, and 31.20. Also of interest is the more fully mythologized picture given in the Younger Avesta (*Vīdēvdāt* 19.28–33, *Hadoxt Nask* 2) and the Pahlavi texts (e.g. *Dādestān ī Dēnīg* 20–21, *Mēnōg ī Xrad* 2.115, *Dēnkart* 9.20.3–4). On these images, see Marijan Molé, "Daēnā, le pont Cinvat et l'initiation dans le Mazdéisme," *Revue de l'histoire des religions* 157 (1960): 155–85, and Herman Lommel, "Some Corresponding Conceptions in Old India and Iran," *Dr. Modi Memorial Volume* (Bombay: Fort Printing Press, 1930), pp. 263–69.

5. *Gorgias* 523A–524A. Compare *Phaedo* 107E–108A and *Republic* 614B–C, where multiple paths and crossroads are also mentioned, but are described in somewhat different fashions.

6. See particularly the tablets recovered at Petelia and Thurii, listed as Fragments 32a and 32f in Otto Kern, *Orphicorum Fragmenta*, 2d ed. (Berlin: Weidmann, 1963), pp. 104–5 and 108, respectively. A different pattern is represented in the older Hipponion Tablet, on which see Gunther Zuntz, "Die Goldlamelle von Hipponion," *Wiener Studien* 10 (1976): 129–51, esp. pp. 137–39, and Walter Burkert, *Orphism and Bacchic Mysteries: New Evidence and Old Problems of Interpretation* (Berkeley: The Center for Hermeneutical Studies in Hellenistic and Modern Culture, 1977), pp. 1–10. The very fact of initiation at Eleusis, rather than any knowledge granted to initiates, was claimed to secure a preferential state in the afterworld, as asserted in the *Homeric Hymn to Demeter* 480–82.

7. Hermann Diels, *Die Fragmente der Vorsokratiker*, 5th ed., revised by Walther Kranz (Berlin: Weidmann, 1934), Fragment B1.

8. This allegoric narrative attributed to Prodikos is preserved in Xenophon's *Memo-*

rabilia 2.1. Although the action is set entirely within this world and there is no question of the hero's death or *post-mortem* fate, many of the details—particularly the two paths and the two women—are strongly reminiscent of Germanic and Iranian funerary geography. See, further, Jan Bergman, "Zum Zwei-Wege Motiv: Religionsgeschichtliche und exegetische Bemerkungen," *Svensk Exegetisk Årsbok* 41/2 (1976–77): 27–56.

    9. *Gorgias* 523A–524A.

    10. *Odyssey* 4.561–69. Plato also drew upon Hesiod, *Works and Days* 167–73, where the Isles of the Blessed are reserved for heroes (*toi . . . olbioi hēroēs*, line 172), and on Pindar, *Olympia* 2.56–80, the earliest text in which ethical qualifications are raised for admission to the favored afterlife. Pindar's discussion is extremely complex, and itself draws on disparate traditions. For while he places conventional heroes—Peleus, Kadmos, and Akhilles—in the Isle (singular) of the Blessed and specifies that the last of these gained entry as a result of the intercession of his mother (the goddess Thetis) and Zeus (lines 78–80), Pindar also states that those faithful to their oaths (*euorkiais*, line 66) and those who have endured three life-cycles while holding their souls apart from injustice (lines 68–70) may gain admission. Heroism, kinship with the gods, perfection in speech-acts, and ethical conduct thus all intermingle, and the last of these ideas appears in the context of reincarnation beliefs that reflect Pythagorean influence.

    11. The political import of this fable is made clear in *Republic* 615C–616A, where Plato observes that it is usually tyrants who are the worst offenders in life and thus deserve the sternest judgment in the otherworld. Presumably, it was just such persons who in the reign of Kronos were able to escape the fate to which their acts, rather than their dress and station, entitled them.

    12. Richard Cleasby and Gudbrand Vigfusson, *An Icelandic-English Dictionary,* 2d ed., revised by Sir William A. Craigie (Oxford: Clarendon Press, 1957), p. 200. Gimlé is mentioned only once in the *Poetic Edda: Vǫluspá* 64, where it is identified as that heaven which emerges after the cosmic catastrophe of the Ragnarǫk, i.e. the new heaven for the worthy people (*dyggvar dróttir*) of a new era. See, further, Paul Schach, "Some Thoughts on Völuspá," *Edda: A Collection of Essays,* ed. Robert J. Glendinning and Haraldur Bessason (Winnipeg: University of Manitoba Press, 1983), 109–10. Vingólf is paired with Valhalla in *Gylfaginning* 20, and in chapter 14 of the same text is said to be ruled over by the goddesses. It thus appears to be that otherworld to which particularly favored women were admitted, possibly those who died in childbirth.

    13. *Gylfaginning* 38. *Gylfaginning* 20 further correlates the name *Valhalla* to Oðinn's epithet "Father of the battle-slain" (*Valfǫðr*), explaining "because his adopted sons are all those who fall in battle". See also *Grímnismál* 8 and the classic treatment of Gustav Neckel, *Walhall* (Dortmund: Wilhelm Ruhfus, 1913).

    14. Avestan *vahišta-* (the superlative of *vohu-* "good") is used with eschatological reference both as a substantive and as an adjective modifying such as nouns as *ahu-* "existence" and *mižda-* "reward." See Christian Bartholomae, *Altiranisches Wörterbuch* (Wiesbaden: Otto Harrassowitz, 1904), col. 1400, and such passages as *Yasna* 30.4, 32.16, 44.2, 47.5, and 49.9. The Middle Iranian derivatives from *vahišta*—Pahlavi *wahišt,* Manichaean Parthian and Manichaean Persian *whyšt*—are the standard terms used to denote "paradise."

15. Fragment B1, line 3. With regard to the shape of the path, Parmenides recounts his passage along "the much-discussed path . . . of the goddess" (*hodon . . . poly-phēmon . . . daimonos*, Fragment B1, lines 2–3) to "the gates of the pathways [plural!] of Night and of Day" (*pylai Nyktos te kai Hēmatos eisi keleuthōn*, Fragment B1, line 11), which he later identifies with the two divergent "paths of inquiry" (*hodoi . . . dizēsios*, Fragment B2, line 2), i.e. the "Way of Truth" and the "Way of Seeming."

16. On the semantics of this verb, see Jaan Puhvel, *Analecta Indoeuropea* (Innsbruck: Institut für Sprachwissenschaft der Universität Innsbruck, 1981), 312–15.

17. Note that the way of moral conduct which entitles one to cross the "Bridge of Separation" and ascend to heaven is called the "path of truth" (*ašahyā . . . paθō*) in *Yasna* 51.13, to which compare the "path of truth" (*pánthā ṛtásya*) that is equated with "the road of heaven" (*śrutír diváḥ*) in *Ṛg Veda* 1.46.11. Mastery of sacred speech-acts is also made a criterion for admission to the favored afterworld in Pindar, *Olympia* 2.66, treated briefly in note 10 above.

18. See, for example, *Chandogya Upaniṣad* 5.10.1–7, *Praśna Upaniṣad* 1.9–10, *Kauṣika Upaniṣad* 1.2–3, and *Bṛhadāranyaka Upaniṣad* 6.2.15–16.

19. Mircea Eliade, *The Myth of the Eternal Return* (Princeton: Princeton University Press, 1954).

20. Bruce Lincoln, *Discourse and the Construction of Society: Comparative Studies of Myth, Ritual, and Classification* (New York: Oxford University Press, 1989), Chapters 1, 2, 3.

21. Note also *Hárbardsljód* 24, where the distinction between the battle-slain and the died-in-bed is explicitly correlated to the social distinction between nobles (*jarla*) and their servant subordinates (*præla kyn*). Here, Oðinn, in the disguise of a ferryman, taunts Thórr as follows:

> I was at the Land of the Slain   and I aided in battles.
> I urged on the kings,   and never made peace.
> Oðinn has the nobles   who fall in battle,
>   And Thórr has the servant-kind.

22. On *druí*, see Christian-J. Guyonvarc'h, "Notes d'etymologie et de lexicographie gauloises et celtiques, V.16., Les noms celtiques du 'chêne,' du 'druide,' et du roitelet," *Ogam* 12 (1960): 49–58; on *waidelotte*, Reinhold Trautmann, *Die altpreussischen Sprachdenkmäler* (Göttingen: Vandenhoeck and Ruprecht, 1910), 454–55. Cf. Old Russian *ved'ma* "witch," Old Norse *vitki* "wizard," Old High German *wīzzago*, and Old English *wítega*, "prophet, soothsayer," from the latter of which we have English *wizard* and *witch*. Note also the observation of Otto Schrader, *Reallexikon der indogermanische Altertumskunde*, 2d ed. revised by Alfons Nehring (Berlin: Walter de Gruyter, 1929), 2:202: "Die verbreiteste und ohne Zweifel altertümlichste Auffassung des Priesters in den idg. Sprachen ist also die vornehmlich an die Wurzel *vid-*, *void-* gebundene als des 'Wissenden' . . . ".

23. See the discussions of R. J. Kent, "The Vedic Paths of the Gods and the Roman Pontifex," *Classical Philology* 8 (1913): 317–26, Gustav Herbig, "Zur Vorgeschichte der römischen pontifices," *Zeitschrift für vergleichende Sprachforschung* 47 (1919): 211–32, and Judith P. Hallett, "'Over Troubled Waters': The Meaning of the Title Pontifex," *Transactions of the American Philological Association* 101 (1970): 219–27.

PART TWO

WAR, SACRIFICE, AND THE SCIENCE
OF THE BODY

TEN

HOMERIC *LYSSA:* "WOLFISH RAGE"

Over the years, a moderate amount of ink has been spilled on the topic of the Homeric feminine substantive *lyssa* (Attic: *lytta*), a term meaning "1. martial fury" and "2. rabies".[1] Most discussion has focussed on etymology and for the most part agreement has been reached that *lyssa* represents an underlying pre-Greek **lyk-ia*.[2] It is here that the argument begins, however, and two camps have emerged. On the one hand, Havers, Specht, Lasso de la Vega, and Theander have wished to derive from Indo-European **leuk-* "to shine, light,"[3] while Ernout, Hartmann, and Porzig have taken it as formed from Gk. *lykos*, "wolf" < I-E **wlkʷo-*.[4] Frisk has prudently refrained from passing judgment on the case, as has Liddell-Scott, while Pokorny has accepted the derivation from **leuk-*.[5] While the feminine gender has caused problems for some authors,[6] there is no real difficulty here. The term is a derivative in **-ya*, a suffix which forms feminines and abstracts.[7] Schwyzer has shown it to be an abstract like *phoxa*, "panic,"[8] and one might also add *aza*, "dryness," and *kissa*, "envy of a pregnant woman," as points of comparison. One need not see them as personifications of some female being or spirit,[9] but can merely take them as terms that express an abstract entity such as an emotion or a general state of being.

This having been established, it may be instructive to examine the occurrences of *lyssa* in the epic, something which—surprisingly—has not been done by any of the authors cited above. The word occurs three times in the *Iliad*, none in the *Odyssey*. The first occurrence comes when Odysseus and Aias have gone to Akhilles, attempting to persuade him to reenter the battle. Odysseus, describing the desperate situation, tells him:

> . . . Hektor, exulting greatly in his might,
> Rages vehemently, relying on Zeus and holding no one in
>   respect,
> Neither men nor gods. And the powerful *lyssa* has entered him.

> *Iliad* 9.237–383

At the conclusion of the same speech, Odysseus mentions *lyssa* again, now trying to tempt Akhilles with thoughts of possible glory:

> For now you might take Hektor, as he would come very near
>   to you,

Possessing the deadly *lyssa*, and he thinks that not one of the
Danaans
Whom the ships brought hither is like unto himself.

Iliad 9.304–6

The third occurrence is when Akhilles storms in front of Troy:

Thus he [Priam] spoke, and they loosened the gates and thrust
back the bolts,
And the gates spreading produced light. Now Apollo
Himself sprang forth in order to ward off destruction from the
Trojans.
And straight into the high-walled city,
Rough in the throat with thirst, and dusty from the plain,
They fled. He [Akhilles] followed impetuously with his spear,
and powerful *lyssa*
Unrelentingly possessed his heart.

Iliad 21.537–43

Two features are particularly vivid in these passages. First, the hero characterized by *lyssa* is viewed as absolutely irresistible. In 9.239, Hektor yields to no one, man or god; in 9.305, he thinks none of the Greeks his equal; and in 21.542, the entire Trojan army breaks and runs before the might of the raging Akhilles. In their fury, both heroes run out of control: Akhilles is described as acting impetuously (*sphedanon*), and Hektor is made so bold that he might even venture to do battle with Akhilles while in this state, for he feels no man can oppose him. Odysseus tries to make use of this to tempt Akhilles into battle, but there is no assurance that he would indeed be able to stop Hektor when the latter is possessed of *lyssa*. It is worth noting that only the two greatest heroes of the epic take on this state, and it increases even their great powers immensely.

Having mentioned possession, we are brought to our second point. It is by no means clear that the hero possesses the *lyssa* or whether the *lyssa* possesses him. In one of our texts, the verb *ekhō,* "to possess," appears as a participle in the nominative case, referring to Hektor and governing *lyssa* in the accusative (9.350). But, in another, *ekhō* appears as a finite verb with *lyssa* in the nominative and the heart (*kēr*) of Achilles as its object (21.542). The powerful (*kraterē*)[10] *lyssa* is again the subject in our third text, and is said to have "entered, made its way into" (*de-dyken < dyō*) Hektor. The usages are ambiguous, and if they are to be understood, we must bear in mind that they refer to an ambiguous situation, a state of wild, uncontrolled rage which is possessed by certain highly gifted warriors, but which also possesses them. This uncontrolled nature of the state can be seen in the adverbs used in connection with the deeds of the man who is acting under its influence: *ekpaglōs,* "vehemently," and *aien,* "unrelentingly."

This phenomenon of a warrior frenzy which a man both possesses and is possessed by is not unknown in ethnography. The rage of the Kwakiutl cannibal dancer, and the *amok* of the Malays are well-known examples.[11] But it is particularly well documented among the various branches of the Indo-Europeans, each of which seems to have given its own peculiar name to this specific state of furor.[12] Perhaps a few examples will show their similarity to the Homeric *lyssa.* First, there is the classic description of the Germanic *Wut,* from the *Ynglingasaga,* chapter 6:

> They went without shields, and were made as dogs or wolves, and
> bit on their shields, and were as strong as bears or bulls; men they
> slew, and neither fire nor steel would deal with them; and this is
> what is called the fury [*wut*] of the berserkr.[13]

The Celts called this state *Ferg,* and it is seen most clearly in the great Irish hero Cúchulainn. In one passage of the *Táin Bó Cúailnge,* the charioteer of a prospective opponent relates a dream to his master, in which he beheld the might of the great Cúchulainn:

> There's a skilled Hound at the helm,
> A fine chariot warrior,
> A wild hawk hurrying his horses southward
> Surely it is Cúchulainn's
> chariot horses coming.
> Who says he is not coming to our defeat?
> I had a dream last year:
> Whoever at the time appointed
> Opposes the Hound on the slope, let him beware.
> The Hound of Emain Macha,
> In all his different shapes,
> The Hound of plunder and battle
> —I hear him, and he hears.[14]

For the Iranians, this fury was known as *aēšma,* and was soundly condemned in the reform of Zarathustra.[15] But descriptions of it still remain, particularly with regard to the god Vərəθraγna, the incarnation of aggressive victory.[16]

> Mithra, lord of wide pastures we worship . . . in front of whom
> flies Ahura-created Vərəθraγna in the shape of a wild, aggressive,
> male boar with sharp fangs and sharp tusks, a boar that kills at one
> blow, is unapproachable, grim, speckle-faced and strong, iron of
> foot, iron of hand, with iron tendons, an iron tail and iron jaws; as
> he catches up with opponents, beset by passion—simultaneously
> by manly valour—, he knocks them down with a toss: he does not
> even think he has struck, nor has he the impression he is hitting
> anybody, until he has smashed even the vertebrae, the pillars of
> life, even the vertebrae, the springs of vitality.[17]

For all their differences, these texts do have many features in common, but perhaps most striking of all is that in each case the warrior possessed of the martial frenzy is depicted as a wild beast. Moreover, this is not just description, they are truly experienced as *being* beasts of prey. The Norse *berserkr* (lit. "those of the bear's shirt") and *úlfhednar* ("those of the wolf's head") dressed and acted as bears and wolves.[18] Cúchulainn was felt to be a baleful hound in battle, and Vərəθraγna a raging boar[19]—as was Herakles, in Hesiod's description of him (*Shield of Herakles*, II. 386–392). Bear, boar, wolf, and hound were all forms taken by the Indo-European warriors, via masquerade, using pelts and specially designed helmets resembling the animal's head.[20] Lion, fox, ram, and stallion may also have played this role.

Of all the powerful or carnivorous animals, though, the wolf seems to have been the most important for the Indo-European warriors. Reflexes of the old word *wlk^wo-*, "wolf," are found in literally hundreds of proper names, and numerous peoples, such as the Luvians, Lycians, Hirpini, Luceres, Dacians, Hyrcanians, and Saka Haumavarka all bear names that tell of their nature as "wolves."[21] Stories of lycanthropy are well known among the Greeks, Romans, Germans, Celts, Anatolians, and Iranians, and these would seem to be traceable to these ancient warrior practices.[22] The ideology is not difficult to understand: as one dons the skin of the wolf, he takes on the lupine mode of being—he becomes as the wolf, wild, ravenous, merciless and irresistible, raging and out of control.

There is, of course, a classical example of this practice in the *Iliad:* the nocturnal mission of Dolon, ably studied from this standpoint by Louis Gernet.[23] Thus, in *Iliad* 10.334, Dolon, like the figures depicted on Scandinavian helmet bronzes[24] or like Caeculus and his men (*Aeneid* 7.688f), is said to have "put on as a covering, the skin of a greyish wolf" (*hessato d'ektosthen rhinon polioio lykoio*). The wolf-skin itself, of course, does not transform the warrior but is only aid or a technique for taking on the wolf-nature. Dolon is not a great warrior, merely being "swift of foot" (*podōkes,* 10.316), and he quickly panics when Odysseus and Diomedes come upon him. The wolf-skin aids him little and he meets his death, for he is not able to take on the animal rage with it that would make him invincible. This rage is accessible only to the greatest heroes, and is known as *lyssa,* "wolfish rage, furor," a term derived from *lykos,* "wolf," and hearkening back to a very ancient Indo-European warrior practice.

This solution also casts light on a problem that bothered Ernout, with regard to the secondary and specialized usage of *lyssa* to denote "rabies." Here he noted that the word was used to describe this illness only in dogs or horses, but never in wolves, and he speculated that this might be because these domestic animals were more easily observed and thus better known and more commented upon than the wild animals.[25] But, if we are correct in our analysis, a simpler answer is possible: one does not speak of the "wolfish rage" of wolves as a disease—wolves are wolfish by nature. It is only when a domesticated species begins to act wolfish that something is wrong—unless of course, the species in question is man himself, in which case his *lyssa* is represented and regarded as if it were heroism.

Notes

1. Henry George Liddell and Robert Scott, *A Greek-English Lexicon* (Oxford, The Clarendon Press, 1961), p. 1067. In Homer, the term always carries the meaning of martial rage, but the usage of the description *kyna lyssētēra* as a metaphor for Hektor in Θ 299 makes it seem highly likely that the usage as "rabid" was known to Homer.

2. Derivation from **lyt-ja,* as suggested by Felix Solmsen, "Zur Tempel-ordnung von Tegea und zum Gottesurteil von Mantineia," *Zeitschrift für vergleichende Sprachforschung* 34 (1897): 447f, has been abandoned for the most part.

3. Wilhelm Havers, "Geister- und Damonenglaube," *Die Sprache* 4 (1958): 23–38; Franz Specht, *Der Ursprung der indogermanischen Deklination* (Göttingen: Vandenhoek & Ruprecht, 1947), p. 344; Jose Sanches Lasso de la Vega, "Sobre la etimologia de *lyssa,*" *Emérita* 20 (1952): 32–41; Carl Theander, "*lykabas, lykambēs,*" in: *Symbolae Philologicae O. A. Danielsson* (Uppsala: A. B. Lundquist, 1932), pp. 349–51.

4. A. Ernout, "*lyssa,*" *Revue de Philologie* 23 (1949): 154–56; Felix Hartmann, "*lyssa,* 'Hundswut,'" *Zeitschrift für vergleichende Sprachforschung* 54 (1926): 287–90; Walter Porzig, *Die Namen für Satzinhalte im Griechischen und im Indogermanischen* (Berlin: Walter de Gruyter, 1942), pp. 349f.

5. Liddell-Scott, p. 1067; Hjalmar Frisk, *Griechisches Etymologisches Wörterbuch* (Heidelberg: Carl Winter, 1970), vol. 2: 147; Julius Pokorny, *Indogermanisches etymologisches Wörterbuch* (Bern: Francke, 1959), p. 687.

6. Thus, Hartmann and Porzig felt the need to derive *lyssa* from the she-wolf, literally the feminine of wolf, and were led to a theory of demonesses causing disease and the like.

7. See P. Chantraine, *La formation des noms en grec ancien* (Paris: Honore Champion, 1933), pp. 97–100, and especially his warning that "cette notion de féminine doit être entendue très largement" (p. 97).

8. Eduard Schwyzer, *Griechische Grammatik* (Munich: Beck, 1939–53), p. 474. See also Specht, p. 387.

9. See above, note 6.

10. On the Indo-Iranian reflexes of this term, and their relation to warrior ideology, see K. Rönnow, "Xratu," *Le Monde Oriental* 26 (1932): 1–90.

11. See Franz Boas, *Kwakiutl Ethnography,* ed. Helen Codere (Chicago: University of Chicago Press, 1966), pp. 271–77 for the Cannibal Dancer. The Malay material is so well known as to have passed into common English usage as "amuck" via the British colonial experience.

12. For a discussion of this, see Georges Dumézil, *Horace et les Curiaces* (Paris:

Gallimard, 1942), pp. 11–26, who mistakenly sees *menos* as the Greek equivalent term. With this exception, the discussion is excellent.

13. W. Morris and E. Magnusson, trans. *Heimskringla* (London: The Saga Library, 1893), vol. 1:16f.

14. Thomas Kinsella, trans. *The Tain* (London: Oxford University Press, 1970), p. 179.

15. On *Aēšma,* see Stig Wikander, *Der arische Männerbund* (Lund: Gleerupska Universitets Bokhandeln, 1938), pp. 57–60; H. Lommel, *Die Religion Zarathustras nach dem Awesta dargestellt* (Tübingen: J. C. B. Mohr, 1930), pp. 78–79.

16. See E. Benveniste and L. Renou, *Vṛtra et Vṛθraγna* (Paris: Imprimerie Nationale, 1934), and Jarl Charpentier, *Kleine Beiträge zur indoiranischen Mythologie* (Uppsala: Akademische Buchdruckerei, 1911), pp. 25–68, for the most important works on this god.

17. *Yašt* 10.70–71. Ilya Gershevitch, trans. *The Avestan Hymn to Mithra* (Cambridge: The University Press, 1959), p. 107, slightly altered.

18. See Otto Höfler, *Kultische Geheimbünde der Germanen* (Frankfurt: Moritz Diesterweg, 1934), pp. 55–65, and Wilhelm Grimm, "Die mythische Bedeutung des Wolfes," *Zeitschrift für deutsches Alterthum* 12 (1865): 203–28, a remarkable article for its time. Also note that Cúchulainn's hound nature is expressed in the first element of his name: *Cú,* "hound."

19. Actually, Vərəθraγna has ten forms, on which see Charpentier.

20. See Mircea Eliade, *Rites and Symbols of Initiation* (New York: Harper & Row, 1958), pp. 81–84; Robert Eisler, *Man into Wolf* (London: Spring Books, n.d.), pp. 149, 176, and passim; Jean Pryzluski, "Les confréries de loups-garous dans les sociétés indo-européennes," *Revue de l'histoire des religions* 121 (1940): 128–45; Richard von Kienle, "Tier-Völkernamen bei indogermanischen Stämmen," *Wörter und Sachen* 14 (1932): 67; Höfler, pp. 55–65 and Gerhard Binder, *Die Aussetzung des Königskindes Kyros und Romulus* (Meisenheim am Glan: Anton Hain, 1964), 91.

21. On proper names, see Eisler, pp. 140–45. On ethnonyms, Eisler, pp. 132–40; von Kienle, pp. 32–39; Paul Kretschmer, "Der Name der Lykier und andere kleinasiatische Völkernamen," *Kleinasiatische Forschungen* 1 (1930): 14–17; Arthur Ungnad, "Luwisch = Lykisch," *Zeitschrift für Assyriologie* 35 (1924): 1–8; Mircea Eliade, "Dacians and Wolves," in *Zalmoxis, The Vanishing God* (Chicago: University of Chicago Press, 1972), pp. 1–20; and Christian Bartholomae, "Beitrage zur altiranischen Grammatik V," *Beiträge zur Kunde der indogermanische Sprachen* 13 (1888): 70f.

22. On lycanthropy in the Greek context, see Richard Preston Eckels, "Greek Wolf-lore" (Philadelphia: University of Pennsylvania dissertation, 1937), pp. 32–68; Wilhelm Kroll, "Etwas vom Werwolf," *Wiener Studien* 55 (1937): 168–72, and "Lykanthropy," *Pauly-Wissowa, Realenzyklopädie,* Suppl. 7 (Stuttgart: 1940), pp. 423–26, and J. A. MacCulloch, "Lycanthropy," in *Hastings Encyclopedia of Religion and Ethics* (New York: 1916), 8:206f. The chief texts are Pausanias 8.2; Lycophron 481; Plato, *Republic* 565 D, and Pliny, *Natural History* 8.22. For Roman materials, see Binder, pp. 78–95 and Joachim Gruber, "Zur Etymologie von Lat. *lupercus,*" *Glotta* 39 (1961): 273–76. The most important texts are Vergil, *Eclogues* 8.95f., and Petronius, *Satyricon* 61. Germanic materials have been treated in MacCulloch, 208f.,

and Höfler, 55–65, 170–72, 197 and passim. Anatolian evidence is in Ungnad, and V. V. Ivanov, "L'organisation sociale des tribus indo-européens d'après les donnés linguistiques," *Cahiers d'Histoire Mondiale* 5 (1960): 794 and n. Iranian evidence is handled in Wikander, 64f., where there are two striking pieces of evidence: the appellation of certain Scythians as *haumavarka,* "those who become wolves through the drinking of the *haoma* (= Skt. *sóma*) intoxicant" (see Bartholomae) and the mention of "the two-footed and four-footed wolves" in *Yasna* 9.18. A treatment of the werewolf problem in general is found in Eisler, 148–59 and passim.

23. Louis Gernet, "Dolon le loup," *Mélanges Cumont* (Brussels: Institut de Philologie et d'Histoire Orientales et Slaves, 1936), pp. 189–208.

24. See the illustrations in Höfler, p. 57. Note also the Mycenaean figure in the so-called "wild style" of a warrior in what seems to be a tiger skin, depicted in Emily Vermeule, *Greece in the Bronze Age* (Chicago: University of Chicago Press, 1972), p. 313, figure j.

25. Ernout, p. 155.

ELEVEN

WAR AND WARRIORS: AN OVERVIEW

For our purposes, war may be defined as organized and coherent violence conducted between established and internally cohesive rival groups. In contrast to numerous other modes of violence, it is neither individual, spontaneous, random, nor irrational, however much—like all varieties of violence—it involves destructive action, even on a massive scale. Being a complex phenomenon, war has multiple dimensions that are deeply interrelated, chief among them being economic, ideological, and social factors.

Of these, perhaps the most obvious and important (at least according to the majority of modern analysts) are the economic factors that precipitate war, war being the most extreme form of competition for chronically scarce resources, such as women, territory, movable wealth (including livestock), and/or the labor power of subjugated populations. One must note, however, that scarce and valued resources are not exclusively of a material nature, prestige being a crucially important example of a nonmaterial resource that is highly desired and that figures prominently in warfare. It is possible, in fact, to speak of a prestige economy that exists not only side by side but intimately interwoven with the material economy of any given people, and warfare provides a convenient means of reaping rewards in both. Thus, for instance, success in raiding was requisite for a Crow warrior to advance his position, for this provided him first with goods—above all, horses—that not only enriched him but also could be used to place others in his debt through a process of redistribution. Further, raiding furnished the successful warrior with a set of heroic deeds of which he could boast on regular, formalized occasions, thereby further elevating his standing in the group. Success in battle also opened up religious prerogatives for him, insofar as many important and prestigious ritual roles were reserved for those who had accomplished specific, highly regarded feats of war, such as touching coup, winning horses, killing an enemy, or leading a successful raiding expedition.

Indeed, accomplishments in battle provide a common means, in many cultures and periods in history, whereby individuals can seek to elevate not only their own individual prestige above that of their peers but also that of their group above others (conquered rivals, as well as those who remain outside the fray). Thus, for instance, among the Jalé-speaking peoples of highland New Guinea, the performance of stereotyped, formulaic songs is a prominent part of every public celebration. These songs, which preserve the memory of past warfare, are a crucial element in the local prestige economy as well as a stimulus to further conflicts, for they celebrate the glory of the group that sings them, while also heaping derision upon their foes:

> The man Wempa will never eat again,
> nor will Alavóm ever eat again.
> But we live to see the sweet potatoes roast,
> The sweet potatoes from Wongele and Tukui.

Koch 1974, p. 85

One may observe similar processes in the well-wrought poetry of praise for successful warriors and blame for those who are less than successful (e.g., Hektor's rebukes of Paris) that figures prominently in the Homeric epic. Moreover, the heroes depicted there are presented as acutely self-conscious with regard to issues of prestige, as is evident, for example, in Sarpedon's speech just prior to the Trojan assault on the Greek camp, an assault that leads to his death. Here we are shown a warrior, himself the son of Zeus, weighing the relative value of the material and nonmaterial rewards of combat and setting greatest stock on the winning of a prominent and enduring reputation. In the last analysis, the pursuit of such a reputation—elsewhere called "the fame that does not decay" (*kleos aphthitos*)—becomes nothing less than a quest for immortality, although, ironically, it is a quest that regularly costs the quester his life. Among the most interesting aspects of this passage, however, is the absence of any tension or contradiction between the warrior's pursuit of material gain (booty, also land and privileged banquet portions) and his pursuit of glory. On the contrary, we see an effective coalescence of the material and the prestige economies, encompassed within an ideology and a poetics that decidedly emphasize the latter:

> Glaukos, why is it you and I are honored before others
> with pride of place, the choice meats and the filled wine cups
> in Lykia, and all men look on us as if we were immortals,
> and we are appointed a great piece of land by the banks of
> Xanthos,
> good land, orchard and vineyard, and ploughland for the
> planting of wheat?
> Therefore it is our duty in the forefront of the Lykians
> to take our stand, and bear our part of the blazing of battle,
> so that a man of the close-armored Lykians may say of us:
> "Indeed, these are no ignoble men who are lords of Lykia,
> these kings of ours, who feed upon the fat sheep appointed
> and drink the exquisite sweet wine, since indeed there is strength of
> valour in them, since they fight in the forefront of the Lykians."
> Man, supposing you and I, escaping this battle
> would be able to live on forever, ageless, immortal,
> so neither would I myself go on fighting where men win glory.

> But now, seeing that the spirits of death stand close about us
> in their thousands, no man can turn aside nor escape them,
> let us go on and win glory for ourselves, or yield it to others.
> Homer, *Iliad*, trans. Lattimore

The assignation of prestige to deeds of valor (the etymological connections between *valor, valiance,* and *value* are significant, as are those between *virtue* and *virility*) is but one means whereby ideological factors influence warfare, albeit a tremendously important one. No less important is the way in which other ideological constructs supply the means necessary to persuade individuals to join in combat, providing them with motivation sufficiently great that they are willing to risk their lives, even in situations (as is true for the vast majority of warriors over the course of history) wherein they stand to reap quite little in the way of personal gain—material or immaterial—from even the greatest of military successes.

It is in this fashion that religion has played a most important role in war throughout history, and the examples of religious justifications that have been used to legitimate even the most tawdry of struggles are legion. Among these we must note calls to convert the heathen (as in the Christian Crusades and more recent European wars of colonial expansion); promises of a favorable afterlife for warriors who die in battle (as within Islam, Shinto, or among the ancient Aztec, Germans, and others); and ethical dualisms whereby warfare is cast as an unremitting struggle between good and evil (as in ancient Iran or the modern United States).

Among most contemporary students of war, ideological factors are generally viewed as subordinate or epiphenomenal to material ones, religion and other forms of legitimation being understood as the convenient or even necessary means that serve to mask or mystify the acquisitive competition that is the primary motivation for armed conflict. Others, however, have challenged this view, particularly with regard to warfare in the ancient and preindustrial world, where (in their view) religious motivations played a much more powerful and directly causal role. A favorite example cited by adherents of this position is the case of Aztec warfare, which they claim was pursued above all else to obtain the victims necessary for the performance of human sacrifice, the central ritual act of the Aztec empire. Such a line of analysis, however, has been rendered untenable by the most recent studies of Aztec sacrifice, which reveal it to have been not an act of transcendent religiosity performed for its own sake and at any cost but, as John Ingham has cogently argued, an expression and an instrument of the same drives for wealth, power, and prestige that prompted Aztec warfare and imperial expansion in general. In Ingham's words:

> Whatever else it may have been, human sacrifice was a symbolic
> expression of political domination and economic appropriation

and, at the same time, a means to their social production. . . . The sacrificing of slaves and war captives and the offering of their hearts and blood to the sun thus encoded the essential character of social hierarchy and imperial order and provided a suitable instrument for intimidating and punishing insubordination. (Ingham 1984, p. 379)

In this case, then, and others like it, one must conclude that, far from having been the ultimate cause of war, religion was intimately bound up with other causal factors more familiar to the world of *Realpolitik*.

Beyond the material and ideological factors, there are also powerful social factors that must be taken into account. Briefly, two social conditions are necessary for the occurrence of war, given the definition proposed above ("organized and coherent violence conducted between established and internally cohesive rival groups"). First, a given group of individuals must understand themselves as a group; that is, they must be bound together in some abiding fashion by sentiments, traditions, kinship ties, institutions, residence patterns, language, and the like. Second, they must understand members of some other group ("the enemy") as radically alien to them, outsiders to whom they are not connected and with reference to whom they need not refrain from violence. As the Jalé put it in a striking proverb: "People whose face is known should not be eaten." Moreover, prior to the outbreak of hostilities or at the very least shortly thereafter, this same set of conditions—internal solidarity coupled with external alienation and hostility—will prevail on the other side as well.

In short, warriors must be persuaded not only to risk their own lives but also to take the lives of others, and not merely random others but those whose otherness is most radically marked. Involving organized and relatively large-scale lethal violence as it does, warfare always poses serious ethical problems within the already thorny set of issues surrounding homicide. As a starting point, we must note that humans kill one another for many reasons and under many sets of circumstances, and all groups possess certain norms regulating how such killings are to be regarded and judged. Sometimes they are defined as murder (i.e., illicit homicide); in other instances they are not, for there are conditions under which the taking of a life is legally, morally, culturally, and/or religiously sanctioned or even (this is particularly relevant to the case of war) celebrated.

A fundamental concern in such adjudications, and one infinitely more complex and malleable than is ordinarily acknowledged, is the question of whether the victim(s) or would-be victim(s) of a given homicide are truly human. In any number of instances (e.g., infants, slaves, prisoners, outlaws, heretics and other social deviants, the aged and infirm, etc.), an individual may conveniently be defined by the killer (and the community that passes judgment upon the killing) as something less than human: a "monster," a "beast," a "vegetable," and so forth. Patterns of verbal abuse, in fact, whereby such persons are referred to as animals, rotting matter ("garbage," "trash"), and the like, regularly accompany and assist the lethal redefinitions whereby it is established that effecting the death of such an individual is a permissible or even a worthy act.

Nor is it only individuals who may be defined as somehow less than human and thus freely killable. On the contrary, social borders are regularly constructed and maintained such that entire groups of others ("aliens" in the fullest sense of the word) are regarded thus by their neighbors and enemies. Such a state of affairs is evidenced, for example, in the frequent occurrence of self-referential ethnonyms by which a given people denote themselves as "humans," implicitly (and in many instances, explicitly) relegating all others to the category of nonhumans—nonhumans who may, moreover, be freely killed as the occasion arises.

An instructive case is that of the Yanoama of the Amazon Basin, who not only call themselves "humanity" (the meaning of their name) and all others "lesser subhuman beings" (*nabä*) but carry the process still further: members of one Yanoama village habitually accentuate the minor differences of dialect (or the like) that separate them from residents of other villages; then they deride the others for being less than fully *Yanoama,* which is to say, somewhat subhuman. Relations between Yanoama villages are always tense, partly as a result of this pattern of marking social borders and partly as a result of pronounced competition over women, for it is the goal of all Yanoama males to retain the women of their own village while obtaining those of other villages through marriage or war. The central value of Yanoama life is *waiteri* ("fierceness"). To survive in this highly competitive atmosphere, a village must ally itself with others to resist the aggression of others still. As a means of overcoming the suspicions that normally prevail between villages, allies seek to bind themselves to one another through trade, marital exchanges, and reciprocal feasting, but the process is never a simple one. To form an alliance is to signal weakness, and allies, sensing this weakness, press ever-increasing demands for women as a condition for the alliance's continuation. Alliances thus often end in enmity, in warfare, or in an act that the Yanoama view as the ultimate form of fierceness and violence, being a parody and an inversion of the fragile festivals of intervillage solidarity: that is, a treacherous feast in which the male guests are all slaughtered and their women taken.

Again, with regard to the radical nature of social boundaries in situations of conflict and war, one may note the case of Anggor in western New Guinea. As Peter Birkett Huber reports, each Anggor village "can be considered a cosmos in itself, an autonomous and essentially harmonious moral system confronted by a uniformly hostile, dangerous, and chaotic outside world. Violence between these villages is consequently not a form of policy or a distinct kind of political situation, but an inescapable feature of man's existential condition" (in Nettleship, Givens, and Nettleship 1975, p. 620). Most violence perpetrated by residents of one Anggor village on those of another takes the form of sorcery, but revenge expeditions are ultimately organized and battles ensue in which Anggor warriors venture from their homes to confront chaos itself and, by means of this confrontation, reassert the solidarity of their group and the order of their cosmos by inflicting retaliatory deaths on their enemies outside.

Although these are somewhat extreme cases, they are by no means unique, and all warfare involves sociopolitical suspensions of the ethical, whereby the otherness of the enemy is radically accentuated, a situation that permits and legitimates their victimization. War is, in truth, that situation in which the killing of other people on a grand (or even total) scale is rendered not only licit but requisite, even glorious, by virtue of the fact that those others belong to a rival group to whom ethical norms do not extend, they having been effectively defined as subhuman or even nonhuman.

Yet another example of these principles is found in the shields that form a crucial part of a warrior's equipment among the several Dayak peoples of Borneo. In general, shields function not only as an important implement of defense in warfare prior to the introduction of gunpowder but also as a movable social border that separates one's self, one's group, and one's territory from the enemy. In an advance, shields mark the incorporation of conquered territory, booty, and prisoners into one's own group; in retreat, they mark the group's contraction, as land, stragglers, and the fallen are left outside. In the classic warfare of the Zulu, for instance, and in other powerful kingdoms of southern Africa, rival armies assumed formation in lines opposite to one another, each warrior holding a five-foot rawhide shield in front of him with his left arm. Standing behind this row of shields, the opponents exchanged insults with one another, verbal combat (in the forms I have discussed) preceding physical. Thereafter, the regiments closed, and each one tried to break through the enemy's walls of shields. Finally, when an army felt itself defeated, its members dropped their shields in token of surrender, whereupon the battle would cease. What was signified in this action was that the vanquished group renounced the social borders that they had previously maintained, thereby relinquishing their independence and accepting incorporation as a subjugated part of the victor's polity.

Dayak shields are used in similar fashion and bear similar significance but are remarkable for the iconographic content of the designs painted and carved upon them. Most noteworthy is the bifurcation of design, for on the inside of most Dayak shields—that is, the side facing the bearer—is the image of two protective ancestral figures; on the outside is a snarling monster. The import of the ancestors is not hard to judge; being the founders of the bearer's social group, they define that group and represent it. Insofar as there are others who descend from these same ancestors, the warrior has comrades who will take up arms together with him to defend their group against outsiders (i.e., those descended from other ancestral lines). The group's sense of identity and solidarity are thus nothing more than the sentiments called forth by the image of these ancestors, and it is such sentiments—much more than the wooden shields—that provide protection and security in battle and beyond.

The monsters on the outer face of Dayak shields are more difficult to interpret, however, for they are susceptible to multiple readings. On the one hand, these ferocious figures, marked most prominently by bulging eyes and exaggerated fangs, would seem to represent the enemy, particularly when considered in juxtaposition to the ancestor figures. Accordingly, one may posit a series of correlated binary oppositions, the effect of which is to dehumanize the enemy (in fashions similar to those discussed above) and thereby render his killing licit:

inside : outside
ancestors : monsters
own group : enemy
protection : menace
solidarity : hostility
deaths suffered must be avenged : deaths inflicted constitute revenge
killings illicit : killings licit or even requisite

In light of such observations as these, I am inclined to propose certain revisions to a classic text of Simone Weil, her justly celebrated meditations on "The Iliad, or The Poem of Force," written in 1940, shortly after the fall of France to Nazi arms and also after her own combat experience during the Spanish Civil War. In this essay, reflecting on death in battle, particularly as described in the epic, Weil came to define force as "that x that turns anybody who is subjected to it into a *thing*," going on to observe, "exercised to the limit, it turns man into a thing in the most literal sense: it makes a corpse out of him. Somebody was here, and the next minute there is nobody at all; this is a spectacle the *Iliad* never wearies of showing us" (Weil, 1983). To be sure, there is a power and a grandeur in so stark a formulation, yet, given what has been outlined above, particularly regarding the nature of social borders in warfare and those patterns of dehumanization whereby an enemy is defined as subhuman, nonhuman, and/or monstrous, one must reject the idea that it is force itself, acting as some sort of quasi-personified agent, that "turns a man into a thing." Rather, the process is quite the reverse, and one can say with more justice and precision, *pace* Weil, that it is only when human actors come to regard others as "things" that they become capable of employing force, particularly lethal force, against them. Force here only completes that process of "turning into a thing" that begins in the sentiments and social patterns of human subjects.

To return to the Dayak shields, however, there is more that can be said.

Thus far, I have suggested that the image of the monster may be taken to represent the enemy, as seen through the dehumanizing gaze of the warrior. Such an interpretation, moreover, is consistent with a view of shields as a marker of social borders, for in this instance we may clearly perceive the tenuous nature of such borders, something that becomes particularly obvious within the situation of battle, for it is then quite literally only the thickness of the shield itself that separates safety from danger, self from other, and the ancestral (representation of) community from the monstrous (figure of the) outside. In addition, there is significant material evidence to support such a view, for in the construction of many Dayak shields the monster images are rendered more grotesque still by the use of human hair as ornament: hair taken from the trophy skulls of slain enemies. Such enemies, having been viewed as monsters, were treated as monsters, and their corpses were used to depict the monsters that they were.

This datum, however, suggests another line of interpretation that may be advanced regarding the complex and polyphonous image of the monster. For it is obvious that the outer side of any shield is directed toward the enemy, especially toward one's immediate adversary in hand-to-hand battle. Further, it is equally obvious that the intended (and also, one assumes, quite real) effect of such an image is to intimidate or even terrify opponents, for in its very material substance (the actual hair of fallen victims), this shield announces the force, the valor, and also the cruelty of its bearer. It supplies graphic and tangible witness to the fact that he has taken enemy lives in the past and stands ready and able to do so once more. The shield thus displays the bearer's face as seen through the eyes of his opponent or (to put it differently) the face that he wishes to present to all enemies: for he becomes a monster against those whom he regards as monstrous, even as they do conversely to him.

We reach here the final paradox of war and the warrior: a corollary to the pattern we have observed whereby one must dehumanize one's enemies in order to employ force against them. In practice, it appears that a warrior must also dehumanize himself before he can become an instrument of slaughter, effectively eradicating such human tendencies as guilt, fear, and compassion. A well-articulated example of this is found in the samurai ideal of "no-mind," this being that psychomental state—cultivated by years of meditation and training in martial arts—in which the sumarai's body and arms act as if automatically, with no hesitation born of thought, weakness, or doubt. Elsewhere, warriors frequently speak of themselves as animals: "lions" or "leopards" (East Africa); "two-footed wolves" (India and Iran); berserkers, or "those who wear the bear's shirt" (Scandinavia); or "crazy-dogs-wishing-to-die" (Crow), to cite but a few examples. To these data one might add the fact that Yanoama warriors march off to battle imitating the noises of a host of carnivorous beasts, from insects on up. The war song of the Yanoama is also noteworthy as a supreme statement of the warrior's auto-dehumanization, being entitled "I am a meat-hungry buzzard."

Bibliography

Not surprisingly, some of the best attempts at academic analysis of the nature and ideology of warfare were made at the time of the Vietnam War. Among the valuable collections that appeared during this period, one should note *Law and Warfare*, edited by Paul Bohannan (Garden City, N.Y.: 1967); *War: The Anthropology of Armed Conflict and Aggression*, edited by Morton Fried, Marvin Harris, and Robert Murphy (Garden City, N.Y.: 1968); *Problèmes de la guerre en Grèce ancienne*, edited by Jean-Pierre Vernant (The Hague, 1968); and *War: Its Causes and Correlates*, edited by Martin A. Nettleship, R. Dale Givens, and Anderson Nettleship (The Hague, 1975). A slightly later work, and in a different vein, is *The Warrior Tradition in Modern Africa*, edited by Ali A. Mazrui (Leiden, 1977). Special attention should also be given to Pier Giorgio Solinas's "Guerra e matrimonio," in *Potere senza stato*, edited by Carla Pasquinelli (Rome, 1986), pp. 21–47.

Among the most important case studies are those drawn from Melanesia, which, given the relatively late date of "pacification" there by colonial authorities, provided an extremely informative field for gathering data. Here, one ought to note Klaus Koch's *War and Peace in Jalémo: The Management of Conflict in Highland New Guinea* (Cambridge, Mass.: 1974); Andrew P. Vayda's *War in Ecological Perspective* (New York, 1976) and M. J. Meggitt's *Blood Is Their Argument: Warfare among the Mae Enga Tribesmen of the New Guinea Highlands* (Palo Alto, Calif.: 1977). Other valuable case studies include Peter Birkett Huber's discussion of the Anggor in *War: Its Causes and Correlates* (cited above), pp. 619–61; Napoleon A. Chagnon's essay on the Yanoama, in *War: The Anthropology of Armed Conflict and Aggression* (cited above), pp. 109–59; and Fred W. Voget's "Warfare and the Integration of Crow Indian Culture," in *Explorations in Cultural Anthropology*, edited by Ward H. Goodenough (New York, 1964), pp. 483–509.

John Ingham's study of Aztec sacrifice is found in his "Human Sacrifice at Tenochtitlan," *Comparative Studies in Society and History* 26 (1984): 379–400. A brief discussion of the Dayak shields is W. Münsterberger's "Die Ornamente an Dayak-Tanzschilden und ihre Beziehung zu Religion und Mythologie," *Cultureel Indië* (Leiden) 1 (1939): 337–43. Simone Weil's essay "The Iliad, or The Poem of Force," translated by Mary McCarthy, can be found in *Revisions: Changing Perspectives in Moral Philosophy*, edited by Stanley Hauerwas and Alasdair MacIntyre (Notre Dame, Ind.: 1983).

WARRIORS AND NON-HERDSMEN: A RESPONSE TO MARY BOYCE

Scholars and Ideology

I have read Mary Boyce's article "Priests, Cattle, and Men"[1] with interest, and for all that I may disagree with this distinguished scholar in important ways, I am pleased that she found my book, *Priests, Warriors, and Cattle*, still worthy of serious discussion some seven years after its publication.[2] Certain of Boyce's detailed criticisms are well-founded, and must be granted at the start. Thus, it is clear that I made too much of such evidence as exists for lycanthropic practices and beliefs among the Indo-Iranians, insofar as I failed to take account of the uncertainties that exist regarding translation and interpretation of Old Persian *haumavarga*, while also mistranslating *Yasna* 9.18.[3] Again, it is clear that the comparison of the Maruts and Fravašis which I drew unduly stressed certain superficial resemblances, while minimizing the differences that exist between these two groups of deities.[4]

Boyce argues that I committed these and other alleged errors because I relied too heavily and uncritically upon Stig Wikander's *Der arische Männerbund*,[5] which reliance led me to misrepresent the role of warriors within Indo-Iranian society. Although I cannot concur with her on this latter point, for reasons that I will spell out below, I am troubled by the matter of Wikander, and welcome the opportunity to discuss it, although I will do so from a different perspective than does Boyce.[6] For it is less the scholarly failings of *Der arische Männerbund* that concern me (although these exist, to be sure) than its extrascholarly dimensions. This is, after all, a book on the topic of "Aryan" war-bands that was written in the late 1930s, just after its author had spent a considerable period of time in Berlin.[7] It begins, moreover, by acknowledging the strong influence of Otto Höfler's Nazi-tinged *Kultische Geheimbünde der Germanen*,[8] and notes with approval the recent upsurge of scholarly interest in Germany on questions of Indo-European religion and society.[9]

For the most part, the ideological underpinnings and resonances of Wikander's book are submerged under detailed discussions of Indic, Iranian, and classical sources. Yet occasionally they peek through more clearly: witness, for instance, the description of Indra as "Führer" of the Maruts,[10] or a dispute with Herman Lommel over whether the disquietingly violent Rudras ought be understood as properly "Aryan" or not.[11] Two passages stand out as particularly direct—and particularly chilling. The first of these is a discussion in which Wikander summarized his results, insisting that behind the various linguistic data he was treating there lay "a reality," a cult

> whose foremost characteristics were worship of the dead, orgiastic sacrificial feasts, the entry into warrior organizations, and a positive attitude [*eine positive Einstellung*] toward the dark and demonic powers of life.[12]

What is one to make of this "positive attitude"? That is, how can one gauge the author's attitude—and the attitude he invites his readers to adopt—toward those of whom such a "positive attitude" is characteristic? A simple answer is not possible, and it does not seem to be the case, here or elsewhere in his published work, that Wikander explicitly advocated Nazi positions or openly celebrated violence. Yet, in his choice of topic and the tone of his diction, particularly in passages such as this, he does appear to celebrate those who (according to his reconstruction) themselves celebrated violence. Moreover, those persons, being ancient Indo-Iranians, might legitimately be termed "Aryans" on the basis of their own self-referential ethnonym (Vedic *árya-*, *árya-*, Avestan *airyō*, Old Persian *ariya-*).[13] But in the moment wherein Wikander wrote, there were others who pointedly called themselves "Aryans," while also evincing "a positive attitude toward the dark and demonic powers of life." One is entitled to ask in what measure he wrote of and for them, and how such persons might reasonably have been expected to receive and react to his discourse.

Such questions as these are also pertinent for the interpretation of a second passage, in which Wikander sought to connect the occasional role of the Maruts as vengeful deities to the position of Männerbünde within other societies:

> Männerbünde stand out quite often as guardians of justice. This can be a Bund's self-appointed justice of force and lynching [*die selbstgenommene Gewalt- und Lynchjustiz*], which is of limited value. But where the Männerbund includes the principal power within itself, it can also establish itself as the representative of an effective order and administration of justice [*als der Vertreter einer wirklichen Ordung und Rechtssprechung*].[14]

Wikander's footnotes refer to studies of men's societies in "primitive" societies, which he took as paradigmatic.[15] Closer at hand, however, and seemingly implicit was the example of the SA and SS.

Like any book, *Der arische Männerbund* ought to be read not only for what it tells us (or does not tell us) about its purported topic, but also for what it does and does not tell us about its author and the times in which he wrote. Like all authors, Wikander had an ideological position, which he articulated only partially and indirectly, and of which, no doubt, he was only partially conscious. Moreover, like all scholarly works, his book was the product of a

dialectic encounter that occurred at a specific historic moment between its author's intellect—something itself extremely complex in its formation, shaped
only in part by ideology—and a body of evidence that, while inevitably perceived and organized through the workings of that intellect, retained nonetheless an independent existence and offered a certain measure of resistance to
distortions, misrepresentations, and radical reshaping. Sorting out the extent
to which "the data" and "the author" each contributed to the final text, remain present in it, and are analytically separable is here (as always) an extraordinarily difficult endeavor, as is judging what within that text retains worth.
Yet so distressed is Boyce at Wikander's overemphasis on the importance of
warrior bands, as well as the specific limitations and/or tendentiousness of his
philological, hermeneutic, and religio-historic argumentation at various points
that she not only categorically denies the value of his book but also denies the
existence of that which it purports to study. On this, however, I believe there
is a good deal more to be said.

The Evidence of the Gāthās

Although a specialized warrior grouping or stratum is attested in most Indic
and Iranian texts (the Vedas, the Younger Avesta, the Indic and Iranian epics,
the Mitanni materials, Scythian legends, e.g.), Boyce would deny that warriors with specialized social identity as such—whom she refers to somewhat
anachronistically as "professional warriors"—were a part of Proto-Indo-
Iranian society. Against those who hold differently, myself included, she advances a theory that she introduced several years ago,[16] arguing first that the
Gāthās treat warriors as a novelty and, further, that this evidence is conclusive
for the reconstruction of Proto-Indo-Iranian society.[17] Although on general
methodological grounds I would not grant so privileged a position to one text
among many, for the sake of argument I will confine myself for the most part
in the discussion that follows to a careful examination of this severely restricted body of evidence, which alone suffices to render Boyce's position
untenable.

Before we can consider these texts, however, there is the thorny problem of
dating them. In her article, Boyce asserts that the Gāthās were composed
around 1400 B.C., a date at which she believes—on rather scant evidence—that
Bronze Age technology was just being introduced to the relative backwater
of eastern Iran. For all that the question of dates is crucial to her argument,
however, Boyce has wavered on it over the years. In her most authoritative
work, published in 1975, she dated the Gāthās to "some time between, say,
1400 and 1000 B.C.,"[18] while in 1979, without explanation (but in a work intended for a more popular audience) she revised this to "some time between
1700 and 1500 B.C."[19] In subsequent publications, she has modified her position again, opting for dates that fall between these two extremes.[20] On no oc-

casion, however, has she offered detailed arguments in support of any given figure or described what factors prompted her shifts of opinion.

Rather, Boyce has usually been content to offer some general observations about the turbulent nature of the age in which the Gāthās were written, and to cite the relatively few other scholars who advocate so early a date. In her most recent discussion,[21] she cites two authors only (in addition to her own earlier writings), neither of whom inspires great confidence, for the first is but the most recent Zoroastrian scholar to defend a hoary date at all costs,[22] and the second is K. F. Geldner's century-old article for the ninth edition of the *Encyclopaedia Britannica*. And, as if to make matters worse, she apparently failed to note that in the *Britannica*'s eleventh edition, Geldner opined that a date of 1000 B.C., "may be too high." [23] Elsewhere, in an attempt to bolster these weak reeds, Boyce cited also the linguistic researches of Paul Friedrich,[24] but not only does Friedrich say nothing in support of a date around 1400, but I can assure her that his study established only that a significant (if indeterminate) length of time separated Younger Avestan from Gāthic, since it was I who carried out the primary research on which he based his conclusions.[25]

Over the course of the last decade and a half, Boyce has thus vacillated, now dating the Gāthās as low as 1000 B.C., now as high as 1700, the latter being a figure with no credence whatever outside the Zoroastrian community, where it is held almost as an article of faith. At present, the majority opinion among scholars probably inclines toward the end of the second millennium or beginning of the first, although there are still those who hold for a date in the seventh century.[26] All specialists, however, are at pains to acknowledge the extreme difficulty of establishing any date with precision. Accordingly, it would seem precarious—not to say tendentious—to base one's line of interpretation upon a presumed date for the Gāthās (particularly one that deviates markedly from the generally prevalent opinions), rather than upon a philologically rigorous examination of their contents.

Men and Warriors

One of the first difficulties Boyce's theory encounters, as she recognized, is the Avestan substantive *nar-*, a word which scholars since Bartholomae have seen to have three separate levels of denotation:[27]

a) an unmarked meaning—"male human being";
b) a more inclusive meaning—"human being," without reference to gender;
c) a more restrictive meaning—"warrior," i.e. that kind of male who exhibits most prominently the characteristics (especially physical force) that were understood to be particularly constitutive of male identity.

Now, all three of these meanings occur commonly in Vedic and in the Younger Avesta.[28] On this there is no argument. Nor is there any doubt that within other Indo-European languages, particularly Italic and Celtic, terms

derived from P-I-E *H_2ner-[29] have a semantic range that includes the idea of
martial force, as for instance Welsh ner, "hero," Irish nert, Breton nerz and
Luvian annari- "strength," and the name of the Latin goddess Neriō, a con-
sort of Mars.[30] Within the Gāthās, however, Bartolomae located only two
verses in which he thought he could recognize nar- in its more restrictive
sense (Yasna 28.8b and 48.10a). About these, Boyce rightly raises questions,
for in neither verse is translation of nar- as "warrior" mandatory, although it
remains perfectly plausible.

There are, however, two other passages in which a stronger case can be
made. The first of these is Yasna 32.10a:

> That nar destroys the doctrines who says the worst to see
> The cow and the sun with his eyes, and who makes the wise into
>   liars,
> Who ravages the pastures and who raises a club against the
>   truthful man.

hvō mā nā sravā mōrəndat	yə acištəm vaēnaŋhē aogədā
gam ašibyā hvarəcā	yascā dāθəng drəgvatō dadāt
yascā vāstrā vīvāpat	yascā vadarə vōiždat ašāunē

Interpretation of the phrase "who says the worst to see the cow and the sun
with his eyes" has proven notoriously difficult, and thankfully there is no need
for us to enter this debate.[31] More important for our present purposes is the
fact that the nar- is identified here as one "who ravages the pastures and raises
a club against the truthful man" (hvō mā nā . . . yascā vāstrā vīvāpat / yascā
vadarə vōiždat ašāunē). Moreover, this description of a nar- stands in conscious and explicit juxtaposition to the description of another type of evildoer,
for Yasna 32.9 and 32.10 both begin with variations on a single formulaic
phrase, the former reading duš.sastiš sravā mōrəndat ("He whose teaching is
evil destroys the doctrines") where the latter has hvō mā nā sravā mōrəndat
("That nar- destroys the doctrines"). And just as it is the nar- who is portrayed committing violence against the herds with a weapon in his hand, so
conversely the duš.sasti- is said to "(destroy) the knowledge of life through
his pronouncements" (hvō [mōrəndat] jyātōuš sənghanāiš xratūm). Speech
acts are thus contrasted to acts of armed force just as the duš.sasti- ("he
whose teaching is evil") is contrasted to the nar-, with the latter hardly being
understood as a "man" and nothing more.

Also of interest are the reflections of Zarathustra that are preserved in Yasna
46.2:

> I know why I am powerless, O wise One:
> Few livestock are mine, and also I am one whose nars are few.
> I lament to you: see it, O Lord,
> Furnishing support as a friend must give to a friend.
> Teach [me] the power of the good mind, along with truth.

vaēdā tat yā   ahmī mazdā anaēšō
mā kamnafšvā   hyatcā kamnānā ahmī
gərəzōi tōi   ā īt (a) vaēnā ahurā
rafəδrəm cagvå   hyat fryō fryāi daidīt
āxšō vaŋhəuš   ašā īštīm manaŋhō

In the second line of this stanza Zarathustra specifies the cause of his difficulty, employing two compounds that share the same first member: mā
kamnafšvā / hyatcā kamnānā ahmī, "Few livestock are mine, and also I am
one whose nars are few." Both the Pahlavi and the Sanskrit translations of
this verse provide glosses that identify the nars in question as fighting men,[32]
and detailed analysis of the Avestan text confirms this conclusion. Thus, it
ought to be noted that the locution kamnafšvā . . . kamnānā depends upon
and transforms in two ways an ancient formula meaning "men and livestock"
(Avestan pasu- vīra- < P-I-E *péku-*wīró-) that is well attested in Indic,
Iranian, and Italic.[33] In the first place, that formula is modified by the addition
of kamna-, a term that appears also in Old Persian, always in phrases that
describe a shortage of fighting men.[34] Second, the Avestan term which would
normally be expected in this formula—vīra—is here replaced by nar-. Semantic renewal of this sort is not uncommon,[35] but presumably has some motivation. In the case at hand, that motivation may be discerned by comparing
Yasna 46.2 with Y. 45.9:

> [I am] wishing to satisfy him for us, together with good mind:
> He who made that which is beneficent and that which is
>   nonbeneficent for us, according to his will.
> By his power, may the Wise Lord place us in [a state of] vigor
> For the increase of our men and livestock
> As a result of the good relation of good mind with truth.

> təm nə vohū   mat manaŋhā cixšnušō
> yə nə usən   cōrət spəncā aspəncā
> mazdå xšaθrā   varəzī nå dyāt ahurō
> pasūš vīrəng   ahmakəng fradaθāi.ā
> vaŋhəuš ašā   haozaθwāt ā manaŋhō

This is as close as Zarathustra comes to seeking redress of that problem
which he identified so clearly in Y. 46.2. There, as we saw, the prophet attributed his state of powerlessness (an-aēšō) to the fact that he possessed
within his group only a few head of livestock and a few of those males whom
he referred to as nar-. In the present verse, however, while announcing himself as desirous of more livestock, he implicitly rejects the corresponding ac-
quisition of nars and seeks instead another kind of male, as he asks "for the
increase of our vīras and livestock," employing the old formulaic diction:
pasūš vīrəng ahmakəng fradaθāi.ā. His point is as subtle as it is forceful, for
having stated that the possession of warriors—nar- in its more restrictive

sense—yields power (aēša-), Zarathustra goes on to assert that he will have none of this, and will instead seek to gather around him vīras, i.e. men more traditionally associated with livestock than are nars. Further, just as he seeks a different sort of man, so also he seeks a different sort of power from that which depends upon the possession of nars, as is seen in his request for "the power (išti-, a term related to, but different from aēša-) of the good mind, along with truth" (vanhə̄uš / ašā ištīm mananhō) in Y. 46.2e. This search for an alternative form of power—one resting on qualities of thought and speech and therefore appropriate to a priest, not a warrior—is also apparent in Yasna 44.17c, where Zarathustra implores the Wise Lord: "for me there should be a powerful voice" (mōi hyāt vaxš aēšō).[36]

Herdsmen and Non-herdsmen

Another term which poses problems for Boyce's theory is the plural substantive a-fšuyantō (a hapax legomenon found in Y. 49.4b), which is formed by addition of a privative prefix a- to the frequently attested noun fšuyant- ("herdsman").

> Those who with an evil will increase furor and cruelty
> By their own tongues—the non-herdsmen among the herdsmen,
> They whose evil deeds one has not yet vanquished with good
> deeds—
> They have established the Daēva-gods: which is [to say] the
> liar's religion!

yōi duš.xraθwā	aēšəməm varədən rāməmcā
x˅āiš hizubīš	fšuyasū afšuyantō
yaēšạm nōit	hvarštāiš vạs dužvarštā
tōi daēvə̄ng dạn	yā drəgvatō daēnā

It is, on the face of it, difficult to reconcile the appearance of a term meaning "non-herdsmen" with Boyce's stated view that in the "bipartite society of the ancient Iranians," all men other than priests were engaged in herding activity.[37] Who then were these "non-herdsmen among the herdsmen" (fšuyasū afšuyantō), who—to make matters more problematic—were clearly engaged in martial violence, as they are said to "increase furor and cruelty" (aēšəməm varədən rāməmcā), these being terms closely associated with the practice of cattle raiding?[38]

To her credit, Boyce acknowledges these difficulties, and struggles with them gamely. In truth, her attempt to establish a specific social and historic context for the Gāthās in large measure derives from and rests upon her interpretation of the phrase fšuyasū afšuyantō. She has commented upon this phrase and its significance several times in recent years, and it is worth citing her discussions in their entirety.

The semi-nomadic Iranians, living close to their animals, on whom their lives depended, were likely to have regarded themselves as "the collectivity of men and cattle together," *pasu vīra* in the Avestan phrase. Apart from priests, adult males are likely to have shared, as the normal activities of manhood, the tasks of herding, hunting and fighting. As herdsmen they would have had to carry weapons against beasts of prey; and if human marauders appeared, it would doubtless have been their accepted duty to stand and fight. In those horseless days it would have been useless to run (as do herdsmen in the Irish sagas) to alert the warriors of the tribe, expecting them to speed after the vanishing foes and cattle. No one could move faster than his own feet would carry him, and so there was no justification for specialised activity. . . . The Gāthās appear to mirror, however, the breaking up of that stable society, through the pressures of a new age. To possess a chariot and teams of horses, with charioteer and grooms, and to acquire weapons of mined and wrought metal, demanded means, but once a man had obtained these things, honestly or otherwise, he could acquire more wealth, by combat or raids, and pass it on to his sons; and so there came into being a new class within the ranks of the *nar-*, that of the "chariot-rider," a man who is no longer accepting the duties of herdsman, but who must often have abandoned his own tribe to seek the service of some noted warrior-chief, devoting himself, with the rest of his retainers, to fighting, feasting and the chase; and thus there evolved the Iranian Heroic Age, with its splendours and miseries. In Zoroaster's terminology such ruthless and acquisitive men were *afšuyantō*, "non-herdsmen" (Y. 49.4), an expression which evidently gained its force from the fact that all honest men had previously borne their part in protecting the tribal herds.[39]

To the present writer it appears from Zoroaster's words in this [sc. Y. 29] and other of his gāthās that he experienced the fierce assault by professional fighting men—"non-herdsmen"—on traditional pastoral society, the unity of "cattle and men," as something not only wickedly cruel and destructive but also new, an attack on established order; but this L[incoln] cannot even consider. . . .[40]

. . . only the *Gāthās,* strictly and piously memorized from the time of their composition, faithfully reflect a fixed point in Indo-Iranian prehistory, a period, it seems, when the traditional pastoral society was still surviving locally on the steppes, but was under attack from new forces generated in the age of bronze, notably the professional war-band with its dangerous mobility, unknown before the evolution of the chariot. In denouncing the members of such war-bands Zoroaster does not use the term *mairya* (the Avestan equivalent of Vedic *márya*), but defines them harshly or negatively, as for instance "non-herdsmen among the herdsmen," that is, *as tribesmen who had abandoned their traditional duty of sharing in the tending of cattle.*[41]

Now, surely this line of interpretation goes beyond what the text itself says, and there are no grammatical grounds on which the privative prefix *a-* in *a-fšuyant-* can be twisted to establish that these are persons who have *abandoned* the practice of herding. Formulaic constructions in which a noun is grouped with its opposite, the latter being marked by a privative prefix, are fairly common in the Gāthās and show no meaning of abandonment. Rather, here—as elsewhere within Indo-European poetic diction—the privative form derives its meaning solely from its juxtaposition and opposition to a positive counterpart, as for example: *gaēmcā ajyāitīmcā*, "life and non-life" (Y. 30.4b); *afšmāni . . . nōit anafšmạm*, "in verse and not non-verse" (Y. 46.17ab); *vīdyå vā ạvīdvå vā*, "knowing or non-knowing" (Y. 31.12b).[42] Nor is there anything in the text that suggests these "non-herdsmen" have but recently left herding behind. And there is another Gāthic passage which renders dubious in the extreme Boyce's repeated assertion that these "non-herdsmen" were just beginning to make their appearance in eastern Iran at the time of Zarathustra. This is a text which should be considered in connection with the question Zarathustra asks the Wise Lord in *Yasna* 44.6e: "For whom did you shape the fertile, luck-bringing cow?" (kaēibyō azīm / rānyō.skəraitīm gạm tašō).[43] That question—which had profound practical as well as religious significance in a society where cattle were not only the means of production but also the primary means of exchange and chief measure of wealth—is answered in a myth recounted at Yasna 31.9–10:

9. Yours was devotion; yours too was the Shaper of the Ox;
Understanding of the spirit [was yours], Wise Lord, when you
    gave her [i.e., the cow] the path
To go either to one who would be a pastor or one who would not
    be a pastor.
10. Then truly, of these two she chose the herdsman-pastoralist
As the truthful lord for herself, the furtherer [?] of good mind.
The non-pastoralist will not have a share of the good message, O
    Wise One, even should he prove his ability [?].

9. θwōi as ārmaitiš   θwə̄ gə̄uš tašā as xratuš
mainyuš mazdā ahurā   hyat ahyāi dadå paθạm
vāstryāt vā āitē   yə̄ vā nōit aŋhat vāstryō
10. at hī ayå fravarətā   vāstrim ahyāi fšuyantəm
ahurəm ašavanəm   vaŋhə̄uš fšəŋhīm manaŋhō
nōit mazdā avāstryō   davạscinā humərətōiš baxštā

Here we are told that the Wise Lord did not create the primordial cow (and consequently, the bovine species) for someone or some group in particular, but rather let her choose between two different sorts of men, who stood (and stand) in direct opposition to one another. Having been given a choice between "one who would be a pastor or one who would not be a pastor" (vāstryāt vā . . . yə̄ vā nōit aŋhat vāstryō, Y. 31.9c), the cow settles upon the "herdsman-pastoralist" (vāstrim . . . fšuyantəm), and in so doing rejects his negative counterpart, the "non-pastoralist" (avāstryō).[44] This contrast of vāstrya- with a-vāstrya- not only parallels closely that of fšuyant- to a-fšuyant- in Y. 49.4b,[45] but also establishes that Zarathustra, far from having viewed the "non-herdsmen" as relative newcomers on the scene, rather considered them to have been long established, indeed to have existed from the time of creation.

Technology and Warfare

Boyce, however, would have it otherwise, and she repeatedly insists that the appearance of a specialized warrior grouping was not only a recent development at the time of Zarathustra, but—more specifically—that it was a social mutation consequent upon the introduction of bronze weaponry and the chariot in eastern Iran.[46] As I lack training to evaluate critically the archaeological evidence pertinent to the early history of these technologies, it would be presumptuous of me to discuss this side of the argument, although I am surprised to find that Boyce has ignored the evidence of Tepe Hissar IIIB, a site just to the southeast of the Caspian Sea, occupied by an Indo-Aryan population toward the end of the third millennium B.C., where great quantities of bronze weapons have been found, as well as bones of domesticated horses and an alabaster cylinder seal on which is inscribed the picture of a horse-drawn chariot.[47] Beyond this, as a general matter of method I would only note that all archaeological dating of "origins" ought to be treated as provisional, since new finds can always force revision upward.

Quite apart from all questions involving the archaeological record of the Iranian and Indo-Iranian peoples, however—many of which remain controversial[48]—there remain textual and linguistic data that are absolutely irreconcilable with Boyce's theory. First, metallurgical technology is clearly and explicitly mentioned in three separate verses of the Gāthic Avesta: Y. 30.7c, 32.7b, and 51.9b, all of which describe the separation of those who are righteous and truthful from evildoers and liars through the agency of fiery metal. Although details of the procedures to which these verses allude are not entirely clear, experts—Boyce included—are in general agreement that the reflect religio-legal practices involving the administration of oaths and ordeals that are considerably older than Zarathustra.[49] Hardly a novelty, the smelting of bronze appears to have been well known at the time these texts were written, as witness the references to "glowing metal" (xᵛaēnā ayaŋhā) in Y. 32.7b and "molten metal" (ayaŋhā xšustā) in 51.9b, in which the word ayah- (cognate to Vedic áyas-, Latin aes, Gothic aiz, and others) denotes copper and bronze, the latter an alloy of copper and tin.[50]

In addition to metals, the chariot is mentioned in *Yasna* 50.6, and other Gāthic verses make reference to the yoking of swift steeds, with obvious reference to chariot racing.[51]

> A knower of sacred formulae, an ally of truth,
> Prayerful Zarathustra lifts up his voice, O Wise One:
> "May the Creator command my direction through good mind
> To be the charioteer of [my] tongue and power of thought."

yō maθrā	vācim mazdā baraitī
urvaθō ašā	nəmaŋhā zaraθuštrō
dātā xratəuš	hizvō raiθīm stōi
mahyā rāzəng	vohū sāhit manaŋhā

Here and in the following verse, one encounters a vocabulary that is drawn from the practice of chariot racing.[52] Far from being a description of chariotry itself, however, this passage appropriates from chariotry a set of images with which to construct a discourse of a more spiritual and allegoric nature. Thus, control of two yoked steeds by one charioteer is compared to the control of thought and speech (*xratəus* / *hizvō*) by one's ordering, directive faculty (*rāzəng*).[53] Chariots, then, were sufficiently familiar to Zarathustra and to his audience that he could employ without fear of miscomprehension a relatively complicated image grounded upon the practice of chariotry.

Of particular interest in this verse is the masculine substantive *raiθī-*, which—as Humbach first recognized[54]—corresponds to Vedic *rathī-* "charioteer," and is constructed upon the base of the Indo-Iranian masculine substantive **ratha-*, "chariot," a term reflected in Vedic *rátha-*, Younger Avestan *raθa-*, Old Persian *u-ratha-* "good chariots," and also in Indo-Aryan proper names recovered from the Ancient Near East, such as that of the Mitanni king *Tuš-ratta*.[55] Insofar as cognate terms in other Indo-European languages—Latin *rota*, Old Irish *roth*, Old High German *rad*, Lithuanian *rātas*, etc.—all have the meaning "wheel," it would appear that a semantic specialization occurred among the Indo-Iranians during their period of unity, whereby an older term for "wheel" came to denote a wheeled vehicle of a rather specific sort, i.e. the two-wheeled war chariot. This is shown not only by the usage of *rátha-* in Vedic and *raθa-* in Avestan but also by the existence of alternate terminology for other sorts of wheeled vehicles in both languages (Avestan *vāša-;* Vedic *ánas-*, explicitly contrasted to *rátha-* at RV 3.33.9). Further, and perhaps most important, there exists another term that permits us to specify just who it was that rode in a **ratha-*. For Avestan *raθaēštā-*, *raθaēštar-*, means most literally "he who stands in a chariot," and in practice denotes a member of the warrior class. What is more, this term—a complex formation in which the first member is the singular locative of *raθa-*[56]—corresponds in every particular to Vedic *rathesthā́-*, which virtually ensures their common descent from a Proto-Indo-Iranian **rathai-sthā́-*.[57]

That Zarathustra does not employ this word or others that are used elsewhere to denote warriors does not mean either that such terms were unavailable to him, or that such warriors did not exist, just as it may not be inferred from his non-use of terms like *haoma-*, *vazra-*, or *daēnu-* that intoxicants, maces, and cows either did not exist or were recent innovations during his lifetime. Rather, the prophet employed a terminology that was both innovative and polemic when referring to men of war. Among other things, he called them "non-herdsmen" (Y. 49.4) and "non-pastoralists" (Y. 31.10), identifying them not by what they were, but by what they were not, thereby condemning them for their omissions instead of celebrating them for their accomplishments.

However innovative Zarathustra's terminology and rhetoric may have been, there is nothing in the texts to suggest that those against whom he polemicized were themselves a novelty. On the contrary, careful consideration of the Gāthās indicates that warriors—like metal and chariots—had been a part of Iranian and Indo-Iranian society for many centuries before those texts were composed, whenever and wherever that may have been.

Scholars and Ideology Redux

Boyce has not, in my opinion, been sufficiently attentive to the details of Gāthic diction in her attempt to reconstruct the social milieu in which these texts were composed. Her vision of a "bipartite society" without specialized warriors rests less on rigorous philology than on tendentious dating, truncation of the textual evidence, circular argument, and—in the last analysis—a desire to see the "professionalization" of violence as a historically specific and (relatively) recent event, contingent upon a given set of technological advancements. This same desire to recover a pacific age prior to that which she calls "heroic"[58] recurs in her implausible assertion about the most martial god of the Vedas: "it is quite possible that in pastoral times"—one might as well say *in illo tempore* or *once upon a time*—"Indra himself was not the strikingly bellicose divinity of the existing traditions, but rather a celestial hero, honoured indeed among the *maryas*, but not yet a being whose chief delight was in war."[59]

In a similar vein—and for similar reasons—Boyce also rewrites the ethnology of East Africa to suit her purposes, repeatedly asserting that among the Nilotic peoples every herdsman was a warrior and every warrior a herdsman.[60] This, however, misrepresents a much more complicated state of affairs. While each separate case has its own particularities, that of the Maasai may serve as an example. According to John Galaty's penetrating analysis,[61] Maasai social identity is constructed along three separate axes: (1) that of gender, which separates males from females; (2) that of practical activity, which separates blacksmiths, hunters, and diviners (i.e. those whose characteristic activities place them in states of special purity or pollution) from other males; and (3) that of age and ritual status, which separates the remaining males into boys (who lack initiation and are barred from herding activity), warriors (initiated but forbidden marriage, who alone undertake the violence of raids), and elders (who are ritually removed from the rank of warriors, whereupon they may marry and devote themselves to peaceful herding activities).[62]

Unfamiliar with such evidence,[63] and unwilling to admit that warriors formed a specialized group, occupying an important position within Nilotic societies, Boyce proceeds to suggest:

> the possibility that cattle-raiding, with the associated large-scale butchery of ordinarily much-valued animals, *is not in fact an integral part of traditional Nilotic pastoralism, but an uncharacteristically violent and wasteful activity that developed incidentally*—perhaps when the tribes increased in numbers and came into closer contact with one another, and with the Bantu. Herdsmen, one may suppose, who had previously used their spears chiefly against wild animals—notably the lion, enjoying the hunt and gaining fame by their prowess in it, then learnt the excitement and potential profit of turning them also against their fellowmen; and the sudden increase in cattle which resulted from a successful raid may have led them to indulge them unlawfully in one of their chief, and ordinarily restricted, pleasures, that of eating meat. If such an explanation approaches the truth, it is possible to regard both cattle-raiding and the meat-feasts as essentially hedonistic activities, so enjoyable that they were indulged in despite of their being at variance with old social and religious codes.[64]

No evidence is adduced in support of these views, which would seem to be based on pure speculation. Yet if such speculations can tell us little about Nilotic society or prehistory, they may tell us much about their author, reflecting as they do a scholar of liberal and utopian bent who would prefer to imagine—here, as in India and Iran—that there existed a time when warfare and specialists in its practice did not yet exist, and to view these latter as something "that developed incidentally." Warfare thus appears not only as a historic accident but more generally as a fall from primordial perfection and a state of grace.

Ideologically attractive, perhaps, such a position runs aground on the evidence of four lexemes: *nar-*, an Indo-European designation of males that was used in the Gāthās, as in Vedic and Younger Avestan, to designate warriors; **rathai-sthā-*, an Indo-Iranian designation of chariot-riding warriors; *a-fšuyant-* and *a-vāstrya-*, Gāthic coinages through which Zarathustra referred derisively to those warriors whom others denoted by other names. On the strength of such evidence, I remain of the opinion that specialized warriors were very much a part of Indo-Iranian society. Beyond this, I would venture—in a formulation that obviously derives in part from ideological considerations, for I am no more a sterile and detachedly "objective" intellect than are Boyce, Wikander, or other human beings—that neither warfare nor warriors are recent in development, but are extremely ancient and have their roots, in Iran as elsewhere, not in specific technological innovations, but in the competition of rival groups and classes over scarce and valued resources.

Notes

1. *Bulletin of the School of Oriental and African Studies* (1988): 508–26.

2. *Priests, Warriors, and Cattle: A Study in the Ecology of Religions* (Berkeley: University of California Press, 1981). The published version was based largely upon my Ph.D. dissertation of similar title, "Priests, Warriors, and Cattle: A Comparative Study of East African and Indo-Iranian Religious Systems" (University of Chicago, 1976). The bulk of the research and writing was carried out between 1972 and 1976, with certain revisions being added in 1979–80.

3. Ibid., pp. 131 and 125–26 respectively.

4. Ibid., pp. 129–30.

5. Lund: C. W. K. Gleerup, 1938. Although published at Lund, where Wikander taught for a short time, this work was his doctoral dissertation at Uppsala University, and produced such heated controversy that at the time of its formal defense twelve different scholars rose to attack it. Others continue to make use of this work, and in addition to those mentioned by Boyce (p. 516, n. 50) one might note Franco Crevatin, *Richerche di antichità indeuropee* (Trieste: Edizioni LINT, 1979), pp. 51–76 ("Aspetti militari delle società indoeuropea e società militari"); Franklin E. Horowitz, "Greek skhétlios, Sanskrit kṣatriyaḥ, and the Indo-European Image of the Warrior," *Studia Linguistica* 29 (1975): 98–108; Willem B. Bollée, "The Indo-European Sodalities in Ancient India," *Zeitschrift der deutschen morgenlandischen Gesellschaft* 131 (1981): 172–91; and Kim R. McCone, "Hund, Wolf, und Krieger bei den Indogermanen," in W. Meid, ed. *Studien zum indogermanischen Wortschatz* (Innsbruck: Innsbrücker Beiträge zur Sprachwissenschaft, 1987), pp. 101–54.

6. Her discussion is found in "Priests, Cattle and Men," pp. 512–15.

7. Wikander, *Der arische Männerbund*, p. vii, makes mention of his two-semester stay in Berlin, where he studied philology at Friedrich-Wilhelms Universität on a Humboldt fellowship.

8. Frankfurt: Mortiz Diesterweg, 1934. Wikander cites this work in the very first sentence of *Der arische Männerbund* (p. vii) as the inspiration for his own research. On the nature and significance of *Kultische Geheimbünde der Germanen*, see Carlo Ginzburg, "Mitologia Germanica e Nazismo: Su un vecchio libro di Georges Dumézil," *Quaderni Storici* 19 (1984): 867–72. One should note that Höfler—who later enthusiastically supported the Nazi régime in Austria and contributed to such publications as the notorious *Forschungen zur Judenfrage*—served as lecturer in German at Uppsala from 1928 to 1934, at which time it is possible that he met and influenced Wikander. The intellectual milieu of Uppsala in the 1930s, where Georges Dumézil also served as lecturer in French (1931–33), deserves careful investigation. Ulf Drobin of the University of Stockholm is currently carrying out research in his area, and has made some preliminary observations on the topic in his article, "Indoeuropeisk kulturteori, språkteori och ideologi," *Häften för Kristika Studier* 19/1 (1986): 61–65.

9. Wikander, *Der arische Männerbund*, p. 1.

10. Ibid., p. 79; cf. p. 103, where the same term is used of Ferîdûn.

11. Ibid., pp. 4–5. The debate is an interesting and complex one, as it is Wikander who accuses Lommel of racism (*die losesten Rassenspekulationen*) for his attempt to classify the Rudras as belonging to a pre-Indo-European Indic stratum (cf. Herman Lommel, *Die alten Arier: von Art und Adel ihrer Gottheiten* [Frankfurt-am-Main: Klosmann, 1935], pp. 193 and 197–203). Wikander, in contrast, was at pains to assert that they, and the violence they represent, have a proper rôle within the Indo-European tradition.

12. Ibid., p. 64 (emphasis added).

13. Most recently on the etymology and significance of this term, see the important article of Françoise Bader, "De sanskrit *anyá-* à sanskrit *árya-:* noms indo-européens de l'autre," *Bulletin de la société de linguistique de Paris* 80 (1985): 57–90.

14. Wikander, *Der arische Männerbund*, p. 78.

15. Ibid., citing Heinrich Schurtz, *Altersklassen und Männerbünde* (Berlin: G. Reimer, 1902), and Hutton Webster, *Primitive Secret Societies* (New York: Macmillan, 1908).

16. "The Bipartite Society of the Ancient Iranians," in *Societies and Languages of the Ancient Near East*, M. A. Dandamayev et al., eds. (Warminster: Aris & Phillips, 1982), pp. 33–37.

17. For her emphasis on the importance of the Gāthās, see "Priests, Cattle and Men," pp. 511–12 and 516.

18. *A History of Zoroastrianism*, vol. 1, *The Early Period* (Leiden: E. J. Brill, 1975), p. 190.

19. *Zoroastrians: Their Religious Beliefs and Practices* (London: Routledge & Kegan Paul, 1979), p. 18.

20. *Textual Sources for the Study of Zoroastrianism* (Manchester: Manchester University Press, 1984), p. 11; "On the Antiquity of Zoroastrian Apocalyptic," *Bulletin of the School of Oriental and African Studies* 47 (1984): 74–75.

21. "Priests, Cattle, and Men," p. 511.

22. H. E. Eduljee, "The Date of Zoroaster," *Journal of the K. R. Cama Oriental Institute* 48 (1980): 103–60.

23. Karl Friedrich Geldner, "Zoroaster," *Encyclopaedia Britannica*, 11th ed. (New York: 1911) 28:1041. Boyce is not above citing obsolete scholarship in attempts to buttress those of her opinions for which no other support is available. Thus, for instance, in support of her interpretation of Avestan *nar-* (on which, see below), she appeals to Wilhelm Geiger, "who long ago studied these ancient texts with a fresh and penetrating eye" ("Priests, Cattle and Men," p. 511, with reference to Geiger's 1882 *Ostiranische Kultur in Alterthum*).

24. "On the Antiquity of Zoroastrian Apocalyptic," *Bulletin of the School of Oriental and African Studies* 47 [1984]: 74–75, citing Paul Friedrich, *Proto-Indo-European Syntax* (Butte, Mon.: Institute for the Study of Man, 1975), pp. 44–46.

25. As Friedrich acknowledged, p. 46.

26. On the date of Zarathustra, see Gherardo Gnoli, *Zoroaster's Time and Homeland* (Naples: Istituto Universitario Orientale, 1980), pp. 159–79, with a review of the earlier literature. A variety of views—but none ranging beyond the end of the second millennium b.c.—may also be conveniently consulted via the listings under "Zeit Zarathustras" in the index of Bernfried Schlerath, ed., *Zarathustra* (Darmstadt:

Wissenschaftliche Buchgesellschaft, 1970). Beyond these sources, one ought also see Kaj Barr, "Irans Profet som Teleios Antthrôpos," in *Festskrift til L. L. Hammerich* (Copenhagen: E. Muuksgard, 1952), pp. 26–27; Otakar Klima, "The Date of Zoroaster," *Archiv Orientalnì* 27 (1959): 556–64; F. B. J. Kuiper, "Remarks on the Avestan Hymn to Mithra," *Indo-Iranian Journal* 5 (1961): 43; and Ilya Gershevitch, "Zoroaster's Own Contribution," *Journal of Near Eastern Studies* 21 (1964): 12–14.

27. Christian Bartholomae, *Altiranisches Wörterbuch* (Berlin: Karl J. Trübner, 1904), pp. 1047–53. Boyce's discussion is found at "Bipartite Society of the Ancient Iranians," p. 33; cf. "Priests, Cattle and Men," p. 511.

28. Hermann Grassman, *Wörterbuch zum Rigveda* (Wiesbaden: Otto Harrassowitz, 1872), pp. 748–50, lists seven different meanings for Vedic *nṛ-*, among them "Kriegsmann, Held" (for which he cited 46 occurrences) and "insbesondere von Göttern, und zwar meist in dem Sinne der Helden" (186 occurrences). Bartholomae, p. 1048, lists 17 occurrences for *nar-* in the Younger Avesta with the meaning "wehrhafter Mann, Kriegsmann; kriegerischer Held" and two others with the meaning "Bezeichnung für den zweiten Stand, 'Krieger, Ritter.'" Also relevant is Old Persian *huvnara* (<*hu-H₂nara-*), which occurs three times, all in the same passage (Darius's inscription at Naxš-i-rustam b, lines 45–51): a passage that, when read with that which immediately precedes it, is seen to have clear martial reference:

> I am trained with my hands and feet. As a horseman, I am a good horseman; as an archer, I am a good archer, both on foot and mounted; as a spearman, I am a good spearman, both on foot and mounted. The Wise Lord bestowed these qualities of a good *nar-* [*ūvnarā*] on me, and I was strong [enough] to bear them, by the will of the Wise Lord. That which has been done by me—I did these things with the qualities of a good *nar-* [*ūvnaraibis*] which the Wise Lord bestowed on me. Boy, make it well known how great I am, how great are my qualities of a good *nar-* [*ūvnarā*], and how great is my superiority.

29. That there is an initial laryngeal, evident in Sanskrit *sūnara-*, Old Persian *huvnara-*, and also in Avestan *kamnā.nar-*, was first recognized by H. Jacobi, "Über Indra," *Zeitschrift für vergleichende Sprachforschung* 31 (1892): 316–19; see further Helmut Humbach, "Der Fugenvokal ā in gäthischen-awestischen Komposita," *Münchener Studien zur Sprachwissenschaft* 4 (1954): 54.

30. See also Suetonius' observations regarding the name *Nerō*—quo sīgnificātur linguā Sabīnā fortis ac strenuus (*Tiberius* 1.2). Consideration of the contrast in Umbrian between *ner* and *ueiro* (see the *Iguvine Tables* Vla 30, Vlb 59 and related passages) is quite helpful, on which see Georges Dumézil, *Idées romaines* (Paris: Gallimard, 1969), pp. 234–38, and Emile Benveniste, *Vocabulaire des institutions indo-européennes* (Paris: Editions de Minuit, 1969), 1:291–92; otherwise—but unconvincingly so—Enrico Campanile, "La dialettologia contemporanea e i problemi della ricostruzione indoeuropea," in *Nuovi materiali per la ricerca indoeuropeistica* (Pisa: Giardini, 1981), pp. 34–36. On the etymology and semantics of various Indo-Iranian terms derived from P-I-E *H₂ner-*, see the detailed discussions of H. W. Bailey, "Analecta Indoscythica: 2.*nṛta-*," *Journal of the Royal Asiatic Society* (1953): 103–16; Dumézil, *Idées romaines*, pp. 225–41; and (with some reservations) F. B. J. Kuiper, "Nōropi Khalkōi," *Medelelingen der Koninklijke Nederlandse Akademie van Wetenschappen* 14 (1951): 201–27. For the related forms in Hittite and Luvian,

see Jaan Puhvel, *Hittite Etymological Dictionary,* vol. 1 (Berlin: Mouton, 1984), pp. 62–63.

31. See, inter alia, Herman Lommel "Die Sonne das Schlechteste?" *Oriens* 15 (1962): 360–73; Ilya Gershevitch, "Die Sonne das Beste," in John Hinnells, ed., *Mithraic Studies* (Manchester: Manchester University Press, 1975), pp. 68–89; Hanns-Peter Schmidt, *Zarathustra's Religion and His Pastoral Imagery* (Leiden: University of Leiden, 1975), pp. 14–15; and Helmut Humbach, "Ahura Mazdā und die Daēvas," *Wiener Zeitschrift für die Kunde Sud und Ost Asiens* 1 (1957): 92.

32. The Pahlavi reads "my heroes and weapons [or: forces] are few" (*gurd ud abzār kam*); Neryosengh's Sanskrit, "my army and weapons are quite insignificant" (*me sainyam śastrānica kiṃcittarāni*).

33. On this formula, see Jakob Wackernagel, "Zum Dualdvandva," reprinted in *Indogermanische Dichtersprache,* Rüdiger Schmitt, ed. (Darmstadt: Wissenschaftliche Buchgesellschaft, 1968), pp. 30–33; Emile Benveniste, "Sur quelques dvandvas avestiques," *Bulletin of the School of Oriental and African Studies* 8 (1935–37): 405–6; Manfred Mayrhofer, "Zwei indische Miszellen: 1. Zu vedisch virapsá-," *Indian Linguistics* 19 (1958): 31–33; Rüdiger Schmitt, *Dichtung und Dichtersprache in indogermanischer Zeit* (Wiesbaden: Otto Harrassowitz, 1967), pp. 213–16 and Calvert Watkins, "NAM.RA GUD UDU in Hittite: Indo-European poetic language and the folk taxonomy of wealth," in Erich Neu and Wolfgang Meid, eds., *Hethitisch und Indogermanisch* (Innsbruck: Innsbrücker Beiträge zur Sprachwissenschaft, 1979), pp. 269–87. Similar conclusions have been reached regarding *kamnafšva . . . kamnānā* by Benveniste, *Le vocabulaire des institutions indo-européennes,* 1:49, and Françoise Bader, "Phraséologie, étymologies, civilisation indo-européennes," *Bulletin de la Société de linguistique de Paris* 73 (1978): 206.

34. Thus, Darius states that he had few men (*kamnaibiš martiyaibiš*) with him when he slew Gaumata the Magus (Behistun Inscription 1.56); that his army was small when he put down the rebellion of Phraortes (*kamnam,* DB 2.19, referring back to *kāra* in the preceding line); and four times he describes kings who, when conquered, fled "with a few horsemen" (*kamnaibiš asabāraibiš* DB 2.2, 2.71, 3.41, 3.71–72). In interpreting Avestan *kamnā.nar-,* one ought also consider its opposite: *pouru.nar-* ("having many *nar*s"), which appears as a modifier of the battlefield wherein warriors ought pray for their horses to be strong and swift (*Yasna* 11.2; cf. Yt. 10.11 and 5.53).

35. Numerous Vedic instances are given by Wackernagel, pp. 32–33. Within Avestan, note the pairing of *vīra-* with *gav-* in Yt. 10.28 and 13.52, and that of *pasu-* with *nar-* in Y. 4.5 and Vd. 13.32. In the Gāthās, the archaic formula is preserved at Y. 31.15c and Y. 45.9d, and in the Younger Avesta, at Y. 9.4, 58.6; Yt. 10.112, 13.12, 19.32, and 13.10; Vr. 7.3; Vd. 10.18 and 6.32.

36. Also relevant is Y. 29.9, where the soul of the ox, struggling to reconcile his desire for a powerful protector with the reality of the seemingly impotent priest to whom he has been consigned, characterizes Zarathustra as "a carer without power" (anaēšəm . . . rādəm), who has only "the voice of a man without strength," (vācim nərəš asūrahyā; *nar-* being used here either ironically or in its unmarked sense). Moreover, the ox contrasts him with the desired "one whose rulership has power" (īšā.xšaθrīm) who would be capable of giving "help that has hands" (zastavat avō). The contrast thus drawn between the priest, whose power resides in his voice, and the warrior, whose power resides in his hands, is strongly reminiscent of the sociogonic

portion of the *Puruṣasūkta* (RV 10.90.11–12), and also *Škend Gumānīg Wizār* 1.20–24, which reads: "And in the microcosm which is man is revealed a likeness to the four social classes of the world. The head is like the priesthood, the hands like the warrior-hood, the belly like the commoners, and the feet like the artisanry" (ud andar gēhān ī kōdak ī hast mardōm, paydāgēnēd pad hōmānāgīh ī ēn cahār pēšagān ī gēhān: ciyōn abar sar, āsrōnīh; abar dašt, artēštārīh; abar aškamb, wastryōšīh; abar pay, hutuxšīh).

37. Boyce, "The Bipartite Society of the Ancient Iranians," pp. 34–35; idem, "Priests, Cattle and Men," pp. 511 and 523.

38. Cf. the recurrence of *rāma-* and *aēšma-* in Y. 29.1 and 48.7 (considering the latter within the full context of Y. 48.5–7), and see further *Priests, Warriors, and Cattle*, pp. 127 and 149–50, together with the literature cited therein.

39. "The Bipartite Society of the Ancient Iranians," p. 35.

40. "Priests, Cattle and Men," p. 525.

41. Ibid., p. 512 (emphasis added).

42. Other examples are cited in Helmut Humbach, *Die Gāthās des Zarathustra* (Heidelberg: Carl Winter, 1959), 1:39. See also the observations of Enrico Campanile, *Ricerche di Cultura Poetica Indoeuropea* (Pisa: Giardini, 1977), pp. 98–103.

43. The same question recurs at Y. 29.1a, where it is the cow herself who asks: "For whom did you shape me?" (kahmāi mā θwarōždūm).

44. On the antiquity and significance of the group of terms that includes *vāstrya-*, see Emile Benveniste, *Hittite et indo-européen* (Paris: Adrien Maisonneuve, 1962), pp. 97–101.

45. The same contrast is expressed a bit differently at Y. 31.15, where the "non-lying herdsman" (*vāstryehyā . . . adrujyantō*) is set against the "lying evil-doer" (*drəgvāitē . . . duš.šyaoθanāi*). Here again a privative a- prefix is used to mark these two differing groups, and an inverse relation is established between them on the basis of two binary variables: occupation (±Herding) and speech conduct (±Lying). One group, championed by Zarathustra, is thus identified as +Herding/−Lying, and the other as −Herding/+Lying. The same two groups are contrasted in abbreviated form (+Herding opposed to +Lying) in the phrase *fšuyəntē drəgvasū* (Y. 29.5c), which is also grammatically parallel to *fšuyasū afšuyantō* in Y. 49.4b.

46. "Bipartite Society of the Ancient Iranians," pp. 35–36; "Priests, Cattle and Men," pp. 508–14 and passim.

47. See the discussion of R. Ghirshman, *L'Iran et la migration des indo-aryens et des iraniens* (Leiden: E. J. Brill, 1977), pp. 14–16, who has emphasized the importance of this seal.

48. It is worth quoting the remarks of E. A. Grantovskij, which were already cited and heartily endorsed by Ghirshman, p. 78: "It is difficult to point to a single study on which a unanimity of opinion could be forged. Contemporary experts propose diametrically opposed solutions for a whole series of cardinal questions."

49. Thus Herman Lommel, *Die Religion Zarathustras nach dem Awesta dargestellt* (Tübingen: J. C. B. Mohr, 1930), pp. 219–22; Jacques Duchesne-Guillermin, *La religion de l'Iran ancien* (Paris: Presses Universitaires de France, 1962), pp. 90–91; Geo Widengren, *Die Religionen Irans* (Stuttgart: W. Kohlhammer, 1965), pp. 87–88; and Boyce, *History of Zoroastrianism* 1:34–36 and 242–44. With regard to metallurgy, Boyce seems to have adopted the position of Eduljee, who refers to "the paucity of references to any metal in the Gathas and the ancient Yashts" (pp. 144 and 147), thus ignoring not only the three Gāthic passages here cited, but also the description of

Mithra's mace (Yt. 10.96), that of the Fravašis' armor and weaponry (Yt. 13.45), and the proper name *Ayō.asti-* "He whose bones are metal" (Yt. 13.112).

50. Thus Alfons Nehring, "Studien zur indogermanischen Kultur und Urheimat," *Wiener Beiträge zur Kulturgeschichte und Linguistik* 4 (1936): 30; Carl Darling Buck, *A Dictionary of Selected Synonyms in the Principal Indo-European Languages* (Chicago: University of Chicago Press, 1949), pp. 611–12; Julius Pokorny, *Indogermanisches etymologisches Wörterbuch* (Bern: Francke Verlag, 1969), pp. 15–16. Derivation is from the verb **ai-*, "to shine." Bartholomae, *Altiranisches Wörterbuch*, p. 159, interprets Avestan *ayah-* as "metall (Eisen)," but iron seems unlikely for a Gāthic text. Further indication that *ayah-* in early sources denotes bronze comes from an old metric passage of the Yašt to Mithra (Yt. 10.96), in which the god's mace is said to be "cast of golden metal" (zarōiš ayaŋhō frahixtəm), with *ayah-* modified by *zairi-*. Whereas copper would be too soft for such a weapon, iron would hardly be "golden." The *R̥g Veda* also mentions weapons—specifically "blades" *dhārā-* made of *áyas-* (RV 6.3.5 and 6.47.10), and similar terminology, reflecting similar technology, recurs in Yt. 10.96, where the Avestan cognate of Vedic *dhārā-* recurs in the compound adjective *satō.dāra-* ("of a hundred blades") used of Mithra's brazen mace.

51. See also *Yasna* 50.7a, 30.10b, and 44.4d.

52. Boyce acknowledges the existence of chariots as attested in these verses, while paradoxically denying the existence of chariot warriors ("Bipartite Society of the Ancient Iranians," p. 33).

53. For interpretation of Avestan *rāz-*, see Jean Kellens, *Les noms-racines de l'Avesta* (Wiesbaden: Ludwig Reichert, 1974), pp. 280–82. The imagistic depiction of proper speech and thought as horses yoked together is also apparent in Y. 50.7, where the "swiftest steeds" (zəvištyə̄ng aurvatō) are said to be "strong with truth and good mind" (ašā / ugrə̄ng vohū manaŋhā). In its general lines, the image is reminiscent of *Katha Upaniṣad* 1.3.3–9, and Plato's *Phaedrus* 246A–247C, yet given the broad divergence of detail among these sources, it would be risky to posit a common origin for them. On the use of imagery derived from chariotry in poetic and ritual speculation, see M. Sparreboom, *Chariots in the Veda* (Leiden: E. J. Brill, 1985), pp. 13–27; Boris Oguibénine, *Essais sur la culture védique et indo-européeune* (Pisa: Giardini, 1985), pp. 171–89.

54. Humbach, *Die Gāthās des Zarathustra* 2:85, pace Bartholomae, *Altiranisches Wörterbuch* p. 1508. See also S. Insler, *The Gāthās of Zarathustra*, pp. 307–8.

55. Manfred Mayrhofer, *Kurzgefasstes etymologisches Wörterbuch des Altindisches* (Heidelberg: Carl Winter, 1956–76), 3:39. On the Mitanni name, see Mayrhofer's discussion, "Zu den arischen Sprachresten in Vorderasien," *Die Sprache* 5 (1959): 78–80.

56. One should note also that the singular locative of *raθa-* takes the form *raθaē* (=Vedic *ráthe*) only in this frozen compound, being elsewhere always *raθoi* or *raiθe*, as was first noticed by Helmut Humbach, "Awestische raθa- 'Wagen' und seine Ableitungen," *Münchener Studien zu Sprachwissenschaft* 36 (1977): 49. Cf. the relation of Av. *dūraē-darštar-*, "who sees in the distance," to Ved. *dūre-dr̥ś-*.

57. *Pace* Boyce's attempt to shrug this important word off as a novel formation since it does not appear in the Gāthās ("Priests, Cattle and Men," p. 512).

58. "The Bipartite Society of the Ancient Iranians," pp. 33–36, with reference to the influential work of H. M. Chadwick, *The Heroic Age* (Cambridge: Cambridge University Press, 1912).

59. "Priests, Cattle and Men" p. 521.

60. Ibid., pp. 516–20.

61. John Galaty, "Pollution and Pastoral Antipraxis: The Issue of Maasai Inequality," *American Ethnologist* 6 (1979): 803–16.

62. It is worth quoting here Galaty's observations regarding this last category. He states (p. 806): "The male Maasai elder—the distinctively 'unmarked' category of Maasai—withholds himself from activities of slaughter, which are performed by hunters or youngers; from warfare, which is performed by warriors; from birth, which is carried out by women; and from circumcision, which is performed by hunters. In other words, he is able to benefit from the necessary processes of blood letting, on which life itself depends, while not involving himself with the degradation of actual contact with those generative events. His purity, then, is purchased at the expense of the pollution of others: hunters, diviners, and blacksmiths, on the one hand; and age-inferiors, women and children, on the other hand." Similar considerations are conceivably relevant to and implicit in the high moral position accorded herdsmen in the Gāthās.

63. By her own admission ("Priests, Cattle and Men," p. 516), Boyce has read nothing about the peoples of East Africa save my summary treatment.

64. Ibid., pp. 518–19.

THIRTEEN

SACRIFICIAL IDEOLOGY AND INDO-EUROPEAN SOCIETY

At present, it is difficult to speak of Indo-European myth, religion, and/or society without invoking the name of Georges Dumézil, whose theory of the "three functions"—that is, the perceived tendency of I-E-speaking peoples to conceptualize their world in terms of (1) religio-magical sovereignty, (2) martial force, and (3) the spheres of production and reproduction—has dominated scholarly debate for the last half century. Yet before Dumézil, there were other important studies in this area, now often overlooked, but still worthy of consideration. In particular, I have in mind the writings of such scholars as Hermann Güntert, Albrecht Götze, and Richard Reitzenstein, who worked on the theme of microcosm and macrocosm, and Kasten Rönnow who—in my view, rightly—related this theme to that of ritual sacrifice, although he was severely criticized for his insistence on the reality and importance of the practice of human sacrifice in ancient India, Greece, and elsewhere.

Over the last few years, I have been reconsidering the importance of sacrifice within Indo-European thought and practice, and I would like to summarize here some of those results, although I can present only a frustratingly small portion of the evidence and argumentation. I shall begin with excerpts from two classic texts drawn from different points in the Indo-European world: the celebrated *Puruṣasūkta* ("Song of Man," RV 10.90), a hymn of the *Ṛg Veda* dating roughly to 900 B.C., and the "Poem on the Dove King," (*Stič o golubinoj knigъ*), an Old Russian folk poem, collected from oral tradition early in the nineteenth century, but mentioned already in texts dating to the thirteenth.

> When they divided Puruṣa ["Man"], how many pieces did they
>   prepare? . . .
> The moon was born of his mind; of his eye, the sun was born;
> From his mouth, Indra and fire; from his breath, wind was born.
> From his navel, there was the atmosphere; from his head, heaven
>   was rolled together;
> From his feet, the earth, from his ear, the cardinal points.
> Thus the gods caused the worlds to be created.
> Seven-mouthed were the sacrificial enclosures; thrice seven
>   bundles of wood were made
> When the gods, performing sacrifice, bound Puruṣa ["Man"] as
>   the sacrificial animal.

Our bright light comes from the Lord,
The red sun from the face of God,
The young shining moon from his breast,
The bright dawn from the eyes of God,
The sparkling stars from his vestments,
The wild winds from the Holy Spirit. . . .
Strong bones come from stones,
Our bodies from the damp earth.

I could dwell on the differences in detail between these two texts, and could add others to the discussion, but I shall restrict myself to some general remarks concerning their similarities. First, we must note the way in which both these accounts break down the universe and the human body into parallel sets of their constituent parts. The sets, moreover, are correlated to one another such that the relations of all parts reflect the more general relation of the body to the universe: the microcosm to the macrocosm. Now, while some of the specific correlations are found only in one text or the other, there is considerable overlap between them, and many items recur in other texts as well: the correlation between sun and eyes, for instance, or those between wind and breath, or stones and bones. When a large number of texts are studied carefully, other such recurrent correlations may be identified: earth and flesh, plants (especially grass) and hair, water and blood (or other bodily fluids), moon and mind, clouds and brain, and also the rim of heaven and the head or skull. Finally, in all these instances, these correlations are not expressed in the form of poetic imagery. The texts do not say "The sun is like the eyes" or "the wind resembles the breath"; rather, we are regularly told of the very creation of the world and its parts from the corresponding pieces of a primordial human body. As the Old Norse *Vafþrúðnismál* has it: "From Ymir's flesh the earth was made, and mountains from his bones. . . ." The two items in any such correlation are thus placed in homologic relation, a fundamental consubstantiality and interchangeability being posited between them. Each item in such a homology is thus seen to consist of and derive from the material substance of the other. The two items are thus what I call *alloforms*—that is, alternative shapes of one another. Viewed thus, flesh and earth—like any other alloformic pair and like the body and the universe more generally—are considered to be composed of the very same essential matter ("undifferentiated flesh-earth stuff" in this case), matter which may be temporarily incarnated in either one of two superficially different forms at any given moment: one bodily or microcosmic form and the other macrocosmic.

In the texts I have cited—with one minor exception—the transformations all move from the microcosm to the macrocosm: that is, these are cosmogonic accounts, stories of how the world was created from the dismembered parts of a primordial victim. What is more, priests within the Indo-European tradition claimed to repeat this process with the performance of every act of ritual sacrifice. Such is clear, for instance, in Herodotus' account of Persian rites (1.131) in which the Magi are said to have chanted a "theogony," i.e., a hymn of creation, during the dismemberment of an animal victim, this being performed for the benefit of heaven, sun, moon, earth, fire, water, and wind: i.e., the elements of the macrocosm. One finds similar beliefs in an Old Irish text (*Senchus Mór* 1.22), where it is said that the Druids "claimed that they made the sky and earth and sea and so forth, the sun and moon and so forth." Indic texts also strike a similar note, as for instance, this set of instructions for the handling of the dismembered bodily parts of animal victims (*Aitareya Brāhmaṇa* 2.6):

> "Cause its eye to go to the sun; send forth its breath to the wind; its life-force to the atmosphere; its ear to the cardinal points; its flesh to the earth." Thus [i.e. with this sacred formula and the accompanying gestures] the priest places this victim into the parts of the universe.

Returning to the myths of creation with which we began our discussion, one can see how these sacrifices consciously and carefully represent the actions described in the cosmogonic accounts, while the cosmogonies conversely represent sacrificial dismemberment. Beyond this, we must now turn our attention to the one exception to the predominantly cosmogonic (and sacrificial) pattern which characterizes the two texts I have cited. This is found in the last lines of the Old Russian "Poem on the Dove King," where we are told *not* that stones were created from bones (i.e., macrocosm from microcosm), but just the reverse: "Strong bones *come from stones,* / Our bodies from the damp earth." And similar, often much more elaborate accounts of the origin of the human body from the material substance of the macrocosm are found in all the European members of the Indo-European language family. Consider, for instance, an insertion to the fifteenth-century Old Frisian *Code of Emsig:*

> God made the first man—that was Adam—from eight transformations: the bone from stone, the flesh from earth, the blood from water, the heart from wind, the thoughts from clouds, the sweat from the dew, the locks of hair from grass, the eyes from the sun, and then he blew in the Holy Spirit. Then he made Eve, Adam's love, from his rib.

The Christianization here—evident at the beginning and end of the passage—is quite superficial, consisting of no more than the use of the name "Adam" for the first man, the substitution of "Holy Spirit" for wind as the alloform of breath, and the addition of Eve's creation from Genesis 2:21–22. But what is most significant is that we see here the mirror image of cosmogony: that is, an anthropogonic account, in which the body of the first man is created from homologous parts of the macrocosm. What is more, we occasionally encounter texts such as the first chapters of the *Aitareya Upaniṣad,* in which cosmogonic and anthropogonic narratives are joined together, it there being recounted how the universe was created from the dismembered body of the primordial man (again called Puruṣa ["Man"]), and then how his body was put back together from its macrocosmic alloforms that had been scattered throughout the universe. The picture presented is that of a cycle, in which cosmogony and anthropogony ceaselessly alternate: the body being created out of the world and the world out of the body, with the creation of the one always implying and resulting from the (temporary and partial) de-creation of the other.

I have spoken of sacrifice as a ritual which effectively repeats the cosmogony, shifting matter from a victim's body to the alloformic parts of the universe in order to sustain the latter against decay and ultimate collapse. But there were other Indo-European rituals which employed these same ideas to repeat anthropogonic processes, transferring matter from the universe to the human body, in order to sustain the latter against the same threats of decay and collapse. Among the clearest of these were healing and the taking of food, actions which also found their religious explanation and legitimation in myths of creation through sacrifice. Consider, for instance, the Middle Persian text *Zad Spram* 3.42–51, which recounts a crucial episode in the first assault of the Evil Spirit Ahriman against the good creation:

> Ahriman came to the cattle. He struggled against the cattle. As the first ox died, because it possessed the nature and form of plants, fifty-seven species of grain and twelve species of healing plants came into being. From every bodily member they grew, just as the details of every one which came from those bodily members are revealed in the *Dāmdād Nask.*

The passage continues to discuss the nature and use of several of these plants: sesame, we are told, "has its origin in marrow and is itself marrow, it is an increasor of marrow." Similarly, the vine comes from blood, and thus wine "is a helper for the healthy nature of the blood." We are thus told that food was *and is* created through an act of sacrifice—a cosmogonic ritual, in which a living being (here the first ox) is transformed temporarily into inert matter. Moreover, through the act of eating, bodies can be re-created once more out of the alloformic matter: wine that was blood can become blood again, for the consumption of food is taken to be nothing other than an anthropogonic reversal of sacrifice. Healing was considered similar, and it seems clear that the lost *Dāmdād Nask* (mentioned as the ultimate source of the text quoted above) discussed in detail the origin, nature, and use of all "fifty-seven species of grain and twelve species of healing plants" that were created from the body of the first sacrificial ox. What becomes clear—and there are similar passages in Indic, Greek, Germanic, Celtic, Baltic, and Slavic texts—is that just as cosmogony and anthropogony complement and alternate with one an-

other, so sacrifice complements and alternates with rituals of an anthropogonic nature: every offering is followed by a meal.

I will not attempt to consider here the detailed applications of the general
system of homologic correspondences and transformations, but I should at
least mention that we find many passages scattered throughout the various
Indo-European literatures in which the attempt was made to work out the
subtle implications of individual homologies in their specificity. The interaction of the alloforms breath and wind, for instance, in yoga, Presocratic philosophy, and elsewhere is used to explain "simple" respiration, i.e. the cycle
of anthropogony and cosmogony in which essential air-breath lifestuff enters
the microcosm with each act of inhalation, only to reenter the macrocosm sec-
onds later with each exhalation.

Again, the homology of hair and plants figures in the widespread practice
of placing shorn hair in the soil, in order to supply matter essential for the
re-creation of hair's macrocosmic alloform, as is made explicit in the formula every Zoroastrian is instructed to recite while burying his hair clippings:
"Make the plants grow" (*Vīdēvdāt* 17.5). Moreover, this process is reversed
in cures for baldness, where one is advised to rub the scalp with solutions of
various plant substances, in an evident attempt to transfer the underlying material substance common to hair and plants (i.e. "hair-plant stuff") from its
temporary residence in the macrocosm to its desired—but equally temporary—incarnation on a balding head.

In truth, we still rub plant solutions upon our hair—herbal shampoos, bal-
sam rinses, and the like—and some people still apply mud packs on their
faces as a means to restore aging flesh. Other homologies also continue to
exert influence or were only recently replaced by more "scientific" explanations. The idea of "lunacy," for instance, grows out of the homology of mind
and moon, and one can still invest the lowly act of urination with a cosmogonic significance through the common expression "to make water." That this
is, in fact, part of the general system under discussion may be confirmed once
more in aspects of yogic practice, for the yogin is taught to master the anthropogonic reversal of "making water," by attaining sufficient control over
his urinary tract that he can draw up water thereby, thus recreating bodily
fluids out of their macrocosmic alloform.

No doubt, we find these vestiges of homologic thought in our modern world
rather amusing: we had not expected to discover cosmic significance in our
choice of shampoo or our excretory euphemisms. What makes them amusing,
however, is that being mere fragments abstracted from the full system in
which they were initially cast, they have lost their real persuasive power. We
tell different stories now to explain the origin and nature of the universe, or to
speculate on the interrelations of human beings and the world around them.
And when our myths have been replaced by others still, such survivals as may
persist will also seem rather amusing.

Within a totalistic and totalizing system of thought, however—a system which centered upon the homology of microcosm and macrocosm, and the complementarity of cosmogony and anthropogony, sacrifice and such anti-sacrificial operations as eating and healing—all pieces of the system were mutually reinforcing. The system thus possessed enormous persuasive power, by virtue of the vast scope and variety of phenomena which could be explained within it. I would note briefly, for instance, the analysis of birth and death which formed an important part of this awesomely inclusive system, for death was regarded as nothing less than a cosmogonic action—a final sacrifice, in which the material substance of the body was transformed into its macrocosmic alloforms, while birth was the anthropogonic reversal of death, in which cosmic matter was reassembled in bodily form. Such a view is summarized concisely, to cite but one example, in a fragment from Empedocles (B9 in the Diels-Kranz collection):

> When the cosmic elements are mixed into man—
> Or into the race of wild animals, or into bushes,
> Or into birds—then people call that "birth."
> And when they separate out, that is called "death."
> That which is correct, they do not call by name, and by habit
>   even I speak in similar fashion.

In this, and other ways, I take Empedocles to have been working within the lines of an extremely ancient, coherent, and finely wrought system of thought common among the Indo-European peoples. It is thus of considerable interest that he—like his counterparts in India, Iran, Scandinavia, and elsewhere—held creation to have resulted from nothing other than an act of sacrificial dismemberment, for as Kasten Rönnow rightly saw some sixty years ago, sacrifice was not only the centerpiece of Indo-European ritual practice but was also the centerpiece of Indo-European speculative thought.

As I mentioned earlier, Rönnow went further and argued for the primacy of human sacrifice, not only for the Germans, Celts, Scyths, and Thracians—where there is significant evidence to support such a claim—but also among Greeks and Indians, where the evidence is quite thin. As a result, he was severely criticized and his works lie largely ignored. I want to return to the issue of human sacrifice but, before doing so, it seems helpful to reflect on issues of theory and method, since before we can safely interpret the evidence of myths and rituals, we must first have some clarity about what we take myth and ritual to be.

For my part, I consider myth and ritual to be stylistically different but complementary and mutually reinforcing modes for the encoding and dissemination of ideology, most often religious ideology, but not necessarily so. In the case at hand, this last qualification is an unnecessary one, for the myths and rituals we have been considering are part of a well-integrated system of religious ideology, and we must thus note that unlike secular ideologies—which they resemble in many ways—religious ideologies regularly offer analyses of the fundamental nature of humanity and of the cosmos itself. But like other modes of ideology, religious ideologies also devote careful attention to the nature and proper order of a third entity intermediate to the microcosm of the individual and the macrocosm of the universe: that is, the meso-cosm of human society. And one cannot, in my opinion, study myth, ritual, and/or religion in pristine isolation: rather, we must take careful account of the society in which these are rooted, a society whose structures and organization they continually re-present in accurate and/or mystified terms, and which they usually—but not always—help to perpetuate.

With regard to the Indo-European themes of creation through sacrifice, there are certain data which can help us to relate myth and ritual to society, for I must now confess that I have not played entirely fair in my presentation of the evidence, for I began by citing *excerpted* passages from two texts that described the creation of the physical universe from the body of a primordial being. The time has now come, however, for me to restore the sections which I earlier deleted, which describe—as an integral part of the same process of creation—the origins of the social universe. Thus, the central section of the Old Russian "Poem on the Dove King" states:

> From this our dear Czars are on earth:
> From the holy head of Adam.
> From this princes and heroes come into being:
> From the holy bones of Adam.
> From this are the orthodox peasants:
> From the holy knee of Adam.

Verses 11–12 of the *Puruṣasūkta* show the same pattern: a vertical hierarchy of social classes, in which relative positions are defined by that portion of the first man's body from which they came when that man was sacrificed and ritually dismembered:

> When they divided Puruṣa ("Man"), how many pieces did they
> prepare?
> What was his mouth? What are his arms, thighs, and feet called?
> The priest was his mouth; the warrior was made from his arms;
> His thighs were the commoner, and the servant was made from
> his feet.

There are other texts one could add to these—one thinks particularly of Plato's tendentious use of the same homologies between bodily parts and social classes in the discussion of *Republic* 440E–441A and *Timaeus* 69D–70A, where he correlates his philosopher-king (the "deliberative" class characterized by reason) to the head, the "defensive" class (characterized by "spirit" [*thymos*] and charged with police and army functions) to the upper torso (i.e.

the region between the neck and the diaphragm), and the "commercial" class (characterized by appetite) to the lower torso. Here, as in all such cases, the duties and privileges of the various social classes—which follow the familiar Dumézilian pattern—are justified ("explained") by reference to their bodily alloform. Czars, priests, or philosopher-kings are entitled to direct and command others because they are, in effect, the head of the sociopolitical body. Warriors fight because of their association to the arms, chest, heart, and lungs (where energy and courage are located), while the lower classes run errands, produce food, and generally support their class superiors because of their proximity to feet, legs, and abdomen. Regarding the lower classes, numerous texts also specify that they are not to be trusted, given their excessive appetites, which derive from their association to the belly and genitals, not to mention their considerable distance from the seat of reason. This is yet another way in which they were regarded as "lowly"—in every sense of the term—but it was this group which formed the bulk of society, a fact which is reflected (one might also say "explained," when the world is seen upside down under the influence of powerful ideological constructs) in the way that the lower torso, the bodily alloform of this group is the largest part of the body, while the smallest (but also the highest) social class has as its alloform the smallest and highest part of the body: the head.

Now, it would be easy to dismiss the inequities within this mythico-ritually encoded ideological system did it stand alone, just as it is easy to be impressed by the brilliance and the grandeur of the cosmic speculations which we considered earlier. But it is an artificial result of my presentation—a heuristic and analytic device only—to view them in separation. On the contrary, the cosmic and the social sides of this religious ideology, as expressed in myth and ritual, and as enacted in social praxis and organization, were both part of one and the same system. And one cannot separate the elegant strands of speculative thought from the brutal facts of social hierarchy and exploitation: it was, and regularly is, the persuasive power of the former which makes the latter possible.

The social system which was buttressed by this ideology was one in which mental labor was reserved for a privileged few, to whom were allotted the greatest shares of valued resources. The others, who engaged in manual work, were further differentiated, some enjoying a considerable measure of power, prosperity, and prestige, while others—the majority—were relegated to lives of service and subordination, bearing further the stigma of impurity. All these results—real, concrete effects, and not gossamer stories—were effectively legitimated by myths of creation through sacrifice, and were also dramatized in the practice of sacrificial ritual, in which members of the highest class presided and—most often—those of the second class served as patrons, while those of the lowest class played minor roles, if any at all.

In their classic *Essai sur le sacrifice,* Henri Hubert and Marcel Mauss argued that all social life is essentially a form of sacrifice, in which individuals offer up portions of themselves for the common good but reap the great rewards of life within society as a result. What these masters of the *école sociologique* failed to realize, however—here, as in all their work—is that far greater sacrifices are required from some members of society than of others, while those who are required to offer the most often reap the leanest rewards. With this recognition, I feel prepared to consider the question which earlier I postponed.

It may well be that Kasten Rönnow—to whose memory I dedicate this essay—may have overestimated the importance of human sacrifice among the Indo-European peoples. For my part, I would prefer to say that he was but overly literal in his formulation of the problem. Indeed, there are more ways than one to sacrifice a human being, and it is not those victims alone who are actually led to the altar who deserve our respect and compassion.

FOURTEEN

THE DRUIDS AND HUMAN SACRIFICE

Scholars have long been uncomfortable with the various Greco-Roman accounts of the foremost members of the ancient Celtic priestly class. For while many of the classical sources accord high praise to the Druids' intellectual accomplishments,[1] others have vigorously condemned them for their complicity in the performance of human sacrifice,[2] while others still have noted both wisdom and barbaric rites alike.[3] In the face of such seemingly contradictory evidence, some modern authorities—those incapable of believing it possible that men gifted in the study of philosophy could also celebrate hideous rituals—have sought to settle the problem by one of two complementary strategies, effectively denying one half of the evidence or the other. Thus, on the one hand, some would have us believe that the ancient praises of Druidic learning were but an ancient version of the romantic and unfounded celebration of the "noble savage" (so-called "primitivism"),[4] and, on the other, some would convince us that the testimonies of Druidic sacrifice were but part of a Roman propaganda campaign in the period after the conquest of Gaul, a campaign aimed at reducing the Druids' role as a center of resistance to Roman rule.[5]

Neither the one nor the other of these attempts can be sustained in the face of the evidence. For although the Roman propagandists certainly exploited the Druids' connection to sacrifice, they relied on Greek sources such as Posidonius's ethnography of the Celts and Sopater's account of them, both of which long predate any propagandistic motive and unflinchingly recount rather grisly Druidic rituals. Still, there surely is a trace of "primitivism" in certain classical authors' expressed admiration for Druidic science even though there can be no doubt that the Celts themselves regarded their priests as masters of wisdom, for the very name "Druid" (OIr. *druí*, gen. *druad*) means nothing other than "He whose wisdom is firm" (from P-I-E *dru-wid-*, where the first element is an intensifying article also attested in toponyms [*Dru-nemeton*, "firm sanctuary"] and personal names [*Dru-talus*, "He whose visage is firm"]).[6]

Happily, there is no need to choose between viewing the Druids *either* as practitioners of wisdom *or* of sacrifice, but not both, for as the great bulk of recent research shows, sacrificial ritual is regularly attended by the most complex structures of thought. And as Mircea Eliade insisted in a short article with the provocative title "Druids, Astronomers, and Headhunters," there is no contradiction in the Greco-Roman testimonies.[7] Rather, the problem begins with the cultural presuppositions of modern students of these texts, who are unable to accept the fact well-known from anthropological research—Eliade cites the classic study of Hans Schärer on the religion of the Ngaju Dayak—that one may perfectly well combine such practices as headhunting, cannibalism, human sacrifice, and the like, with extremely sophisticated and intelligent religio-philosophical systems and rationales.

There is a methodological problem in the use of such far-flung comparative evidence, however, which is not resolved in Eliade's study. For while such comparisons may establish that it is possible to combine philosophical speculation and the practice of human sacrifice, they do not and cannot establish that the Druids did, in fact, do so. For this conclusion to legitimately emerge, only evidence directly relevant to the Druids themselves will suffice. Such evidence, however, can be located, and I hope to do so in this essay, thus putting an end to the fruitless and fundamentally misguided debate on whether the Druids were sages or butchers.

It is within the writings of those authors who borrowed from the now-lost Celtic ethnography of Posidonius that we find the fullest and clearest descriptions of the sacrifices performed by the Druids, and the usual scholarly tendency has been to rely most heavily upon three of the earliest such sources: Caesar's *De Bello Gallico* 6.16, Strabo 4.4.5, and Diodorus Siculus 5.32.6, all of which were written in the first century B.C.[8] Yet it is within the works of an author writing a century later, who also relied heavily upon Posidonius, that certain crucial points emerge most clearly: Pomponius Mela's *De Situ Orbis* 3.2.18–19, written between 41 and 44 A.D.:

> [The Gauls] are arrogant and superstitious, and at one time they were so savage that they believed a man to be the best and most pleasing sacrificial victim for the gods. Vestiges of their past ferocity remain, so that while they refrain from the final dismemberments [*ultimis caedibis*], nonetheless they take off a little portion [from the victims] when leading the consecrated ones to the altars. Still, they have their own eloquence and their masters of wisdom, the Druids. These ones profess to know the size and form of heaven and earth, the motion of sky and stars, and what the gods desire. They instruct the noblest of their race in many things secretly and at length, twenty years, either in a cave or in remote woodlands. One thing which they teach has slipped out to the general public, and it is clear that they should be better in war [because of it]: that souls are eternal and there is another life among the Manes. Therefore, they burn and bury with the dead that which is appropriate to living people. Formerly, the settlement of business affairs and the collection of debts were carried down into the underworld, and there were those who willingly threw themselves onto the funeral pyres of their relatives, as if expecting that they will live together thereafter.

Certain details clearly indicate that this text was composed in a time when Roman policy had adversely affected the Druids. Their teaching, we are told, now took place in secret, and they had been forced to renounce one of the central figures of sacrificial ritual: dismemberment of the victim.[9] But with the exception of these items, there is little in Mela's account which does not already appear in the writings of earlier authors who also made use of Posidonius. In particular, many of Mela's phrases are strongly reminiscent of Caesar's discussion of the Druids in *De Bello Gallico* 6.14:

> The Druids habitually are absent from war, do not pay tributes along with the rest, and have freedom from military service and immunity in all things. Excited by such great rewards, many enter instruction, sent by their parents and relatives or by their own free will. There, they are said to learn a great number of verses by heart, and *some spend twenty years in instruction.* They do not consider it right to commit these [verses] to writing, but in almost all other things, in public and private matters, they make use of Greek letters. They seem to me to have established this [practice] for two reasons: they do not wish their knowledge [*disciplinam*] to be disseminated to the masses, nor that those who rely on letters devote themselves less to the art of memory. It usually happens that with the aid of letters, people relax their diligence in learning things thoroughly and also in the art of memory. Above all, *they wish to convince people that souls do not perish, but after death they pass from some bodies to others, and this they believe to excite courage most greatly, the fear of death being neglected. Beyond this, they dispute concerning the stars and their motion, the size of the world and of lands, the nature of things, and the immortal gods and their power,* and this they teach to their youths.

Careful comparison of these two passages reveals a strong tendency in Caesar to depart from his source and to insert his own speculations: to reorganize materials taken from Posidonius in light of his own interests. Thus, as a military man, he maintains that youths entered Druidic training in order to avoid military service, something attested in no other source that has come down to us. Again, he speculates on the reasons why the Druids rejected writing, introducing his own conjectures with the phrase *id mihi duabus de causis instituisse videntur.*[10] In contrast, Mela at one point carefully preserved Posidonius's organization of data where Caesar abandoned it, for Mela continued the discussion of postmortem existence to include such phenomena as grave gifts, suicide, and settlement of debts in the otherworld, as did also Diodorus Siculus 5.28.6, while Caesar—ever the general—was content to mention only that the doctrine of metempsychosis increased courage in battle.[11]

In both Caesar's account and that of Mela, two topics emerge as central to the druidic system: the immortality of the soul (also attested in numerous other sources)[12] and the nature of the cosmos. This latter concern is voiced most generally by Caesar, who tells of the Druids' interest in "the nature of things" (*de rerum natura*), a phrase reminiscent of other authors' specification that the Druids studied *physiologia*, "natural philosophy," a sphere of inquiry that spanned the nature of the human body (whence modern *physiology*) and that of the universe (whence modern *physics*).[13] A more precise statement is given, however, that describes the Druids' special studies of the motion of heavenly bodies and the dimensions of the cosmos. Although these topics are listed in reverse order in Caesar and Mela, the wording is extremely close and undoubtedly derives from their common source in Posidonius:

Caesar: *de sideribus atque eorum motu*
Mela: *motus coeli ac siderum*
Caesar: *de mundi ac terrarum magnitudine*
Mela: *terrae mundique magnitudinem et formam.*

It is of the greatest significance for our present investigation, moreover, when we note that Mela discussed these cosmic preoccupations of the Druids immediately after he had offered a summary of their sacrificial practices. Here again, Mela's organization of his data diverges from that of Caesar, and one must ask which is closer and more faithful to their common source. The evidence of other classical authors also dependent on Posidonus indicates that it is Mela, once more, who is most conservative.[14] Thus, in a passage from Diodorus Siculus (5.31.2–4), one finds the same grouping of topics as is found in Mela, sacrifice and physiology (in the ancient sense) being discussed together:

There are some men who are philosophers and theologians, who are greatly honored, whom they call "Druids."

And they consult them as diviners, deeming them worthy of great approbation. And they foretell what is destined through the interpretation of birds and of sacrifices of victims, and they hold all the multitude attentive. Above all, when they consider something major they have a custom that is unbelievable, incredible. For having consecrated a man, they strike him above the diaphragm with a sacrificial knife, and when the man struck has fallen, they know destiny [*to mellon*] from his fall, from the dismemberment [or: trembling][15] of his limbs [*tou sparagmou tōn melōn*], and from the flow of his blood, for they trust to ancient and time-honored observance in these things.

It is not their custom to make a sacrifice without a philosopher, for they say that thank offerings to the gods ought to be offered by those who are acquainted with divine nature [*tēs theias physeōs*], as it were, speaking the same language as the gods, and they believe that it is by them that good things ought to be requested.

It is obvious that this passage offers general support for the connection between Druidic sacrifice and physiological speculation as attested in Mela. Beyond this, we must note a highly significant detail hidden in a bit of Greek wordplay. Thus, Diodorus tells us that it is possible to know destiny (*to mellon*) from the arrangement of the victim's limbs (*tōn melōn*) after that victim had been killed and dismembered (or perhaps from the trembling of the victim's limbs in the throes of death: see note 15). He thus indicates that a subtle connection was felt to exist between the two, and as a result, one possessed of sufficient knowledge could perceive the pattern of the future—or perhaps it is better to say, the pattern inherent within nature (*physis*)—by studying the (sundered?) members of a sacrificial corpse (*ek tēs ptōseōs kai tou sparagmou tōn melōn, eti de tēs tou haimatos rhyseōs to mellon noousi*). One recalls also that, in Mela's account of sacrifice, significant attention is given to the practice of dismemberment, which while suppressed, could not be dispensed with altogether.

Further still, we must note the great diffusion of myths describing the creation of the physical universe from the dismembered body of a primordial victim. This theme is attested among a great many of the world's populations, and—as I have demonstrated elsewhere—plays a prominent role in the religious, philosophical, sociopolitical, and proto-scientific speculation of the various Indo-European peoples.[16] Of the many examples that might be cited, let me offer two. The first is from a Middle Persian text written in the ninth century of our era, *Škend Gumānīg Wizār* 16.8–13:

> This also is said (by the Manichaeans): the bodily, material creation is of the Evil Spirit—all the bodily creation is of the Evil Spirit. More precisely, the sky is from the skin, the earth is from the flesh, the mountains are from the bone, and the plants are from the hair of the demoness Kūnī.

To this, we may compare a verse from the poetic Edda, dating to the period just before the conversion of Iceland to Christianity in the year 1000, *Vafþruðnismál* 21:

> From Ymir's flesh   the earth was made
>   and mountains from his bones;
> Heaven from the skull   of the rime-cold giant
>   and from his blood, the sea.

One could cite other cosmogonic accounts of the various peoples who spoke Indo-European languages, in which it is similarly described how the physical universe was created from the dismembered body of a primordial victim (sometimes human, sometimes divine, sometimes animal, sometimes a giant or demon), with certain consistent homologies being posited: earth from flesh, mountains from stones, etc. With this evidence, we come a good deal closer to the world of the Celtic Druids than we were with the Ngaju Dayak. For if consideration of the Dayak evidence was sufficient to establish that it is possible to practice human sacrifice and exalted philosophy side by side, the Indo-European data establish the probability that the Druids did so, the Celts and their priests being among the most conservative members of the Indo-European family, as was demonstrated by Joseph Vendryes in a celebrated article of some seventy years past, in which sacrificial themes play a prominent part.[17]

To establish full certainty, however, only Celtic evidence proper will suffice, and several important Irish texts do preserve the theme of creation through sacrificial dismemberment, although not on a full-fledged cosmic scale.[18] Among these, for instance, there is a myth of the origin of healing herbs. The story tells how Dian Cecht, physician of the Tuatha De Danaan, killed his son, Miach, when the latter outshone him in medical skill (*Cath Maige Turedh* 33–35):

> That cure (performed by Miach) seemed evil to Dian Cecht. He let loose his sword on the head of his son, cutting his scalp down to the flesh. The youth healed that, through the exercise of his skill. He struck again, cutting the flesh to the bone. The youth healed that by the same exercise. He hewed a third cut, to the membrane of the brain. The youth healed that by the same exercise. He hewed a fourth cut, and reached the brain so that Miach died, and Dian Cecht said that there was not any physician who could heal that blow.
>
> After that, Miach was buried by Dian Cecht, and three hundred and sixty-five healing herbs grew up through his grave, according to the number of his joints and sinews.

The number three hundred sixty-five signifies a totality (= the number of days in the year), and the totality of medicinal herbs is thus homologized to the totality of bodily connectors ("joints and sinews"), these being the places where injury is most critical and occasional repair most necessary. For each separate joint or sinew, there is thus a separate healing herb, and knowledge of medical practice consists of knowing which herb to apply for injury to any given bodily part. The logic is clear: a given herb has the power to heal one and only one bodily member because that herb had its origin from the same part of Miach's body. Here, as elsewhere, esoteric knowledge consists in understanding the relation between microcosm and macrocosm, or—as Caesar puts it—"the size and form of heaven and earth," the latter term designating the small world, and the former the large.

Healing, in fact, is a process precisely inverse to that of sacrifice, at least as the two were practiced by the Celts and other Indo-European peoples. Thus, while a sacrificer employed matter taken from a victim's dismembered body to restore the cosmos, the healer used matter from the universe to restore a damaged body. What is more, both of these practical operations reflected a mythic ideology in which body and cosmos were understood as homologous. It is this ideology, moreover, which was the basis of that unified discourse which the Greeks and Romans called "physiology."

Among the Celts we find not only the survivals of a myth of creation through sacrifice, and testimonies that the Druids practiced human sacrifices while studying philosophy, but, more precisely, that their studies centered on "physiology." Further, in an extremely conservative legal text (*Senchus Mór* 1.22) we learn that the Druids "claim that they themselves created heaven and earth and sea, etc., the sun and the moon, etc."—that is, they considered themselves to be repeating the cosmogony in their ritual acts. To this we may add one further piece of evidence: a creation myth that sets forth the system of homologies between the human body and the universe, but which is anthropogonic rather than cosmogonic in its orientation. This is the story of the "Seven Part Adam" as told in an Old Irish manuscript of the thirteenth or fourteenth century A.D. (London, Additional MS. 4783, folio 7a):

> There is this to be known concerning the creation of Adam from seven parts. The first part is from the earth, the second part from the sea, the third part from the sun, the fourth part from the clouds, the fifth part from the wind, the sixth part from stones, the seventh part from the Holy Spirit.
> The part of earth, that is the body of man. The part of the sea, that is the blood of a man. The part of sun is his face and countenance; the part of cloud, his thought; the part of wind, the breath of man; the part of stones, his bones; the part of the Holy Spirit, his soul. . . .[19]

While the contents of this text have been superficially Christianized, its relation to the myths of Miach, Kūnī, and Ymir is obvious. All derive from a religious system in which microcosm and macrocosm were set in homologic relation to one another, in which cosmogony was accomplished by a primordial act of sacrificial dismemberment and each successive sacrifice reenacted that cosmogonic event. Further, anthropogony—the creation of the first human being—was a reversal of cosmogony, in which bodily members were created from matter drawn out of their macrocosmic homologues. Finally, every act of healing was a reenactment of the anthropogony (and a reversal of the cosmogony), in that healing transferred material substance from the macrocosm to the microcosm. These processes may be represented graphically as in figure 14.1 below, where parallel arrows represent reciprocal processes and parallel lines represent parallel processes.

Masters of healing arts as much as of sacrifice, the Druids thus emerge as a

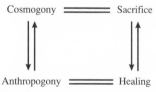

Figure 14.1: Cosmic processes as represented in myth and ritual

priestly group possessed of an esoteric knowledge: a knowledge centered on physiological lore, that is, the science of homologic connections between the bodily microcosm and the macrocosm beyond. This knowledge was encoded and transmitted in myths of creation (cosmogony and anthropogony), and enacted in such rituals as healing and human sacrifice. It should thus be obvious that the latter rite was not just barbaric slaughter, but was also a serious intellectual exercise, presided over by priests who considered themselves to have mastered the very secrets of the universe, secrets which they employed for the wellbeing—indeed, for the continued existence—of the universe.

The above discussion extends and reinforces the arguments contained in Eliade's earlier article, for if he demonstrated that people can perform human sacrifice and also hold elevated ideas, I hope to have shown that the Druids did, in fact, do just that. Moreover, I would make a more radical argument still, for it seems to me that this must always be the case. Indeed, those authors who sense a contradiction between the Druids' reputation for learning and their purported involvement in savage rites, in my opinion totally misunderstand not only the immediate sources under discussion, but the whole interrelation of thought and action in human history. That people perform ghastly deeds while holding lofty ideas should come as no surprise to anyone who surveys history from the latter half of the twentieth century, for one must observe that it is precisely when people are supported by a powerful ideological system that they are most disposed to perpetrate atrocities. And it is, I maintain, one of the chief functions of religion, as of other ideological systems, to lend legitimacy to those purportedly necessary but unpleasant actions which might otherwise go undone.

The question "why" people behave in any given fashion will always evoke multiple responses, some of them stressing ideological factors and others social and material. Thus far, I have tended to dwell on the former at the expense of the latter, but in my view no explanation is complete that does not take account of both. Crucial to any materialist interpretation of Druidic sacrifice is recognition of the fact consistently noted in our classical sources that the victims were regularly prisoners of war and criminals.[20] We must further take account of certain ecologic and socioeconomic factors, for in an economy that is not particularly labor-intensive, criminals and prisoners of war present an acute problem: they must either be released (after which they pose a threat) or kept (in which case they must be fed). Whereas large-scale agricultural societies may solve this problem by turning captives into slaves, thus gaining a cheap supply of productive labor, small-scale agriculturalists and pastoralists like the ancient Celts, Scyths, Germans, and others are afforded no such easy solution. Human sacrifice provides a way out of this dilemma, and the practice is made more palatable when it is decked out in religious trappings. Indeed, when the soul was believed to be immortal, and sacrifice nothing less than a repetition of cosmogony, one could despatch another human being secure in the knowledge that "to kill a man was the most religious act" (Pliny, *Natural History* 30.13).

Notes

1. This attitude is particularly characteristic of those authors who derive their information from Timagenes and/or Alexander Polyhistor rather than from Posidonius. Note, inter alia, Diogenes Laertius, *Lives of the Philosophers* 1, Prologue, 6; Ammianus Marcellinus 15.9.8; Dio Chrysostom, *Oratio* 49; Clement of Alexandria, *Stromateis* 1.15.71; Hippolytus, *Philosophoumena* 1.25.

2. Condemnation of Druidic sacrifice is most fervent in the writings of Roman authors of the first century A.D., when Claudius and Tiberius were suppressing the Druids (who constituted a focal point of resistance to Roman rule). Human sacrifice was the convenient rationale offered for this suppression. Among Roman denunciations, note Tacitus, *Annals* 14.30; Pliny, *Natural History* 30.13; Lucan, *Pharsalia* 1.444ff. and 3.399ff.; Dionysius of Halicarnassus 1.38.2; and Justinus 26.2.2. For earlier mentions of human sacrifice, see Athenaeus, *Deipnosophistai* 4.160E (quoting Sopater), and Cicero, *Pro M. Fonteio* 14 (31–32). On the motives and rhetoric for Roman suppression of the Druids, see Nora K. Chadwick, *The Druids* (Cardiff: University of Wales Press, 1966), pp. 70ff., and Françoise Le Roux, "Introduction générale a l'étude de la tradition celtique, 1," *Ogam* 19 (1967): 324–26, *pace* the older (but still influential) views of Fustel de Coulanges, "Comment le druidisme a disparu," in his *Nouvelles recherches sur quelques problèmes d'histoire*, ed. C. Jullian (Paris: Hachette, 1891), pp. 81–215.

3. The most important works which fall in this category are those which have Posidonius as their chief source: Caesar, *De Bello Gallico* 6.14 (on Druidic learning) and 6.16 (on sacrifice); Strabo 4.4.4 (learning) and 4.4.5 (sacrifice); Diodoros Siculus 5.28.6 (learning) and 5.32.6 (sacrifice); and Pomponius Mela 3.2.18–19 (learning and sacrifice together). On Caesar's attitudes, see most recently, G. Ch. Picard, "César et les Druides," in *Hommage à la mémoire de Jerome Carcopino* (Paris: Société Les Belles Lettres, 1977), pp. 227–33.

4. To a greater or lesser extent, this attempt was made by T. D. Kendrick, *The Druids: A Chapter in Keltic Prehistory* (London: Methuen, 1927), pp. 104–23; Henri Hubert, *Les Celtes et l'expansion celtique* (Paris: Éditions Albin Michel, 1973 [first pub. 1932]), p. 27; Ferdinand Lot, *La Gaule* (Paris: Arthème Fayard, 1947), pp. 276–80; J. J. Tierney, "The Celtic Ethnography of Posidonius," *Proceedings of the Royal Irish Academy* 60 (1960): 214–15, 222–23; and Stuart Piggott, *The Druids* (New York: Thames & Hudson, 1968), pp. 91–99.

5. Again, authors have varied in the extent to which they have sought to advance this position. See, inter alia, Alexandre Bertrand, *La religion des Gaulois* (Paris: E. Leroux, 1897), p. 68; Émile Bachelier, "Les druides en Gaule romaine," *Ogam* 11 (1959): 175; Chadwick, *The Druids*, pp. 28–30, 36–38, 45–46, 84–85; Le Roux, "Introduction générale," pp. 320, 329–30; Le Roux, *Les druides*, 2d ed. (Rennes: Celticum, 1978), passim.; Le Roux, *La civilisation celtique* (Rennes: Ogam-Celticum, 1982), p. 37; Jan de Vries, *La religion des Celtes* (Paris: Payot, 1977), p. 232; and Jean Markale, *Les Celtes et la civilisation celtique* (Paris: Payot, 1969), pp. 341–47.

6. See Christian-J. Guyonvarc'h, "Notes d'etymologie et de lexicographie gauloises et celtiques, V.16., Les noms celtiques du 'chêne', du 'druide', et du 'roitelet','' *Ogam* 12 (1960): 49–58, pursuing a suggestion first advanced by Rudolf Thurneysen, "Italisches," *Zeitschrift für vergleichende Sprachforschung* 32 (1893): 562–64. Note, however, that Thurneysen himself later rejected this idea in "Allerlei Keltisches: 10. Palinodie," *Zeitschrift für celtische Philologie* 16 (1927): 276–78. The older etymology, to which Thurneysen reverted, interprets *Druid* as "Knower of the Oak," but this view rests on nothing on nothing so much as Pliny's folk etymologizing connection of *Druid* with Greek *drus* (*Natural History* 16.249). This must be rejected on phonologic grounds, for as Guyonvarc'h has shown, given that the Celtic names of the oak take the form **derwo-*, we ought to expect **derwo-wid-* for "knower of the oak," not **dru-wid-*. It remains possible, however, that the name for the oak is itself an augmented grade formation from the particle **dru-*, designating this tree as that which is "great," "hard," or "firm." See further Émile Benveniste, "Problèmes sémantiques de la reconstruction," *Word* 10 (1954): 257–59, which remains preferable to Paul Friedrich, *Proto-Indo-European Trees* (Chicago: University of Chicago Press, 1970), pp. 140–49. Also relevant is Karl Horst Schmidt, *Die Komposition in gallischen Personennamen* (Tübingen: Max Niemeyer, 1957), pp. 197–98.

7. Mircea Eliade, "Druids, Astronomers, and Head-hunters," in Giulia Piccaluga, ed., *Perennitas: Studi in Onore di Angelo Brelich* (Rome: Ateneo, 1980), pp. 173–83. His discussion of Dayak materials is based on Hans Schärer, *Ngaju Religion* (The Hague: Martinus Nijhoff, 1963). Recent work on sacrifice strongly supports Eliade's point of view. See, inter alia, Jean-Pierre Vernant and Marcel Detienne, eds., *La cuisine du sacrifice en pays grec* (Paris: Gallimard, 1979); John Ingham, "Human Sacrifice at Tenochtitlan," *Comparative Studies in Society and History* 26 (1984): 379–400; Valerio Valeri, *Kingship and Sacrifice: Ritual and Society in Ancient Hawaii* (Chicago: University of Chicago Press, 1985); and the articles collected on the theme "Sacrificio, organizzazione del cosmo, dinamica sociale," *Studi Storici* 25 (1984): 829–956, and *L'Uomo* 9 (1985): 3–298.

8. For the reliance of these authors on the 23rd book of Posidonius's *History,* a work written some time between 100 and 60 B.C., see Tierney, "The Celtic ethnography of Posidonius", *Proceedings of the Royal Irish Academy* 60 (1960), and M. Truscelli, "I *Keltika* di Posidonio e loro influsso sulla posteriore etnografia," *Rendiconti della reale Accademia dei Lincei* (1935), 609–730.

9. Latin *caedes* "a cutting down, slaughter, massacre," refers not to nondescript acts of force or violence, but to those which involve cutting action (cf. the compounds in -*cīdō* derived from the same verbal root, *caedō*, "to cut, hew, lop": *abscīdō*, "to separate, cut apart"; *circumcīdō* "to cut around, circumcise"; *concīdō* "to cut up, cut in pieces, annihilate"; *excīdō* "to cut out, excise"; *praēcīdō* "to cut off, cut short, abbreviate"; *recīdō* "to cut off, cut away, retrench"; *succīdō* "to cut down, cut under"). When used with reference to animals, *caedes* denotes the violent tearing apart of their bodies (cf. Ovid, *Metamorphoses* 2.442, 11.371, 15.106), often in a sacrificial context (thus Horace, *Carmen* 3.23.14, Martial 14.4, and Ovid, *Metamorphoses* 15.129, the latter two with implied condemnation of the act). On the importance of dismemberment within the sacrificial rituals of the Indo-European peoples, see my discussion in "Of Meat and Society, Sacrifice and Creation, Butchers and Philosophy," *L'Uomo* 9 (1985): 9–29, and, more broadly, *Myth, Cosmos, and Society: Indo-*

European Themes of Creation and Destruction (Cambridge: Harvard University Press, 1986).

10. Moreover, Caesar's speculations on this topic were quite inadequate to the true depth and complexity of Druidic ideas, on which see Georges Dumézil, "La tradition druidique et l'écriture: Le vivant et le mort," *Revue de l'histoire des religions* 122 (1940): 125–33.

11. On the more extreme practices which follow from the beliefs in metempsychosis and immortality of the soul (also attested in Athenaeus 4.145C; Valerius Maximus, *Factorum et Dictorum Memorabilium* Liber Novem 2.6.10; and Lactantius Placidus, *Commentarius in Stati Thebaida* [1898], × #793), see the classic treatment of Marcel Mauss, "Sur un texte de Posidonius: le suicide, contre-prestation suprême," in his *Oeuvres*, vol. 3, *Cohésion sociale et divisions de la sociologie* (Paris: Editions de Minuit, 1969), pp. 52–57.

12. Diodorus Siculus 5.28.6; Strabo 4.4.4; Ammianus Marcellinus 15.9.8; Lucan, *Pharsalia* 1.454–58.

13. Druidic concern with *physiologia* is specified in Strabo 4.4.4 and Cicero, *De Divinatione* 1.41.90. The latter passage is worth citing, for it is one of the very few passages in classical literature which claims to draw directly on the testimony of a Druid himself. Cicero writes:

> The reckoning of divination is not neglected among barbarian peoples, since the Druids are in Gaul. Among them is the Aeduan Divitiacus, your guest and eulogizer, whom I know myself. He proclaimed that that reckoning of nature which the Greeks call *physiologia* is known to him, and he told what would come to pass, sometimes by means of auguries and sometimes by means of inferences.

14. A similar judgment has been reached independently by Giuseppe Zecchini, *I Druidi e l'opposizione dei Celti a Roma* (Milan: Editorial JACA, 1984), pp. 40–41, 42.

15. Translation here is less than fully certain. The most common meaning of Gk. *sparagmos* is "tearing, rending, mangling," with derivation from *sparassō*, "to tear, rend, pull to pieces." Occasionally, however, *sparagmos* can denote a violent, involuntary, and pathological shudder or trembling in which the body seems to be on the point of dismembering itself (cf. the technical medical term *sparaxis*, "convulsion"). The fact that there is mention of one knife blow only might indicate that the latter sense is preferable (unless, of course, there were further operations on the corpse after death), yet the use of *sparagmos* in this sense is extremely rare, and of the passages cited in Liddell-Scott, *Greek English Lexicon* (Oxford: Clarendon Press, 1968), 1624, only one—Aeschylus, Fragment 169 [Nauck]—is convincing; in the others (Sophocles, *Trakhiniai* 778 and 1254), translation by "rending" remains preferable. On balance, I think it is best to retain the common sense of the term.

16. See above, Chapter 13, "Sacrificial Ideology and Indo-European Society," and for a fuller discussion, *Priests, Warriors, and Cattle: A Study in the Ecology of Religions* (Berkeley: University of California Press, 1981), pp. 69–95.

17. J. Vendryes, "Les correspondances de vocabulaire entre l'indo-iranien et l'italo-celtique," *Mémoires de la Société de linguistique de Paris* 20 (1918): 265–85.

18. In addition to the materials presented here, see my discussion of the final scene

in the *Táin Bó Cúailnge* in *Priests, Warriors, and Cattle,* pp. 87–92, and William Sayer's analysis of the oath sworn by Fergus within that same epic, "Fergus and the Cosmogonic Sword," *History of Religions* 25 (1985): 30–56. Note also Diego Poli, "La distribuzione nel banchetto Celtico," *L'Uomo* 9 (1985): 75–97.

19. Text from Whitley Stokes, *Three Irish Glossaries* (London: Williams & Norgate, 1862), xi–xlii. Other Celtic versions of this anthropogony (often with eight parts rather than seven) are cited and discussed in H. L. C. Tristram, "Der 'homo octipartitus' in der irischen und altenglischen Literatur," *Zeitschrift für celtische Philologie* 34 (1975): 119–53.

20. Caesar, *De Bello Gallico* 6.16; Diodorus Siculus 5.32.6; Tacitus *Annals* 14.30; Livy 38.47.12; (on the Asian Galati); and Athenaeus 4.160E (citing Sopater on the Galati again: this is the earliest mention of human sacrifice among the Celts, and POWs are specified as the victims). On similar Scythian practices, see Chapter 16, "Debreasting Disarming, Beheading: Some Sacrificial Practices of the Scyths and Amazons."

FIFTEEN

ON THE SCYTHIAN ROYAL BURIALS

In a recent article with the provocative title "Les scythes imaginaires," François Hartog set forth a major challenge to traditional interpretations of the *locus classicus* for matters Scythian: Book Four of Herodotus' *Histories* (Hartog 1979). His position is as brilliant as it is bold, forcefully arguing that Herodotus tells us less about the Scyths than about the Greeks for whom he wrote, from whom he gathered the bulk of his information, and among whom he must himself be numbered. Essentially, Hartog maintains that it was the freedom of the nomadic Scyths, along with their constant motion, that so fascinated the *polis*-dwellers. Nor were the Greeks in this simply indulging a taste for things exotic or alien, but their fascination with the Scyths had its sources in the military exigencies and tactics of Athens during the Persian Wars (490 and 480 B.C.), and later in the decade before the onset of the Peloponnesian War (440–430 B.C.). For in the Scyths' successful resistance to Darius's invasion—characterized by constant withdrawal and refusal to offer battle over any given piece of land—Hartog sees a model for Athenian willingness to retreat to fortifications or the fabled "wooden walls" of the fleet, abandoning fields temporarily to the enemy.

Much is to be gained from this radical shift in critical perspective, and Hartog's astute reading enriches our appreciation of Herodotus considerably. Yet there is a danger in carrying the basic principle of his article too far. For if texts are best read for what they tell us about their author and primary audience—not for what they say about their purported subject matter—then Hartog's article itself tells us less about Greeks of the fifth century (*les grecs imaginaires*), than it does about modern French scholars and readers of the *Annales*. Moreover, those who read the present discussion may learn more about American scholars and readers of *Festschriften* than about the French, less still about Greeks or Scyths. Applying this hermeneutical principle, we rapidly move further and further from our initial object of study, fleeing the Scythians much as they—supposedly—once fled Darius's troops.

Is this inevitable? Or is there some way to halt the *fuga perpetua?* In truth, I believe there is, and in the case at hand, archaeology comes to our rescue, for by considering material remains, we break the infinite chain of literary mediations and come as close as possible to the *Dingen an sich* of Scythian culture.[1]

For all that Herodotus emphasized the mobility of the Scyths—which he saw as resulting from their lack of sentimental attachment to any specific places, with a consequent readiness to live in and travel through all geographic space—he did stress, in a passage absolutely central to the story of Darius's defeat, that there was one spot which commanded the Scythians' loyalty and affection. Within this passage (Hdt. 4.127), the Scythian king Idanthyrsus responds to Darius's demand that he halt his flight and either give battle or submit, saying:

> Thus it is with me, O Persian. I never yet fled, fearing any man—neither before, nor do I flee you now. And what I have done is nothing novel, but that which I am accustomed to do in peace. And this is why I do not give battle to you straightaway: I will explain it. We have neither towns nor planted land, and fearing neither that you will capture the one nor raze the other, we need not join you in battle any sooner. But if you wish to accomplish this goal speedily at any cost, the tombs of our ancestral fathers [*taphoi patrōioi*] will suit your purpose. Come: discover these and just try to destroy them! Then you will know if we will give battle for these graves or if we will not give battle!

If this passage may be trusted, it appears that there was a still point in the Scyths' turning world, a lone landmark that stood out from homogeneous, undifferentiated space: the royal burial grounds. For the graves in question are not those of any ancestral fathers. Rather, it is the king, Idanthyrsus, who speaks of *his* ancestral fathers, and elsewhere Herodotus calls the same graves "tombs of the kings" (*taphoi . . . tōn basileōn*), placing them near the confluence of the rivers Gerrhos and Borysthenes, i.e. on the lower stretches of the Dniepr (4.71, see also 4.56). That there was a subgroup of Scyths who identified themselves as Royal Scyths is known from linguistic data, particularly the form given in Greek as *Sakaurakoi* (Lucian, *Macrobius* 15), which reflects an underlying Iranian **Saka-ura-ka-*, the **ura-* element being equivalent to Khotan Saka *rre* "King," as is confirmed by the Chinese rendition of this name: *Sək-wang*, "Kingly Scyths" (Altheim 1951, 95; Kothe 1968, 97; on the Khotan Saka form, see Bailey 1979, 368). But whether the Royal Scyths had their own burial grounds is not something that linguistics can tell us. For this, the testimony of the spade is indispensable.

Within recent decades, extensive Soviet excavations have been staged throughout the territories inhabited by the Scyths, and their results—now ably and conveniently summarized by Renate Rolle—show a dense concentration of graves bearing marks of high status (well-built mounds more than five meters high; associated burials of sacrificial victims; numerous grave goods, including luxury items and signs of prestige) very much where Herodotus places the royal tombs: the lower bends of the Dniepr, especially where it meets the Kondo at Kamskoe gorodišče (Rolle 1979; see 33–35, 47–48, 157, and 160–64). Most scholars now agree that in such burial sites as the kurgans of

Čertomlyk, Ordžonikidze, Alexandroppolь, and Ogyz we may see the palpable remains of the Scythian royal tombs, for which Idanthyrsus was prepared to stand and fight.[2]

It is not the mere existence of these tombs, however, which is confirmed by archaeological data. Herodotus also gives us a detailed account of the funerary rituals performed for the Scythian kings (4.71) and of elaborate ceremonies performed on the first anniversary of each king's death (4.72). The latter are decidedly spectacular, involving the sacrifice of fifty men and fifty horses, which—so the Father of History tells us—were stuffed and set in a ring around the tumulus of their dead sovereign. Thus far, material evidence has not emerged to confirm that such macabre merry-go-rounds were constructed. Yet negative evidence cannot force a negative conclusion: the most we can say is that on the strength of such data as are now available in the Lower Dniepr region, one is not disposed to give credence to Herodotus's account in 4.72, while future excavations may yet force revision of this opinion.

No such hesitation is necessary regarding the funerary rituals described in 4.71. The passage is sufficiently detailed to warrant citing it in full.

> The tombs of the kings are in the land of the Gerrhoi, at a place where the Borysthenes is accessible. Here, whenever their king passes on, they dig a great square pit in the earth, and having made this ready, they take up the corpse, the body having been covered with wax, its cavity having been cut open and purified, filled with cut galingale, incense, celery seed, and anise, then sewn together again. Then they carry it off in a wagon to other people [*ethnos*]. And those who receive the corpse once it has been carried away do the very same things as the royal Scyths: they cut off their ears, shear their hair, make cuts around the arms, rend their foreheads and noses, and thrust arrows through their left hands. Then they carry away the king's corpse in the wagon to another people over whom [the kings] rule. And when they have gone around to all, carrying the corpse, they are in the land of the Gerrhoi, who dwell at the outermost bounds of those peoples whom they rule, and [they are also] at the graves. Then, when they place the corpse in these tombs on a bed of straw, having fixed spears on both sides of the corpse, they stretch beams over it and cover these with wicker. And having strangled one of the [king's] concubines, they bury her in the remaining open space, and also his wine-steward, butcher, groom, man-servant, messenger, horses, first-fruits of all other things, and golden cups [*phialās*], for they have no need of silver nor bronze. And having done these things, they all heap up a great mound, striving and competing to make it most great.

Most of these details find material confirmation in the largest and wealthiest (i.e., those which are presumably royal) burials of the Lower Dniepr region.

Square chambers, high mounds, funerary sacrifice of attendants and horses, drinking vessels as grave goods, are all abundantly attested (Rolle 1979, passim, esp. pp. 41, 68, 89–90, 132). Inferential evidence also supports Herodotus' description of a forty-day cortège throughout the Scythian lands, although this is less certain.[3] Finally, although there is no evidence of embalming in the burials of the Lower Dniepr, this is attested for the burials of eastern Scyths at such sites as Pazyryk, Bašadar, and Sibė (Rolle 1979, 82–88; Rudenko 1970, 279–83). For all that Herodotus may have been speaking to Greeks, with Greek interests uppermost in his mind, he still seems to have been extremely well-informed regarding the funerary practices of the Royal Scyths.

What Herodotus does not tell us, however—and what mere remains cannot tell us—is *why* Scythian kings were buried in this fashion, and what it meant for them to be treated thus. Most maddening of all is the fact that our archaeological and literary data alike are mute on the rationale for human sacrifice at the king's death. Surely, the most commonly offered interpretation—which posits that victims were to wait on the deceased king in the next world—is wrong. Not only does Herodotus make no mention of expectations that the king would enter another world, nowhere in his entire treatment of the Scyths is there the slightest mention of a belief in another world or any form of *post mortem* existence,[4] nor is there anything in the archaeological record which would require us to posit such a belief. Yet if we cannot adopt this facile solution, are we able to locate other motives which might have prompted such funerary sacrifices? Or, must we simply resign ourselves to ignorance?

In an attempt to avoid the latter alternative, I suggest we consider the general relations of king and community. For the Scythian king in life was not merely a political authority but is more accurately described as having been the very center of the total Scythian society, as well as its defining member.[5] Conversely, the Scythian people are to be understood in some measure as having been the extension or projection of their king. This may be seen from any number of data reported by Herodotus.

Among these, we may begin with the Scyths' ethnonym, formed from the name of their first king. This is attested directly by Herodotus 4.6—*sympasi de einai ounoma Skolotous, tou basileos epōnumiēn*—and also follows from analysis of the name Scyths called themselves: *Skolotoi*, a plural formation in *-t-* (like the ethnonym of the Ossetes) built on the name of their eponymous first king, **Skolo xšaya* (King Skolo), a name which appears in Hellenized form as *Kolaxais* in Herodotus 4.5–7 (Christensen 1918, 138; Benveniste 1938, 534–35; Brandenstein 1953–55, 196–99).[6] Further, when Greeks told the story of Scythian origins, they called the first king *Skythēs* to conform with the Greek form of the ethnonym *Skythai*, thus preserving the direct relation between the name of the king and that of his people (Hdt. 4.6 and 10; Diodorus Siculus 2.43).

The content of the Scyths' creation account (Hdt. 4.5–6) is also of the greatest interest, for as several authors have observed, it is not so much a cosmogony as it is a regiogony: a story of the origins of kingship, which tells how the world of the Scyths effectively came into existence with the appearance of their first king (see Christensen 1918, 137–38; Dumézil 1930, 114–19; Benveniste 1938, 529–37; Grantovskij 1960, 17–20; Widengren 1965, 156; Xazanov 1975, 36–52; Lincoln 1986, 156–58). Essentially, this myth tells us how fiery golden objects fashioned by the gods came down from the sky, each of which signified a characteristic activity and social grouping (*ethnos*) of the Scythian people: a yoke and plow for herding and agriculture, a sword for war, and a libation cup (*phialē*) for ritual (see also Curtius Rufus 7.8.16–18). These objects were then seized by the youngest of three brothers—Kolaxais—whose older brothers had failed in an attempt. By virtue of possessing all four golden objects, Kolaxais became king, for in him were thus concentrated all the cultural gifts that made Scythian life possible, as well as all the Scythian *ethnea*.

There is also a ritual face to this myth, reported by Herodotus (4.7), following straight on his account of the myth:

> The kings guard that gold, which is sacred, most well. Propitiating it, they offer great sacrifices every year. And if one who has with him the sacred gold should fall asleep at that feast in the open air, it is said among the Scyths that he will not live out the year, and they give him as much [land] as he can ride around on horse in a single day.

The gift of land is apparently an attempt to compensate the unfortunate man for his artificially shortened life, but other aspects of this ritual are of greater interest than this detail. First, we must note that Scythian kings continued to hold possession of the sacred gold from which their kingship ultimately derived. Second, they displayed this gold publicly every year, renewing it—and by extension the legitimacy of their rule—with sacrifice and feasting. Finally, the life of every Scythian depended on proper reverence toward that sacred gold and the kingship which it embodied. Nor was it the case that a lapse in such reverence brought about execution: rather, after such a failure, life simply became impossible. The guilty party—who was the object of sympathy rather than wrath, as is seen from the gift of land given him—would automatically die within a year, which is to say, before the next celebration of the royal gold could take place. It thus appears that well-being and even life itself were felt to flow from the sacred gold through the king to the Scythian people, any interruption of this flow having dire results.

The tie between king and people was expressed in other ways also. The most solemn oaths of the Scythians were sworn by the royal hearth (Hdt. 4.68), which was the affective and ritual center of the whole Scythian people, just as the domestic hearth was such a center for the family unit, as is true among most Indo-Europeans.[7] Moreover, should such an oath be forsworn, the king's health would be imperiled, and with his health, the well-being of the entire people (Hdt. 4.68).

When the king did fall sick, a general crisis was provoked. A group of three diviners was consulted, and almost invariably they reported that the cause of this illness was that a given individual had forsworn an oath taken by the royal hearth. When that man denied the accusation—as was usual—six more diviners were consulted, and if they confirmed the initial accusation, the accused was beheaded straightaway. But if there were disagreement between the two teams of diviners, more diviners still were consulted, the issue being finally resolved by majority vote. And were the accused ultimately acquitted, the first diviners were all drawn and quartered (Hdt. 4.68–69).

The entire procedure is a fascinating one, but what is perhaps of greatest interest in the present context is the sentence with which Herodotus concludes his description (4.69), stating: "And when the king has them executed, he does not leave their children behind, but puts all the males to death, and does no injustice to the females."

To a modern eye, this practice may seem but a callous instance of ancient *Realpolitik,* whereby kings extinguished whole lineages rather than risk smoldering resentments and subsequent revenge. This, however, strikes me as a superficial reading. Rather, I take the practice to derive from two interrelated aspects of Scythian social structure. The first of these is the predominance of corporate social identity—the sense that one's personhood derives primarily from membership in a well-defined group—over individual. The second is the tendency for such groups to center on and derive their identity from focal representatives. Within the family unit, the focal representative was the father; within the larger national unit, it was the king.

Returning to the specific question of executions, we see what happens when the focal representative of a corporate group was judged guilty of a capital offense. Not only was it necessary for him to die, but what is more, all those who derived their identity from membership in the group which he incarnated had to die with him. Perhaps it was thought that they shared his guilt, perhaps not: it is difficult to be certain. In either event, the father's crime and subsequent death were tantamount to—and the direct cause of—the disappearance of the entire social unit centered on him. Without him, life for the other group members became impossible, his female descendants being spared—not out of any sense of chivalry, as Herodotus implies—but because the Scyths were patrilineal (see Hdt. 4.114); women's corporate identity derived from their present or future husbands, not from their fathers.

Other data also reveal that social identity among the Scyths was largely corporate, and that social groups possessed focal representatives. Among these is the fact that close retainers (*tōn hepomenōn hoi pleistou axioi*) were required to take any oaths sworn by their leader as a sign of solidarity with him (Hdt. 4.70).[8] Moreover, the Scythian sense of corporate identity was given a stunning metaphoric description by Herodotus, as was recognized by Seth

Benardette (Benardette 1969, 114). For whereas Darius was able to take an accurate census of his 700,000-strong army by requiring each man to place a single pebble on a common pile (Hdt. 4.87 and 92), a similar attempt by the Scyths failed. For the Scythian king Ariantas commanded every Scyth to bring him, not a pebble, but a bronze arrowhead, and these he melted down and cast into an enormous *amphora,* six times greater than the largest vessel known to the Greeks, and six fingers thick on all sides (Hdt. 4.81). This colossal vessel was nothing less than the tangible representation of Scythian society: a corporate whole in which all individuals merged: a totality called into existence by the king.

What happened, however, when a king died? As Hertz recognized long ago, any death provokes a crisis in society such that those who are left behind must detach the ties which bound them to the deceased, then reintegrate their social field in such a way as to compensate for the loss (Hertz 1960). In all deaths these are difficult and delicate tasks, but it should be clear that the loss of the focal representative who defines and incarnates a corporate group must be particularly problematic. It is just these problems which the Scythian royal funerals attempted to resolve.

Consider, for instance, the way in which the forty-day cortège served to reintegrate the total Scythian people. For the funeral tour, by stopping at each Scythian group (*ethnos*), effectively defined the inclusive bounds of Scythendom. Moreover, by receiving the corpse and its entourage, each group acknowledged that it was a part of that totality which had its focus in the king but which remained cohesive in spite of his death—paying honor to him, but ready for the accession of a new king. The corpse itself also became an item in a circle of exchange that united the various *ethnea,* for each group that received the corpse had to convey it to the next, where they gave over the corpse and received hospitality in return. Each group, moreover, reacted to the corpse in identical fashion—a further sign of their common membership in a corporate whole—with stereotyped expressions of grief and acts of self-mutilation.

These mutilations—which including lopping off ears, tearing one's flesh, and piercing one's self with arrows, as well as the more sedate shearing of hair (Hdt. 4.71)—must be considered as acts of (limited) self-sacrifice, much like the animal sacrifices offered upon the death of lineage-chiefs among the Issedones, said to be neighbors of the Scyths by Herodotus (4.26), but in all likelihood themselves a Scythian people.[9] In both instances, the crisis posed by the death of a corporate group's focal representative was resolved in similar ways. For while members of that group felt the demand to die along with their leader—their identity being largely derived from (and submerged in) his— they honored that demand only in limited fashion, dying a little bit via acts of self-sacrifice.[10] By such mechanisms, they freed themselves to continue living and to resume their identity in a group with a new focal representative.

In certain instances, however, things were not so simple, as we have seen when considering male descendants of those condemned to death. Another such case is the fate of those who by virtue of their sustained, direct, and intimate contact with a king were unable to detach their identity from his at the time of this death via acts of limited self-sacrifice. I refer here to his immediate household staff.

A detail from Herodotus' account of the Scythian royal funerals (4.71) which has not been given sufficient attention in the past is that those who were sacrificed were exclusively persons who had been in direct attendance upon the king: his concubine (*pallakē*), wine-steward (*oinoxoos*), butcher (*mageiros*), groom (*hippokomos*), man-servant (*diēkonos*),[11] and messenger (*angeliēphoros*). For such individuals, the sense of corporate identity in a community focused on the king was most acute, their entire existence having been passed in the closest proximity to him and all of their labor having been devoted to his personal service. Upon his death, their own lives thus became unfocused, aimless, impossible: having no other options, they followed their leader into death.[12] Whether they believed they were headed for some realm beyond is impossible to say; no evidence survives which forces this conclusion.

To reflect on the fate of these unfortunate victims, so far away and so long ago, is not without poignance, and—I believe—a certain importance as well. In order to study the complex forces which led Scythian concubines, wine-stewards, butchers, and the like to their sacrificial deaths, we have had occasion to consider literary and historical texts, etymologies, myths, rituals, patterns of social organization, legal procedures, and tangible physical remains. Of these, the last are hardly least important, for not only do they supply us with invaluable information, they also serve as a grisly reminder that the stations people occupy and the unspoken assumptions they accept about the nature and value of society itself profoundly shape the lives they live, and also the deaths they die.

Notes

1. One must, of course, grant that one never actually reaches *die Dingen an sich*. Even material remains are mediated by the sensory apparatus and receiving intelligence of the archaeologist who studies them, both of which have been culturally conditioned from his/her birth.

2. Since the appearance of Rolle, note Rybakov (1979, 104–68), and Mozolevskij (1980). I have not been able to make use of Grac (1980), but understand that it includes a chapter on funerary ritual.

3. This rests primarily on the presence of wheeled vehicles that might have been used to transport the corpse within certain burials, plus estimates of the amount of labor which would have been required for construction of a tomb such as Grave #2 of the Melitopolʹ Kurgan. When calculations allow for the transport of materials (especially stone) brought from considerable distances (40 km to the nearest quarry), a fig-

ure of forty days' time, as specified in Herodotus 4.71, becomes entirely plausible according to Rolle (1979, 74–75).

4. Note, for instance, that in the list of Scythian deities given by Herodotus 4.59, there is no mention of any god or goddess of the underworld.

5. Among the Indo-Europeans more broadly, such focal members of social groups were denoted by formations with *-no-* suffixes, as in Latin *dom-i-nu-s, tribu-nu-s,* Germanic **teuta-no-s* (Gothic *þiudans,* etc.), **druxti-no-s* (old Norse *dróttinn,* etc.). See Benveniste (1969, 1:301–4). That the Royal Scyths considered themselves to be *the* Scyths par excellence is established in Hdt. 4.20, on which see the discussion of Scythian social categories in Lincoln (1985).

6. Note also the name of a later Scythian king which is but a by-form of **Skolo-: Skyles,* who is mentioned in Herodotus 4.78–80.

7. The importance of the hearth to the Scyths is also apparent from the inclusion of a goddess identified with the Greek Hestia in their pantheon (Hdt. 4.59). The Iranian form of her name, which Herodotus gives as *Tabiti,* reflects a feminine singular nominative of the present participle of the Proto-Indo-European verb **tep-* (Avestan *ā-tāpaite,* Sanskrit *tāpati,* Latin *tepeō,* etc.), thus: "The Warming One."

8. The passage is worth citing in full for its evocation of corporate identity as dramatized in oath, commensality, and ritual consanguinity:

> The Scyths make oaths thus when they make them. Pouring wine into a large ceramic *kylix,* they mix it with the blood of those who are cutting the oath, having struck themselves with an awl or having sliced a small part of their body with a sacrificial knife. Then they dip into the *kylix* a Persian sword [*akinakēn*], arrows, a Scythian sword [*sagarin*], and a javelin. And when they do these things, they pray for many things, and then they drink—those who are themselves making the oath, and the most worthy of their followers.

9. On the Issedones and their relation to other Scythian groups, see the discussion in Pauly-Wissowa. The passage from Herodotus (who states elsewhere [4.13] that his information comes from Aristeas of Proconnessus), is worthy of more thorough consideration than is possible here. It reads as follows:

> The Issedones are said to live following these customs. When a man's father dies, all those who are connected to him in some way bring forth animals, which they sacrifice and cut into pieces. And they cut up the deceased father of him who entertains them, and mixing all the meat together, they set forth a sacrificial banquet.

10. It might also be possible to consider these funerary sacrifices as constituting a gift to which the deceased cannot offer a counter-gift. By thus creating a failure of reciprocity, they dissolve the relations which bound members of the corporate group to their focal representative.

11. Gk. *diēkonos* (from which, English *deacon*) may also mean minister, but given that all other people named within this list waited upon the king in some capacity of physical service, it seems most logical to translate man-servant or personal attendant here.

12. Compare the case of the *silodouroi* of the Gallic Sotiani, as reported by Caesar (*De Bello Gallico* 3.22) and Athenaeus (*Deipnosophistae* 6.249B). These 600 atten-

dants of the king pledged to live and die with him, sharing his powers, his presence, his dress, and his habits, but also committing suicide on his death should they not fall beside him in battle.

References

Altheim, Franz. 1951. *Aus Spätantike und Christentum*. Tübingen: Max Niemeyer.

Bailey, H. W. 1979. *Dictionary of Khotan Saka*. Cambridge: Cambridge University Press.

Benardette, Seth. 1969. *Herodotean Inquiries*. The Hague: Martinus Nijhoff.

Benveniste, Emile. 1938. "Traditions indo-iraniennes sur les classes sociales." *Journal asiatique* 230:529–49.

———. 1969. *Le vocabulaire des institutions indo-européennes*, 2 vols. Paris: Éditions de Minuit.

Brandenstein, Wilhelm. 1953–55. "Die Abstammungssagen der Skythen." *Wiener Zeitschrift für die Kunde des Morgenlands* 52:183–211.

Christensen, Arthur. 1918. *Le premier homme et le premier roi dans l'histoire légendaire des Iraniens*, vol. 1. Uppsala: Archives d'études orientales.

Dumézil, Georges. 1930. "La préhistoire indo-iranienne des castes." *Journal asiatique* 216:109–30.

Grac, A. D. 1980. *Drevnie Kočevniki v Centre Azij*. Moscow: Izdalьstvo Nauka.

Grantovskij, E. 1960. "Indoiranische Kastengliederung bei den Skythen." *Twenty-fifth International Congress of Orientalists*. Moscow: Verlag für orientalische Literatur.

Hartog, François. 1979. "Les Scythes imaginaires: espace et nomadisme." *Annales: Economies Sociétés Civilisation* 34:1137–54.

Hertz, Robert. 1960. *Death and the Right Hand*. Translated by R. and C. Needham. Oxford: Oxford University Press.

Kothe, Heinz. 1968. "Die Königlichen Skythen und ihre blinden Knechte." In *Das Verhältnis von Bodenbauern und Viehzüchtern in historischer Sicht*, pp. 97–110. Berlin: Akademie Verlag.

Lincoln, Bruce. 1985. *The Tyranny of Taxonomies*, Occasional Papers of the University of Minnesota Center for Humanistic Studies, No. 1.

———. 1986. *Myth, Cosmos, and Society: Indo-European Themes of Creation and Destruction*. Cambridge: Harvard University Press.

Mozolevskij, B. N. 1980. "Skifskie Kurgany v Okrestnostjax g. Ordžonikidze na Dnepropetrovšine (Raskopki 1972–1975)." In *Skifija i Kavkazi: Sbornik Naučnix Trudov*, pp. 70–154. A. I. Terenožkin et al., eds. Moscow: Izdatelьstvo Naukova Dumka.

Rolle, Renate. 1979. *Totenkult der Skythen*, 2 vols. Berlin: Walter de Gruyter.

Rudenko, Sergei. 1970. *Frozen Tombs of Siberia*. Berkeley: University of California Press.

Rybakov, Boris A. 1979. *Gerodotova Skifija: Istoriko-Geografičeskij Analiz*. Moscow: Izdatelьstvo Nauka.

Widengren, Geo. 1965. *Die Religionen Irans*. Stuttgart: W. Kohlhammer.

Xazanov, A. M. 1975. *Sošialьnaja Istorija Skifov*. Moscow: Izdatelьstov Nauka.

SIXTEEN

DEBREASTING, DISARMING, BEHEADING: SOME SACRIFICIAL PRACTICES OF THE SCYTHS AND AMAZONS

In this chapter I will be discussing certain practices that are reported for a set of interrelated peoples in antiquity: the Scythians, the Amazons whom certain Scythian youths are said to have married, and the Sauromatians who supposedly descended from this union.[1] Our information about the practices that concern me comes chiefly from two important texts: the *Histories* of Herodotus and a medical work of the Hippocratic corpus entitled *On Airs, Waters, and Places,* that—like Herodotus—was written in the middle of the fifth century.[2] At the outset, I should note the possibility that some of these practices, like some of these peoples (particularly the Amazons), were more imaginary than actual, although as François Hartog, Page duBois, and others have shown us, this in no way diminishes their interest or importance, for one can learn much from the imaginary practices of an imaginary people, particularly regarding the thoughts and values of those whose imaginations they inhabit.[3]

I should also make clear that rather few of the practices I will discuss were actually called "sacrifices" by the authors who wrote about them or by the people (if any) who performed them. Some of the other practices that interest me here might be called executions, mutilations, tortures, surgical, or even cosmetic procedures. Yet in spite of this broad divergence of terminology, I believe it makes sense to group them together for reasons that should become clear by the end of the chapter. Moreover, this regrouping has the ancillary benefit of raising questions about the category of "sacrifice" itself, which— like all categories—brings some things together by excluding others, thereby simplifying and clarifying some matters, but also precluding alternative conclusions that might otherwise emerge.

Of Arms, Breasts, and Amazons

There is a great deal more that could be said here, but I would prefer not to get bogged down in talking about theories of sacrifice, theories of theories of sacrifice, or theories of theories.[4] Rather, let me forego such a meta-discourse in favor of more directly engaging the relevant primary sources, beginning somewhat arbitrarily with chapter 17 of the Hippocratic treatise, which provides the earliest and most thorough explanation that we have of how and why it was that the Amazons were supposed to have acquired their characteristic physical mark:[5]

> These women have no right breast, for in their infancy their mothers take a bronze instrument that is constructed for this very purpose, and after making it red-hot, they place it on the [daughter's] right breast and cauterize it *so that its growth is destroyed, and it surrenders all its strength and fullness to the right shoulder and arm.*

Although it is often said elsewhere that this debreasting was done so that in maturity Amazons might be able to draw bowstrings unimpeded across their chests,[6] the passage I have quoted offers a different explanation, one that is less narrowly pragmatic in character. For it is said that they cauterize the breast—and we will have to return and consider why this particular method of debreasting was specified—"so that its growth is destroyed, and it surrenders [*ekdidonai*] all its strength and fullness to the right shoulder and arm."[7] A breast is thus negated for the benefit of the arm, a soft bodily member for one that is hard, and one that is weak, nurturant, and sustaining of life for one that is strong, martial, and—in martial contexts—a bringer of death. In short, a member that is considered to be categorically female is sacrificed to augment the power of one that is similarly regarded as categorically male (see figure 16.1).

Breast	Arm
Soft	Hard
Weak	Strong
Nurturant	Martial
Life	Death
Female	Male

Figure 16.1: Symbolic associations in the Amazons' mastectomies, as described in the Hippocratic treatise *On Airs, Waters, Places*, ch. 17.

To the set of binary oppositions that is assembled under the master categories of the breast and the arm there is one more pair that should also be added, for it is absolutely central to the broader concerns of this Hippocratic text, for all that it may strike us as initially opaque.[8] This is the contrast of the moist and the dry, and in order to appreciate its significance for the materials we have been considering, a bit of background is necessary.

The treatise *On Airs, Waters, and Places* is an early work of medical ecology, explicitly devoted to demonstrating that a region's climate shapes the bodies and characters of its residents in the same manner that it shapes the topography itself.[9] At a not-so-very subtextual level, however, this is advanced less as a general theoretical proposition than—in the wake of Greek victories in the Persian wars—as the practical basis for comparing Europeans and Asians (under which category were included all non-Europeans), to the general detriment of the latter.[10] To this end, the text poses the argument that the greater variability of their seasons makes Europeans hardier, more energetic, wilder, and more warlike than Asians, while conversely the greater uniformity of their climate makes Asians milder, gentler, more beautiful, and also more torpid than their European counterparts.[11] Going further, the text observes that Asians are not all alike, and proceeds to subcategorize them according to whether their climates are marked by consistent heat and dryness, as in the case of Egyptians and Libyans,[12] or by an equally consistent cold and moisture, as in that of the Scythians, who "breath[e] a moist, thick air and drink water from snow and frosts," and therefore have bodies that are "thick, fleshy, jointless, moist and slack, and their bowels are the moistest of all bowels" (*On Airs, Waters, and Places*, 19). This system of contrasts, as graphed below in figure 16.2, thus identifies the Scythians as that people who are, by virtue of their climate, the moistest of all Asians, which is to say the weakest of the weak, and flabbiest of the mild.

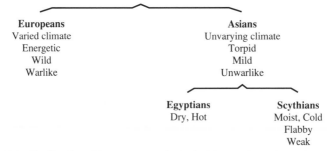

Figure 16.2: Classification of the world's peoples in the Hippocratic treatise *On Airs, Waters, and Places*

If the text sees nature as having made Scythians weak, it also notes that they developed certain techniques for rectifying this unfortunate condition. As chapter 20 of the Hippocratic treatise tells us:

> You will find that the majority of the Scythians . . . have been cauterized on the shoulders, arms, wrists, breasts, hips, and loins, *for no reason other than the moistness and the softness of their bodies.* For they are not able to draw their bows, or to throw their javelins from the shoulder due to their moistness and enervation. But as soon as they cauterize, most of the moisture in the joints is dried up and their bodies become more sinewy, better nourished, and very well knit.

The weakness of the Scythians was thus traced to a bodily moistness that was itself seen as a product of the climate in which they lived, and this moistness was therefore treated—cured—with fire. In contrast, the weakness and moistness of the Amazons was located less in their environment (they being recent immigrants to the north) than in their gender. For like women everywhere, Amazons lactate, something which permitted this text (and others like it) to argue that as a portion of female bodies—the breast—is given over to moisture, females are therefore inherently softer, weaker, and more phlegmatic than men. Unlike other women, however, the Amazons were said to have treated one of their breasts the same way that Scythians treated much of their bodies, cauterizing it in order to dry up its inherent moisture. Cauterization may thus be understood as a medico-physiological practice that was informed by a set of cosmological theories: theories in which, moreover, a racist and patriarchal position was thoroughly embedded. Obviously, one recoils at even the imaginary use of red-hot bronze to negate breasts in favor of arms, but equally offensive—and even more insidious—is the use of purportedly "scientific" discourse to advance the project of negating not just the moist in favor of the dry, but also the female in favor of the male, the Asian in favor of the European, and the weak in favor of the strong.

Of Arms, Blood, and Enemies

If Amazons and Scyths supposedly took pains to strengthen their arms for use in battle, the latter group is also said to have performed operations designed to take away the strength of their enemies' arms, as may be seen from Herodotus' account of the Scythian sacrifices to Ares, their god of war. Such rituals were celebrated at his shrines, which were found in every Scythian district and took the form of great wooden pyramids surmounted by an ancient iron sword of characteristically Scythian shape that Herodotus says was the god's "image" or "representation" (*agalma*).[13] Vast sacrifices of sheep and horses were brought to this sword on a yearly basis, and there were also other victims. Of these, Herodotus recounts:

> Out of every hundred men whom the Scythians might capture in battle, they sacrifice one man, not in the same manner as they use for sheep, but differently. For they pour wine over the heads of these men, and they cut their throats over a vessel, then bear this vessel up on top of the pile of firewood, and they pour this blood over the sword. They carry this blood atop, and down below, alongside the shrine they do these things: they cut off the right arms of those men whose throats had been cut, together with their hands, and they throw these into the air. And when they have finished with the rest of the victims, they depart. And the hand lies where it has fallen, apart from the body. (Herodotus, 4.62)

At its most basic level, this grisly ceremony may be understood as a theater of cruelty that impressed on its audience, as on its victims, the power of those who staged the performance and who benefited from the fear it inspired. Beyond this, however, the ritual was informed by a whole system of cosmological speculation, as becomes clear from a close reading of its details and central sequences.

To begin, we might note that the victims are described not just as having been killed, but also dismembered, for two very specific parts of their bodies were violently separated from the rest in the course of the ritual. Most obvious is the case of their shockingly literal dis-armament, to which I will shortly return. First, however, there is the curious treatment of their blood, which is particularly striking given the fact that in no other Scythian sacrifices was blood shed, nor were any libations poured.[14] Here, however, the shedding of blood and the pouring of libations form part of a clearly articulated ritual sequence in which wine was first poured over the top of the victims' heads as they stood at the base of the shrine. Next, blood was made to flow from their throats (i.e. the base of their heads) into an *aggos* (a vat or pitcher for holding liquids, especially wine), in which it was then carried to the top of the shrine, where it was poured over the sword's tip (i.e. the "head" of Ares' image). Actions in the above—that is, atop the shrine—thus depended upon actions in the below, to which they also held relations of parallelism and inversion. For whereas the victim and the recipient were both bathed in fluids, that which was poured over the god's head had just been drained from the victim's throat, the wine of the initial libation having been thus transmuted into human blood, which was in turn transmuted into Ares' wine.

Insofar as the Scythians were an Iranian people, it is tempting to connect this ritual sequence with the pattern of creation mythology that is well attested in Iranian sources, as well as those of other ancient peoples who spoke languages of the Indo-European family. Here, the universe—in its cosmic as well as its social manifestation—is said to have been created through a primordial act of sacrifice, in which the victim's dismembered body was transformed into the material substance of all else. With regard to the universe, for example, the victim's flesh is said to have become earth, its hair plants, its eyes the sun, and—according to some variants—its blood to have become wine, which thereafter when drunk served to renew and to fortify the blood.[15] Similarly, with regard to society, it is told how the properly hierarchic social order came from the same victim, whose dismembered head became the class of sovereigns—priests or kings—while his hands and arms became warriors, and his lower bodily parts the mass of the common people.

Heads of Enemies, Heads of State

The performance of sacrifice among other Iranians was clearly understood as a repetition of the acts of creation, as Marijan Molé was the first to recognize.[16] And in their treatment of the prisoners whom they offered to Ares, it would appear that Scythians gave ritual reenactment to that section of their creation myths which told how the warrior class originated from the dismembered arms of the first victim, thereby seeking to secure the reproduction of their own martial power from the bodies of those who in the recent past had unsuccessfully opposed that same power on the battlefield.

Other Scythian practices show similar concerns and seem to draw on the same mythic ideology. Thus, Scythians who were defeated in single combat are said to have had their right hand cut off,[17] and regarding Scythian warriors' treatment of enemies whom they slew in battle, Herodotus recounts (4.64): "Many of them flay the skin off the right hands of enemy corpses, with the nails still attached, and make these into the sheaths of their quivers." This passage then goes on to state that these same warriors drank the blood of the fallen (as if it were wine),[18] and that they also severed their victims' heads, which they delivered to the Scythian king as a precondition for receiving a share of the booty.[19]

Just as Scythian warriors negated their enemies' arms in practices based on a cosmogonic myth that were designed to augment their own power, Scythian kings thus seem to have done the same with their enemies' heads. Other practices also show that heads were taken from victims with the conscious intent of thereby sustaining the kingship. For not only were enemy soldiers decapitated, but select others who in some fashion stood opposed to the kingship were also treated in like fashion. Thus, beheading was the punishment for anyone convicted of forswearing an oath by the royal hearth, for these were the most solemn of all oaths, any violation of which would imperil the health of the king and the well-being of the realm.[20]

Similarly, when the Scythians found that one of their kings, Scyles, had turned apostate by secretly embracing the Mysteries of Dionysus, they deposed him from the kingship and replaced him on the throne with his brother, who then had him beheaded. Here, Scyles figures as something of an anti-king: that is, someone who came to the throne, but betrayed his office and was rightly deprived of it, after which the kingship he had damaged was renewed with the offering of his head.[21]

Coda

In the preceding discussion, I have had occasion to consider the Amazons' debreasting and a wide variety of practices attributed to the Scythians, including their therapeutic cauterizations, their offerings to Ares, their mutilation of opponents slain in battle, their execution of perjurers, and finally their treatment of a deposed king. All of these may be understood—following Franz Kafka even more than Michel Foucault—as various means for writing cosmologically and politically significant messages upon people's bodies in so emphatic a fashion that those bodies (or significant portions thereof) are destroyed in the process.[22]

But are they sacrifices?

If the final word on this deceptively simple question must remain with our sources, then the answer is unambiguously no, for only with reference to the prisoners offered to Ares do the texts we have considered employ any of the standard Greek terminology for "sacrifice." Yet no point of method obligates us to accept the views and categories of those whom we study, however much we *are* obliged to take them seriously. Rather, we do better to treat these indigenous categories as themselves providing data for studies in which we may seek to discover the criteria from which these categories were constructed and the role that they played in organizing the practices of those people who constructed them. Clearly, that which sets the offerings to Ares apart from the other materials, and that which led Herodotus and others to regard it as a "sacrifice," is the presence of a god, which is to say that here and here alone did the acts of violence we have considered find legitimation in the fiction of a divine presence, if only that of the fetishized sword.[23] Most modern students of sacrifice, however, would view the (purported) presence of divine recipients as an accidental rather than an essential feature of sacrifice, i.e. one variable among many, but hardly *sine qua non.*

I should like to suggest a model of sacrifice that is sufficiently broad to cover all the examples I have treated (whose similarities far outweigh their differences), and a variety of other data besides. To that end, I would argue that sacrifice is most fundamentally a logic, language, and practice of transformative negation, in which one entity—a plant or animal, a bodily part, some portion of a person's life, energy, property, or even the life itself—is given up for the benefit of some other species, group, god, or principle that is understood to be "higher" or more deserving in one fashion or another. By this logic, animals are regularly sacrificed for humans (in research as in rituals), humans for gods (including such gods as "freedom," "higher profits," and "the national interest"), perjurers for kings (subversives for the state), breasts for arms (butter for guns), and the moist for the dry (fat for muscle, "no pain, no gain").

There are many distinguished scholars who take a rather benevolent view of sacrifice, stressing the way in which it furthers the construction of community or assists in the canalization of violence, to cite two influential examples.[24] Yet I continue to be troubled by the radical asymmetry that exists between the sacrificer and the sacrificed, or between those who call for sacrifices and those who bear the costs. In theory, the logic, language, and practice of sacrifice are accessible to a great many people for a great many purposes, many of which I could comfortably endorse. Yet more often than not, the calls to sacrifice which prove effective strike me as offensive and the performances that are actually staged seem little short of criminal, particularly when those categories of person who already enjoy disproportionate shares of all that this life has to offer—men, victorious warriors, or kings, e.g.—are able to define themselves and their favored entities as "higher" than others, and to reproduce their power and their privilege through the sacrifices they impose on those other, "lower" beings.

Notes

1. The classic account of the relations between Amazons and Scyths is found in Herodotus 4.110–17. Among the more important recent scholarship in Western languages on the Amazons, see William Blake Tyrrell, *Amazons: A Study in Athenian Mythmaking* (Baltimore: Johns Hopkins University Press, 1984); Page duBois, *Centaurs and Amazons: Women and the Pre-History of the Great Chain of Being* (Ann Arbor: University of Michigan Press, 1982); S. Rocca, "Dalle Amazzoni alla militia Phoebes," in *Misoginia e maschilismo in Grecia e in Roma* (Genoa: Istituto di Filologia Classica e Medievale, 1981), pp. 97–119; Jeannie Carlier, "Voyage en Amazonie grecque," *Acta Antiqua Academiae Scientiarum Hungaricae* 27 (1979): 381–405; idem, "Les Amazones font la guerre et l'amour," *L'Ethnographie* 74 (1980): 18–22; and P. Devambez, "Les Amazones et l'Orient," *Revue archéologique* (1976): 265–80. On the Scyths and Sauromatians, see: François Hartog, *The Mirror of Herodotus: The Representation of the Other in the Writing of History* (Berkeley: University of California Press, 1988); Renate Rolle, *The World of the Scythians* (London: B. T. Batsford, 1989); idem, *Totenkult der Skythen* (Berlin: Walter de Gruyter, 1979); Edmond Lévy, "Les origines du mirage scythe," *Ktema* 6 (1981): 57–68; K. F. Smirnov, "Sauromate et Sarmates," *Dialogues d'histoire ancienne* 8 (1982): 121–41; Georges Dumézil, *Romans de Scythie et d'alentours* (Paris: Payot, 1979); and W. D. Blawatsky and G. A. Kochelenko, "Quelques traits de la religion des scythes," in *Hommages à M. J. Vermaseren*, vol. 1 (Leiden: E. J. Brill, 1978), pp. 60–66. More generally, but with important reference to these peoples and the texts in which they are described, see also Brent D. Shaw, "'Eaters of Flesh, Drinkers of Milk': The Ancient Mediterranean Ideology of the Pastoral Nomad," *Ancient Society* 13–14 (1982–83): 5–31, esp. pp. 8–13; and Michèle Rosellini and Suzanne Saïd, "Usages de femmes et autres *nomoi* chez les 'sauvages' d'Hérodote: Essai de lecture structurale," *Annali della Scuola normale superiore di Pisa* 8 (1978): 949–1005, esp. pp. 998–1003.

2. Also useful is Lucian's *Toxaris*, although it is written much later than the other two sources noted above (2nd century A.D.).

3. That the image of the Amazons was produced for the most part by inverting the givens of Athenian patriarchy has been argued persuasively by Carlier, duBois, Tyrrell, and others. Unlike the Amazons, however, the Scythians were a very real people, with whom Herodotus and the author of *On Airs, Waters, and Places* had direct contact in the Black Sea port of Olbia. Still, Hartog has emphasized the degree to which Herodotus' representations were strongly inflected by the Athenian predisposition to see in Scythian nomadism the antithesis of their own *polis*-life. In general, Hartog's position, like that of others who read ethnographic reports with an eye toward their authors and audiences rather than toward the people whom they purport to describe, seems to me a useful principle but one which can produce oversimplifications. Preferable, in my view, is to understand such reports as suspended by their authors between the audience for whom and the people of whom they write. As such, ethnographic texts are surely conditioned by the interests of the audience and the author, but not

wholly determined by them. Rather, within such texts a set of complex negotiations is staged between lives as they are lived by actors, observed by ethnographers, heard about by readers, and imagined by all of the above. Regarding the nature of Greek-Scythian relations, see A. M. Khazanov, "Les Scythes et la civilisation antique: Problemes des contacts," *Dialogues d'histoire ancienne* 8 (1982): 7–51.

4. The most thorough and incisive review of current debates on the topic of sacrifice is offered by Cristiano Grottanelli, "Uccidere, donare, mangiare: problematiche attuali del sacrificio antico," in C. Grottanelli and N. F. Parise, eds., *Sacrificio e società nel mondo antico* (Rome: Laterza, 1988), pp. 3–53, a work which deserves much wider notice than it has thus far received. Theories of sacrifice tend to emphasize either the killing or the eating of the victims, and accordingly follow lines of analysis introduced either by Sir James George Frazer on the one hand, or W. Robertson Smith on the other. Yet to stress one of these aspects at the expense of the other is to divorce consumption from production, a move that makes no more sense in studies of ritual than it does in those of political economy.

5. In antiquity the name *Amazōn* was interpreted as derived from a form *a-mazos,* "one without a breast" or "the de-breasted one," with privative *a-* ($<$ Proto-Indo-European *n̥-*), plus *mazos* (= the Ionian form of *mastos,* "breast"). See, e.g., Diodorus Siculus 2.45.3 and Scholium bT to *Iliad* 3.189. Modern philology tends to treat this as a folk etymology, however, since it fails to account for the final suffix. To date, no alternate interpretation of the term's derivation and significance has gained scholarly acceptance.

6. E.g., Diodorus Siculus 2.45.3; Scholium bT to *Iliad* 3.189; Apollodorus, *Bibliotheca* 2.5.9; Strabo 11.5.1; Justinian, *Epitome* 2.4; Curtius Rufus 6.5.28.

7. Cauterization is also specified as the means of debreasting by Hellanicus, fragment 16 in Jacoby, *Fragmente der griechische Historiker* 3B45, Diodorus Siculus 2.45.3, Curtius Rufus 6.5.28, and Dionysius Scytobrachion, as quoted in Diodorus Siculus 3.53.3.

8. On this text, see C. Calame, "Environnement et nature humaine. Le racisme bien tempéré d'Hippocrate," in *Sciences et racisme* (Lausanne: Payot, 1986), pp. 75–99; Alain Ballabriga, "Les eunuques scythes et leurs femmes. Stérilité des femmes et impuissance des hommes en Scythie selon le traité hippocratique *des airs,*" *Métis* 1 (1986): 121–39; A. Thivel, "L'explication des maladies dans le traité hippocratique *Des airs, des eaux et des lieux,*" *Annales de la Faculté des Lettres et Sciences humaines de Nice* 50 (1985): 129–38; Jackie Pigeaud, "Remarques su l'inné et l'acquis dans le *Corpus Hippocratique,*" in F. Lasserre and P. Mudry, eds., *Formes de pensée dans la Collection Hippocratique* (Geneva: E. Droz, 1983), pp. 41–55; S. Frederick, *Hippocratic Heritage: A History of Ideas about Weather and Human Health* (New York: Pergamon Press, 1982); Jacques Jouanna, "Les causes de la défaite des Barbares chez Eschyle, Hérodote et Hippocrate," *Ktéma* 6 (1981): 3–15; and W. Backhaus, "Der Hellenen-Barbaren-Gegensatz und die hippokratische Schrift *Peri aerōn hydatōn topōn,*" *Historia* 25 (1976): 170–85.

9. For direct statements of these concerns see, e.g., chapters 1, 2, and 13.

10. Chapter 12 of the Hippocratic treatise announces this as its *topos:* "I plan to show how greatly Asia and Europe differ from each other in every way, and how their peoples differ in [bodily] form, so much so that one resembles the others not at all."

11. See esp. chapters 12, 16, and 24.

12. The situation of the Egyptians and Libyans is discussed briefly in chapter 18 and at the beginning of chapter 13. It seems to have been treated at length in a now-missing portion of chapter 12. The Scythians are discussed in chapters 18–22.

13. Herodotus 4.62. In contrast to his treatment of all other Scythian deities, Herodotus gives no indigenous name for that god he calls by the Greek name of "Ares," whose worship is quite anomalous in numerous ways. See further Herodotus 4.59 and the discussion of Hartog, *The Mirror of Herodotus*, pp. 188–92. On the distinctive nature of the Scythian sword, see W. Ginters, *Das Schwert der Skythen und Sarmaten in Südrussland* (Berlin: 1928).

14. Herodotus 4.60. Cf. Lucian, *Toxaris* 45, which states that Scythians think it an act of *hybris* to pour libations of wine.

15. On this pattern in general, see Bruce Lincoln, *Myth, Cosmos, and Society: Indo-European Themes of Creation and Destruction* (Cambridge, Mass.: Harvard University Press, 1986). The relations of wine and blood, as described in the Zoroastrian text *Zad Spram* 3.46, are treated at pp. 66 and 196–97.

16. Marijan Molé, *Culte, mythe, et cosmologie dans l'Iran ancien* (Paris: Presses universitaires de France, 1963); see also *Myth, Cosmos, and Society*, esp. pp. 41–64, 141–71.

17. Lucian, *Toxaris* 10, where this treatment is described as a "penalty" (*epitimion*).

18. A number of Scythian practices show that blood and wine were regarded as alloforms of one another, i.e. the macro- and microcosmic shapes taken by the same basic substance. Thus, for example, an annual feast was held in which wine was served only to those who had slain enemies in battle (Herodotus 4.66), and oaths of friendship were taken by drinking a mixture of blood and wine (Herodotus 4.70, Lucian, *Toxaris* 37). Such concerns may also have been involved in the well-known Scythian predilection for drinking their wine unmixed, a practice considered scandalous in antiquity.

19. Herodotus 4.64. Iconographic and archaeological evidence also attests to head-hunting and to the dismemberment of enemy dead. Cf. Rolle, *World of the Scythians*, pp. 82–86.

20. Herodotus 4.68. See, further, Chapter 15, "On the Scythian Royal Burials."

21. Herodotus 4.79–80. A similar story, involving the decapitation of a (foreign) king who had by his conduct shown himself unworthy of his office is told at length by Lucian, *Toxaris* 44–55. Particularly noteworthy is the fact that the king is beheaded in the temple of Ares, as he is about to swear a somewhat questionable oath. See esp. chapter 50.

22. In many ways, Kafka's haunting story "In the Penal Colony" can be read as a precursor of Foucault's *Discipline and Punish*. Both works contain much that is useful for an understanding of sacrifice. Dante, of course, provides a still earlier antecedent, as does Plato, *Gorgias* 525C–E, where one finds the appealing, but mystificatory notion that it is most often the rich and powerful whose bodies in Hades will have painful lessons written upon them.

23. Lucian, *Toxaris* 38, also describes worship of the Scythian sword but makes no mention of "Ares." Rather, it is there asserted that Wind and Sword are themselves gods (*theoi*) by whom Scythians swear oaths "because Wind is the source of life, and Sword is that which causes to die." Fabio Mora, *Religione e religioni nelle storie di Erodoto* (Milan: Editoriale Jaca, 1985), pp. 125–27, has gone so far as to argue that

Herodotus misrecognized the sword as an image of Ares, and consequently further misunderstood this ritual—which Mora prefers to view as a ceremony terminating the annual period of warfare—as a sacrifice.

24. Marcel Mauss and Henri Hubert, *Sacrifice: Its Nature and Function* (Chicago: University of Chicago Press, 1964); René Girard, *Violence and the Sacred* (Baltimore: Johns Hopkins University Press, 1977).

SEVENTEEN

PHYSIOLOGICAL SPECULATION AND SOCIAL PATTERNING IN A PAHLAVI TEXT

The study of ancient science is frequently rewarding, for in certain instances it may furnish convincing evidence of culture contact and influence. Thus, some forty-odd years ago, Sir Harold W. Bailey was able to recognize the traces of Aristotelian and Hippocratic thought within discussions of the nature of the human body in several Middle Persian texts.[1] In this study, among the most striking pieces of evidence which Bailey cited was a passage (*Zādspram* 30.14) concerned with the "watery" (*ābīg*) elements of the body,[2] said to be four in number, which, as he showed, closely parallel the four humors of Hippocratic theory.[3] Although other elements of Bailey's broader argument may remain subject to debate, in this specific datum the influence of Greek learning in an Iranian milieu is incontestably evident.

There are, however, other reasons for studying ancient speculation on the nature and workings of the natural world, not least of which is the way in which they occasionally encode concerns of a distinctly sociopolitical nature. Such, I hope to show, is true in the case of the Iranian theory of the four humors, as becomes clear when one considers the full *Zādspram* passage in which they are treated.[4] Although Bailey provided a transliteration of this text (Zsp. 30.14–19), he neither translated it nor discussed any of its contents beyond the names given the four bodily fluids in Zsp. 30.14. The sole translation available, to the best of my knowledge, is that of Anklesaria, in which certain misunderstandings so distort its sense as to make the text quite incomprehensible.[5] It thus seems worth providing a new rendition of *Zādspram* 30.14–19, paragraph by paragraph, with a detailed analysis of its content.

> 14. There are four essential fluids in the body, which are: Blood, Phlegm, Red Bile, and Black Bile.[6]

Although similar lists of bodily fluids can be found in other Middle Persian texts, it is in this passage that the closest correspondence can be found to the system which is common in Hippocratic medicine.[7] Thus, if one compares Zsp. 30.14 to the Hippocratic text "Concerning the Nature of Man" (*Peri Physios Anthrōpou*) chap. 4, one finds virtually the same fluids listed in identical order: first blood (Pahl. *xōn;* Gk. *haima*), then phlegm (Pahl. *drēm;* Gk. *phlegma*), and last black bile (Pahl. *wiš ī syā;* Gk. *kholēn melainan*). The sole divergence is that in the third position, where the Greek has "yellow bile" (*kholēn xanthēn*), the Iranian has "red" (*wiš ī suxr*), and even this minor difference is made more minimal still by the specification that the color of "red bile" is "variable from red to yellow" (*gōn suxr ō zardīh wardišnīg* [*Zādspram* 30.15]).

Also of interest is the term that is used to describe these fluids as a set: *āb mādagwar*, which I have translated "essential fluids," following established practice.[8] As is plainly evident, however, *mādagwar* is derived from *mādag* "female" (cf. Avestan *mātar*, Sanskrit *mātṛ*, Latin *māter*, Old High German *muotar*, etc.), and "essential" fails to capture this dimension of its meaning. Nyberg attempted to clarify things by arguing that the broader semantic range of *mādag* included an abstract dimension (thus "the essential element of anything, its core, essence; materials");[9] conversely, however, the designation of certain things as *mādagwar* includes an element of (gender-specific) concretion, such things being in some sense "maternal." The importance of this will become evident when the four "essential/maternal" fluids are brought in conjunction with another, decidedly nonmaternal fluid.

> 15. The nature of blood is warm and moist, its color red, its taste sweet, and its dwelling is in the liver.[10] The nature of phlegm is cold and moist, its color white, its taste salt, and its dwelling is in the lungs. The nature of red bile is warm and dry, its color is variable from red to yellow, its taste bitter, and its dwelling is in the gall bladder. The nature of black bile is cold and dry, its color black, its taste sour, and its dwelling is in the spleen.[11]

The first piece of information that is given regarding each of the fluids is its "nature" or "substance" (*gōhr*).[12] More precisely, an analysis is offered for each fluid as to whether it possesses warmth or cold, moisture or dryness. Classification along these lines yields a quadripartite taxonomy, as shown in figure 17.1.

	Moist	Dry
Warm	Blood	Red Bile
Cold	Phlegm	Black Bile

Figure 17.1: Classification of the four humors based upon their "nature"(I)

While accurate enough, such a representation is not the most instructive way to arrange these data, for the system does not really employ four variables but only two, dryness being simply the absence of moisture, and cold the absence of warmth. Thus the taxonomy is actually constructed upon two binary oppositions, in proper Lévi-Straussian fashion. Moreover, there is a hierarchic dimension to this taxonomy, for in both cases the presence of the taxonomizing property is considered preferable to its absence, moisture and warmth being regarded as beneficent and sustaining of life (i.e. Ohrmazdian) in Zoroastrian theology, while dryness and cold are evil, being characteristic of death and stagnation (i.e. Ahrimanian).[13] Thus, an initial distinction is apparent between those benign fluids which possess moisture (blood and phlegm), and those which do not (red bile and black bile), the latter being classified as "bilious" or "poisonous," for the term that is translated "bile" (Pahlavi *wiš*) means more generally "venom, poison."[14] Further subdivision of the benign and bilious fluids according to the presence or absence of warmth yields the full system of relations that is shown in figure 17.2.[15]

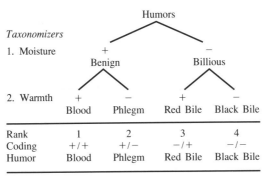

Figure 17.2: Classification of the four humors based upon their "nature"(II)

Beyond the question of "nature" (*gōhr*), the four humors are described in terms of three other variables: color (*gōn*), taste (*mizag*), and bodily locus or "dwelling" (*kadag*). The result is a sixteen-item square (four humors × four variables), in which the properties of the four humors are carefully set forth, without overlap or duplication, save in a single instance: the common color of blood and red bile. Even here, the text is at pains to establish a clear differentiation, specifying that the latter fluid may vary in hue from red to yellow (*gōn suxr ō zardīh wardišnīg*), as we have already noted. The system in full is shown in figure 17.3.

	Nature	Color	Taste	Dwelling
Blood	Warm Moist	Red	Sweet	Liver
Phlegm	Cold Moist	White	Salt	Lung
Red Bile	Warm Dry	Red-Yellow	Bitter	Gall Bladder
Black Bile	Cold Dry	Dark	Sour	Spleen

Figure 17.3: Properties of the four humors

Having established the differences among these four fluids, the text continues, in a somewhat less successful—if no less interesting—attempt to work out their complex interrelations.

16. Blood, the foremost of these elements, goes to the liver, and then in agitation goes mountain-climbing toward the head [?];[16] otherwise it collects and the phlegm awakes. Then the gall bladder, which is above the liver, draws up that which is thin and quick-flowing, which becomes red bile. It always keeps its mouth open. Red bile flows over the stomach, which digests food. That coarseness which remains is thrown down into the spleen, and becomes black bile.[17]

Blood, earlier said to have its "dwelling" in the liver (Zsp. 30.15), is here brought into association with a second bodily locus: the head, to which it travels in the course of normal circulation. When this second "dwelling" is considered alongside the loci assigned to the other humors (none of which is assigned such a secondary locus), a vertical mapping becomes apparent that parallels the hierarchy already established among the fluids based upon their "natures" (compare figure 17.4 to the rank order set forth in figure 17.2).[18]

1. Head (Blood)
2. Lungs (Phlegm)
3. Gall Bladder (Red Bile)
4. Spleen (Black Bile)

Figure 17.4: Vertical mapping of the bodily loci associated with the four humors

Should the blood (or a portion of the blood) not ascend to the head, this sets in motion a complicated set of events. For when blood does not rise from the liver, the result is phlegm, although it is not made clear just how this residual blood catalyzes the production of phlegm in the lungs. Rather, we are simply told that when the blood "collects" (*cinēd*) then the phlegm "awakes" (*guhrāyēnēd*). In contrast, the relation of residual blood to the two kinds of bile is thoroughly explicated. For just as blood is made up of two parts—one which rises and one which does not (the latter being connected, somehow, with phlegm)—so also the residual blood consists of two similar parts. One of these, we are told, is thin, subtle, or rarefied in nature (Pahl. *bārīg*), and is thus capable of upward motion from the liver to the gall bladder (*zahrag ī azabar jagar be jahēd, ān ī bārīg ī tēz ul āhanjēd*), where it becomes red bile. The other portion, in contrast, is coarse and heavy (Pahl. *stabrīh)* and thus falls downward to the spleen (*stabrīh ī abāz mānēd frōd ō spul*), where it becomes black bile. These interrelations may be graphed as in figure 17.5.

Having named the four "essential/maternal fluids" (Zsp. 30.14), discussed the differences among them (30.15), and their interrelations (30.16), the text now proceeds to consider their unification within a fifth fluid, thus far unnamed.

17. Then, seeds from all four elements, which are in the top of the head, the place of the brain, go to the spinal cord. A libation, made up of all four fluids in proportion to their accomplishments, is drawn back to the head. That bodily being which is gathered up

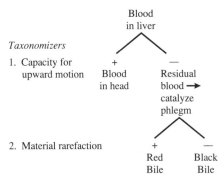

Figure 17.5: Interrelations of the four humors

in that libation [comes] from all the body; its essence is made firm and it is poured forth in the form of seed. And from this there is the coming into being and the birth of mortals.[19]

There is much that remains unclear here. One is given no clue as to how the "seeds" (*tōhmagān*) of the four humors come to be in the brain, nor what is meant by the specification that they are joined in a mixture that is somehow "in proportion to their accomplishments" (*passāxtīh rāy paymānagīg*). The identity of that mixture, however, is no mystery, for it is nothing other than semen (*tōhm*),[20] here viewed as being nothing other than an aggregate of the four fundamental fluids. We are told, moreover, that—apparently as a result of its aggregate nature—semen possesses within itself the very essence of all bodily matter, drawn from all parts of the body (*az hamāg kirb, tan ī pad zōhr ī abar cinēd, andar cihrag ōstīgān be kunēd*), and it is this which makes it capable of producing new life, being in effect a microcosmic version of the body to be created. The "essence" (*cihrag*) contained within semen, moreover, is quite different from that of the four "essential" fluids. For whereas the latter were "essential/maternal" (*mādagwar*), semen is—of course— "essential/paternal," for *cihrag* means, most literally, "(male) seed."[21]

One further item in Zsp. 30.17 is noteworthy: the metaphoric description of seminal fluid as a "libation" (*zōhr*) that, apparently, is poured forth from its place of origin in the brain, through the spinal cord, down to the reproductive organs.[22] In this fashion, the attempt is made to associate a physiological process—albeit one that is misunderstood by our standards—to a ritual action that is viewed as being no less creative: the pouring of libation offerings into the sacrificial fire.[23] Sexual reproduction is thus presented as a sacred action, in which the male role—nothing similar is said of the female—is akin to that of the priest who presents a libation offering. This is the first point at which the text moves beyond its consideration of strictly physiological entities and processes, relating this area of concern to another: that of social relations. Of this, there is more to come.

18. These four elements, which are different in their nature and different in that which they do, [are like] the four social classes, which are: the Priest, who is a teacher; the Warrior, who is a fighter; the Pastoralist and Agriculturalist, who is a table-servant; and the Artisan, who is a menial-servant.[24]

Here, the four humors are correlated to the old Iranian social system of four hierarchially differentiated classes based upon occupation, which are also organized in a hierarchic set.[25] No argument is advanced for a relation of analogy or homology between specific classes and corresponding humors, although with some difficulty elements of such an argument might be inferred.[26] Instead of focusing upon any perceived or imagined similarities between a given fluid and a correlated social class, however, the text is at pains to compare rather the hierarchic *system* under which two sets are organized. The correspondences as set forth in this text are as shown in figure 17.6.

Rank	Fluid	Social Class	Activity
1	Blood	Priests	Teaching
2	Phlegm	Warriors	Fighting
3	Red Bile	Pastoralists & Agriculturalists	Serving Food
4	Black Bile	Artisans	Menial Service

Figure 17.6: Correlations between the four humors and the four social classes

Representation of the social order as if it were but one example of a pattern also encountered in the natural world is quite common within Iranian texts, as in those of many other peoples.[27] As such, it is a classic means of legitimating rigidly hierarchic and exploitative systems, the contingent natures of which are masked as they are made to appear but one expression among many of a natural—and therefore incontestable, immalleable, and perhaps even divine—order. Having thus dealt with the social order, the text concludes with a brief (albeit pointed) discussion of the central political institution in ancient Iran.

19. Semen is above those four [fluids] as the king is above the [four] social classes.[28]

That this is the key point, toward which the entire discourse was structured, is signalled by the fact that the opening words of this sentence were written in red ink in one of the two surviving manuscripts of *Zādspram*. Discussion of bodily fluids, far from being a topic of purely intrinsic interest, provided also the means to make a point more sociopolitical than physiological in nature.[29] For we are told that just as semen is a master fluid, in which the others unite, making possible the (re-)production of life, so the king stands above the social classes, uniting all of them in his very being, and it is he who makes possible the ongoing life of society. Moreover, a subtle point of gender politics is also advanced, for just as the four "essential/maternal" (*mādagwar*) fluids, which all have their origin in the lower parts of the body, were set in contrast to the unique "essential/paternal" (*cihrag*) semen, which has its origin in the brain, so the king stands apart from and above (*abar*) his people, with whom he may enter into fruitful relations, if the text is to be believed, but only as the dominant—i.e. male—partner. These relations are graphed below in figure 17.7.

Semen : Four Humors ::
King : Four Classes ::
Male : Female

Figure 17.7: Concluding analogies as presented in *Zādspram* 30.14–19

Notes

1. H. W. Bailey, *Zoroastrian Problems in the Ninth Century Texts* (Oxford: Clarendon Press, 1943), pp. 78–119.

2. *Zādspram* 30.3 asserts that "The body is threefold: the bodily being which is bone, and [that which is] of water, and [that which is] of wind": *tanīg 3 ī ast tanīgardīg ud ābīg ud wādīg*. There then follows an analysis of these three categories of bodily substance, of which the passage under consideration here is a part.

3. Bailey, p. 105.

4. As is so often the case, secure dating of the *contents* within a Middle Persian text composed in the ninth century of our era is virtually impossible. Given certain of the details within the passage to be considered, it seems most plausible to me that its key concepts are rooted in the Sassanian period, but I see no secure way to preclude either an earlier or later dating.

5. Behramgore Tehmurasp Anklesaria, *Vichitakiha-i Zatsparam, with Text and Introduction* (Bombay: Trustees of the Parsi Punchayet Funds & Properties, 1964), p. cvi–cvii. Bailey's transliteration is found at pp. 211–12.

6. The full text is found in Anklesaria, p. 112, line 5, to p. 114, line 2.

112.5. āb[ān] andar tan mādagwar 4, ī hast *xōn

    6. ud drēm ud wiš ī suxr ud wiš ī syā.

Textual Notes

112.5 *mādagwar*, not *mādagwarīhā*, following the TD MS, pace Anklesaria and Bailey. The term is adjectival, modifying *āb*. It is possible that the *-īhā* suffix might signify the plural, in which case, however, we ought expect *āban*.

112.5 Both of the manuscripts (TD and BK) omit *xōn* here, and the TD MS had *3* instead of *4*, in keeping with this omission. BK, however, has *4* in accord with the full set of bodily fluids spelled out in the discussion that follows (Zsp. 30.15–19).

112.6 *wiš* "bile" is homographic with *wēh* "good." Anklesaria consistently misinterprets it as the latter term.

7. Thus, the set of four humors given at *Dēnkart* 3.263 (MS. B 211.12–13) fails to differentiate between the two types of bile, and adds "breath" (*wād*) to fill out the set. A vague association is also there advanced between the humors—breath, blood, bile, and phlegm—and the four "worldly elements of the body" (*gēhān āmēzišnīg tan*

ristān): fire (*ādur*), wind (*wād*), moisture (*nām*), and clay (*gil*). Although it is not spelled out, one probably ought correlate fire to blood, wind to breath, moisture to phlegm, and clay to bile.

8. Thus D. N. MacKenzie, *A Concise Pahlavi Dictionary* (London: Oxford University Press, 1971), p. 53; Henrik Samuel Nyberg, *A Manual of Pahlavi* (Wiesbaden: Otto Harrassowitz, 1974), 2:129.

9. Nyberg, 2:129 (under *mātakīk*).

10. Thus the text, although Anklesaria consistently translates *jagar* by "heart," in keeping with what is now known about the circulation of the blood. That this is the liver, however, and not the heart, is made certain not only by the etymology of Pahlavi *jagar* (cf. Avestan *yākarə*, Sanskrit *yakṛt*, Persian *jigar*, Greek *hēpar*, Latin *iecur*, Lithuanian *jaknos* [pl.]), but also by the specification later in the text that the gall bladder (*zahrag*) is located *above* the *jagar* (*zahrag ī azabar jagar be jahēd*).

11. 112.7. xōn gohr garm ud xwēd, uš gōn suxr, uš

    8. mizag šīrēn, uš kadag pad jagar. drēm sard ⟨ud⟩ xwēd,

    9. ud gōn spēd, mizag sōr, uš kadag pad suš. wiš ī

    10. suxr garm ⟨ud⟩ hušk ud gōn suxr ō zardīh wardišnīg, uš

    11. mizag taxl, uš kadag pad zahrag. ud wiš ī syā

    12. sard ⟨ud⟩ hušk, uš gōn syā, uš mizag *trufš, uš

    13. kadag pad spul.

Textual Notes

112.7 *garm*, the reading of the BK MS is preferable to that of TD (*drēm*), pace Anklesaria.

112.10 Again *garm* and not *drēm*, following the BK reading, pace Anklesaria.

12. On this term, see Bailey, pp. 89–90.

13. See, for instance, *Greater Bundahišn* 181.6, *Dēnkart* 3.105, 123, 162, and 390, and the discussion of Mansour Shaki, "Some Basic Tenets of the Eclectic Metaphysics of the *Dēnkart*," *Archiv Orientálni* 38 (1970): 295–96.

14. MacKenzie, p. 92. Nyberg, 2:215, does not even list the more specialized meaning "bile." Derivation is from the Avestan *viš-*, *viša-* "poison"; cf. Sanskrit *viśa-*, Greek *īos*, Latin *vīrus*, Irish *fí*.

15. For further discussion of this means of representing classificatory systems, and on the hierarchic nature of classification in general, see Bruce Lincoln, *Discourse and the Construction of Society* (New York: Oxford University Press, 1989), pp. 131–141.

16. This sentence employs imagistic language to describe imaginary physiological processes, making it extremely difficult to interpret with any certainty.

17. 112.14. pēšōbāy az āmēzišnān xōn ō jagar šawēd,

    15. ud pas andar ayārdēnišn kōf be sar abganēd enyā

  113.1 cinēd ud be ō drēm guhrāyēnēd. pas zahrag ī azabar

    2. jagar be estēd, ān ī bārīg ī tēz ul āhanjēd

    3. be ō wiš ī suxr bawēd, bāstān dahān wišād

    4. dārēd. wiš ī suxr abar kumīg rēzēd, ī xwarišn

    5. gugārēd, pas stabrīh ī abāz mānēd frōd ō *spul

    6. *abganihēd be ō wiš ī syā bawēd.

Textual Notes

112.14 Both MSS have what amounts to a misspelling here, showing '*mzšn'n* for '*mycn'n* (in transliteration).

112.14 Where TD has *jagar* ("liver," i.e. the original dwelling place of the blood according to the preceding discussion), BK has *sar* ("head," i.e. the blood's destination, according to the following line, where both MSS have *sar*). Graphically, the two are very easily confused, given the close resemblance of the ligature y + k in *jagar* (*ykl*) to the letter samek in *sar* (*sl*).

    18. The relative positions of the gall bladder and spleen are established in Zsp. 30.16, where they are said to be above and below the liver respectively.

    19. 113.7. pas az ēn harw 4 āmēzišnān tōhmagān, kē pad

        8. bālist ⟨ī⟩ sar, andar mazg gāh, pad ān rahag pad pušt

        9. abar šawē⟨n⟩d. zōhr-ē ī az harw 4 passāxtīh rāy

      10. paymānagīg, abāz ō sar āhanj⟨ih⟩ēd, az hamāg kirb, tan ī

      11. pad zōhr ī abar cin⟨ih⟩ēd, andar cihrag ōstīgān be kunēd,

      12. pad tōhm ēwēnag frāz rēzīhēd, [uš] bawišn ud zayišn ī

      13. mardōmān az-iš bawēd.

Textual Notes

113.10 Pace Anklesaria and Bailey, the *sar* of MS. BK is preferable to TD's *jagar*.

113.11 *pad* is omitted in MS. BK. When this is so, *zōhr* functions as the subject of the sentence and the active form of the verb is proper. With *pad* present, however, *tan* becomes the subject and a passive form (**cinihēd*) is required.

    20. Nyberg, 2:194; Bailey, pp. 106, 109. The view advanced by Shaki, "Some Basic Tenets," 289–91, that *tōhmag* denotes "substance" in a technically Aristotelian sense strikes me as overly restrictive, as do his interpretations of *mādag* (p. 279, n. 15) and *cihr* (p. 303). In stressing the abstract semantic range of these terms as they are employed in discussions of cosmogony, Shaki systematically ignores their grounding in the physiology of human reproduction, which—as some of the texts he cites make clear—provided a model of creative processes (cf. GBd. 16.1–9 and *Dēnkart* MS. B 82a 18–83b, cited at pp. 310 and 281–83 respectively).

    21. MacKenzie, p. 22; Nyberg, 2:55 (under *cihr*). MacKenzie, apparently following Christian Bartholomae, *Altiranisches Wörterbuch* (Berlin: Walter de Gruyter, 1961 [orig. 1904]), pp. 586–87, differentiates two homographic Pahlavi terms ¹*cihr* (derived from Avestan ¹*cithra-*) "form, shape, appearance, face," and ²*cihr* (from Av. ²*cithra-*) "seed, origin, nature, essence," *cihrag* being derived from the latter.

    22. See further Jacques Duchesne-Guillemin, "Le Xvarənah," *Annali dell' Istituto Orientale di Napoli, Sezione Linguistica* 5 (1963): 19–31, esp. 25–26.

    23. On sacrifice as *the* quintessentially creative act, see Marijan Molé, *Culte, mythe, et cosmologie dans l'Iran ancien* (Paris: Presses Universitaires de France, 1963).

    24. 113.14. ān 4 āmēzišn⟨ān⟩ ī jud-cihrag jud-kār be ō

      15. 4 pēšag ⟨ī⟩ mardōm ī hēnd hammōzgār āsrōn ud zadār

      16. artēštār ud *frawārdār wāstaryōš [ud] paristār *hutuxš.

Textual Notes

113.16 Reading *frawārdār for *frawardār*.

113.16 Parallelism requires a connective particle between *wāstaryōš* and *paristār*, since the bipartite designators of the other three classes (action-describer plus formal title) are all separated by *ud*. The TD MS contains an error, with the *ud* preceding *wāstaryōš* instead of following it.

    25. A half century later, the classic works on the ancient Iranian social order remain Georges Dumézil, "La préhistoire indo-iranienne des castes," *Journal asiatique*

216 (1930): 109–30; Émile Benveniste, "Les classes sociales dans la tradition avesti-que," *Journal asiatique* 221 (1932): 117–34; and idem, "Traditions indo-iraniennes sur les classes sociales," *Journal asiatique* 230 (1938): 529–49. More recently, see my *Priests, Warriors, and Cattle: A Study in the Ecology of Religions* (Berkeley: University of California Press, 1981), pp. 134–39.

26. This is easier as one moves toward the bottom of both hierarchic sets, for just as two types of bile occupy the third and fourth positions within the system of four humors, so two types of servant are similarly placed within the social order. And just as the higher type of bile is concerned with the digestion of food (Zsp. 30.16), so the higher type of servant—the pastoralist-herdsman, whose chief activity is the production of food in its animal and vegetable forms—is called a *frawārdār,* a "servant" from the verb *frawārdan* "to serve," with particular reference to the presentation of meals. For its part, *paristār,* the term used for the activity of the artisan class, is derived from the verb *paristīdan* "to serve, to worship," and denotes not so much a specific activity as the enormous gulf which separates this kind of servant from the one who is served. Correlations between the upper two classes and the upper two humors are more difficult (if not impossible) to establish and the text wisely makes no such attempt.

27. In *Myth, Cosmos, and Society: Indo-European Themes of Creation and Destruction* (Cambridge, Mass.: Harvard University Press, 1986), I have studied this pattern among the literatures of Indo-European-speaking peoples. While common enough in this culture area, this ideological and rhetorical style is hardly unique to them; cf. the brief but insightful remarks of William J. Goode, *The Celebration of Heroes: Prestige as a Control System* (Berkeley: University of California Press, 1978), p. 147.

28. 114.1. **TOHMAG ABAR** awēšān ciyōn *šahryār abar 4

    2. pēšagān.

Textual Notes

114.1 **TOHMAG ABAR**: In MS. BK, these words are written in red ink.

29. One ought not, however, unduly and anachronistically dichotomize these two discursive spheres. Discussions on the interrelation of the individual body and that of the body politic (or social body) continues well into the early modern period. See, inter alia, the classic work of Ernst Kantorowicz, *The King's Two Bodies: A Study in Mediaeval Political Theology* (Princeton: Princeton University Press, 1957).

EIGHTEEN

EMBRYOLOGICAL SPECULATION AND GENDER POLITICS IN A PAHLAVI TEXT

In the preceding chapter, I tried to show how a Middle Persian text, *Zād Spram* 30.14–19, that is explicitly concerned with aspects of human physiology also (and more important) encodes social and political ideology. Physiological and sociopolitical discourses merge and interpenetrate in numerous other Pahlavi texts, as for instance in those where the nature of conception, the supreme mystery of the origins of life, is at issue. Let us consider one such text in detail, the *Indian Bundahišn* 16.1–6,[1] which begins as follows:

> 1. Regarding the nature of birth, it is said in the Religion: From the time a woman comes forth from her menses until ten days and nights (have elapsed), men go to her before she becomes pregnant.
> 2. When she is clean from her menses and it is time for her to become pregnant, whenever the man's seed is more powerful, then there is a son. When the woman's seed is more powerful, there is a daughter. And when the two seeds are equal, then twins and triplets come into being.[2]

The text begins by differentiating between those times when sexual intercourse will result in conception and those when it will not, specifying ten days after the cessation of menstrual bleeding as the fertile period. No attempt is made, however, to establish why this is so. Rather, it is simply asserted as a fact, after which the discussion moves to differentiate those pregnancies which result in the birth of a boy from those which produce a girl, and to offer a causal explanation for this bifurcation. Thus, it states that whereas a male child follows from an act of insemination in which the seed (*tōhm*) supplied by the father is somehow "more powerful" (*nērōgōmandtar*) than that of the mother, a female child is conceived through the opposite state of affairs. Sexual union and conception thus involve a test of sorts, in which the seeds of the parents vie quite literally to "overpower" each other, with the gender identity of the resulting child as the prize in this contest. Within the logic of this explanatory system, there remains one final possibility, i.e. that case in which the seeds of both parents are precisely equal in power. Such an eventuality, it is maintained, results in the phenomenon of multiple births.[3] The three logical possibilities entertained within this system are, then as presented in figure 18.1.

It should be noted that no inherent superiority in "power" is attributed to

Male seed more powerful	→	Birth of male child
Female seed more powerful	→	Birth of female child
Both seeds equal in power	→	Birth of twins, triplets

Figure 18.1: The role of gender in conception according to *Indian Bundahišn* 16.1

either male or female seed, and although the text is silent in this regard, it might be assumed from the fact that female births are approximately equal to male in number, that female seed must therefore be more powerful than male in about 50 percent of all conceptions, and vice versa. This apparent egalitarianism, however, is belied by the next portion of the text.

> 3. If the man's seed comes first, it grows in the woman and she becomes stout [i.e. pregnant]. If the woman's seed comes first, it turns to blood and the woman is thereby weakened [i.e., she does not conceive, but menstruates].[4]

Whereas the preceding verse seemed to establish a rough equality of the two seeds, each of which could produce a child of its own gender when present in a form more "powerful" (*nērōgōmandtar*) than its counterpart, this verse is at pains to assert the superior nature of the male seed. In order to do so, it employs the imagery of sequential order, for apparently more is necessary for conception than an act of correctly timed parental intercourse. In addition, it is asserted, in order for procreation to result, the male seed must arrive first (presumably at the womb; alternatively, it might be that male orgasm must precede female in order for conception to occur). The primacy of male seed—in temporal terms, rather than those of relative "power"—is thus established as a necessary precondition for any birth, for only when male seed comes first, is life possible. Figure 18.1 must be modified accordingly, as shown in figure 18.2.

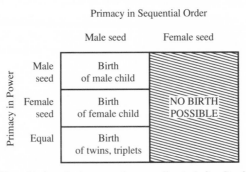

Figure 18.2: The role of gender in conception according to *Indian Bundahišn* 16.1–3

These points established, the text moves on to consider the essential and contrasting natures of the two gender-specific seeds:

> 4. Women's seed is cold and moist, and its flow is from the ribs: its color is red and yellow. Men's seed is warm and dry, and its flow is from the brain. Its color is white and dark.[5]

Male and female seed are thus differentiated, first on the basis of four physical properties: warmth, cold, moisture, and dryness. These properties, far from being chosen at random, are of fundamental importance in Zoroastrian thought. For as is evident in numerous other sources, moisture and warmth are considered to be inherently Ohrmazdian in nature: that is, they are beneficent and sustaining of life. Conversely, dryness and cold are Ahrimanian, characteristic of death and stagnation. These Ahrimanian properties, however, upon closer analysis are less categories of being than of non-being, for they are in essence nothing other than the negation of their Ohrmazdian counterparts, for cold is the absence of warmth, and dryness the absence of moisture.[6] Male seed is thus characterized by the presence of warmth and the absence of moisture, while female seed is just the reverse, as is shown in figure 18.3.

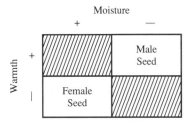

Figure 18.3: Classification of the two seeds according to the presence or absence of moisture and warmth

It is thus clear that the two seeds—one of which possesses warmth, but lacks moisture, while the other possesses moisture, but lacks warmth—are both morally ambiguous mixtures of Ohrmazdian and Ahrimanian properties, and accordingly neither one is capable of creating and sustaining life in and of itself.[7] Rather, the union of the two is necessary for procreation to occur, so that each one can liquidate the other's (Ahrimanian) lack. Conception via sexual union is thus represented as a classically dialectic process, in which two opposite entities confront one another and generate a third, different from either of its antecedents, but derivative of both, as is shown in figure 18.4.

As for classification of the seeds by color, the text implies that female seed, being red *and* yellow, includes, but is not limited to menstrual blood,[8] while male seed similarly includes, but is not limited to semen, insofar as it is white *and* dark.[9] Presumably, pains are being taken here to avoid a straightforward identification of female seed with blood, for the latter fluid is elsewhere said to be both warm and moist: that is to say, wholly Ohrmazdian and capable of sustaining life in and of itself (Zsp. 30.15). By assigning two colors to each

	Moisture	Warmth
Male Seed (Thesis)	−	+
Female Seed (Antithesis)	+	−
Union of the two (Synthesis)	+	+

Figure 18.4: Interaction of the two seeds in conception

seed, the text avoids this pitfall, while also correlating the two seeds to the four humors, for through their color codings, each seed is brought into association with one benign humor (female to [red] blood, male to [white] phlegm) and one that is destructive or poisonous (female to that bile which is "variable from red to yellow," [10] and male to black bile).

Beyond their differing physical properties, the two seeds are also said to have their origin in different parts of the body. Thus, we are told that while female seed flows from the ribs, male flows from the brain, and the means whereby the latter makes its way from the brain to the testicles via the spinal column is spelled out in a number of other sources. [11] More important for our present concerns, however, is the system of vertical relations whereby the male element is set dramatically above the female in a fashion that encodes and re-presents a social hierarchy. [12]

Association of male seed with the brain further serves to identify males as those who are, *ab origine,* possessed of thought, while conversely thought is identified as something quintessentially male. Also we must note that in Pahlavi, one word (*mazg*) denotes "brain" and "marrow" alike, the brain being understood as an organ composed entirely of marrow. Marrow, for its part, is viewed as the innermost core of bodily existence, surrounded by bone, which in turn is surrounded by flesh, fat, veins, skin, and hair. [13] In their contrastive original loci (brain and ribs), the two seeds are thus also contrasted as marrow is to bone: the former being that which is absolutely central, and the latter that which is—somewhat, if only slightly—peripheral. This system of oppositions is mapped out in figure 18.5.

Male	Female
Brain	Ribs
Above	Below
Superior	Subordinate
Thought	Body
Marrow	Bone
Center	Periphery

Figure 18.5: Binary contrasts following upon the opposition of brain to ribs according to *Indian Bundahišn* 16.4

With this established, the text continues:

> 5. All female seed comes first and holds on in the womb. The male seed is above, and makes the place of the womb full. All that [seed] which is superfluous turns back into blood. It goes into the woman's veins and becomes milk in her breasts when the child is born, as all milk comes from men's seed and all blood from that of women.[14]

Strikingly, this portion of the text openly contradicts a point made only a bit before, where it was claimed that male seed must come first for conception to result (IndBd. 16.3). The very fact of such a contradiction is itself instructive, however, revealing as it does, how little concerned this passage is with the physiology of reproduction in the last analysis. For if it is able to reverse itself on physiological details, it is nonetheless quite consistent in its ideological formulations which are alternately presented in a code of sequential order and one of vertical relations. For if the present verse negates the earlier specification that male seed must come "first" if there is to be a fruitful conjunction, it replaces that notion with the equally novel, equally fallacious, and equally tendentious idea that male seed sits somehow "above" (*azabar*) the female when the two commingle in the womb.

Equally striking is the discussion of what becomes of that portion of the mixed seed which is superfluous (*harw ce az-aš be parrēzēd*), i.e. that which is left over after the fetus has been formed. This excess, we are told, returns to the mother's bloodstream, where at the time of the child's birth, the two gender-specific seeds separate once more, the mother's remaining in the form of blood (perhaps the blood of parturition), while the father's is transformed into milk. Although this line of analysis may have been suggested by the system of color classification that posits (in part) Male : Female :: White : Red, there are serious consequences which follow from it. For when these views are accepted, nourishment—from the moment of birth onward—is identified as a paternal gift, and the very milk that flows from a mother's breasts is appropriated by male ideology.

Having pursued its consideration of life's origins from the moment when conception becomes possible through to the feeding of the newborn, the text shifts its focus, moving from an embryological discourse to one that is cosmological.

> 6. These four things are said to be male and female respectively: Sky, metal, wind, and fire come into being as male and never otherwise. Water, earth, plants, and fish come into being as female, and never otherwise. The rest of creation may come into being male and female.[15]

Here, at the culmination of the entire passage, appears the definitive coding of sex hierarchy, in which the very cosmos is classified according to gender.

Two basic distinctions are advanced, the first being that between those things which have a fixed gender and those which do not.[16] Of this latter group, nothing further is said, it being no more than the residual class which fills out the taxonomic system. In contrast, all those items which have gender are individually named as they are divided into the subcategories of male (sky, metal, fire, and wind) and female (water, earth, plants, and fish), as is shown in figure 18.6.

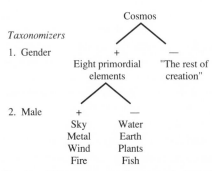

Figure 18.6: Classification of the cosmos according to gender in *Indian Bundahišn* 16.6

As always, there is more. For of the eight gender-specific elements that are mentioned here, four recur in the list of "Six Original Creations" in the *Bundahišn*'s cosmogonic account (IndBd. 1.28, GBd. 1.54). When the two texts are considered together, we find that the first element of creation is male (sky), the second, third, and fourth (water, earth, plants) are female, and the last two (cattle and humanity) lack gender specificity.[17] Further, five of the eight also figure in the set of "Beneficent Immortals" (*Aməša Spəntas*), Zoroastrian divine beings each of whom is associated with one specific element of the created universe. These figures, moreover, are always listed in a regular, canonic order, as follows: 1) Vohu Manah ("Good Thought"), patron of (non-gender specific) livestock; 2) Aša Vahišta ("Best Truth"), patron of (male) fire; 3) Xšaθra Vairya ("Choice Dominion"), patron of (male) metal; 4) Spənta Armaiti ("Beneficent Devotion"), patroness of the (female) earth; 5) Haurvatāt ("Wholeness"), patron of (female) water; and Amərətāt ("Immortality"), patron of (female) plants. As in the case of the "Six Original Creations," so here, the sequential order encodes gender hierarchy such that male items always precede female, although non-gender-specific items may come either at the head or the tail of the total list.

Just as sequential order encodes hierarchy, so also do vertical relations, as we saw in the embryological discourse of IndBd. 16.1–5. The same holds true in the cosmological discourse of 16.6, for the four creations which are there said to be male are all associated with the above: sky, metal (of which the sky is made, according to the *Bundahišn*),[18] fire (associated, above all, with the sun), and wind. Conversely, the four female creations are all associated with the below: earth, plants, water, and fish.[19] One can correlate all of these codes—embryological and cosmological, sequential and vertical—in one master list, as in figure 18.7.

		SEQUENTIAL CODINGS		VERTICAL CODINGS	
EMBRYOLOGICAL DISCOURSE	**Male Seed**	Must come first for conception		Flows from brain	Lodges above womb
	Female Seed	Must come second for conception		Flows from ribs	Lodges in womb
COSMOLOGICAL DISCOURSE	**Male Elements**	Sky first created	Beneficent Immortals # 2 & 3 (Fire, Metal)	Locus in the above (Sky, Metal, Fire, Wind)	
	Female Elements	Water, earth, plants created 2nd, 3rd, 4th	Beneficent Immortals # 4, 5, 6 (Earth, Water, Plants)	Locus in the below (Earth, Plants, Water, Fish)	

Figure 18.7: Interlocking representations of gender hierarchy in *Indian Bundahišn* 16.1–6

This completes the analysis offered by the *Bundahišn*, and that which I offer for this rich and complex text, a text that mixes multiple levels of discourse with equal skill and tendentiousness. In antiquity, as in the present, there are those who maintain that the making of babies is a cosmic and not merely an individual matter; a question of religion as well as biochemistry. If nothing else, I hope to have demonstrated that speculation on this topic—the origins of life, in the ontogenetic sense—has, on occasion, been a sociopolitical and gender hierarchic issue as well.

Notes

1. My translation is based upon the text established by Ferdinand Justi, *Der Bundehesh, zum ersten Male herausgegeben* (Leipzig, 1868) page 38, line 12 to 39.13. The corresponding passage of the *Greater Bundahišn* is extremely close (the few minor variants have been noted), but contains two long and intrusive excursuses, dealing primarily with the reproductive processes of various animal species (GBd. 15.1–3 and 15.8–16, at TD$_2$ MS. 109.6–11 and 110.11–112.14 respectively). These excursuses are signalled at the start of the chapter by insertion of the phrase *zāyišnān ī az harw sardag* (TD$_2$ MS. 109.3: "Regarding the nature of *the births of every species*") where IndBd. has only *zāyišnīh:* "Regarding the nature of birth"). English translations of these passages are available in E. W. West, *Pahlavi Texts*, vol. 1 (Oxford: Clarendon Press, 1880), pp. 60–61 (IndBd.) and B. T. Anklesaria, *Zand-Akāsīh: Iranian or Greater Bundahišn* (Bombay: Rahnumae Mazdayasnan Sabha, 1956), pp. 139–43 (GBd.).

2. 38.12. abar ciyōnīh ⟨ī⟩ zāyišnīh gōwēd pad dēn kū.

13. zan ka az daštān be āyēd tā 10 rōz šab, ka-š

14. ō šawēnd pēš ābustan bawēd. ka-š

15. az daštān šust ēstēd ka ābustan zamān [*ka]
16. estēd. hamē ka tōhm ī mard nērōgōmandtar
17. pus, ka ān ī zān nērōgōmandtar duxt, ka harw
18. rāst tōhm 2-gānag ud 3-gānag az-aš bawēd.

Textual Notes

38.12 *zāyišnīh:* GBd. has *zāyišnān ī az harw sardag* (TD₂ MS. 109.3). See above, note 1.

38.13 *āyēd:* GBd. has *šāyēd* (MS. TD₂ 109.5).

38.14 *ō šawēnd:* GBd. has *ō nazdīkīh šawēnd* (TD₂ MS. 109.5). Thus: "they go *near to* her," a clearer euphemism for sexual intercourse.

3. The problematics of gender are not pursued here: one might, for example, expect hermaphroditic or asexual children to result from parental seeds of equal power, given the logic of the system. It would seem that twins of opposite sexes, i.e. a situation in which precise gender balance is maintained, were taken as the paradigm of all multiple births, so that the text is spared the difficulty (and embarrassment) of working out the causal factors that result in the birth of same-sex triplets, for instance.

4. 38.18.   agar tōhm ī
19. nar pēš āyēd ō mādag abzāyēd, uš
20. frabīh bawēd. agar tōhm ī mādag pēš āyēd xōn bawēd,

39.1. mādag az-aš nizārīhēd.

Textual Notes

38.19: GBd. inserts *pīh bawād* "it would become fat" between *āyēd* and *ō* (TD₂ MS. 109.15), thus specifying that it is the male seed which is actually growing and causing pregnancy.

5. 39.1.   tōhm ī mādag sard ud xwēd, tazišn az
2. pahlūg ud gōnag [spēd] suxr ud zard. tōhm ī narān garm
3. ud hušk, tazišn az mazg ī sar, gōnag spēd ud xašēn.

Textual Notes

39.1 *spēd* is lacking in the corresponding passage of the Greater Bundahišn (TD₂ MS. 110.3). Its presence here seems to be a scribal error, since it disrupts the logic of the analysis.

39.3 *ud xašēn* is omitted in GBd. (TD₂ MS. 110.5), physiological observation prevailing over schematic representations, and white semen only being recognized. Since all manuscripts preserve two colors of female seed (red *and* yellow), it seems likely that male seed—which balances female in all other respects—also had two colors attributed to it.

6. See, for instance, GBd. 181.6, Zsp. 30.15, *Dēnkart* 3.105, 123, 162, and 390, and the discussion of Mansour Shaki, "Some Basic Tenets of the Eclectic Metaphysics of the *Dēnkart*," *Archiv Orientalnì* 38 (1970): 295–96.

7. Note that the existence of an unambiguously Ohrmazdian sexual fluid (i.e., +Warmth/+Moisture) is not entertained by the text, nor is one that would be unambiguously Ahrimanian (−Warmth/−Moisture).

8. Note also that female seed is said to revert to blood either if conception does not occur or if there is more seed than is necessary for conception (IndBd. 16.3, 5).

9. This last point is subject to modification if the reading of the GBd. is to be preferred here. See above, note 5, textual note to line 39.3.

10. *gōn suxr ō zardīh wardišnīg,* Zsp. 30.15.

11. E.g., Zsp. 30.17. See further Jacques Duchesne-Guillemin, "Le X᾽arǝnah,"

Annali dell' Istituto Orientale di Napoli, Sezione Linguistica 5 (1963): 19–31, esp. 25–26.

12. Compare *Dēnkart* 3.163, where the king's supremacy to the various priests is asserted by associating the former to the brain and the latter to skin, flesh, bone, tendon, heart, and liver. On the quasi-universal use of vertical imagery to discuss social hierarchy, see Barry Schwartz, *Vertical Classification* (Chicago: University of Chicago Press, 1981).

13. See Zsp. 30.4. When it is necessary to differentiate the brain from marrow in general, the former is referred to as *mazg ī sar,* "marrow of the head."

14. 39.4. hamāg tōhm ī mādagān pēš be āyēd andar kadag gāh
   5. gīrēd, ud tōhm ī narān *azabar ān be ēsted. ān
   6. kadag gāh purr be kunēd. harw cē az-aš be
   7. parrēzēd abāz ō xōn bawēd. pad rag⟨ān⟩ ī mādagān
   8. andar šawēd, pad handām kē be zāyēd šīr bawēd.
   9. uš parwarēd ciyōn hamāg šīr az tōhm ī narān bawēd,
   10. xōn ān ī mādagān.

Textual Notes

39.4 *kadag gāh:* here and in line 6, where this seemingly senseless phrase ("house dwelling"?) recurs, Anklesaria transliterates *kadagīhā,* which is no improvement. The context demands that it be understood as a euphemism for the womb or some part thereof. West translates "womb"; Anklesaria, "fallopian tubes." Can it be a scribal error for *mādag gāh* (or *mādagīhā*)?

39.5 *gīrēd:* GBd. has *frāz gardēd* (TD₂ MS. 110.5–6).

39.5 **azabar ān:* GBd. has *abar* (TD₂ MS. 110.6).

39.7 *rag⟨ān⟩ ī mādagān:* GBd. has the plural, but omits the izafat, thus: *ragān mādagān* (TD₂ MS. 110.8).

39.8 *handām kē be zāyēd:* GBd. has *handām ī zāyišn.* That this phrase refers to the breasts is confirmed by a gloss inserted after *šīr,* which reads: *abāz peštān āyēd* "it goes back to the breasts" (TD₂ MS. 110.8).

15. 39.10.   ēn 4 tis nar mādag gowēd
   11. asmān ayōxšust wād ātaxš nar hagriz juttar
   12. nē bawēd. ān āb ud zamīg ud urwar ud māhīg mādag hagriz
   13. juttar nē bawēd. abārīg dahišn nar ud mādag ōh bawēd.

16. It is not clear whether we are to understand that the members of the latter group are mixed or variable in gender, although it may be significant that the text says that they "may come into being male *and* female" (*nar ud mādag ōh bawēd*), not "male *or* female" (*nar *ayab mādag*). This, however, is a less than compelling argument, and one might reasonably expect some explicit mention of mixture, given the importance this state has in Zoroastrian theology. Perhaps it is best to leave the question unresolved.

17. One should note that while cattle and humanity in general may be of either sex, the first human (Gayōmard) and the first bovine (Evāgdād) were male.

18. GBd. 1A.6, 3.16, 34.5, etc. Note also *Yašt* 13.2 and the discussion of H. W. Bailey, *Zoroastrian Problems in the Ninth Century Books* (Oxford: Clarendon Press, 1971), pp. 124–34.

19. Further subclassifications may be suggested here, as the male elements may be divided into the heavenly (sky, metal, fire) and the atmospheric (wind), female elements into the terrestrial (earth and plants) and the aquatic (water and fish).

PART THREE

POLEMIC PIECES

NINETEEN

SHAPING THE PAST AND THE FUTURE

A review of Georges Dumézil, *L'oubli de l'homme et l'honneur des dieux: Esquisses de mythologie*. Paris: Editions Gallimard, 1985.

I

There is much for which Georges Dumézil must rightly be praised. His erudition, perspicacity, and originality are monumental; his perseverance and boldness, no less prodigious. More than any other individual, he helped rescue two important fields of study from the discredit into which they had fallen: comparative mythology, which had become a laughingstock toward the end of the nineteenth century, and Indo-European studies, which was deeply tainted by Nazi racism. To these, he brought rigor and dispassion, producing results that commanded international attention and respect.[1]

Most famous among Dumézil's contributions is his reconstruction of the tripartite ideology through which speakers of ancient Indo-European languages perceived the world and (occasionally) organized their society in three functional categories: (1) the sacred, represented on the human plane by priests, (2) physical force, represented by warriors, and (3) production and reproduction, represented by herdsmen, agriculturalists, merchants, artisans, and the like.[2] Now in his eighty-eighth year, he has written some sixty or seventy books, all serious, scholarly, and deserving of careful attention. Yet throughout his career, he has been a center of controversy.

In recent years, Dumézil has pursued two complementary projects: an attempt to give definitive shape to his past, via new, revised editions of earlier works ("to provide the most presentable corpse for the inevitable autopsy"),[3] and an attempt to influence the future through "mythological sketches" (*esquisses de mythologie*), in which he identifies problems for further research and suggests probable lines for their solution. The current volume, like two predecessors,[4] contains twenty-five such sketches, the bulk of them devoted to Greek and Roman myth and ritual, others to Welsh, Indic, and Iranian data, or to scholarly polemic.

Modest claims notwithstanding, these "sketches" are best considered as virtuoso exercises: brief, dazzling displays of technical mastery and insight. Some (like those on the death of Herakles, the dialogue of Solon and Croesus, or the Buddha's begging bowl) treat rich and complex narratives, laying bare their structure, ideology, and relation to other materials. Others (like those on the Roman deity Vacuna, or the war costume of Darius III) treat a seemingly minuscule or obscure bit of data, in which is revealed a world of meaning.

II

A case in point is the title essay (pp. 135–50), a study of the Roman *evocatio:* the ritual through which the Carthaginian gods were induced to abandon their city (Macrobius, *Saturnalia* 3.9.7–8).[5] Here, Dumézil focuses on one word, an adjective (Latin *proditi*) describing the gods upon their departure. Although ambiguous in derivation and meaning, it is regularly translated as "having come forth [from Carthage]," but Dumézil argues for the alternate interpretation: "having been put forth, expelled."

While possible, this rendition is usually rejected for its seeming contextual inappropriateness.[6] Hardly "expelled," the gods rather desert their city, thus ensuring its fall. Yet, in Dumézil's view, this is the nub of the problem, for it is the goal of the *evocatio* not just to appropriate enemy deities, but to do them no implicit dishonor in the process: one does not make gods into traitors. He thus calls attention to an earlier phrase, where the gods are implored to produce "fear, terror, and forgetfulness" in the Carthaginians, the last of which curses—he argues—refers to forgetfulness of the cultic obligations which bind together a people and their gods. As a consequence of their devotees' negligence, artificially induced though it be, the gods are relieved of their reciprocal obligations. Effectively driven forth (*proditi*), they retain their honor by provoking the forgetfulness of men.

Given this analysis, the *evocatio* acquires new and deeper import. No longer may one view it simply as a magical weapon used by superstitious generals against obstinate cities. Beyond this, it is shown to contain an elegant (if casuistic) logical structure, as well as profound reflections on the nature of the divine and the human.

As an inquiry into a neglected aspect of Roman religion, this study is a tour de force of the sort familiar to Dumézil's readers. One senses, however, that the category of memory bears more than academic interest for him, as evidenced in an earlier discussion of the *evocatio* found within the *Discours de réception* he delivered upon the occasion of his long-awaited admission to the Académie Française:

> The past, honestly preserved and meditated upon in its grandeurs and its frailties, has defended more than one people from dissolution, even those enslaved or dispossessed of their language. . . . When a Roman general, at the end of a siege, attempted to seduce, to lead into his camp the city's gods, in whom the almost-vanquished nation placed its highest hope, he asked them—as in any battle—to cast fear and panic over those whom

they previously protected, but in this case he added: forgetfulness. . . . All the forgetfulness: forgetfulness of those very gods,
who thus gave themselves the appearance of being betrayed by
those whom they in reality betrayed; forgetfulness of the past, of
myths, paradigms (*exempla*), and ancestors (*maiores*). . . .

Whoever today gives himself over to the traditional works of
the spirit lives in a messianic perspective: like Cardinal Bessarion,
we know that our Constantinople will soon fall, and in those
remaining free islands of our Aegean, we feverishly copy the
manuscripts which at the time of a Renaissance, in which we
also persist in believing, will reanimate somewhere in the world
our Greece and our Byzantium, that is to say, the letters and sciences of Europe. That suffices to preserve in us an ardor and a
confidence. . . .[7]

Memory here appears as the last, best defense against chaos. The apocalyptic flavor is unmistakable: barbarians at the gates and decadence within, the
fate of civilization hanging on a faithful few. The vision (or parable?) evokes
other *Götterdämmerungen,* and prompts many questions.[8] What is it, precisely, that must be preserved and remembered? Who are the menacing enemies? The amnesiac many? And who the mindful, messianic "we"?

III

Dumézil discussed only one other ancient datum in his *Discours de réception,*
and this also receives a chapter in *L'oubli de l'homme* (pp. 246–53): the story
of a constitutional debate held prior to Darius's accession, in which a certain
Otanes championed democracy; Megabyzos, oligarchy; and Darius himself,
monarchy (Herodotus 3.80–82).[9] Whereas most consider this a Greek rhetorical exercise in Persian garb, Dumézil demurs, noting that the hierarchic rank
of each functionally defined stratum in a tripartite society varied inversely
with its size, priests being a small minority and warriors a somewhat larger
group, while the third function formed the great mass of the population.[10]

With this in mind, he suggests that the Herodotean debate presents an Indo-
Iranian ritual sequence as misunderstood by a fifth-century Greek. In Iranian
terms, he argues, modes of government were not at issue but rather social
strata, Otanes representing not democracy but the masses of the third function, and Megabyzos the elite few of the first two functions.[11] Kingship then
emerges as the transcendent institution in which all strata were integrated and
the tensions among them resolved, just as in certain sequences from the royal
installation ceremonies of ancient India.

Surely the suggestion is daring and dramatic. Yet however justified it might
be (and there are details which give one pause), studying this episode without
reference to the broader Herodotean narrative (3.60–87) raises problems.

Thus, Dumézil ignores Herodotus' critique of Darius and of monarchy, whereby Darius is presented as a cheat (3.85–87), a liar (3.72), and a would-be traitor (3.71), while the case he makes for kingship hardly rebuts the charges (tyranny, *hybris,* etc.) raised by his adversaries. In effect, Herodotus casts the Persians' choice of monarchy as misguided, leading ultimately to conflict with and defeat by the democratic Greeks.[12] Moreover, behind Herodotus' tendentiousness stands that of Darius, for the royal proclamations from which the broader Herodotean narrative derives are nothing other than Darius's (successful) attempt to mask his crimes of regicide and usurpation.[13]

In his attempt to recover an ancient and edifying royal ideology, Dumézil thus overlooks the text-critical principle that every discourse is an exercise in persuasion, wherein the past enters discussion always for reasons of the present.[14] This holds for Herodotus. It holds for Darius. It holds for Indo-Iranian rituals, and it also holds for Georges Dumézil, to judge from his meditations on Darius elsewhere:

> Herodotus tells how . . . Darius and the others deliberated on the respective merits of régimes: popular, aristocratic, monarchic. They have had many imitators, down to Montesquieu and beyond, and this is not the place to add a variant to that rhetorical collection. Nor must we decide between Joffre's Order of the Day after the Battle of the Marne: "The Republic can be proud of the soldiers she has prepared," and the amendment Charles Maurras proposed for this decree: "For forty-three years, Alsace-Lorraine has been Queen of France." Nor must we examine if frequent changes of regime renew or injure nations. In November 1918, during the night that would be the last of the war, the batteries of my regiment went into the line. . . . During a halt, some comrades and I approached a half dozen prisoners [being taken to the rear] and we set to chattering in our bad German. Uncharitably, one of us chastened them for their pending defeat: from other Frenchmen, they learned that Wilhelm II and the crown prince had fled to Holland. Then one became insolent and, in French, hurled in my face: "You—Republic, Emperor, King, Republic; We—Emperor." That was his way of crying at me: Caramba! I admired this and did not reply: our column had already departed. I have often thought afterward of this aborted academic colloquium on a roadside in Lotharingia. Three regimes have succeeded, on one side as on the other. And where are we?[15]

Where, indeed? More specifically, where lie Dumézil's own opinions on "the respective merits of régimes," and how deep runs his admiration for the speech of the German prisoner? Moreover, have his personal views influenced his reading of the Herodotean text or of Indo-European thought and institutions? And why does Charles Maurras—founder of the militantly Royalist, violently anti-Semitic *Action Française*, later ideological master to Vichy France—enter so strangely into this passage?[16]

IV

Although Dumézil's writings have often excited controversy, early debate was traditionally academic, focused on details of his proposals and the general legitimacy of his comparatism.[17] More recently, attention has shifted to the ideological underpinnings of his life and work.

Thus, toward the end of the 1970s, concern emerged regarding Dumézil's connections to the "New Right" of Alain de Benoist, which courted him, hoping to appropriate his views and prestige for their own purposes (mobilization of European solidarity via the Indo-European past; rejection of "Judeo-Christian" ideas as foreign to European traditions; creation of an anti-egalitarian society).[18] For his part, Dumézil lent his name to the patronage committee of *Nouvelle école*, a New Right publication, granted an indiscreet interview to de Benoist, and received the dedication of a popularizing book, in which a thinly veiled "Aryan" racism was evident.[19] He managed to extricate himself from these embarrassments, however, by breaking with *Nouvelle école* and by making vague disclaimers in several interviews.[20] Others, including Claude Lévi-Strauss, rallied to his defense, and the controversy abated for a time.[21]

Interest in Dumézil's politics has been rekindled, however, by Arnaldo Momigliano, who suggested in a recent article that Dumézil's strained relations in the 1920s and 1930s with Henri Hubert, Marcel Mauss, and others of the school of Durkheim resulted from political differences, the Durkheimians having been of the left and Dumézil (the son of an eminent French general) of the right.[22] In his most aggressive passage, Momigliano writes:

> Neither Dumézil . . . nor his French exegetes have told us much about the political opinions of the young Dumézil. But the dedication of his first book *Le festin d'immortalité* [1924] to Pierre Gaxotte suffices in itself to indicate where he stood politically. Gaxotte, later a member of the Académie Française, was secretary to Maurras and chief editor of *Candide*, an organ of the extreme right: later he was among those who opposed resistance to Nazism in 1938–39. Dumézil's book of 1939, *Mythes et dieux des Germains* contains clear traces of sympathy for Nazi culture. In politics, there was evidently an abyss between Dumézil on one side and Mauss and his friends on the other.[23]

To this, Dumézil replies spiritedly in the final "sketch" of the volume under review (pp. 329–41). While acknowledging his difficulties with some of the Durkheimians, he attributes these to his desire to remain independent of any "school." Of his political views—past and present—he has this to say: "I have not made and I do not have to make disclosures regarding my philosophical, political, or esthetic opinions, which I have held all my life to be malleable and provisional, like all that rises up out of opinions (*doxa*) that are inevitably subjective." [24] One here encounters a stone wall: he will tell us nothing, except that his ideas have changed, a stipulation which guards against any potentially embarrassing revelations.

V

To the two specific data exhumed by Momigliano—the matter of Pierre Gaxotte and that of *Mythes et dieux des Germains*—Dumézil had no choice but to respond more fully. Regarding the latter, there has since been a fuller exchange between Carlo Ginzburg and Dumézil, with inconclusive results. [25] What is clear is that Dumézil could write in 1939 of the SA and the "dynamic economy" of the Third Reich without explicit disapprobation. Whether this reflects tacit sympathy or dispassionate inquiry is a question perhaps incapable of resolution, depending as it does upon the interpretation of silence. Regarding Gaxotte, things are different.

Dumézil relates that having been friends as students at the elite École Normale Supérieure, he and Gaxotte shared an "entente particulièrement confiante" until the latter's death in 1982. His defense of the latter rests on two points: (1) Gaxotte took from Maurras only "an unflagging intellectual attachment to the dynastic principle. . . . Is this to be of the extreme right?" and (2) his advocacy of appeasement was a matter of tactics only, for "after German rearmament of the Rhineland in 1936, . . . conscious of the military unpreparedness and the political impotence of the country, he thought that salvation—if it was still possible—required that one gain time to rectify all of that." [26]

This will not do. First, it is clear that Gaxotte was fully and intensely loyal to Maurras and his ideas. Consider, for instance, his statement of January 1941, in the Vichy-published *Almanach de la France nouvelle:* "Tomorrow, Maurras will be read in all the schools, and children will recite the pages he has written as they recite Racine or Bossuet. He will remain for us the master who rediscovered the great laws that make states prosperous and powerful: it is in [his] principles that France seeks her salvation today." [27] Similarly slavish sentiments—hardly limited to the question of "dynastic principle"—appear into the 1960s. [28]

Second, as early as three years before rearmament of the Rhineland, Gaxotte already favored appeasement, not for reasons of tactics but for those of ideology, Hitler being the scourge of his own enemies: Marxists and Jews. Consider these early excerpts from his lead column to *Je suis partout,* a scabrously reactionary publication of which he was chief editor from its inception until June of 1937:[29]

> As for us, we are not disposed to take pains [*faire du zèle*], nor to risk so much as a hair for the Communists who suffer from the tyranny of M. Goering. . . . "No war of propaganda! No war of the democracies!" Such should be the slogan of patriots against the warlike Marxist International. (29 April 1933)

> The International is dead: Marxism is moribund. Hitler, who has no love for France, has at least done this service for us and for the world. The consolidation of Fascism, its success and its social works had already shaken orthodox socialism. But it is Hitler who struck the decisive blow. (26 August 1933)

> France is pursuing the policy of the Bolsheviks and the refugees. . . . It is the trio [of Léon Blum, Jules Moch and Oreste Rosenfeld] who lead the Quai d'Orsay [and think that] France ought to avenge the Jews of Germany, and that young Frenchmen ought to take up rifles because Hitler booted the little cousins of Blum, Moch, and Rosenfeld in the derrière. One has to be blind not to see that the coalition France-Israel-the Soviets is not a league of peace. It is a disquieting coalition, it is the crusade of the Internationals, it is the hope of universal pillage. France is separated from Germany by a certain number of things: while keeping our forces intact and our army strong, a truly pacific diplomacy would employ lubrication and courtesy to sweeten the points of friction, to avoid searching out occasions for quarrels. No more! (15 September 1934)[30]

For one who values memory so highly, Dumézil is peculiarly amnesiac concerning these matters. Were he just making the best case for a flawed but departed friend, one might forgive his distortions of the record. But Gaxotte entered the discussion only when Momigliano, seeking to uncover the political views and associations of Dumézil's youth, called attention to the dedication of his doctoral thesis to one Pierre Gaxotte. In defending Gaxotte, Dumézil thus defends himself, by minimizing the extent to which he and his friends were influenced by Maurras and the Action Française.

Alongside his journalistic endeavors, Gaxotte wrote popular volumes of history, in which he constructed the past along openly Maurrasian lines.[31] Much as Herodotus saw in Darius what he wanted to see and was prepared to see, so Gaxotte's ideological orientation shaped his treatment of such figures as Louis XIV and Robespierre, to cite the most obvious examples. And although the scholarship of Georges Dumézil is infinitely more disciplined, rigorous, and carefully reasoned than that of Gaxotte, one may still ask whether his studies are not colored by similar ideological predispositions. How relevant, for instance, to Dumézil's discussion of memory is Maurras' dictum: "Democracy is forgetting"?[32] Among other themes worth exploring are Dumézil's view of the lower social orders ("the third function"), the interrelation of religious and political authority, and the "enemy within," i.e. figures like Loki or Gullveig, who threaten their adoptive societies, much like the four classes of "aliens" (Jews, Protestants, Masons, and *métèques*) who so obsessed Maurras.

Most important is the question of the tripartite ideology in its social application. For beyond his unexceptionable identification of three functionally defined strata, Dumézil posits as the Indo-European ideal that the society built from these strata ought be both rigidly hierarchic *and* harmoniously integrated.[33] Is it accident that this has a familiar ring? Momigliano suggested possible influence from Fascist ideas of the "corporate state," noting that the first exposition of Dumézil's theory came in 1938.[34] Closer than this, however, is Maurras' "integral nationalism," wherein one finds the same contradictory conjunction of hierarchy and harmony, as well as the vision of kingship ensuring this happy (if improbable) combination. The similarity to the Indo-European system of Georges Dumézil is considerable and, I am persuaded, less than coincidental.

Notes

1. The best introductions to Dumézil's work remain two of his books from the 1950s: *L'idéologie tripartie des indo-européens* (Brussels: Collection Latomus, 1958), and *Les dieux des indo-européens* (Paris: Presses Universitaires de France, 1954), which are preferable to such treatments as those of C. Scott Littleton, *The New Comparative Mythology,* 3d ed. (Berkeley: University of California Press, 1982), or Jean-Claude Rivière, "Pour un lecture de Dumézil: introduction à son oeuvre," in Rivière, ed., *Georges Dumézil: à la découverte des Indo-européens* (Paris: Éditions Copernic, 1979). The latter volume contains a number of articles devoted to Dumézil's oeuvre, as does the collection entitled *Georges Dumézil: Cahiers pour un temps* (Paris: Centre Pompidou, 1981).

2. Within the volume under review, Dumézil offers an extremely interesting and quite precise formulation of the nature of the three functions: "[I] mastery of the sacred and of knowledge, together with that form of temporal power founded upon them; [II] physical force and warrior valor; [III] fecundity and abundance, together with their conditions and consequences" (*L'oubli de l'homme,* p. 94).

3. Thus, new editions of *Heur et malheur du guerrier* (1st ed. 1968) and *Loki* (1st ed. 1948) have recently been issued by Flammarion, while a work such as *Les dieux souverains des indo-européens* (Paris: Gallimard, 1977) is largely a reworking of materials from *Mitra-Varuṇa* (Paris: Gallimard, 1940) and *Le troisième souverain* (Paris: Maisonneuve, 1949).

4. *Apollon sonore* (Paris: Gallimard, 1982) and *La courtisan et les seigneurs colorés* (Paris: Gallimard, 1983).

5. The standard work on the *evocatio* is Vsevolod Basanoff, *Evocatio: étude d'un rituel militaire romain* (Paris: Presses Universitaires de France, 1947). The passage from Macrobius is the longest description of the rite, but not without its problems, emphasized by the article in Pauly Wissowa (vol. 6, pt. 1, pp. 1152–53). Those other sources in which the ritual figures—Livy 5.21.3–7, Pliny, *Natural History* 28.18, Servius's commentary on *Aeneid* 2.351, Propertius 4.2.2–6, and Ovid, *Fasti* 3.843–44—make no mention of the theme of memory and forgetfulness that is so emphasized by Dumézil.

6. See, for instance, Fritz Heussler, "Evocatio," *Museum Helveticum* 36 (1979): 168–69.

7. *Discours de réception de M. Georges Dumézil à l'Académie française et réponse de M. Claude Lévi-Strauss* (Paris: Gallimard, 1979), pp. 35–36.

8. Ibid., p. 33, Dumézil indicates that it is the decline of Europe in the face of "the oriental empires which haunted Napoleon's gloomy hours" and "our old partners across the Mediterranean who, due to deposits of organic debris in the earth's crust, have restored at our expense these last decades, the system of ransoms." He has also reflected on the decline of Europe in a number of interviews, most notably in *Le Figaro* 20 April 1979, p. 20; and in *Georges Dumézil: Cahiers pour un temps*, p. 41.

9. The passage has been much discussed. Inter alia, see: J. Enoch Powell, "Notes on Herodotus II," *Classical Quarterly* 29 (1935): 153–54; F. Lasserre, "Hérodote et Protagoras: Le débat sur les constitutions," *Museum Helveticum* 33 (1976): 65–84; Fritz Gschnitzer, *Die sieben Perser und das Königtum des Dareios* (Heidelberg: Carl Winter, 1977), esp. pp. 30–40; J. A. S. Evans, "Notes on the Debate of the Persian Grandees in Herodotus 3,80–82," *Quaderni urbinati di cultura classica* 36 (1981): 79–84; and John Hart, *Herodotus and Greek History* (New York: St. Martin's Press, 1982), pp. 45–49.

10. Dumézil, *L'oubli de l'homme*, p. 251. A similar suggestion, albeit more vague, was advanced by Hans Drexler, *Herodot-Studien* (Hildesheim: Georg Olms, 1972), p. 143.

11. Actually, it is not entirely clear whether Megabyzos' position is meant to represent the first two functions together or the second only (in which case Darius's position might represent the first). The matter is further complicated by Dumézil's labored and unconvincing suggestion (pp. 252–53) that Otanes might represent the third function in the debate scene but the first function at that moment when he withdraws from competition for the kingship.

12. See the discussions of Hans-Friedrich Bornitz, *Herodot-Studien* (Berlin: Walter de Gruyter, 1968), pp. 201–20; and Klaus Bringmann, "Die Verfassungsdebatte bei Herodot 3.80–82 und Dareios' Aufstieg zur Königsherrschaft," *Hermes* 104 (1976): 266–79.

13. On this there is now broad agreement, if not unanimity on all details. See M. A. Dandamaev, *Persien unter den ersten Achämeniden* (Wiesbaden: Ludwig Reichert, 1976); E. J. Bickerman and H. Tadmor, "Darius I, Pseudo-Smerdis, and the Magi," *Athenaeum* 56 (1978): 239–61; and Clarisse Herrenschmidt, "Les historiens de l'empire Achéménide et l'inscription de Bisotun," *Annales Économies Sociétés Civilisations* 37 (1982): 813–23. Different, however, are the views of Josef Wiesehofer, *Der Aufstand Gaumatas und die Anfänge Dareios I* (Bonn: Rudolf Habelt, 1977).

14. It is interesting to observe that in the very first course of Marcel Granet's which Dumézil followed (1934–35), Granet being he whom Dumézil acknowledges as his foremost mentor, the emphasis was on how in certain Chinese texts "persuasion (with an eye toward a conversion of the reader) is obtained without any attempt at demonstration, thanks to the employment of an extremely small set of symbolic themes (forming a definite and coherent enough system) . . ." The stress on symbolic systems remains with Dumézil always, to his great benefit; that on persuasion did not, to his detriment. This datum was uncovered by Ricardo di Donato, "Di *Apollon Sonore* e di alcuni suoi antenati: Georges Dumézil e l'epica greca arcaica," *Opus* 2 (1984): 402–3.

15. *Discours de réception de M. Georges Dumézil à l'Académie française,* pp. 39–41.

16. On Maurras, see: Michael Curtis, *Three against the Third Republic: Sorel, Barrès, and Maurras* (Princeton: Princeton University Press, 1959); Eugen Weber, *Action Française: Royalism and Reaction in Twentieth Century France* (Stanford: Stanford University Press, 1962); Emil Nolte, *Three Faces of Fascism,* trans. L. Vennewitz (London: Weidenfeld and Nicolson, 1965); and Colette Capitan-Peter, *Charles Maurras et l'idéologie d'Action Française* (Paris: Éditions du Seuil, 1972). Among Maurras's own works, note his *Enquête sur la monarchie* (Versailles: Bibliothèque des oeuvres politiques, 1928); *Mes idées politiques* (Paris: A. Fayard, 1937); and *La contre-révolution spontanée* (Lyon: H. Lardanchet, 1943).

17. In *L'oubli des hommes,* p. 316, Dumézil supplies a convenient listing of the earlier criticisms (by H. J. Rose, Angelo Brelich, John Brough, Pierre Smith and Dan Sperber, Jan Gonda, Paul Thieme, and Henrik Wagenvoort) and his responses to them.

18. On the "Nouvelle Droit," see Julien Brunn, ed., *La Nouvelle droite: le dossier du "procès"* (Paris: Nouvelles Éditions Oswald, 1979); Alain Schnapp and Jesper Svenbro, "Du Nazisme à "Nouvelle école": repères sur la prétendue Nouvelle droite," *Quaderni di Storia* 6 (1980): 107–20; and P. A. Taquieff, "L'héritage Nazi: Des Nouvelles Droites européennes à la littérature niant le génocide," *Les Nouveaux cahiers* 64 (1981): 3–22. Among their own publications, note, for example, Alain de Benoist, *Vu de droite: Anthologie critique des idées contemporaines* (Paris: Éditions Copernic, 1977), or Pierre Vial, ed., *Pour une renaissance culturelle* (Paris: Éditions Copernic, 1979).

19. Dumézil's name appeared on the "Comité du patronage" of *Nouvelle école* until 1973. A rather inoffensive interview with him appeared in number 10 of the same journal (September 1969), and another—in which he was led to state, inter alia, that the hierarchy of the three functions was established only by force, and that he looked forward to the day when the French would show the same interest in the Indo-Europeans as do Germans—appeared in *Le Figaro Dimanche* 29–30 April 1978, p. 19.

Jean Haudry's *Les indo-européens,* which appeared in the popular "Que sais-je" series of the Presses Universitaires de France (1981), prompted a major outcry, as in its scathing review by Bernard Sergent, "Penser—et mal penser—les indo-européens," *Annales Économies Sociétés Civilisations* 37 (1982): 669–81. The first footnote of this volume reads: "Je remercie M. Georges Dumézil d'avoir bien voulu lire le manuscrit de ce livre; il va de soi que j'en reste seul responsable," but the precise significance of this intentionally ambiguous statement remains uncertain. The racist views of Haudry, founder and editor of the *Études indo-européennes*, are made clear in his article "L'origine des indo-européens," *Nouvelle école* 42 (1985): 123–28.

20. Dumézil's withdrawal from the *Nouvelle école* patronage committee came directly after number 21–22 (Winter 1972–73), a special issue devoted to "Georges Dumézil et les études indo-européennes." Here, an introductory article ("Itinéraire," pp. 7–12, unsigned but probably by Alain de Benoist) hailed the "Indo-European fact" as the means whereby Europeans can find a model for their future, a future which features the domination of lower social strata (the "producers" of the third function) by upper-class elites (the "predators" of the first and second). Significantly, this article was dropped when the issue's other contents were published as *Georges Dumézil à la découverte des Indo-européens* (Paris: Éditions Copernic, 1979).

In an interview published in *Le Figaro* on the eve of his admission to the Académie Française (20 April 1979, p. 20), Dumézil was asked to comment on those who drew "abusive conclusions" from his theories. In response, he differentiated three groups who have made use of his work: (1) conscientious scholars, (2) "des esprits plus lyriques que critiques," and (3) scholars motivated by political agendas. Of these, he stated that only the first is of interest to him; the second he discourages, and the third is wholly foreign (*étrangère*) to him. Given Dumézil's ongoing connections with Benoist, it is clear that the latter is hardly "foreign," and thus must fall in the second category, which is treated quite gently, all things considered. Moreover, this is the closest Dumézil has ever come to repudiating his admirers of the New (or Old) Right. Elsewhere (e.g. interviews in *Georges Dumézil: Cahiers pour un temps* [Paris: Centre Pompidou, 1981], pp. 39–40, or *Nouvel Observateur* 14 January 1983, p. 23), his remarks have been strategically couched to preserve maximum ambiguity: he makes no disavowals of anyone, stating only that he takes no responsibility for what others have written unless he cites it with approval.

21. "Réponse de M. Claude Lévi-Strauss," in *Discours de réception de M. Georges Dumézil à l'Académie française*, pp. 73–74.

22. Arnaldo Momigliano, "Premesse per una discussione su Georges Dumézil," *Opus* 2 (1983): 329–41. Momigliano's article was the opening presentation at a seminar on "Aspects of the Work of Georges Dumézil," held at the Scuola Normale Superiore of Pisa in January 1983. Five other articles from this seminar were published in the same issue of *Opus*, of which the very different presentations of John Scheid, "G. Dumézil et la méthode experimentale" (pp. 343–51), and Cristiano Grottanelli, "Temi Duméziliani fuori dal mondo indoeuropeo" (pp. 365–89), are particularly interesting.

23. Momigliano, "Premesse," p. 331.

24. Dumézil, *L'oubli des hommes*, p. 306. Similar remarks are found in the interview published in *Nouvel observateur* 14 January 1983, p. 24.

25. Carlo Ginzburg, "Mitologia Germanica e Nazismo: Su un vecchio libro di Georges Dumézil," *Quaderni Storici* 19 (1984): 857–82. Dumézil answered in "Science et politique. Réponse à Carlo Ginzburg," *Annales Économies Sociétés Civilisations* 40 (1985): 985–89.

26. Dumézil, *L'oubli des hommes*, p. 307.

27. Cited in Weber, *Action Française*, p. 442.

28. See, for instance, the introduction Gaxotte contributed to a reprint edition of

Maurras's *Mes idées politiques* (Paris: A. Fayard, 1968), where he states "there does not exist in this last third of the twentieth century a richer, closer, stronger, nor more lively thought" than that of Maurras (p. 14).

29. Gaxotte became chief editor of *Candide*, another highly aggressive publication following the Maurrassian line, shortly before he was succeeded at *Je suis partout* by Robert Brasillach, who was his protégé there. Gaxotte continued to write the lead column for the latter publication until January 1939, by which time it was apparent that under Brasillach it had become more Germanophile than Maurras could countenance. On Gaxotte's position in the 1930s and the important role of *Je suis partout*, see: Weber, *Action Française*, especially pp. 503–8; J. Plumyène and R. Lasierra, *Les fascismes français 1923–1963* (Paris: Éditions du Seuil, 1963), pp. 103–9; and Pierre Marie Dioudonnat, *Je suis partout, 1930–1944: Les Maurrassiens devant la tentation fasciste* (Paris: La table ronde, 1973). Important information can also be found in Charles A. Micaud, *The French Right and Nazi Germany 1933–1939* (New York: Octagon Books, 1964); and William R. Tucker, *The Fascist Ego: A Political Biography of Robert Brasillach* (Berkeley: University of California Press, 1975).

30. Quotations could easily be multiplied, and it is difficult to overstate just how offensive *Je suis partout* was in its editorial policy. Truly, there is no substitute for reading the full run of this vile publication, but to cite a single example of its orientation, consider Gaxotte's response to those who felt France ought to boycott the Berlin Olympics of 1936:

> There was a time when the current ran in the direction of democracy; today it is running toward fascism. Parliamentary and socialistic democracy is an outdated thing that lives on only in a few very backward, very primitive countries. If it is forbidden for France to consort with states organized according to the nationalist formula, we will finish by finding ourselves alone with Spain, the Soviets, and the Republic of Liberia. But might not one affirm that there could be a surprise one day soon in Spain? (30 May 1936)

Gaxotte's position on all the major foreign policy issues of the 1930s is consistent: he opposed a Franco-Soviet alliance, French acceptance of refugees, sanctions against the Italian invasion of Ethiopia, and resistance to German rearmament of the Rhineland, while championing Franco's forces in the Spanish Civil War, the Austrian Anschluss, and abandonment of Czechoslovakia at Munich.

31. See, for instance, Gaxotte's *La révolution française* (Paris: A. Fayard, 1928); *La siècle de Louis XV* (Paris: A. Fayard, 1933); or *La France de Louis XIV* (Paris: Hachette, 1946). So clear are his prejudices that the English translator (whose own ideological orientation is quite transparent) for the first of these volumes was moved to comment:

> M. Gaxotte's book, then, is interesting, apart from its merits as a work of art, as a manifesto of a school of political thought which is likely to gain increasing influence in French intellectual circles. It is interesting, too, as yet another manifestation of the revolt against the principles and practice of representative democracy which has long been gathering force in all the Latin countries, and in nearly all of them has resulted in the establishment of some form of dictatorship. Among the motives behind this tendency there has been the fear of Communism. . . . M. Gaxotte holds that

Communism is the logical outcome of the principles of the Revolution, and in this he is at one with the Communists themselves, who regard Robespierre as one of the chief apostles of their creed. (Walter Alison Phillips, translator for Gaxotte's *The French Revolution* [New York: Charles Scribner's Sons, 1932], pp. xii–xiii)

32. Charles Maurras, *Kiel et Tanger* (Paris: Nouvelle Librairie Nationale, 1921), p. 213. A similar line of thought is evident in Gaxotte's column entitled "Souvenir" (*Je suis partout*, 9 February 1935), in which he observes: "It is true that democracy has done everything to separate the working class from the nation. French children are taught to hate or to scorn their ancestors. The schools steal from their hearts all those sentiments which make of man something other than a machine for production: love of the *patrie*, respect for family, and pride in the past." In particular, he denounces those who point to Notre Dame or Versailles as instances in which the upper estates exploited the labor of the working class for their own glorification, instead of viewing these as triumphs of the total French nation under the leadership of Church and King.

If memory is an ideologically charged category for Maurras and his heirs, it is also worth noting that the conflict of Carthage and Rome is fraught with significance for the New Right, providing a coded reference for the struggle of Semites and Aryans. See, for instance, Alain de Benoist, *Vu de droite*, pp. 53–55.

33. Cf. pp. 94 and 202 of *L'oubli des hommes*, the former passage emphasizing hierarchy and the latter harmony. The two are brought together in the 29–30 April 1978 interview with de Benoist in *Le Figaro Dimanche:*

The Indo-Europeans considered that the proper order [*la bonne marche*] of the world implied an "organization" in which the representatives of the first function commanded, while others fought and defended the community, and the largest number worked and produced. In their eyes, there was a harmony necessary for the smooth functioning of the cosmos as of society. It is a sort of Indo-European form of the "Social Contract."

Beyond this, Dumézil added that the relation of the first to the second function was similar to that between elders and youths, while that between the upper two functions and the third was like that of men to women.

34. Momigliano, "Premesse," p. 331. Momigliano advances this suggestion somewhat tentatively, and undercuts it by imagining (p. 337) that he sees a vaguely Marxist influence in Dumézil's *Le troisième souverain* (Paris: Maisonneuve, 1949). The outlandishness of this latter idea is not lost on Dumézil, who uses it to disqualify in general any attempt to identify a political dimension in his writings (*L'oubli des hommes*, p. 311).

TWENTY

KINGS, REBELS, AND THE LEFT HAND

Religion, Politics, and Scholarship

For some years now, I have struggled to persuade professional (and not-so-professional) students of religion that there is a significant political dimension to all religious discourse, and that it is not only possible but important to render this visible so that it may be subjected to critical analysis. I am embarrassed to confess, however, that it was not so long ago that I was myself persuaded that a similar state of affairs prevails with regard to another discourse that has occasionally made claims to a privileged status, not on the basis of its transcendent nature, but on an equally mythic self-representation as disinterested and "objective." Yet scholarship too has its political dimensions, which may also be rendered visible and subjected to critical analysis.

It may be that I am now overly sensitive to such issues as a result of the fact that much of my own work has been conducted within the area of Indo-European studies (also known, more chillingly, as "Indogermanische," or "Aryan" studies in decades past), the political dimension of which has played a particularly abhorrent role in the history of our century. Yet however extreme the case of this subdiscipline may be, I would contend that it differs from others more in degree than in nature. Accordingly, its example may prove instructive, exhibiting with particular clarity, as it does, certain features that characterize scholarship in general. More specifically, one may observe here how scholars actively construct that which they study through their selection of evidence, a process in which they systematically disarticulate certain data from their original context while ignoring others, and rearticulate those so chosen within a novel context of their own devising. These novel contexts, moreover, are inevitably, if most often unconsciously, conditioned by the interests of their authors (taking "interests" in its bland, as well as its more pointed meaning), for even discourse about the past and the exotic enters the present always and only for reasons of the here and now. These points I hope to illustrate, by reexamining some classic studies of "Indo-European" myths.

"Le borgne et le manchot"

At the center of these studies are the accounts of two Roman heroes: Horatius Cocles and Mucius Scaevola, whose deeds figured prominently at that time when Romans, as Florus 1.10 put it, "took up the first arms for liberty (*pro libertate*) after the expulsion of the kings from the city (*pulsis urbe regibus*), when Porsenna, king of the Etruscans, descended with vast forces and sought to restore the Tarquins by force."

By way of background for those unfamiliar with Roman history, Tarquin the Proud (Tarquinius Superbus) was the last Roman king, who was driven from his throne and from the city as a result of outrages committed by himself and his sons. Being of Etruscan descent,[1] the Tarquins took refuge with an Etruscan monarch, where, as Livy tells it:

> Mixing advice and entreaties, now they pleaded with Porsenna not to permit persons of Etruscan descent, of the same blood and name as himself, to live destitute in exile, and now they admonished him not to allow the expulsion of kings [*pellendi reges*] to go unpunished. Liberty [*libertatem*] itself is sweet enough that unless kings defend their thrones as strongly as the [republican] states covet them, the highest would be made equal to the most lowly and there would be nothing lofty, nothing that stands out over others, in the states of the future. The end of kingship, the finest thing among gods and men, was approaching. (Livy 2.9.1–3)

Swayed by these arguments, Porsenna set forth to make war against the newly established Roman Republic, in defense of kinship and kingship alike. And, as the Romans lacked sufficient forces to oppose his host in open battle, they took refuge behind their city's defenses, the single weakest link of which was the Pons Sublicius, the wooden bridge spanning the Tiber, which gave direct access to the city. Here, as the Etruscans stormed forward, their advance was checked by a single man: Horatius Cocles, whose cognomen brands him "the one-eyed" or "Cyclops."[2] Fighting against a swarm of Etruscans with miraculous success, and intimidating them with his ferocious manner,[3] he held them at bay long enough for his comrades to cut down the bridge, whereupon Cocles leapt into the Tiber and swam to safety in full armor, lest anything be shamefully abandoned to the enemy.[4]

Thus ended Porsenna's attempt to take Rome by assault, after which he settled in for a siege. Facing starvation now, as well as superior forces, the Republic was rescued for a second time by the unprecedented acts of a single, low-ranking soldier: Gaius Mucius, who infiltrated the Etruscan camp with a hidden dagger, but—being ignorant of what Porsenna looked like—managed only to assassinate the latter's secretary in his place, and directly was taken captive. By a stratagem improvised in the course of his interrogation, however, Mucius was able to accomplish his goals, for he hinted to Porsenna of a broader plot against the latter's life, and when the king threatened to have him burnt alive at a nearby altar, the young Roman calmly thrust his right hand into the fire (*dextramque accenso ad sacrificium foculo inicit,* Livy 2.12.13), ostensibly to demonstrate his contempt for pain and suffering. At a deeper level, however, this gesture must be understood as a complex inversion of oath-taking procedures, in which the sacrifice of the right hand renders credible a false testimony, while simultaneously doing penance for this violation of *fides* ("faith, confidence, trust," and also those qualities which merit and call forth these responses, i.e., "trustworthiness," and the like).[5] Awed by this gesture, Porsenna set Mucius free, whereupon the latter—now given the cognomen Scaevola, "Lefty" (from *scaevus*, "left," "the left-hand")—further embroidered his story, telling his gullible benefactor that he was but one of three hundred Romans sworn to kill him, having been chosen by lot to make the first attempt. In the wake of this, on fuller reflection, Porsenna decided to make peace.[6]

It was Georges Dumézil's merit to have recognized in his studies of these materials, first, that these accounts were better viewed as myth than as history; second, that the two together form a set; and third, that this set can profitably be compared to two myths of the ancient Scandinavian gods Oðinn and Tyr, the first of whom gave up an eye in an act of self-sacrifice, through which he gained magical powers, including, perhaps, the ability to render enemy troops powerless and hold them at a distance.[7] Matching this mutilation, just as that of Scaevola matches that of Cocles, is Tyr's loss of his hand, which he, like Scaevola, gave up in order to make a false testimony seem true and to win thereby the salvation of his people. For when the gods wished to bind down the monstrous Fenris-wolf, whose very existence threatened them and the universe, the only way they could do so was by fabricating a magical cord from such things as a woman's beard and a mountain's roots, so that it would be incredibly strong while also barely visible. The problem, however, was how to place this apparatus on the beast's neck, for when they asked him to test it—"just for sport"—the wolf agreed to do so only upon the condition that one of the gods put a hand in his mouth as a pledge of good faith. This only Tyr was willing to do, losing his right hand (*hǫnd sína hægri*) as a result (*Gylfaginning* 25 and 34).

Over the course of four decades, Dumézil returned repeatedly to these materials, examining numerous other data that resembled them in one fashion or another.[8] Ultimately, however, he concluded that none were of equal value and importance. In his view, that which was essential was the association and parallelism of a one-eyed and a one-handed god or hero. For all that one might find one or another such figure here or there, it was their occurrence in tandem—found nowhere else—that struck him as crucial. Moreover, he accorded the Scandinavian data (preserved in texts of the tenth and thirteenth century C.E.) primacy over the Romans, arguing that the "Republican orientation" of the latter obscured an Indo-European tradition, in which two complementary sides of sovereignty were described: (1) magic, as represented by a one-eyed visionary god able, inter alia, to render his enemies' weapons ineffective, and (2) legal, as represented by a one-handed deity given to absolute, if occasionally deceptive fidelity to the demands of oaths, pledges, contracts, and the like.[9]

There are details here with which one could argue, and there are those who have done so, with greater and lesser degrees of success.[10] I will proceed somewhat differently, however, concentrating upon the ways in which his selection of data prefigured the conclusions that Dumézil reached, while also suggesting that this selection was itself prefigured by other factors. In order to do this, let me examine three items to which Dumézil gave consideration at one point or anther, but which he ultimately judged irrelevant to his studies of the "borgne et manchot" theme.

The Loss of a Leg

While Livy has Horatius Cocles escape from his heroic stand virtually unscathed, other authors make mention of numerous wounds, one of which in particular—a debilitating wound to his lower body—they dwell upon in considerable detail. As Dionysius of Halicarnassus 5.24.3 tells it, "there was one spear blow in particular that afflicted him with pains and disabled his step, passing through one of his buttocks over the top of the thigh."

We are thus told that Horatius lost the use of a leg, and it is this, and not his lack of an eye, that is at times explicitly paired with Mucius Scaevola's loss of a hand. Thus, for instance, when considering whether Antony's attempt to crown Caesar king was justified, Cicero is said to have invoked the heroes who put an end to kingship and established the Republic: "No, by the rods of Valerius [Publicola] and the law of Porcius. No, *by the leg of Horatius and the hand of Mucius.* No, by the spear of Decius and the sword of Brutus."[11] Dumézil, however, taking his cue from Dionysius's observation (5.25.3) that this leg wound rendered Cocles "useless in the remaining affairs of the city as a result of the crippling of his step," dismissed it as little more than an afterthought: a convenient device through which certain authors sought to explain the hero's disappearance from later Roman history.[12]

Things are not so simple, however, and the importance of this wound is underlined by Plutarch, who confirms Dionysius's testimony that Cocles "was hit in the buttock by an Etruscan spear,"[13] and goes on to tell that this wound figured prominently in the honors which Rome subsequently bestowed upon Cocles, specifying "they erected a bronze image of him in the Temple of Vulcan, consoling him with honor for the lameness caused by his wound."[14]

That the statue of the lamed hero should be placed in the Temple of Vulcan is something of considerable interest, and its significance is not difficult to decipher, for Vulcan, like other Indo-European deities associated with metalworking, artisanry, and the lower social classes, was said to have suffered an injury or deformity that deprived him of the use of one leg. Obvious comparisons are the Greek Hephaistos, the Old Norse Vǫlundr, and the English Wayland, all of whom—like Cocles in his relation to Porsenna—were artisans lamed by kings who aimed to subordinate them, and with whom they struggled, sometimes successfully and sometimes not.[15]

Similar also is the Irish god Lug, who is portrayed as a member of the artisan class, and who assumes a one-eyed and one-legged form to oppose an oppressive foreign king, in which task he cooperates with a one-armed hero. For in "The [Second] Battle of Mag Tuired," one of the chief texts in which pre-Christian Celtic mythology has been preserved, we are told how Lug gained admission to the company of the gods (the Túatha Dé Danann), announcing himself first as a builder, then as a smith, later as a champion, harpist, poet, historian, sorcerer, physician, cupbearer, brazier, and ultimately as one who practices all of the practical arts, as a result of which status he bore the epithet *Samildánach,* "Skilled in many arts," a title reminiscent of Caesar's description of Lug (whom he identified with the Roman Mercury) as "inventor of all the arts" (*omnium inventor artium*).[16] Further, when the Túatha Dé confronted their former king (of whom we will shortly have more to say) in battle, Lug contributed to the gods' success by reciting a magic spell while hopping on one foot and holding one eye shut, i.e. becoming one-eyed *and one-legged,* albeit temporarily.[17]

Including these materials in the comparison has much to recommend it, although expansion of our dossier inevitably forces certain shifts of emphasis in the interpretations that can be offered. But it is clear that serious consideration of Cocles's leg wound and his connection to Vulcan leads one to other data that focus upon the opposition of the lower social orders—smiths, artisans, and common soldiers (for neither Cocles nor Scaevola were officers, and the latter was of a plebeian family)—to domination by kings.

The King's Lost Hand and the Foreign King

When speaking of the Irish account of the Second Battle of Mag Tuired, I mentioned in passing that a one-handed figure appears there beside Lug.[18] This is "Núadu of the Silver Hand" (*Núadu Argetlám*). King of the Túatha Dé Danann, Núadu lost his right arm in the First Battle of Mag Tuired, and as a result was forced to renounce his kingship, for as the text emphatically states: "Núadu was not fit for kingship after the cutting off of his hand" (*ar nirb' inrighae Núadoo iar mbéim a láime de*).[19] The point that is made here is not just that in order to rule a king must be whole in body, although this broader custom, attested among Celtic peoples as elsewhere around the globe,[20] is less banal than is commonly thought, often deriving from complex speculations on the king's body as a perfect microcosm of society and the universe at large. More specifically, however, the right hand—which signifies power (i.e. the ability to employ direct, open, and effective physical force), honor (a pattern of actions consistent with and constrained by the requirements of established norms), and legitimacy (official sanction and validation for one's position)—is shown to be necessary for any king.[21] And, as the myth makes clear, the negation of the right hand is equivalent to the negation of kingship.

The general problematic of proper and improper kings is pursued in the account of Núadu's successor: Bres ("the Beautiful"), whose reign provides a negative model of proper kingly rule. This may be seen at the outset from the facts of his birth, for Bres was the issue of an illicit union between a Fomoire man and a woman of the Túatha Dé, a fact which made him both a bastard and a foreigner, a resident alien among those over whom he ruled.[22] Bres's selection as king of the Túatha Dé Danann (his mother's people, but not his father's) thus represents a tilt toward matriliny, in contrast to the Celtic patrilineal norm. Moreover, we are told that it was the women among the Túatha Dé who moved to make Bres king, arguing—against the men's opposition— that such a step would secure better ties for them with the Fomoire (*Cath Maige Tuired* 14). And when subsequent episodes of the myth show this unprecedented act of female initiative in the political sphere to result in the disastrous reign of an unfit king, patriliny and patriarchy were both reasserted, their alternatives having been entertained (at the narrative level) only in order that they might be disqualified forever.

Disastrous, indeed, was Bres's reign, and among his failings three are emphasized: (1) he took beyond what a king should take, extracting tribute and permitting the Fomoire to do so as well; (2) he degraded the warrior champions of the Túatha Dé, relegating them to the most menial work; and (3) he did not give as a king should give, showing no generosity, hosting no banquets, and extending only the meagrest of hospitality.[23] Of these, it was this last offense which proved his undoing, for when Bres received the poet Coirpre in particularly niggardly fashion, so outraged was the latter that he composed Ireland's first satire at the king's expense, with such devastating effect that directly thereafter Bres was deposed in favor of Núadu, whose hand had meanwhile been miraculously restored.[24] All of this forms the background to the Second Battle of Mag Tuired, in which the Fomoire (his father's people) sought Bres's restoration, and were opposed in this by the Túatha Dé under the leadership of the (previously) one-handed Núadu and the (temporarily) one-eyed and one-legged Lug.

Although Dumézil initially included these Irish myths alongside the Roman and Scandinavian materials, he later came to minimize their importance as a result of his misgivings about the nature of Lug's one-eyed status: "only a magical grin," as he put it, "not a mutilation."[25] Perhaps this is sufficient reason to exclude these data from consideration: surely their inclusion complicates the comparative enterprise. Yet if one does choose to include them, there are certain points that remain obscure in the narrower comparison that come to figure more prominently in broader discussion. Chief among these is the nature of the enemy whom the one-eyed, one-handed, and one-legged gods or heroes oppose, for both Bres and Tarquin are described as foreigners who ascended to the throne, ruled oppressively and exploitatively, and as a result were rightly deposed, whereupon their patrikin waged war for the tyrant's restitution.

Again, when one chooses to accord the Irish materials more than a marginal place in the study, different emphases emerge. In particular, the similarities between the reign of Bres and that of Tarquin make it clear that kingship is a central issue in these myths, which treat it as a highly problematic institution. Yet here a difference is apparent, for whereas the Irish myth treats Bres's reign as an aberration, and resolves the problem of tyranny through the restoration of a more proper, but equally royal, rule, the Roman texts treat Tarquin not as an aberration but as one whose excesses reveal the tyrannical potential ever present within kingship. Resolution lies thus not in kingship reestablished, but in its definitive termination.

The Left-handed Assassin

In this regard, it is a story from the Old Testament that resembles the Roman account most closely, as Cristiano Grottanelli has convincingly argued in an impressive series of publications.[26] The text in question is Judges 3:12–30, which tells how in that period shortly after the return from Egypt, when "there was no king in Israel and every man did what was right in his own eyes,"[27] there arose a situation in which the Israelites came under the domination of Eglon, king of the Moabites, who extracted heavy tribute from them. God, however, raised up a judge, i.e. a non-royal hero-savior: Ehud, son of Gera of the tribe of Benjamin, a man said to be "restricted with regard to his right hand" (*'tr jd jmnw*), a phrase which at the very least marks him as left-handed, but more probably as one with some prior mutilation or deformity of his right hand.[28] And when Ehud was sent at the head of a deputation bringing tribute to Eglon, he hid a short sword under his clothing, strapped to his right thigh, where he could reach it easily with his left hand, and where it might escape search by the king's guards. This gambit succeeding, he, like Mucius Scaevola and also like Tyr, employed a misleading speech-act to gain advantage against his adversary, telling Eglon "I have a secret message for you, O king. . . . I have a message from God for you" (3:19–20). This "message" he delivered directly the Moabite ruler had dismissed his guards to receive the revelation in private, whereupon Ehud drew his sword and thrust it deep in the tyrant's belly, a belly grown hideously fat on tribute extracted from his subjects.[29] Making good his getaway by a further ruse, Ehud rallied the men of Israel and led them in a massacre of the Moabites, ushering in a period of peace and independence eighty years in duration.

When he was forced to consider this story in the course of a celebrated debate, Dumézil dismissed it summarily, as part of his insistence in holding Indo-European mythic traditions separate from those associated with other linguistic (and ethnic?) groups. More specifically, he argued that the resemblances between this biblical story and the myth of Mucius Scaevola were superficial only, such as might characterize any tale of assassination, and where the two seemed most similar, he found them quite different, for whereas Scaevola lost his right hand in the course of his deed, Ehud bore no mutilation, being only left-handed.[30]

Details of philology aside—and here, Grottanelli has refuted Dumézil's position, showing that he misunderstood the Hebrew text, under the influence of the Greek of the Septuagint[31]—such a stance fails to recognize that the narrative of Ehud, that of Núadu Argetlám, and that of Mucius Scaevola, are all variant representations of the same logical-symbolic formulation in which the negation of the right hand, with all its associations, is seen to be equivalent to the negation of kingship. What is more, the difference between those narratives where the king loses both his hand and his throne (Ireland) and those where royal rule is ended by a commoner who loses (or lacks the use of) his right hand (Israel and Rome) reflects a corresponding difference of sociopolitical structures and attitudes. Thus in medieval Ireland—where kingship was the central institution and was taken to be a fundamental good—the narrative sets out the problem of a bad king, and resolves it with the restoration of a proper monarch. Israel during the time of the Judges and Rome under the Republic, however, had no kings, and their narratives portrayed kingship itself as the problem, a problem which is resolved by a heroic act of liberation. The heroes who accomplish this, moreover, are sharply contrasted to kings, and employ powers such as those of ruse, deception, bluff, and assassination: i.e., powers that are unofficial and unexpected, such that they may seem (particularly to those against whom they are deployed) illegitimate and dishonorable: sinister, in the fullest sense of this term. Moreover, lacking a right hand as they do, there is no danger that they will ever become kings: rather they are, in their body and in their actions, the very antithesis of kingship.

A Discourse on Method

My point in the above discussion is not that Dumézil was objectively and categorically wrong in choosing to exclude Cocles's leg wound, the Second Battle of Mag Tuired, or the story of Ehud from his study of "le borgne et le manchot." On the contrary, I mean to assert that there exists no Archimedean point from which to judge "right" from "wrong" in such a matter. Scholarship, like myth, is an arena of discourse wherein those who participate are continually constructing and reconstructing the very ground on which they tread. As such, it is inevitably and inescapably, although not exclusively or always obviously, a site of political struggle and maneuver.

To make such an assertion at a high level of abstraction is easy enough. Beyond that, I have tried to show, through a concrete example, how one scholar's choices about which data were and which were not relevant to a given problem helped shape the conclusions he ultimately reached. For by his insistence that the myths of Cocles and Scaevola ought be compared first and foremost to those of Oðinn and Tyr, Dumézil was not only able to posit a single (Indo-European) prototype for them, but to argue that the significance of this prototype was its schematic presentation of ideal sovereignty as something both magic and legal alike.

Given the materials which he studied, such a line of interpretation is fair enough, and has met with broad, if not universal, acceptance. To arrive at such conclusions, however, it was necessary for him to strip the stories of Cocles and Scaevola from their Republican context and to stress their resemblance to less overtly political Scandinavian myths, while excluding from consideration other materials in which arise such issues as the contributions made and wounds suffered by members of the lower classes; the offenses and extractions characteristic of kingly rule; and the value of liberating action, even that which employs left-handed methods.

Finally, it is worth pointing out that the choices one makes about what to include and what to leave out have their sources as well as their consequences. In each instance, Dumézil cited reasons—always plausible, if not always compelling—for the exclusion of those data which I would prefer to include in any comparative study of the myths of Horatius Cocles and Mucius Scaevola. Still, one must marvel at the almost magical way in which he was able to transmute Roman stories celebrating the end of kingship and defense of the Republic into "Indo-European" myths celebrating the nature of a sovereign power which he depicted as both legal and magic in nature. And, although I would not stress the point unduly, it is perhaps relevant to note that this feat was accomplished by a man who was closely associated with the Action Française in his youth, and one who remained throughout his life a confirmed royalist and self-proclaimed "man of the right." [32]

My intent is not simply to point the finger of accusation at a distinguished scholar, but to illustrate a general principle by a particularly clear example. For the analyses and interpretations which Dumézil offered of the myths of Horatius Cocles and Mucius Scaevola, however persuasive they may be, are hardly definitive. Rather, they are but one possible construction of select data, and I have been at pains to show just how problematic is the fact and the process of selection. Other constructions remain possible, and it remains advisable to subject all such constructions to a critical and an analytical reading, employing as it were, one's left eye in the process.

Notes

1. The family tree of the Tarquins is actually rather complex, for the first of the line, Tarquinius Priscus, was himself the son of a Corinthian father and an Etruscan mother. As such, he was regarded by the Etruscans of his natal city (Tarquinii, whence the family name) as a foreigner, and at his wife's urging, he moved to Rome, where foreigners would have more opportunity to advance (Livy 1.34). There, he became king, and he and his line were regarded as of Etruscan origin. The importance of patrilineal descent, however, is underlined in the story by the fact that the kingship of the Tarquins was ended by Lucius Junius Brutus, whose social identity and political loyalties were defined by his Roman father and not his mother, herself the daughter of Tarquinius Superbus. See diagram below.

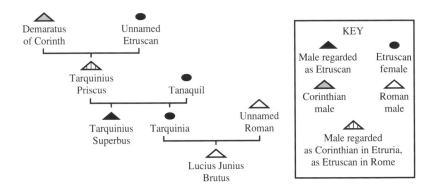

2. See Dionysius of Halicarnassus 5.23.2, Servius's commentary on *Aeneid* 8.649, and Plutarch, *Publicola* 16.5, the last with a rationalizing explanation of Horatius's one-eyed status. The relation between Cocles and the Cyclopes is explored extensively, with a diffusionist hypothesis, by Giorgio Camassa, *L'occhio e il metallo: Un mitologema greco a Roma?* (Genoa: Il Melangolo, 1983).

3. Dumézil placed great emphasis upon Livy's characterization of Cocles as "casting about wild looks in menacing fashion" (2.10.8: *circumferens . . . truces minaciter oculos*), which, in his opinion, established a connection between the hero's one-eyed nature and his ability to hold the enemy at bay through a quasi-magical power of the eye. There are numerous problems with such an argument, however, and I am inclined to accord it little weight, while still accepting in general the comparison of Cocles to Oðinn and Lug.

4. Accounts of these deeds are found in Livy 2.10.1–13, Dionysius of Halicarnassus 5.23.2–5.25.3, Plutarch, *Publicola* 16.4–7, Florus 1.10, Polybius 6.55.1–3, and Valerius Maximus 3.2.1.

5. On the explicit and powerful association of the right hand to Fides (the abstrac-

tion personified as a goddess), see Pierre Boyancé, "La main de Fides," in *Hommages à Jean Bayet* (Brussels: Collection Latomus, 1964), pp. 101–13. Note also, however, that within the Roman practice of divination, the left hand was considered auspicious, a fact which even the Romans found puzzling at times. On this, see François Guillaumont, "Laeva prospera, remarques sur la droite et la gauche dans la divination romaine," in Raymond Bloch, ed., *D'Héraklès à Poséidon: Mythologie et protohistoire* (Paris: Librairie Champion, 1985), pp. 159–77.

6. This story is found in Livy 2.12.1–2.13.5, Florus 1.10, Plutarch, *Publicola* 17.1–5, and Dionysius of Halicarnassus 5.27.1–5.30.3, although the last of these sources omits the central motif of the sacrificed right hand.

7. That Óðinn possessed such powers is clear enough (see, e.g. *Havamál* 150). What is not clear, however—for no text states so explicitly—is that he gained them through the sacrifice of his eye or that they are associated with his one-eyed status in any way. This is an issue with which Dumézil struggled repeatedly, but which (in my view, at least), poses no insuperable difficulties for the comparison of Cocles to Óðinn, and also to Lug. The most important sources for the Norse god's loss of an eye are *Vǫluspá* 28 and *Gylfaginning* 15. Most recently on these materials, see Françoise Bader, *La langue des dieux, ou l'hermétisme des poètes indo-européens* (Pisa: Giardini, 1989), pp. 29–31, 39. 44.

8. See, inter alia, Georges Dumézil, *Mitra-Varuna: Essai sur deux représentations indo-européennes de la souveraineté*, 1st ed. (Paris: Presses universitaires de France, 1940), pp. 111–28; ibid., 2d ed. (Paris: Gallimard, 1948), pp. 163–88; *L'heritage indo-européen à Rome* (Paris: Gallimard, 1949), pp. 159–69; "Mythes romains," *Revue de Paris* (Dec. 1951): 105–15; *Mythe et epopée* I (Paris: Gallimard, 1968), pp. 423–28; *Mythe et epopée* III (Paris: Gallimard, 1973), pp. 267–86; " 'Le Borgne' et 'Le Manchot': The State of the Problem," in G. J. Larson, ed., *Myth in Indo-European Antiquity* (Berkeley: University of California Press, 1974), pp. 17–28. After numerous revisions of his views, Dumézil ultimately concluded that while Irish and Iranian counterparts to the stories of Tyr and Scaevola existed, nowhere outside Rome and Scandinavia was there a corresponding version of the one-eyed deity or, *a fortiori*, of the one-eyed and one-handed figures in tandem.

9. See, for instance, his statements in *Mythe et epopée*, 3:275–76 and " 'Le Borgne' et 'Le Manchot': The State of the Problem," pp. 18–21. The quotation is taken from *Mitra-Varuna*, 2d ed., p. 168; cf. *Mythe et epopée*, 1:427.

10. The fullest critiques to date are those of Cristiano Grottanelli, discussed below, and that of Marie Delcourt, "Horatius Coclès et Mucius Scaevola," in *Hommages à Waldemar Deonna* (Brussels: Collection Latomus, 1957), pp. 169–80. See also the critical remarks of C. Scott Littleton, *The New Comparative Mythology*, 3d ed. (Berkeley: University of California Press, 1982), pp. 86–88, and his retraction at p. 99. Broader criticisms of Dumézil's "magical sovereign" and "legal sovereign" have been voiced by Paul Thieme, Jan Gonda, and others.

11. Dio Cassius 45.32.3. Cf. idem 46.19.8, and also 45.31.1, where Horatius is singled out as the savior of the Republic, and set in marked contrast to Antony, its would-be destroyer.

12. *Mythe et epopée*, 3:269.

13. *Publicola* 16.6. This wound is also mentioned by Servius, in his commentary

on *Aeneid* 8.646. Polybius 6.55.2 states that Cocles suffered numerous (unspecified) wounds, and alone reports that the hero died in this encounter (6.55.3). Also of interest are the descriptions of two heroes in Caesar's army, Gaius Acilius and Cassius Scaeva, who are clearly patterned after Mucius Scaevola and Horatius Cocles. Thus, Acilius lost his right hand in combat, while Scaeva—like Cocles—lost an eye and received disabling wounds of the shoulder and thigh (Plutarch, *Caesar* 16; Suetonius, *Divus Iulius* 68.4). Regarding these figures, see further Gérard Capdeville, "Le centurion borgne et le soldat manchot," *Mélanges de l'École Française de Rome* 84/1 (1972): 601–21.

14. *Publicola* 16.7. The connection of Horatius Cocles to Vulcan was recognized already by Ettore Pais, *Storia di Roma* (Rome: 1898), 1:472–76, who took the hero to be a doublet of the god. The statue is mentioned by Dionysius of Halicarnassus 5.25.2 and Livy 2.10.12, who place it more generally in the Forum and the Comitium, the southeast corner of which was occupied by the temple of Vulcan. Aulus Gellius 4.5 also places it in the Temple of Vulcan, and gives a plainly mythic account, derived from earlier sources, of how it was moved thence from the Comitium. The views of Delcourt regarding this statue, pp. 172–74, are unconvincing.

15. Cf. *Iliad* 1.590–600, *Vǫlundarkviða, Déor's Lament*. On the theme of the limping smith, see Giorgio Camassa, "I segni del fabbro," *Annali della Facoltà di Lettere e Filosofia della Università di Perugia* (1980–81): 153–60, and Ferdinand Sokolicek, "Der Hinkende im brauchtümlichen Spiel," *Festschrift für Otto Höfler* (Vienna: Verlag Notring, 1968), 2:423–32, esp. pp. 431–32. The opposition of smiths and artisans to tyrannical, even monstrous kings is also evident in the myths of Daedalus and Minos, Prometheus and Zeus, Kāva and Zohāk, on the last of which, see Arthur Christensen, *Smeden Kâwäh og det gamle persiske Rigsbanner* (Copenhagen: A. F. Høst, 1919). Also similar is Thersites, Agamemnon's lower-class antagonist, who is described in *Iliad* 2.217 as "lame in one foot" and *pholkòs*, a hapax legomenon which the ancient scholia interpret as meaning "squinty-eyed." If these are to be trusted, Thersites would then be a figure with deformities of eye and leg, much like Horatius Cocles.

16. *De Bello Gallico* 6.17. The entry of Lug to the company of the gods, and the significance of his epithet Samildánach are described in *Cath Maige Tuired* §§53–71.

17. *Cath Maige Tuired* §129. In researches that, to the best of my knowledge, remain unpublished, Udo Strutynski has noted that a one-legged figure also appears alongside others who are one-eyed and one-handed (Gunther, Hagen, and Walther respectively) in the minor Germanic epic *Waltharius*. Still more striking is the portion of *Scéla Mucce Meic Dathó* ("The Tale of Mac Datho's Pig") in which Cét mac Mágach recounts the wounds and disgraces he has inflicted upon various heroes of Ulster. These include injuries to (A) two men of royal status, Éogan mac Durthacht, one of whose eyes he put out, and Cúscraid Mend Macha mac Conchobair, whose vocal cords he severed; (B) one man of warrior status, Láme Gábaid, whose hand he cut off; and (C) one described as a herdsman, Salchad father of Mend, whose heel he cut off, rendering him "one-footed" (*oínchoisseda*), and one of unspecified status, Celtchair mac Uithechair, whom he castrated. This distribution, whereby wounds of the head (eye and voice) correspond to sovereign figures, of the arm or hand to warriors, and of the lower torso (foot and genitals) to the lower social strata is reminiscent of socio-

gonic myths in which these same social orders are said to have been created from the same bodily parts. See further my discussion in *Myth, Cosmos, and Society: Indo-European Themes of Creation and Destruction* (Cambridge, Mass.: Harvard University Press, 1986), pp. 4–5 and 141–63.

18. On this text, see the splendid discussion of Elizabeth A. Gray, "Cath Maige Tuired: Myth and Structure," *Eigse* 18 (1981): 183–209; 19 (1982): 1–35 and 230–62; idem, *Cath Maige Tuired: The Second Battle of Mag Tuired* (Dublin: Irish Texts Society, 1982). Also useful are Alwyn and Brinley Rees, *Celtic Heritage* (London: Thames & Hudson, 1961), pp. 31–38; Jan de Vries, *La religion des Celtes* (Paris: Payot, 1977), pp. 157–64; and Jarich G. Oosten, *The War of the Gods: The Social Code in Indo-European Mythology* (London: Routledge & Kegan Paul, 1985), pp. 115–33.

19. *Cath Maige Tuired* §14. That it was his right hand which Núadu lost is specified in the "First Battle of Mag Tuired" §§56 and 58, the text and translation of which may be found in *Eriu* 8 (1915): 52–53 and 56–57, and in a poem quoted within the *Lebor Gabála Érenn* §290 and 297.

20. Thus, for instance, the Welsh heir to the throne traditionally must be free of three blemishes: he must be whole in his limbs, not deaf or dumb, and not insane (T. P. Ellis, *Welsh Tribal Law and Custom in the Middle Ages* [Oxford: Clarendon Press, 1926], p. 29). Similar provisions are expressed regarding Irish kings in the *Ancient Laws and Institutes of Ireland* (Dublin: Royal Irish Academy, 1865–1902), 1:73 (from the *Senchus Mór*), and 3:83 (from the *Book of Aicill*). The last of these sources is perhaps the most interesting, for it tells how Cormac was deposed from the kingship of Tara *after losing one eye*, and how he became a lawgiver and teacher of wisdom thereafter.

21. On the significance of the right hand, see the essays collected in Rodney Needham, *Right and Left: Essays on Dual Symbolic Classification* (Chicago: University of Chicago Press, 1973); Raoul and Laura Makarius, "Le symbolisme de la main gauche," in *Structuralisme ou ethnologie?* (Paris: Editions anthropos, 1973), pp. 195–233; and Serge Tcherkézoff, *Le roi nyamwezi, la droite et la gauche* (Cambridge: Cambridge University Press, 1983), as well as the article of Boyancé cited above. One should stress, however, that within the various Indo-European languages, no particularly pejorative association is attached to the left hand, which is designated, rather, as the "better" (Greek *aristerós*), "choice" (Avestan *vairyastāra*), "friendlier" (Old High German *winistar,* Old Norse *vinstri,* Old English *winestra*), or "more winning" (Latin *sinister;* cf. Sanskrit *sánīyas*) hand, in contrast to the "more skillful" right (Latin *dexter,* Greek *dexiterós,* Irish *dess,* Gothic *táihswō,* Sanskrit *dákṣiṇa-,* Avestan *dašina-,* etc.).

22. The story of Bres's conception is of sufficient importance that it is not only told at length (*Cath Maige Tuired* §§15–23), but figures as a subtitle of the text, which is called in full "The [Second] Battle of Mag Tuired and the birth of Bres, son of Elatha and the kingship" (*Cath Maige Turedh an scél-sa sís ocus genemain Bres meic Elathain ocus a ríghe*). That Bres, for all his ambiguity, is ultimately and definitively to be seen as of the Fomoire is established not only by his father, but also by his son, Rúadan, who sides with the Fomoire in the Battle of Mag Tuired (*Cath Maige Tuired* §124). The parentage and consequent social identity of Bres and Rúadan is implicitly contrasted to that of Lug, which is its precise opposite, i.e. he is the child of a man of the

Túatha Dé and a woman of the Fomoire, who have been properly joined in marriage. See diagram below.

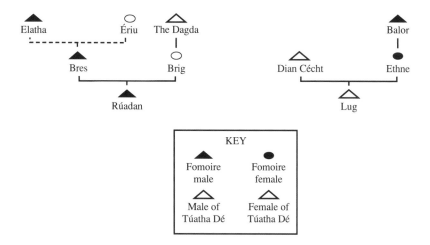

23. *Cath Maige Tuired* §25, 36–38. This should be compared to the speech in which Brutus catalogued the offenses of the Tarquins, Livy 1.59.9.

24. *Cath Maige Tuired* §39. See also Vernam Hull, "Cairpre mac Edaine's Satire upon Bres mac Eladain," *Zeitschrift für celtische Philologie* 18 (1929): 63–69.

25. "'Le borgne' et 'le manchot': The State of the Problem," p. 21. For his earlier views, see *Mitra-Varuṇa*, 2d ed., pp. 181–88.

26. Cristiano Grottanelli, "Un passo del libro dei Giudici alla luce della comparazione storico-religiosa: Il giudice Ehud e il valore della mano sinistra," *Atti del primo convegno italiano sul vicino oriente* (Rome: Centro per le antichità e la storia dell'arte del vicino oriente, 1978), pp. 35–45; "The Enemy King Is a Monster: A Biblical Equation," *Studi Storico Religiosi* 3 (1979): 5–36; "Temi dumeziliani fuori dal mondo indoeuropea," *Opus* 2 (1983): 365–89, esp. pp. 381–84.

27. This statement is made at Judges 21:25 (RSV) as a summation of the entire period prior to the foundation of the monarchy under Saul. Similar statements are found at Judges 18.1 and 19.1.

28. The *Targum Jonathan*, for instance, refers to Ehud as "a person with a shriveled right hand." One should also note a consistent association of the tribe of Benjamin with the left hand, as at Judges 20:16, where seven hundred left-handed Benjaminites armed with slings are mentioned, and Genesis 35:16–18, where the story of Benjamin's birth is related. The last of Jacob's twelve sons, Benjamin's delivery caused the death of his mother (Rachel), who as she died gave to him the name Ben-oni "Son of my sorrow." For this, however, Jacob substituted the more auspicious name Ben-jamin "Son of the right hand." The narrative thus contrasts the mother's sorrow at her death to the father's joy at the birth of his son. This contrast is encoded within the two names which they give to the child, each of which implies another term, thus filling out a system of

binary oppositions, in which—as is seen in the diagram below—Benjamin is understood, from his mother's point of view, to be her "son of the left hand."

Viewpoint	Mother	Father
Experience	Death	Birth
Sentiment	Sorrow	Joy
Name$_1$	"Son of my sorrow"	["Son of my joy"]
Name$_2$	["Son of the left hand"]	"Son of the right hand"

29. Judges 3:17 and 3:22 emphasize Eglon's corpulence and filth in ways that clearly serve not only to degrade him personally, but also—and more importantly—to criticize that system which permitted him to rule and grow fat on the labor of others.

30. *Mythe et epopée,* 3:348n. The story of Ehud was brought to Dumézil's attention by John Brough, "The Tripartite Ideology of the Indo-Europeans: An Experiment in Method," *Bulletin of the School of Oriental and African Studies* 22 (1959): 69–85, esp. p. 75. This detail played only a minor part in their exchange, an exchange in which both parties seem to me to have been equally misguided. Thus, Dumézil insisted, as always, on the unique (i.e., privileged) status of the Indo-European peoples, here contrasting them to the Semitic peoples in a fashion reminiscent of the racism of nineteenth-century theoreticians such as Renan (on whom, see Maurice Olender, *Les langues du Paradis. Aryens et Sémites: un couple providentiel* [Paris: Gallimard, 1989], esp. pp. 75–111). For his part, Brough was at equal pains to establish that myths do not really treat tensions between social strata, but only seem to do so when misconstrued and misrepresented by devious scholars.

31. Grottanelli, "Un passo del libro dei Giudici," p. 37 n. 6.

32. On Dumézil's politics and its relation to his scholarship, see Chapter 19, "Shaping the Past and the Future," and the literature cited there. While Dumézil was always quite guarded in discussing his sociopolitical opinions, one can get some sense of them from a careful reading of *Discours de reception de M. Georges Dumézil à l'Académie Française* (Paris: Gallimard, 1979), from interviews which appeared in *Le Figaro Dimanche* 29–30 April 1978, *Le Figaro* 20 April 1979, and *Nouvel observateur* 14 January 1983, and from his *Entretiens avec Didier Eribon* (Paris: Gallimard, 1987).

TWENTY-ONE

MYTH AND HISTORY IN THE STUDY OF MYTH: AN OBSCURE TEXT OF GEORGES DUMÉZIL, ITS CONTEXT AND SUBTEXT

To date, no one has attempted to compile a definitive bibliography of the writings of Georges Dumézil, and to do so would be a formidable task in light of the scores of books and hundreds of articles which comprise his massive oeuvre.[1] Still, given the intense scrutiny that his work has received and the acute self-consciousness with which he reflected upon his output, it is quite a surprise to come across a piece of Dumézil's that has received absolutely no mention whatsoever, either by Dumézil himself or by anyone else. Yet this is true of a short article with the intriguing title "De quelques faux massacres," published in the *Revue turque d'anthropologie* for 1927, that I happened upon quite by chance, and that strikes me as worthy of further attention.[2]

On the title page of this article, Dumézil is listed as "Professor of History of Religions at the University of Istanbul," a position which he held from 1926 to 1931, and in order to have appeared in early 1927, this article must have been written during the first year of his tenure. Dumézil found himself in Turkey, according to his own account, as the result of his inability to obtain an academic position in France upon completion of his dissertation in 1924. This, in part, seems to have been due to the failure of Antoine Meillet, whom Dumézil regarded as his patron, to help pave the way for his career, and in part to the opposition of Henri Hubert, with whom he had had his difficulties. In 1925, however, Jean Marx—who had succeeded Hubert at the École pratique des hautes études and also held responsibility for the placement of French scholars in positions overseas—helped him to obtain a newly created chair in the history of religions at the University of Istanbul.[3]

The creation of this chair, again according to Dumézil, constituted one small part of Kemal Ataturk's campaign to modernize and secularize the Turkish nation, and followed upon Ataturk's having been impressed in his youth by Ernest Renan's writings, which convinced him that the academic and comparative study of religion in France had helped to reduce the influence of the Catholic church in that country.[4] Dumézil's position in Turkey thus had its problems and complexities, insofar as the purposes of the state which had hired him were quite antithetical to those of the Faculty of Islamic Theology to which it appointed him, and from which it was necessary for him to be discreetly removed in 1927, when his chair was transferred to the Faculty of Letters.[5] Beyond this, there were other difficulties. Library resources were poor, especially in the area of Indo-European studies, but Dumézil sought to make the best of things, opening up new lines of inquiry where possible and drawing on his previous researches where he could, while holding open the possibility of finding academic employment in France or elsewhere in Europe.[6]

For their part, the French were pleased to send young academics to Turkey, as relations between the two former enemies warmed considerably during the late 1920s. In particular, the French were interested in gaining increased influence over the republic that Ataturk was building, and as a corollary to this, in obtaining greater access to Turkish markets. Within French popular opinion, however, there lay obstacles to such a rapprochement, for reports of Turkish atrocities—above all, the massacre of more than a million Ottoman subjects of Armenian nationality in 1915–17—had been given wide publicity in France and elsewhere, provoking virtually universal shock and indignation.[7]

This is not the place to consider in any detail this, the first deliberate and systematic campaign of genocide to be backed by the technological and bureaucratic resources of a twentieth-century state.[8] It is worth noting, however, that the deliberate annihilation of a minority from whom they were separated by ethnic, linguistic, and religious differences was part of the Young Turks' project of transforming the multi-ethnic Ottoman empire into a modern nation-state possessed of a homogeneous and unified population, a project which was inherited and completed by Ataturk. The crimes which they perpetrated in pursuit of that end—and the reports issued during the war by such persons as Arnold Toynbee, Hans Morgenthau, and Johannes Lepsius left no doubt about the extent and barbarity of those crimes[9]—led to virtually universal sympathy for the "starving Armenians" and condemnation of the Turkish government. Following the end of the war, world outrage found political expression in the Treaty of Sèvres, signed in August 1920, which recognized an independent Armenia that was expected to come under the protective mandate of the United States.

Events, however, played out rather differently. Retreating into isolation after the war, the U.S. declined to play any role in support of the Armenian republic. Further, Ataturk had come to power in 1919, and while he distanced himself from the Ottoman and Young Turk rulers, he shared the nationalist vision of the latter group, to which an independent Armenia posed unacceptable threats. As a result, in September 1920 he dispatched troops into Armenian territory and forced the fledgling republic to renounce the Sèvres agreements. Further massacres of Armenians followed and elicited no more than token protest from any foreign nation. Turkish power having thus been dramatically reasserted, there followed negotiations to replace the Sèvres treaty. These negotiations were concluded in July of 1923 with the Treaty of Lausanne, in which the

Western democracies established final peace with Turkey and, bowing in this to Turkish insistence, omitted any mention whatsoever of Armenia or Armenians. Since that time, the Turkish government has been steadfast in denying that any massacre of Armenians ever took place, and has exerted considerable pressure on any other government or any international body that has attempted to address or even acknowledge these crimes against humanity.[10]

As Ataturk thus made clear from the outset, the price of doing business with Turkey was turning a blind eye to the fate of the Armenians. France and the Western powers showed themselves willing to do this at Lausanne in 1924, and it was in the wake of this treaty that Georges Dumézil made his way to Istanbul, where the first article he published after arrival took up the topic of *false* massacres. That he was aware of the way Christian Armenians had been eliminated from their homeland in the Caucasus—and that other atrocities had also been committed there by the Turkish state—is clear from certain remarks Dumézil made in his preface to *La langue des Oubykhs,* a work that was published in 1931 after he began teaching in Uppsala, but which was based upon field research he had carried out in Turkey:

> The general war, but above all the Turkish war of independence [by which, presumably, he means Ataturk's struggle to take power] tried the Oubykh villages dearly. The Greeks had occupied the region for many years, and the Oubykhs had made compromises during their stay for which they paid dearly after Ataturk's victory: many young people fled with the retreating Greek army, and many others were shot or hung. Even those who had done nothing for which they could be reproached suffered for the faults of others and for the new regime's distrust of the entire "Circassian element," which was guilty of having remained faithful to the Sultanate too long. Finally, *now that there were no longer any Christians in Anatolia,* the policy of Ankara was above all to "turkify" rapidly all of the non-Turkish Muslims: Lazes, Georgians, Kurds, Cherkess, Ossetes, etc.[11]

That aspect of the Ankara government's policy of "Turkification" which most immediately concerned Dumézil, as he went on to explain, was its campaign to suppress the Oubykh language. Accordingly, in 1929 and 1930 he struggled to record and analyze the structure of this little-known Caucasian language before it became fully extinct, and later, upon discovering a community of Oubykh-speakers previously unknown to him, he made annual trips to Turkey from 1954 to 1972 in order to continue his study.[12]

The history of Dumézil's work on the Caucasian languages has recently been retraced by Georges Charachidzé, a pupil of Dumézil's and an authority in Caucasian studies, in an *éloge funèbre* presented to the Société de Linguistique de Paris on 15 November 1986, and published in 1987.[13] Charachidzé reminded his audience of the eighteen books dedicated by Dumézil to Caucasian linguistics, and the fact that of his one hundred and thirty articles, more than half are dedicated to various linguistic problems, especially aspects of Caucasian languages, but also some on Quechua and Armenian, the only Indo-European language on which Dumézil did etymological work proper. As an Indo-Europeanist who came to reside in a country where the only Indo-European language that was commonly spoken happened to be Armenian, the latter took on considerable importance for him, although he rapidly developed interest in the largely unstudied Caucasian languages such as Oubykh, Laz, Circassian, and Ingush.

Armenian, however, according to Charachidzé, remained important to Dumézil in spite of his Caucasian researches. He studied Armenian in Turkey and, after returning to Paris, he taught Armenian in the École de Langues Orientales for more than a decade, starting in 1937. Moreover, Armenian was, according to his *élève,* the only Indo-European language in which Dumézil did philological work proper, for in all other Indo-European fields, he limited his researches to social, religious, and mythological data.[14] Armenian was thus that Indo-European area which Dumézil studied throughout his career predominantly at a linguistic level, and least of all at other levels, with the exception of Tocharian.[15] His interest in the Armenian language may also reflect the fact that this was a prime area of specialization that had been developed by Antoine Meillet, who had been his mentor. His lack of interest in the "social, religious, and mythological facts" of the Armenians is more difficult to explain however. And regarding the fate of Armenians in the teens and twenties, the phrase cited above, to the best of my knowledge, constitutes his only published comment.

Regarding massacres, Dumézil did have something to say, for this was a topic that he had treated in his "thèse complémentaire," *Le crime des lemniennes,* a work in which he attempted to apply the theories of Frazer's *Golden Bough* to the traditions attested in Apollonius of Rhodes and elsewhere that the men of Lemnos had been murdered *en masse* by their wives, a murder that was annually commemorated in a ritual period of mourning when the Lemnian women were separated from their men.[16] Essentially, Dumézil argued that the ritual, while real enough, was nothing more than a ceremony of seasonal renewal, like many attested elsewhere, while the myth, far from preserving historic memory, set the contents of the ritual within a narrative form which it then projected into an imaginary and absolutely ahistoric past.

To this example of a "pseudo-massacre," Dumézil now added two others. The first of these he took from the biblical account of how Esther had caused Haman's plans to backfire, producing a situation in which it was the Jews who massacred their enemies throughout the Achaemenian empire, an event commemorated thereafter in the Purim festival. Second, he considered the story told in the *Mahabhārata* of the Brahmin Paraśurāma, who, in order to avenge his father—the latter having been unjustly slain by a warrior—killed all members of the warrior or Kṣatriya class, as part of a huge sacrifice he offered to the god Indra. The details of neither case need concern us here, for Dumézil's arguments are much like those he developed for the Lemnian data: that is, he consistently took mythic narratives to be aetiological constructions that serve to justify ritual practices, while considering myth and ritual alike as having only fictive and specious connections to any historic events.

Beyond the individual examples Dumézil treated, one might inquire why he chose these three and not others, and through what logic they are juxtaposed in his text. A clue may be found in an observation he makes almost in passing: "That which in myth is only the mass suppression of all 'evil elements,' all calamities and plagues, as the Chinese say on like occasions, becomes in history (1) the massacre of one people by another, or (2) of one class by another class, or elsewhere (3) of one sex by the other." [17] Thus, each of the three accounts which make up his study describes conflict along one of the three different lines of social cleavage here identified, the story of Esther and Haman focusing on antagonisms of nationality, ethnicity, and religion; that of Paraśurāma on those of caste or class; and that of the Lemnian women and their husband-victims on those of gender. Yet from the ideological perspective of the "integral nationalism" of Charles Maurras that so influenced him in the 1920s,[18] Dumézil was committed to the notion that all the competing segments of society and their potential for disruptive violence were to be kept in check by state power, preferably that of a king. It is surely in connection with this political view that, having assembled a set of sources which describe the massacre of more powerful groups by their normal subordinates [19]—men by women, warriors by priests, and Aryans by Jews—Dumézil set things back in order by asserting that the unity of the respective societies was never really endangered, because there were in actuality no such acts of violence, rebellion, disorder, and massacre: only "myths" of "pseudo-massacres."

In his treatment of the book of Esther, Dumézil plays at the edges of anti-Semitism, but ultimately maintains a position that is rational and dispassionate, if circumspect. Thus, he quotes as an example of an opinion shared by "the most objective historians," Edouard Montet's sneering description of the book as being characterized by an "unhealthy spirit" (*l'esprit malsain*) involving "fanaticism, spiritual narrow-mindedness, and a thirst for vengeance." [20] Yet toward Montet—whose book he describes as excellent, albeit a work of popularization—and toward this position, he strikes an ambiguous posture. Thus, while he seems to grant Montet's characterization of Esther, he initially grants it only for the sake of argument ("*Soit*") and ultimately concludes that although the "esprit malsain" is indeed present in the book, it is not unique or original to the Jews, but derives from various peoples throughout the Achaemenian empire.[21]

Dumézil's circumspection on this particular point is as nothing, however, to that which one can detect in the article as a whole, where the fate of the Armenians is discussed without ever being mentioned explicitly. For the piece is characterized by an indirect style of discourse, in which Dumézil's treatment of ancient texts permitted him to comment obliquely upon recent events—or nonevents, as some would have it. His presentation, then, may be understood as a political intervention which refused to acknowledge itself as such, but which provided comfort and support to those who knew how to read it, while affording its author deniability in the face of any criticism from those who held opposing views. In three separate examples, he thus repeated the by no means disinterested or innocent argument that reports of a massacre are not the same thing as a massacre itself.

In the eyes of the Turkish audience for whom it was intended, this line of argument would inevitably conjure up the reports of an Armenian massacre, against acceptance of which it could well be understood to caution a too-credulous European public.[22] Yet the article includes other passages that seem to be intended for other audiences, in which other arguments are also advanced. For the "false massacre" discussion is encapsulated within a prologue and an epilogue of a rather different nature, each of which consists of a single sentence. Thus, the article begins with the observation "One would be ill advised, even in this year of grace 1927, to deny that the past, present, and future history of mankind is full of massacres, verifiable and authentic, or probable and foreseeable."[23] Here, the author speaks in another voice from that of scholarly skepticism that is heard through the body of the article. And with this voice of humanitarian concern, he acknowledges—albeit briefly and with tactful lack of specificity—that even within recent memory real blood has been seen flowing in the streets. In truth, it seems almost as if he wished for a moment to signal his regret should any readers outside of Turkey chance upon this piece: regret for the victims, and for the circumstances which kept him from speaking more openly of their fate. Yet in the very next sentence— "All the more reason for not aggravating the case of our poor species"—he transforms the acknowledged reality of such events into an argument for treating critically the reports of others like them.

At the end, the concerned voice with which Dumézil opened his essay is heard once more, and speaks once again with direct reference to the situation that author and reader alike confront in the present: "The world has known enough authentic slaughters that one can let rest [*pour qu'on laisse dormir*], in the pacific treasure-trove of human fictions, those massacres that can only be understood as myths."[24] Here, once again it is as if the author wished to signal that he possessed both knowledge and compassion, but also to represent himself as philosophical and worldly-wise in his resignation and sorrow. Yet for all that, his attempt rings hollow, and the advice which he offers in the immediate context of real genocidal slaughter—*qu'on laisse dormir*—remains shocking some sixty-odd years later.

Notes

1. Extensive bibliographical listings and discussions of Dumézil's oeuvre may be found in Jean-Claude Riviére, ed., *Georges Dumézil: À la découverte des indo-européens* (Paris: Éditions Copernic, 1979); *Georges Dumézil: Cahiers pour un temps* (Paris: Centre Pompidou, 1981); and C. Scott Littleton, *The New Comparative Mythology: An Anthropological Assessment of the Theories of Georges Dumézil*, 3d edition (Berkeley: University of California Press, 1982). A "Bibliography of Georges Dumézil, authorized by the author," appears in *La Nouvelle Revue de Paris*, no. 1 (March 1985): 28–30.

2. G. Dumézil, "De quelques faux massacres," *Revue turque d'anthropologie* 3ᵐᵉ année, no. 4 (March 1927): 39–46. This article has been recently reprinted in *Quaderni di Storia* 32 (1990): 19–30.

3. For Dumézil's reflections on this period, see his *Entretiens avec Didier Eribon* (Paris: Gallimard, 1987), pp. 52–60.

4. Georges Charachidzé, "Nécrologie" for Georges Dumézil, *Bulletin de la Société de Linguistique de Paris* 82/1 (1987): xvii.

5. Dumézil, *Entretiens avec Didier Eribon*, p. 53.

6. While Dumézil was teaching in Turkey, the prospect of return came to seem rather remote. Meillet, who had never been fully supportive, now abandoned him utterly, and delivered the following brutal advice: "Tâchez de faire carrière à l'étranger, il n'y a pas de place pour vous en France." Accordingly, when the chance of going to Sweden presented itself in 1931, Dumézil seized it, giving up his position as Professor of History of Religions for the much less elevated post of Lecturer in French at Uppsala University. See ibid., pp. 59–60.

7. Official French policy during the First World War unambiguously backed Armenian claims against the Turkish government and made use of this issue for propaganda purposes. See, for instance, the statement of then prime minister and foreign minister Aristide Briand in November 1916: "When the hour for legitimate reparations shall have struck, France will not forget the terrible trials of the Armenians, and in accord with her Allies, she will take the necessary measures to ensure for Armenia a life of peace and progress" (*Le Temps*, 7 November 1916, cited by Richard Hovannisian, *The Armenian Genocide in Perspective* [New Brunswick, N.J.: Transactions Books, 1986], p. 31). Among the most influential single works in the formation of French popular opinion was the translation of Johannes Lepsius's compelling eyewitness accounts, *Le rapport secret sur les massacres d'Arménie* (Paris: Payot, 1918); also available at that time was Herbert Gibbons, *Le page plus noire de l'histoire moderne: Les derniers massacres d'Arménie* (Paris: Berger-Levrault, 1916). For a bibliographical survey of archival sources and writings on the massacre, see Richard G. Hovannisian, *The Armenian Holocaust: A Bibliography Relating to The Deportation, Massacres, and Dis-*

persion of the Armenian People, 1915–1923 (Cambridge, Mass.: National Association for Armenian Studies and Research, 1980).

8. Among the numerous recent works on these events, see Dickran Boyajian, *Armenia: The Case for a Forgotten Genocide* (Westwood, N.J.: Educational Book Crafters, 1972); Jean-Marie Carzou, *Un Génocide exemplaire: Arménie 1915* (Paris: Flammarion, 1975); Yves Ternon, *Les Arméniens: histoire d'un génocide* (Paris: Editions du Seuil, 1977); Vahakn N. Dadrian, "A Theoretical Model of Genocide with Particular Reference to the Armenian Case," *Armenian Review* 31 (1979): 115–36; Gérard Chaliand and Yves Ternon, *Le Génocide des Arméniens* (Brussels: Editions Complexe, 1981); Leo Kuper, *Genocide: Its Political Use in the Twentieth Century* (New Haven: Yale University Press, 1982); Gérard Chaliand, ed., *Le crime de silence: Le génocide des Arméniens. Tribunal permanent des peuples* (Paris: Flammarion, 1984); and Richard G. Hovannisian, ed. *The Armenian Genocide in Perspective* (New Brunswick, N.J.: Transaction Books, 1986).

9. Arnold J. Toynbee, "A Summary of Armenian History up to and including 1915," in *The Treatment of Armenians in the Ottoman Empire: Documents Presented to Viscount Grey of Fallodon, Secretary of State for Foreign Affairs* (London: H.M.S.O., 1916), pp. 591–653; Henry Morgenthau, *Ambassador Morgenthau's Story* (Garden City, N.Y.: Doubleday, Page, 1918). The French translation of Lepsius's book has been cited above. The German version, *Bericht über das Schicksal des armenischen Volkes in der Türkei während des Weltkrieges* was first published in Potsdam in 1916, and came out in an expanded version in 1919 under the title *Der Todesgang des armenischen Völkes*.

10. On the continuing pattern of Turkish denial, and the response of subsequent generations of Armenians in diaspora, see Yves Ternon, *La cause arménienne* (Paris: Editions du Seuil, 1983), and the following articles in Hovannisian, *The Armenian Genocide in Perspective:* Marjorie Housepian Dobkin, "What Genocide? What Holocaust? News from Turkey, 1915–1923: A Case Study" (pp. 97–109); Richard G. Hovannisian, "The Armenian Genocide and Patterns of Denial" (pp. 111–33); Vigen Guroian, "Collective Responsibility and Official Excuse-Making: The Case of the Turkish Genocide of the Armenians" (pp. 135–52). Also useful are Pierre Vidal-Naquet's Preface to *Le crime de silence*, and—on the broader issue of revisionism in general— his book *Les assassins de la mémoire* (Paris: Éditions La Découverte, 1987). Formal Turkish denials continue to be made, as in *Armenian Allegations: Myth and Reality. A Handbook of Facts and Documents Compiled and Edited by the Assembly of Turkish American Associations,* 2d revised edition (Washington, D.C.: The Assembly, 1982).

11. Georges Dumézil, *La langue des Oubykhs* (Paris: Librairie Honoré Champion, 1931), pp. xiv–xv (emphasis added). On the title page, he is listed as "Lecturer at the University of Uppsala."

12. Dumézil spoke of his work on Oubykh in an interview that was published in *Nouvel observateur* (14 January 1983), p. 22, and also in his *Entretiens avec Didier Eribon*, pp. 56–58, 86–89, making prominent mention in both sources of the determined resistance of the Oubykh people to the Russians both prior to and following the 1917 Revolution, a fact which seems to have particularly endeared them to him. See *Nouvel observateur*, p. 22, and *Entretiens*, p. 57; cf. *La langue des Oubykhs*, p. xi.

13. *Bulletin de la Société de Linguistique de Paris* 82/1 (1987): xvi–xxiii.

14. Ibid., p. xix. Dumézil's eleven articles on Armenian philology, published between 1938 and 1978, are listed in *Georges Dumézil: Cahiers pour un temps*, p. 348.

15. The bulk of Dumézil's non-linguistic work on Armenian is to be found in a 1938 article "Vahagn," *Revue de l'histoire des religions* 117:152–70. Tocharian, of course, had not been recognized as an Indo-European language at the time when Dumézil received his training.

16. Georges Dumézil, *Le crime des lemniennes. Rites et légendes du monde égéen* (Paris: Paul Geuthner, 1924).

17. Dumézil, "De quelques faux massacres," p. 44 (numbers added). His line of argument is, then, that in myth natural evils are represented as social enemies. In the strategic discourses through which real historic antagonisms are inflamed, however, it is social enemies—and would-be victims—who are often represented as embodying natural evils, as when Huguenots were referred to as "vermin" in the period leading up to the St. Bartholomew's Massacre, or when Jews and Gypsies were led to gas chambers, the purpose of which was metaphorically described as "delousing." See further Natalie Zemon Davis, *Society and Culture in Early Modern France* (Stanford: Stanford University Press, 1975), p. 181; Bruce Lincoln, *Discourse and the Construction of Society* (New York: Oxford University Press, 1989), pp. 99–100, and the discussion above in Chapter 11, "War and Warriors: An Overview."

18. Between 1920 and 1925 Dumézil had direct personal dealings with Maurras, the founder of the Action Française and chief ideologist of the French right during the first half of this century. At that time, he was highly impressed by Maurras, and sixty years later still spoke strongly of his support for the "pure kernel" (*le noyau pur*) of Maurras's doctrines. See *Entretiens avec Didier Eribon*, pp. 205–8. On the influence of those doctrines in Dumézil's later writings, particularly with regard to his theory of the three functions, see Chapter 19 above, "Shaping the Past and the Future."

19. The three cases are not absolutely identical in this regard. For whereas in two cases (the Lemnian women, Esther) the massacre is said to have been perpetrated by a group that was both less powerful and hierarchically subordinate to those who were massacred, in the third case (Parásuráma), a priest is said to have massacred those who were possessed of much greater physical and political power than he, but were still his hierarchic inferiors under the givens of the caste system. In marked contrast to all of these examples, however, the Turks' massacre of the Armenians was perpetrated by the dominant segment of society against persons who were their subordinates by all conceivable measures.

20. Dumézil, "De quelques faux massacres," pp. 41–42, quoting Edouard Montet, *Histoire de la Bible* (Paris: Payot, 1924), p. 46.

21. Ibid., pp. 42–44. This unwillingness to adopt a stance of anti-Semitism, however fashionable it might have been, is consistent with Dumézil's declaration to Didier Eribon that, among the things that kept him from joining the Action Française, in spite of his sympathy for the *noyau pur* of Maurras's doctrine, was the latter's insistence on the guilt of Dreyfus (*Entretiens avec Didier Eribon*, pp. 207–8). For Dumézil states that he had grown up among army officers—the colleagues of his father, General Jean-Anatole Dumézil (1857–1929), who ended the First World War as inspector-general of the French artillery corps—who were staunch Dreyfusards.

22. One may infer the identity of the article's primary audience from the fact of its

publication in the *Revue turque d'anthropologie* (Constantinople), a journal with a very limited circulation outside of Turkey. Yet from the fact that it was published in French, it is also clear that Turks wished to reach a European audience, or at the very least wished to believe that they were capable of reaching such an audience through this vehicle. In considerable measures, the contradictions and discontinuities within Dumézil's text may be seen to result from the peculiar situation of the author vis-à-vis his audience. For at a subtextual level, Dumézil was trying to persuade Turks that he was trying to persuade Europeans of things that would be helpful to the Turkish cause. One cannot know whether Dumézil himself believed that any non-Turkish eyes would ever fall upon these pages, but it is clear that in later years he was content to erase this piece from his oeuvre.

23. Dumézil, "De quelques faux massacres," p. 39.

24. Ibid., p. 46.

ACKNOWLEDGMENTS

Chapter 1, "Indo-European Religions: An Introduction" is previously unpublished. It was written in 1983 at the request of Crossroads Press for a projected volume on the pre-Christian religions of Europe.

Chapter 2, "On the Imagery of Paradise," was written in 1979 and was published in *Indogermanische Forschungen* 85 (1980): 151–64.

Chapter 3, "The Lord of the Dead," was written in 1979, and was published in *History of Religions* 20 (1981): 224–41.

Chapter 4, "Waters of Memory, Waters of Forgetfulness," was written in 1978 and was published in *Fabula* 23 (1982): 19–34.

Chapter 5, "The Ferryman of the Dead," was written in 1979, and was presented at a conference on "The Transformation of Europe," that was held in Dubrovnik in September 1979. It was published in the *Journal of Indo-European Studies* 8 (1980): 41–59.

Chapter 6, "Mithra(s) as Sun and Savior," was written in 1978 and was presented at a conference on "The Soteriology of the Oriental Cults in the Roman Empire" that was held in Rome in September 1979. It was published in the proceedings of that conference: Ugo Bianchi and M. J. Vermaseren, eds., *La Soteriologia dei Culti Orientali nell'Impero Romano* (Leiden: E. J. Brill, 1982), pp. 505–26.

Chapter 7, "The Hellhound," was written in 1979, and was published in the *Journal of Indo-European Studies* 7 (1979): 273–86.

Chapter 8, "The House of Clay," was written in 1980 and was published in the *Indo-Iranian Journal* 24 (1982): 1–12.

Chapter 9, "The Two Paths," is previously unpublished. It was written in 1988, based on research that had been begun and abandoned in 1983.

Chapter 10, "Homeric *lyssa:* 'Wolfish Rage'," was written in 1975, and was published in *Indogermanische Forschungen* 80 (1975): 98–105.

Chapter 11, "War and Warriors: An Overview," was written in 1986. It was published in Mircea Eliade, general ed., *Encyclopedia of Religion* (New York: Macmillan, 1987), volume 15, pp. 339–44.

Chapter 12, "Warriors and Non-herdsmen: A Response to Mary Boyce," is previously unpublished. It was written in 1988.

Chapter 13, "Sacrificial Ideology and Indo-European Society," is previously unpublished. It was written in 1985 and was presented as a lecture at the Universities of Uppsala, Siena, Stockholm, Oslo, Lund, and Copenhagen between February and May 1985, and at Columbia University in March 1986.

Chapter 14, "The Druids and Human Sacrifice," was written in 1984. Different versions of it were presented as lectures at the École pratique des hautes études, the Università degli Studi di Siena, and the Universities of Stockholm, Lund, Copenhagen, and Uppsala between February and May 1985. It was published in M. A. Jazayery and W. Winter, eds., *Languages and Cultures: Studies in Honor of Edgar Polomé* (Berlin: Mouton de Gruyter, 1988), pp. 381–95.

Chapter 15, "On the Scythian Royal Burials," was written in 1984 and was presented as a lecture at the University of Oslo in April 1985. It was published in Susan Skomal and Edgar Polomé, eds., *Proto-Indo-European: The Archeology of a Linguistic Problem, Festschrift for Marija Gimbutas* (Washington: Journal of Indo-European Studies Monograph Series, 1987), pp. 267–85.

Chapter 16, "Debreasting, Disarming, Beheading: Some Sacrificial Practices of the Scyths and Amazons," is previously unpublished. It was written in August 1990 and was first presented at a Conference on "Sacrifice" held at the Gest Center for the Cross-Cultural Study of Religion, Haverford College, 6 October 1990. Thereafter, it was presented at Ohio State University and Wesleyan University in January 1991.

Chapter 17, "Physiological Speculation and Social Patterning in a Pahlavi Text," was written in 1987. It was published in the *Journal of the American Oriental Society* 108 (1988): 135–40.

Chapter 18, "Embryological Speculation and Gender Politics in a Pahlavi Text," was written in 1987. It was published in *History of Religions* 27 (1988): 355–65.

Chapter 19, "Shaping the Past and the Future," was written in 1986. It was published in the *Times Literary Supplement* (3 October 1986), pp. 1107–8. A Swedish translation, in which the footnotes omitted in the *TLS* were included, appeared in *Häften för Kritiska Studier* 19 (1987): 62–73.

Chapter 20, "Kings, Rebels, and the Left Hand," is previously unpublished. It was written in 1989 and was presented at the University of Chicago in May of that year and at the University of Florence in May 1990.

Chapter 21, "Myth and History in the Study of Myth: An Obscure Text of Georges Dumézil, Its Context and Subtext," was written in 1990. An Italian version was published in *Quaderni di Storia* 32 (1990): 5–18.

INDEX LOCORUM

INDEX VERBORUM

INDEX OF SUBJECTS